7 8.00

W9-CNH-114

RECORDS

OF THE

ENGLISH BIBLE

THE DOCUMENTS

RELATING TO THE TRANSLATION AND PUBLICATION OF THE BIBLE IN ENGLISH, 1525–1611

EDITED, WITH AN INTRODUCTION, BY

ALFRED W. POLLARD

DAWSONS OF PALL MALL

ISBN : 0 7129 0631 2
First published by Oxford University Press 1911
Reprinted by Wm. Dawson & Sons Ltd. 1974

Printed in Belgium by Jos Adam
for Wm. Dawson & Sons Ltd.,
Cannon House, Folkestone, Kent, England

PREFACE

In writing a Bibliographical Introduction to the Oxford University Press reprints of the English Bible of 1611 I found myself constantly hampered by the lack of such a collection of original documents as has here been brought together. Quite a large number of important documents had never been printed in full; others were available only in books now out of print or for other reasons difficult to obtain. Many of the books, moreover, were extremely bulky, and when it was desired to consider afresh the evidence of several different documents in order to straighten out some small tangle, the difficulties of remembering where each was to be found and getting hold of the right books were somewhat harassing. I was thus moved, when my Introduction was nearing completion, to suggest to Mr. Frowde that a collection of original documents relating to the making, printing, and publishing of the English translations of the Bible, from Tyndale's New Testament of 1525 to the appearance of the version of 1611, would be as appropriate a commemoration of the Tercentenary as could well be conceived. Mr. Frowde cordially agreed, and the volume was accordingly put in hand. The natural desire of publisher and editor that it should be available for the use of those taking part in the Tercentenary Celebrations in March 1911 will be no defence if any serious fault should be found, but may perhaps be allowed some weight by readers who would have liked fuller notes to some of the documents, or see room for minor improvements in other respects.

Although the documents here printed are mainly those which I used in writing my Introduction[1] they take a considerably wider range. The personal element which the bibliographer was bound to leave very imperfectly indicated here crops up at every turn, and in their own words in prefaces and letters, or in the narratives and comments of contemporaries, we get intimate glimpses into the characters of many of those who played their part in the century which it took to determine the great question as to what Bible the English people should be allowed to read. Another point which the documents emphasize is the political importance attached to that struggle. Just as the documents relating to the quarrel of Tyndale and Joye have little bearing on the main history of the English Bible, and yet are worth all the pages they fill because of their human interest, so the long reports of Hackett to Wolsey, or, again, the diplomatic correspondence about the Bible of 1539, which takes us so far away from text and translators, are yet thoroughly relevant as showing the immense importance attached by the statesmen of the day to stopping or forwarding the supply of the Scriptures in English, according as their policy dictated.

I have already indicated in my Introduction my belief that after the accession of Queen Elizabeth the question of what Bible the English people should be allowed to

[1] In reprinting this, marginal references by their numbers have been given to the documents used.

read was almost as keenly contested as before. The documents kindly supplied to me by Mr. Charles Rivington, just in time for insertion (see Nos. LVI and LXI), justify far stronger language than on the evidence at first before me I ventured to use. As long as he lived Archbishop Parker kept the Geneva Bible from being printed in England, and secured a monopoly for the Bishops' Bible, and for Jugge as its printer. We now know that it was within three weeks of Parker's death that Jugge's monopoly was broken down and that not more than three days later, at the instance of seven members of the Privy Council, Christopher Barker was allowed to enter the Geneva Bible ' for his copy ' at Stationers' Hall. In 1577, when Jugge died, the office of Queen's Printer was conferred on Barker by a patent which gave him the most absolute control over Bible-printing in England, and until the accession of Whitgift this patent was used to secure a monopoly for the Geneva version as rigorous as that which Parker had obtained for the Bishops'. To the reasons I have given in my Introduction for believing that after a few years of grace recourse was had to the methods of Archbishop Parker to support the version of 1611 as against that of Geneva, I should like to add here that the real triumph of the 1611 version came in the days of the Commonwealth, when its hold on the affections of the people proved so strong that its supremacy remained undisturbed. The leaders of the two great parties in the Church had loyally co-operated in making it, and after the experience of a third of a century it was recognized as the Bible of the whole Church and the whole Nation.

It only remains to acknowledge some personal obligations. The heaviest of these is to my friend Mr. H. R. Plomer, by whom the greater part of the documents were transcribed.[1] Mr. Plomer took the keenest interest in the work, and without his experienced helpfulness I could have done nothing. Like most other students of the subject, I have found Anderson's *Annals of the English Bible* (1845) of great use despite its vehement partisanship. I also owe many valuable references to Professor Arber's introduction to his facsimile of the Grenville fragment of Tyndale's New Testament of 1525 ; to Mr. J. A. Kingdon's privately printed monograph on *Two Members of the Grocers' Company, Richard Grafton and Thomas Poyntz* ; to the admirable *Historical Catalogue of Printed Bibles* by Messrs Darlow and Moule ; and to that standard work, *A General View of the History of the English Bible* by the late Bishop Westcott, as edited by Dr. Aldis Wright.

ALFRED W. POLLARD.

---

[1] With the exception of a few in Episcopal Registers all documents have been transcribed from, or collated with, the originals. These have been transcribed as they stand, but contracted forms have been written out. In some documents the form ' & ' has been expanded ; in others it has been allowed to stand.

CONTENTS

INTRODUCTION

CHAPTER   PAGE

   I. The Earlier English Translations (1380–1582)   1

  II. The Bible of 1611   37

 III. The Later History of the Bible of 1611   .   65

RECORDS

NUMBER

   I. Prohibition of English Translations of the Bible from the time of Wyclif unless authorized by a Bishop or a Provincial Council   79

  II. Sir Thomas More on the Prohibition .   .   81

 III. More's Plan for a Limited Circulation .   .   84

 IV. Tyndale's Translations   86

  V. Tyndale's Story of his Translation   .   .   93

 VI. The Printing of the first New Testaments .   99

 VII. The News sent to the King   .   .   .   108

VIII. The supposed Trial Version of St. Matthew   110

 IX. The Beginning of Tyndale's Prologue to the first New Testament   111

  X. Tyndale's Epilogue to the second New Testament   114

 XI. Henry VIII's belief that Tyndale was instigated by Luther   117

 XII. Tyndale on his fellow 'apostate' William Roy   119

XIII. An Expert Criticism of Tyndale's Version .   122

XIV. The Criticisms of Sir Thomas More .   .   126

NUMBER		PAGE
XV.	Episcopal Prohibition	131
XVI.	The Search for English New Testaments and other Heretical Books at Antwerp, and endeavour to get their Printers punished	135
XVII.	The Bishop of London buys New Testaments	150
XVIII.	The Bishop of Norwich refunds the Archbishop part of his outlay on New Testaments	153
XIX.	The Confession of Robert Necton that bought and sold New Testaments in English	155
XX.	Bishop Nix implores the King's help .	159
XXI.	The King consults his Council and the Bishops	161
XXII.	The King's Proclamation, June 1530 .	163
XXIII.	Tyndale's Terms of Submission . .	169
XXIV.	Frith's Defence of Tyndale and his Work	172
XXV.	George Joye's Letter to the King and Queen	174
XXVI.	The Bishops' Petition for an English Bible	175
XXVII.	George Joye's unauthorized Revision of Tyndale's New Testament :	
	A. Tyndale's Complaint . . .	178
	B. George Joye's Answer . .	185
	C. The Reconciliation breaks down .	188
	D. Joye's Narrative . . .	190
XXVIII.	Tyndale's Work as a Translator . .	195
XXIX.	The Projected Bishops' Version . .	196

NUMBER		PAGE

XXX. Financial help given to Coverdale by Jacob van Meteren . . . 198

XXXI. Coverdale's Bible, 1535 :
    A. End of Dedication . . . 200
    B. Beginning of the Address to the Reader 202

XXXII. Coverdale's Latin-English New Testament following the Vulgate Text :
    A. Dedication to the First Edition . 206
    B. Preface to the same Edition . 210

XXXIII. The Licensing of Matthew's Bible :
    A. Letter from Cranmer to Cromwell, August 4, 1537 214
    B. Cranmer to Cromwell, August 13, 1537 216
    C. Cranmer to Cromwell, August 28, 1537 216
    D. Richard Grafton to Cromwell, August 28, 1537 218
    E. Richard Grafton to Cromwell, after August 28, 1537 . . . 219

XXXIV. Fox's Account of the Printing of the Great Bible of 1539 . . . 223

XXXV. The French King's Licence . . . 232

XXXVI. Reports of Progress :
    A. Letter of Coverdale and Grafton to Cromwell, June 23, 1538 . . 234
    B. Letter of Edward Whitchurch to Cromwell (undated) . . . 236
    C. Letter of Coverdale, Grafton, and W. Gray to Cromwell, August 9, 1538 237

NUMBER   PAGE

XXXVI.   Reports of Progress—*continued*:

    D. Coverdale and Grafton to Cromwell, September 12, 1538 . . 238

    E. Bishop Bonner to Cromwell, October 7, 1538 240

XXXVII. The King's Proclamation, November 16, 1538 240

XXXVIII. More Reports from Paris :

    A. Grafton to Cromwell, December 1, 1538 243

    B. Coverdale to Cromwell, December 13, 1538 245

XXXIX.   The Bibles Confiscated : Cromwell's Efforts to obtain their release :

    A. Citation of François Regnault for Printing the Bible at Paris, December 17, 1538 246

    B. Castillon, the French Ambassador in England, to the Constable of France, December 31, 1538 . . 249

    C. Extract from Letter of the Imperial Ambassador in England to Charles V, January 9,1539 . . 251

    D. Postscript of a Letter from the French Ambassador, Charles Marillac, to the Grand Constable of France, May 1, 1539 . . . 254

    E. Extract from a Letter from the Grand Constable of France to the French Ambassador, May 6, 1539 254

    F. Extract from a Letter of the French Ambassador to the Constable, July 5, 1539 . . . 255

CONTENTS

NUMBER   PAGE

XL.   The Price and Copyright of the Great
        Bible   257

XLI.   Patent for Bible Printing granted to
        Cromwell   258

XLII.   Anthony Marler and the Privy Council .   260

XLIII. The King's Proclamation for the English
        Bible to be set up in Churches .   .   261

XLIV.   The Reading of the Bible :

        A. Draft for a Proclamation   .   .   265

        B. An Admonition and Advertise-
            ment given by the Bishop of London
            to all Readers of the Bible in the
            English Tongue. 1542 .   .   .   267

        C. The Narrative of William Maldon
            of Newington   268

XLV.   The Great Bible condemned .   .   .   272

XLVI.   Preface to the Geneva New Testament .   275

XLVII. Preface to the Geneva Bible .   .   .   279

XLVIII. Privilege and Licence to John Bodley
        for printing the Geneva Bible for
        seven years   284

XLIX.   Parker and Grindal on the Renewal of
        Bodley's Privilege   285

L.   The Preparation of the Bishops' Bible :

        A. Letter of Richard Cox, Bishop of
            Ely, to Cecil   287

        B. Parker invites Cecil to take part
            in the Revision   287

        C. Strype's Summary of other
            Correspondence   288

LI.   Parker announces to Cecil the completion
        of the Bishops' Bible   291

NUMBER		PAGE
LII.	Presentation of the Bishops' Bible to the Queen, and Story of the Revision :	
	A. Archbishop Parker to Cecil .	292
	B. Archbishop Parker to Queen Elizabeth	294
	C. Parker's Note as to the Translators	295
LIII.	The Inception of the Rheims New Testament	298
LIV.	Preface to the Rheims New Testament .	301
LV, LVI.	Jugge and Barker and their Patrons : .	
	A. The High Commissioners' Order taken between Richard Jugge and others of the Stationers' Company	313
	B. The Beginning of the Bible Stock .	314
	C. Barker's Satisfaction to Jugge .	318
LVII.	Barker establishes his Monopoly . .	322
LVIII.	Barker's Circular to the City Companies	326
LIX.	Draft for an Act of Parliament for a New Version of the Bible . . .	329
LX.	The Attempt to provide for the Translators of 1611 :	
	A. Bishop Bancroft circulates a Letter from the King . . .	331
	B. Bancroft's Exhortation to the Bishops to subscribe . . .	334
LXI.	The Bible Stock in 1606 . . .	335
LXII.	Report on the Making of the Version of 1611 presented to the Synod of Dort .	336
LXIII.	Preface to the Version of 1611 . .	340
INDEX	. . . .	379

INTRODUCTION

I. THE EARLIER ENGLISH TRANSLATIONS
(1380–1582)

MAINLY, no doubt, because of the predominance of French as the language of educated people in England from the time of the Norman Conquest until the middle of the fourteenth century, the Bible, as a whole, remained untranslated into English, until the last years of the life of Wyclif. A version was then made, about 1380–3, and some years later this was revised and substantially rewritten in a simpler style by another hand. That the reformer himself took any personal share in either of these versions which pass popularly under his name is unlikely, and in the case of the second is not seriously contended. We know from a manuscript at the Bodleian Library, Oxford, that Nicholas of Hereford, who up to the time of the final defeat of Wyclif's cause at Oxford (June 1382) figured as one of his strongest supporters at the University, was the author of the first version as far as Baruch iii. 20, where it breaks off in the manuscript abruptly, presumably because of Hereford's flight. The authorship of the rest of this version is unknown, and being unknown has been ascribed to Wyclif himself, with more piety than probability, since the master does not often take up the work of the disciple, and Wyclif, after June 1382, was both old and ill. The authorship of the second version was tentatively ascribed to one of Wyclif's followers, John Purvey, by Daniel Waterton in 1729

The Wyclifite Bibles.

B

(*Waterton's Works*, vol. x, p. 361), and although Waterton says himself that he merely guessed and ' pitched upon ' Purvey as the author, and his reason for doing so has not been confirmed, the suggestion was accepted by Forshall and Madden in their splendid edition of the two versions in 1850, and is now frequently stated as a fact.

A name which long before Waterton's time was connected with an English version of the Bible was that of John of Trevisa, of whom Caxton wrote in the preface to his edition of Higden's *Polychronicon* that at the request of ' one Sir Thomas lord barkley ', to whom he acted as priest, he had translated the *Polychronicon*, the Bible, and the *De Proprietatibus Rerum* of Bartholomaeus Anglicus, one of the best known of mediaeval encyclopaedias. The first and third of these translations survive. Of that of the Bible (mentioned also, probably on Caxton's authority, in the preface to the Bible of 1611) nothing is known, unless it can be identified either with the completion of the first version begun by Nicholas of Hereford or with the second version which has somewhat lightly been assigned to Purvey. For our present purpose it is unnecessary to enter further into these questions of authorship. It is sufficient to note that the translator of the second of the two extant versions worked, according to his own account, ' with diverse felawis and helpars ' and had ' manie gode felawis and kunnynge at the correccioun of his translacioun '. It thus seems certain that there was something of the nature of an informal board or company of translators, and if piety did not constrain us to speak of these two versions, not indeed as the Wyclif, but as the Wyclifite Bible, we might well have been content, as the present writer suggested ten years ago, to have called this the Oxford Bible, since it was with the reform party at Oxford that it took its inception and, despite its origin among Wyclif's followers, there was no attempt in either version to translate in any party spirit, or to do anything else than give a faithful rendering of the Vulgate Latin.

As early as 1397 at least one copy of this English Bible was in the possession of a royal duke, and the names of other noble owners during the fifteenth century, as well as fine manuscripts decorated so as to be worthy of such ownership, remain on record. In 1408 the Convocation Record i, held at Oxford had forbidden the possession of any iii. English version of the Bible without licence from a bishop, but it is plain that such a licence could be procured, and we even hear of a copy belonging to such an eminently orthodox community as the Bridgetine house of Sion, at Isleworth. But the existence of Lollardy had reawakened such fears as Aelfric had expressed lest his epitome of the Pentateuch should entrap the unwary to believe in the lawfulness of polygamy, and a reader of the merchant class who had asked his priest to get him a licence to own an English Bible towards the end of the fifteenth century would probably have met but small encouragement. Add to this the fact that by this time the language of the Wyclifite versions was fast becoming obsolete, and also the vast expense of such an enterprise, and we have no reason to wonder that Caxton neither printed either of the existing translations, nor set himself to procure, or (hardened translator as he was) to make, a new one. But a generation later, other ideas had sprung up, and at least one man in England, William Tyndale, was determined that there should be an English Bible which not merely merchants but ploughboys could buy and read.

William Tyndale had come to London, with a trans- Tyndale's lation of a speech of Isocrates as a proof of his ability, in New the hope of finding encouragement from the Bishop of Testa- ment.

London (Cuthbert Tunstall) to make a new translation of the New Testament not, as the ' Wyclifite ' translators had done, from the Latin Vulgate, but from the original Greek. Erasmus had published his famous edition of the Greek Testament in 1516, and this had been revised and reprinted in 1519 and 1522. Along with it he had printed a new translation into Latin. Tyndale had probably heard Erasmus lecture at Cambridge, and he must have been prepared, if Tunstall had given him any encouragement, to make his English version in the spirit of Erasmus. But there was no room for a translator of iv, v. the Bible in the Bishop's house, nor indeed, as Tyndale said bitterly, in all England, so in 1524 he betook himself to Hamburg, with the help of a subsidy of £10 given him by a generous and devout London merchant, Henry iv, note 4. Monmouth, and completed his translation undisturbed. viii, xiii, There are references to what may have been trial issues xix. of Matthew and Mark, but if, which is doubtful, these ever had a separate existence, no traces of them remain. vii. But before December 1525 copy had been handed to a Cologne printer, probably connected in some way with vi. the important printing house of Peter Quentell, founded some fifty years earlier, and ten quires (eighty pages) of an edition of 3,000 copies in small quarto had been printed off, when an anti-Lutheran controversialist, Johann Dobneck,[1] better known as Cochlaeus, anxious to ingratiate himself with the king of England, persuaded the magistrates of Cologne to interfere. To escape arrest, Tyndale and his amanuensis, William Roy, fled along the Rhine to Worms, taking the printed quires with them,

[1] Dobneck has left three accounts of his exploit, of which he seems to have been more than a little proud, written respectively in 1533 and 1538 and (the fullest) in his *De actis et scriptis Martini Lutheri* of 1549 (see Record vi).

and it was thus at Worms, not at Cologne, that the first
printed edition of the New Testament in English was
brought out.

By a lucky chance a single copy of eight of the ten
quires of Tyndale's New Testament printed at Cologne
has been preserved, wanting only the first leaf, and is
now in the British Museum, to which it was bequeathed
by Thomas Grenville. According to Dobneck, a quarto
edition was published at Worms, but whether this incor-
porated and completed the sheets printed at Cologne, or
was entirely reset, is unknown, as no copy has survived.
Our knowledge of Tyndale's Testament in its unrevised
form thus rests on an octavo edition which has been
identified from its types and illustrations as printed at
Worms by Peter Schoeffer, the second son of the Schoeffer
of the same name who had helped to make the art of
printing a practical success at Mainz some seventy years
before. This has survived in a copy at the Baptist x.
College, Bristol, lacking only the first leaf, and another,
much more imperfect, at St. Paul's Cathedral. According to Dobneck, Tyndale printed 6,000 New Testaments
at Worms ; it is thus probable that both the Worms
quarto edition and the octavo, like the projected Cologne
quarto, consisted of 3,000 copies.

The thirty-one leaves still extant of the Cologne
fragment contain Tyndale's Prologue and the text of
St. Matthew down to the middle chapter xxii. To the
text are attached marginal notes, some of them vehe-
mently anti-Roman. In the Worms octavo the marginal
notes have been removed, but the prefaces are largely
based on those of Luther, and the translation of the text
shows abundant traces of Luther's German version. It
is clear that Tyndale worked with this, the Vulgate, the
Latin version of Erasmus, and the Greek text all before

him, but it is also clear that it was primarily from the
Greek that he translated, and that the other three books
were only aids in the use of which he exercised his own
very competent judgement. We have his personal assurance ('I had no man to counterfet, nether was holpe
x. with englysshe of eny that had interpreted the same,
or soche lyke thinge in the scripture beforetyme') that
among his aids there was no copy of either of the 'Wyclifite' versions, and though some resemblances have been
quoted between his translation and these, they are not
sufficient to cast any doubt on his statement. On the
other hand, Tyndale's own work fixed, once for all, the
style and tone of the English Bible, and supplied not
merely the basis of all subsequent Protestant renderings
of the books (with unimportant exceptions) on which he
laboured, but their very substance and body, so that
those subsequent versions must be looked upon as
revisions of his, not as independent translations.

After the octavo printed at Worms, no fragment of the
text of any subsequent edition earlier than August 1534
is known to exist. Tyndale was at work on the Old
xxvii c. Testament and refused all requests to supervise reprints
of his version of the New. Copies of this are heard of as
selling in England as early as the spring of 1526, and they
xv. were episcopally denounced in the following autumn.
We hear of English Testaments sold the next year at five
xix. and seven groats apiece (1s. 8d. and 2s. 4d., answering
to a modern value of ten or twelve times as much), and
the profit on these prices may have been sufficient of
itself to evoke unauthorized reprints, though it is equally
probable that the unauthorized reprinters were enthusiasts
who did not make pecuniary profit their chief object.
According to George Joye, the editor of the unauthorized
xxvii c. edition of August 1534, 'anon after' Tyndale's own

issue (i. e. of 1525), the 'Dutchmen' got a copy and printed it again in a small volume, adding the Kalendar at the beginning, concordances (i. e. references to parallels) in the margins, and a Table at the end.[1] A second reprint was in a larger form, and with larger type [2] and with figures, i. e. wood-cuts, in the Apocalypse. Of these two editions there were about 5,000 copies printed and these were all sold out some time in 1533. A third reprint, consisting of 2,000 copies, Joye was asked to revise, but refused. When, however, yet another was in preparation, rather, according to his own account, than allow 2,000 additional copies to be placed on the market with the errors which by this time a succession of Dutch compositors had introduced, he undertook to correct the edition which appeared in August 1534. For doing this he was paid at the rate of $4\frac{1}{2}d.$ for sixteen leaves, a small enough sum even when multiplied by ten to give it its modern value, but probably the full market-price of press-correction at that day. Unhappily, Joye did not confine himself to press-correction, but not only botched Tyndale's English in places where he thought it obscure,

[1] This edition was apparently printed at Antwerp in 1526 by xvi A, Christoffel van Endhoven, who was in trouble about it with the note 2. city authorities by the end of the year, and in 1531 died in prison at Westminster as a result of trying to sell Testaments in England. Endhoven also called himself Van Ruremond (in various spellings), and until Mr. Gordon Duff cleared up the matter in his *Century of the English Book Trade*, much confusion was caused by the natural assumption that the two names belonged to different men.

[2] This may be the edition of 1532 of which Dr. Angus possessed a mutilated title-page. Joye certainly seems to be enumerating all the editions of which he knew, and, although he may have used one or more which actually appeared, statements like that of Anderson (*Annals of the English Bible*), that there were six editions before the end of 1530, seem based on very slender evidence.

but in certain passages gave practical effect to views which he had expressed in private controversy with Tyndale, by substituting the words ' the life after this ' and similar phrases for Tyndale's ' the resurrection '. This edition was very neatly printed in sexto-decimo at Antwerp by the widow of Christoffel van Endhoven, whose husband's share in Bible printing has been already mentioned in a note to page 7.

Meanwhile, Tyndale himself had at last revised his translation, and his new edition was printed as an octavo at Antwerp in November 1534 by Martin Emperour, xxvii A. otherwise known as Martin Caesar or Keysere. Tyndale had time to insert into this a vigorous and deserved denunciation of Joye, whom, however, he probably wronged in depicting him as actuated by merely mer- cenary motives. In 1904 the British Museum, which possesses both these editions, was fortunate enough to acquire yet another, previously unknown, ' prynted now agayne at Antwerpe by me Catharyn wydowe [the words ' of Christoffel of Endhouen ' appear to have dropped out] in the yere of our lorde M. ccccc. and xxxv, the ix. daye xxvii B. of Januarye.' This contains a letter from Joye ' Unto the Reader ' written at a moment when friends had brought the two men together, and Tyndale had agreed to withdraw his ' uncharitable pistle ', as Joye calls it, and substitute a ' reformed ' one in which they were both to ' salute the readers with one salutacion '. But the reconciliation was shortlived, the appearance of Joye's new edition being probably itself a fresh cause of offence ; Tyndale drew back, and on February 27, 1535, xxvii C. Joye sent to press an *Apology*, in which he made out the best case he could for himself and incidentally tells us that Tyndale was paid £10 for his edition of November 1534.

In December 1534 the Upper House of Convocation of xxvi.
the province of Canterbury had departed so far from its
attitude of mere resistance as to petition the King that
the Bible might be translated by authorized translators,
and the progress which this denotes accounts for the
rapidity with which one edition of Tyndale's New Testament follows another at this period.   Tyndale himself
revised one more, printed for him by G. H., i. e. Godfrid
van der Haghen, ere he was enticed from the house of
the English merchants at Antwerp in May 1535, with the
result that once beyond the walls of the free city he was
arrested by the imperial authorities and carried to imprisonment and death at Vilvorde.   Yet another 1535
edition may be noticed (probably printed by Hans van
Ruremond), because its strange spellings (faether,
moether, &c.) at one time were imagined to have been
adopted to assimilate its language to the dialect of the
ploughboys for whom Tyndale had declared that he would
write.   More prosaic commentators attributed it to the
vagaries of Flemish compositors. But several similar spellings are found in a letter written this year by Tyndale's
friend, Thomas Poyntz, with whom he lodged at the
' English house ' at Antwerp, and it is possible that they
should be looked upon as among the phonetic devices by
which many bookish people in the sixteenth century tried
to express their views on pronunciation.   All these
phonetic devices without exception were bad, and it
would be well if we could get rid of them, but while many
remained to trouble us in the twentieth century, some
were rejected very quickly, and those of the Antwerp
press-corrector (possibly Thomas Poyntz himself) were
among those which never obtained currency.   It may
be noted that the Van der Haghen edition of 1535 has
sometimes been confused with this which has the strange

spellings, and also that the spellings are repeated in a reprint known only from a fragment in the British Museum. Seven different issues or editions of Tyndale's New Testament appeared in 1536, the year of his martyrdom (October 6), and between 1525 and 1566, when the last dated edition was issued, more than forty editions were printed, of which definite evidence has been preserved. From the fact that many of these are known only from a single copy, or fragment of a copy, we may be sure that other editions have perished entirely.

Cover-dale's Bible.

Had Tyndale escaped his enemies for but a few more years he would assuredly have translated the whole Bible. He had published an English Pentateuch in January 1530 [1531 ?], purporting to be printed by Luther's favourite printer, Hans Luft, not at Wittenberg but at ' Malborow [Marburg] in the land of Hesse ' (an imprint of which the genuineness has been alternately accepted and denied by bibliographers for a fatiguing number of years [1]), and a second edition of this without date, or imprint (? Antwerp, Martin Keysere, 1531) ; also, ' The prophete Ionas, with an introduccion before, teachinge

---

[1] The recent investigations of Mr. Steele have tended to connect the types and ornaments with some firm at Antwerp, but Fox states circumstantially that Tyndale took his translation to be printed at Hamburg, lost the manuscript by shipwreck on the coast of Holland, and when he reached Hamburg in another ship was obliged to begin his work anew, completing it with the aid of Miles Coverdale. There are some difficulties in this account, but the hue and cry for Lutheran books raised by Wolsey's agents in Antwerp at the end of 1526 and beginning of 1527 make it not at all improbable that a press and materials may have been shipped from Antwerp to Hamburg (also a Free City and under ordinary circumstances comparatively safe) in 1527, and that books may have been produced there until printing at Antwerp could be resumed. The attribution of them to Luther's printer would have gained ready credence at the time, as Tyndale's adversaries had greatly exaggerated Luther's influence on his work.

to understande him and the right use also of all the scripture.' To his New Testament of November 1534, moreover, he had appended English versions of all the lessons from the Old Testament appointed to be read in the liturgy instead of Epistles. As we shall see, he had also left behind him, in all probability, a manuscript xxviii. translation of the Old Testament as far as the end of Chronicles. But the completion of an English Bible was reserved for a man of far less scholarship, but an equally happy style, Miles Coverdale, a Yorkshireman born in 1488, and educated at Cambridge, where he had taken the degree of Bachelor of Canon Law as recently as 1531.

The most explicit information which Coverdale's Bible offers as to its provenance is that of its colophon, which reads: 'Prynted in the yeare of oure LORDE M.D.XXXV. and fynished the fourth daye of October.' Its earliest title-page begins with the word ' Biblia ' in roman majuscules, followed in German script type of various sizes by the explanation : ' The Bible, that ‖ is, the holy Scripture of the ‖ Olde and New Testament, faith ‖ fully and truly translated out ‖ of Douche and Latyn in to Englishe ‖ M.D.XXXV. Subsequently this was replaced by another title in English black-letter with the shortened formula, ' faythfully translated in ‖ to Englyshe.' The whole of the text of the book is in a small German script, and it had originally preliminary leaves in the same type (of which only one has survived) ; these, however, were reprinted in English black-letter at the same time as the title-page.

In his dedication to the king Coverdale protests ' I xxxi. haue nether wrested nor altered so moch as one worde for the mayntenaunce of any maner of secte : but haue with a cleare conscience purely and faythfully translated this out of fyue sundry interpreters, hauyng onely the

manyfest trueth of the scripture before myne eyes '.
Investigation has shown that of the five ' interpreters '
here mentioned two must have been ' Douche ' i.e.
(i) the Swiss-German version of Zwingli and Leo Juda,
first printed at Zurich by Christopher Froschouer in the
years 1527–9, and (ii) Luther's German, of which the
New Testament was printed in 1522, the Old Testament
as far as the Song of Songs in 1523–4, and a complete
edition in 1534 ; two Latin, i.e. (iii) the new rendering
of Sanctes Pagninus, an Italian Catholic theologian,
published with papal sanction at Lyons in 1527–8,
and (iv) the Vulgate ; and one English, i.e. (v)
the New Testament and Pentateuch translated by
Tyndale.

Coverdale graduated as Bachelor of Canon Law at
Cambridge in 1531, but thereafter until 1536 his move-
ments are unknown.[1] There has consequently been much
dispute as to where and by what firm his Bible was
printed in 1535. Early in the 18th century, however,
Humphrey Wanley, the librarian of Robert Harley, Earl
of Oxford, suggested that the printer was probably
Christopher Froschouer of Zurich, who fifteen years later
produced another edition of it. Investigation showed
that two of the larger types of the English Bible of 1535
were in the possession of Froschouer, but these were
used also by other German printers, and the matter
remained undecided until, in his article on Coverdale in
the *Dictionary of National Biography*, Mr. H. R. Tedder
by the kindness of Dr. Christian Ginsburg was enabled
to state that he had seen two leaves of a Swiss-German
Bible printed in the same German type as the text of

xxx.   [1] If the story that he was subsidized while translating by Jacob
van Meteren of Antwerp be believed he was probably part of the
time at Antwerp.

Coverdale's English version. The complete book, an un-recorded edition of 1529–30 from the press of Froschouer, had once been in Dr. Ginsburg's possession, but I learn from Dr. Ginsburg himself that this disappeared from his library in a very painful manner, and only these leaves remain. While it is regrettable that the complete evidence can no longer be produced, they may be taken as sufficiently establishing that it was at Zurich and by Froschouer that the first printed English Bible was issued.

The problem presented by the reprinted preliminary leaves is not very difficult. These, as printed at Zurich, probably did not exceed four, of which the first was occupied by the title with a list of the books of the Bible printed on the back, the second and third by Coverdale's Prologue, the fourth by the statement as to ' The first boke of Moses, called Genesis, what this boke con-teyneth '. When it was ascertained that the book would be allowed to circulate in England it was very desirable to distinguish it from the Antwerp New Testaments which had brought such trouble on their purchasers. The word ' Douche ' was therefore elimi-nated from the title-page (' Latyn ' going with it),[1] a dedication to the king was inserted and the whole quire was printed in English black-letter, almost certainly by James Nycholson at Southwark, first with the date M D X X X V on the title, afterwards with that of the following year. There would be the less difficulty in doing this, as under an Act passed in 1534 books printed

[1] The space thus saved was devoted to extending the third of three texts quoted in the title by an additional two lines. It has been contended that the mention of ' Douche and Latyn ' was removed expressly to make room for this. Such a view surely reverses the relative importance of the two changes.

abroad could not be imported into England ready bound, but only in sheets (so that English binders might make their profit off them), and there was thus no need to pull the book to pieces in order to make the change. In the revised form the preliminary quire was made up as follows :

1ᵃ, title; 1ᵇ, blank; 2ᵃ–4ᵃ, an Epistle ‖ Unto the Kynges Highnesse ; 4ᵇ–7ᵃ, A prologe ‖ To the reader ; 7ᵇ–8ᵃ, The bokes of the hole Byble ‖ how they are named in Englyssh, etc. ; 8ᵇ, The first boke of ‖ Moses, called ‖ Genesis ‖ what this book conteyneth.

Coverdale's version was reprinted in folio and quarto by James Nycholson in 1537, each edition bearing on its title, not over truthfully, the words ' newly ouersene and corrected ', or, as the last word stands in the quarto, ' correcte.' The quarto title, which must thus be the later of the two, bears also the still more reassuring announcement, ' Set foorth with the Kynges moost gracious licence.' When as much favour was shown to it as this, it is surprising that this text of 1537 was not taken as the official version, since Coverdale was a much suppler and more conciliatory translator than Tyndale, and whereas the latter had consistently substituted (even going out of his way, at times, to do so), the less eccle-

xiii, xiv. siastical terms *congregation, elder, favour, knowledge, love, repentance,* for *church, priest, grace, confession, charity,*
xxxii B. *penance,* Coverdale was ready to use either or both.
Matthew's While, however, his folio and quarto were being printed
Bible.   at Southwark, a new Bible was being set up, almost certainly at Antwerp, which used Coverdale's version of the Old Testament from the end of Chronicles, including the Apocrypha, but Tyndale's New Testament, as revised by him for the edition of May 1535, and also his Pentateuch and a hitherto unprinted version of Joshua

—2 Chronicles, which has been conjectured with every appearance of reason to be Tyndale's continuation of his translation to the point, or very near the point,[1] which he had reached at the time of his arrest. This version was corrected for the press by Tyndale's disciple, John Rogers, and was put forward as 'truly and purely translated into Englysh by Thomas Matthew[1], a probably fictitious and certainly deceptive attribution, the name serving at the time to cover the share of Tyndale, but being afterwards unequivocally treated as the alias of the real editor, Rogers.

Almost childish as the device of attributing a translation of the Bible made up of the work of Tyndale and Coverdale to a fictitious or man-of-straw Thomas Matthew[2] now appears, it served to save the face of the king and the bishops by the pretence that this was a new version, and so one which might be considered to have been made in compliance with the petition sent to the king by the Upper House of Convocation in December 1534. Cranmer had originally planned that

[1] According to Halle's *Chronicle*, printed by Richard Grafton xxviii. in 1548, Tyndale also translated Nehemiah, ' the Prophet Jonas and no more of the holy scripture.' Why Coverdale's version was preferred to his for Nehemiah is hard to see, but the statement strongly confirms the attribution of Joshua—2 Chronicles to Tyndale. The manuscript of this may have been handed by Thomas Poyntz, Tyndale's host at Antwerp, either to Rogers, the editor, or to the two English printers, Grafton and Whitchurch, who are known to have superintended the production of the edition. Poyntz and Grafton were both members of the Grocers' Company, at this time apparently very favourable to Protestantism. The attribution of the edition to a press at Antwerp is confirmed by Grafton sending Bibles to Cromwell by the hands of a servant who, as he tells Cromwell, had just arrived from Flanders.

[2] A few years earlier a real Thomas Matthew lived at Colchester. xix, note 8.

xxix. such a version should be made by the English bishops, sharing the task between them, and his correspondence shows that some steps in this direction had actually been taken. But while some of the bishops had little fitness for such a task, others had still less inclination, and the work made no progress. Thus when the Matthew Bible xxxvii. A. was submitted to Cranmer, he wrote urgently to Cromwell (August 1537), entreating him to use his influence to get from the king ' a license that the same may be sold and redde of every person withoute danger of any acte, proclamacion or ordinaunce hertofore graunted to the contrary, untill such tyme that we the Bishops shall set forth a better translation, which I thinke will not be till a day after Domesday '. The petition thus made was granted, Cromwell's goodwill having apparently been already secured, and, with a lightheartedness which is really amazing, official sanction was given to a Bible largely made up of the work of Tyndale, and which included his markedly Protestant Prologue to Romans (based on Luther), and equally Protestant side-notes, some of them supplied by Rogers from the version of the French reformer Olivetan. In his letter to Cromwell Cranmer characterizes the book as ' a Bible in Englishe both of a new translation [which, save for the portion Joshua—2 Chronicles, from Tyndale's unpublished manuscript, it was not] and of a new prynte [Antwerp !], dedicated unto the Kinges Majestie, as farther apperith by a pistle unto His Grace in the begynnyng of the boke ', and further remarks, ' as for the translation, so farre as I haue redde therof I like it better than any other translation hertofore made.' No doubt in 1537 the king had moved a long way in the direction of Protestantism— for the moment—but considering his character, the whole transaction bore a remarkable resemblance to playing

with gunpowder. From a letter of Grafton's it appears xxxiii E.
that 1,500 copies of this Bible were printed, and that it
had cost him £500.

As was inevitable, the Matthew Bible was quickly The Great
superseded, but its importance was very great, since it Bibles.
formed the starting-point of the successive revisions
which resulted in the version of 1611, a matter for sincere
congratulation, as it contained (save for the rejection of
his version of Nehemiah, Jonah, and the ' Epistles ' from
the Old Testament) the greatest possible amount of the
work of Tyndale, who was a far better scholar than
Coverdale. It was, however, to the latter, who is known
to have been in England early in 1538, that the task of
revising it, and expunging all controversial annotation,
was entrusted. It was intended, at first, to substitute xxxvi c.
new notes, but although signs drawing attention to these xxxviii B.
xxxiv.
were printed, the notes themselves were suppressed.
For the revision of the text, great use was made in
the Old Testament of a new Latin translation from
the Hebrew by Sebastian Münster, published in 1534-5,
while the New Testament was compared afresh with the
translation of Erasmus and the Complutensian Polyglott.
No English office being considered sufficiently well xxxv,
equipped to produce so large a book in a handsome xxxix B.
manner, or with the speed desired, it was resolved to
have recourse to the great Paris firm of François Regnault, who up to 1534 had been accustomed to print
service-books for the English market. Coverdale and
Grafton went to Paris to see the work through the press,
and an edition of 2,000 copies was put in hand, the funds xxxix B, C.
being provided wholly or mainly by Cromwell. Letters
written by Coverdale and Grafton to Cromwell in June,
August, and September, 1538, speak of the rapid progress xxxvi C, D.
of the book, and its arrival in England seemed to be only

xxxvii. a matter of a few months. In November the king issued a proclamation which reflects the scandal caused to the less progressive Churchmen by the notes and prologues in Matthew's Bible. The contents of the earlier sections are thus summarized by Mr. Robert Steele (*Bibliography of Royal Proclamations of the Tudor and Stuart Sovereigns*, No. 176) :

> In consequence of the import of certain printed books from abroad and the publication of others here ' with privilege ' containing annotations in the margins, &c., imagined by the makers and printers of these books, dissension has been set up concerning the sacraments, &c. It is therefore ordered (1) that no English books printed abroad be brought into the country on pain of forfeiture of all goods and imprisonment. (2) No person to print any English book except after examination by some of the Privy Council or other persons appointed. The words ' cum privilegio regali ' not to be used without ' ad imprimendum solum ', and the whole copy or the effect of the licence to be printed underneath. No copies of Scripture with annotations to be printed except they are first examined, but only the plain sentence with a table. No translations to be printed without the name of the translator, unless the printer answer for it as his own. (3) No printer to publish any books of Scripture in English till they are examined by the King, or one of the Privy Council, or a bishop.

While these provisions were clearly directed to prevent a recurrence of the scandal of 1537, some of them naturally xxxviii A. caused great alarm to Grafton and Coverdale, who wrote at once to Cromwell to know how they were to be met. But a heavier blow was awaiting them. The relations between England and France were becoming critical, and the French ambassador, learning of Cromwell's personal xxxix c. interest in the English Bible which was being printed at Paris, wrote home suggesting that it should be seized. On December 9 the crisis was intensified by the execution of Cardinal Pole's relations on a charge of treason. On

December 13 Coverdale became alarmed and wrote to xxxviii B.
Cromwell that he had deposited some of the printed
sheets (quantity unspecified) with the English ambassador,
Bishop Bonner, that something at least might be saved
from the threatened wreck. Four days later the In- xxxix A.
quisitors were let loose on the printing office, Regnault
was arrested, the English correctors had to flee for their
lives, and all the stock on the premises was seized for
conveyance to the custody of the University of Paris.
As early as December 31 we find Cromwell asking the xxxix B.
French ambassador in London to secure its return. He
had spent, he said, £400 on the work, and any good
offices rendered in this matter should meet with due
acknowledgement. Mention of the Bibles recurs in the
ambassador's correspondence, and as late at least as
July 1539 it is evident that the stock still lay at the xxxix F.
University, and that the negotiations for its return were
at a standstill. Yet the printed copies of the book
bear a colophon which reads : 'The ende of the New
Testament and of the whole Byble. Fynisshed in
Apryll Anno M. CCCCC.XXXIX. A domino factum est
istud.'

It seems probable that in the colophon just quoted
there was at least a touch of bravado. Doubtless the
completion in any form of the edition in April 1539 was
indeed 'the Lord's doing', and doubtless its editors
desired that it should appear marvellous in the eyes of
their enemies. But it is far from certain that the
existence of the colophon denotes the existence of
sufficient copies for an edition to have been issued anywhere near the date named. In the later editions of his
Actes and Monumentes, John Foxe added to his 'Story xxxiv.
of the L[ord] Cromwell' a section 'Of the Bible in
English printed in the large volume', and although

almost every statement in this which can be tested can
be shown to be inexact, his account of what happened in
Paris is worth quoting :

And so the printer went forward and printed forth the booke
euen to the last part, and then was the quarell picked to the
printer, and he was sent for to the inquisitors of the fayth, and
there charged with certaine articles of heresie. Then were sent
for the Englishmen that were at the cost and charge thereof,
and also such as had the correction of the same, which was
Myles Coverdale, but hauing some warning what would folow
the said Englishmen posted away as fast as they could to saue
themselves, leauing behynd them all their Bibles, which were
to the number of 2500, called the Bibles of the great volume,
and neuer recouered any of them, sauing that the Lieftenaunt
criminal hauing them deliuered vnto hym to burne in a place
of Paris (like Smithfield) called Maulbert place, was somewhat
mooued with couetousnes, and sold 4 great dry fattes of them
to a Haberdassher to lap in caps, and those were bought againe,
but the rest were burned, to the great and importunate losse
of those that bare the charge of them. But notwithstandyng
the sayd losse after they had recouered some part of the foresayde bookes, and were comforted and encouraged by the Lord
Cromwell, the said Englishmen went agayne to Paris, and there
got the presses, letters, and seruaunts of the aforesayd Printer
and brought them to London, and there they became printers
themselues (which before they neuer entended) and printed
out the said Bible in London, and after that printed sundry
impressions of them ; but yet not without great trouble and
losse, for the hatred of the Bishops, namely, Steven Gardiner,
and his fellowes, who mightily did stomacke and maligne the
printing thereof. (*Acts and Monuments*, newly recognised and
inlarged by the Authour, John Foxe, 1583, page 1191).

It is clear from this narrative that the French authorities, while holding the bulk of the stock as an asset in their
negotiations with Cromwell, made a pretence of burning
it, and that of the copies set aside to be burnt, Grafton
rescued a certain number, possibly sixty or eighty, as it
would need a large vat to hold more than a score of them.

Add the copies deposited with Bonner before the raid, and there may have been a hundred or so available for issue, enough for distribution, but not a quantity which could be put on the market. When, therefore, on the arrival of type and printers from France, the missing sheets were printed and the first edition finished, a new one, answering to the first page for page, so that sheets would be interchangeable, was put in hand, at the expense this time, not of Cromwell, but of a member of the Haberdashers' Company, Anthony Marler. In November 1539 there is good evidence that Grafton was once more in Paris, and nothing is likely to have taken him there save the business of the Bible. It seems probable that this time he succeeded in rescuing the remains of the confiscated stock, and that this first Great Bible was thus ready for issue some time before the end of the year 1539, which, it must be remembered, answered to March 24, 1540, the more prevalent English reckoning at this time being from the Incarnation, not the Nativity, nor the Jan. 1 of the Roman Civil Year. Thus the issue of 'April 1539' was probably followed within a few weeks by that of April 1540, and this by a third in July, and a fourth in November, while yet others followed in May, November, and December, 1541, making seven Great Bibles in all. Only by an output on this scale could it be possible for every parish church to supply itself with a copy, as Cromwell had bade in the Injunctions which, as Vicar-General, he issued (before the trouble in Paris) in September 1538, and as the king commanded afresh by a proclamation of May 6, 1541, the limit of date being then fixed at the feast of All Saints (November 1), under penalty of a fine of forty shillings for each month's delay. In order to lighten the obligation, the price of the book was fixed as low as 10s. unbound, or 12s. well

xxxiv, note 10.

xliii, note 1.

xliii.

and sufficiently bound, trimmed and clasped. This price of ten shillings was only formally imposed by the xlii. Privy Council on April 25, 1541, but as early as November xl. 1539 we find Cranmer writing to Cromwell that Berthelet (the king's printer) and Whitchurch had been with him, and that he had sanctioned a charge of 13s. 4d., but that as the printers understood that Cromwell desired it to be 10s., they were contented to sell them for that, if they could be protected against competition. This Cromwell xli. effected the same day, by getting a patent from the king made out to himself, which enabled him to make the authorized printers and publishers his deputies. All the same, the substitution of 10s. for 13s. 4d. as the price must have hit the producers rather heavily, as from a curious lawsuit decided—such were the law's delays in Tudor times—in 1560, it appears that Anthony Marler had actually agreed to repurchase Bibles from a stationer named Philip Scapulis at the rate of 10s. 4d. apiece, or 4d. more than the price which he was himself allowed to charge (see 'Anthony Marler and the Great Bible', by H. R. Plomer. *The Library*, 3rd Series, i. 200–6). If he had made many such contracts the vellum copy of the issue of April 1540, which Marler presented to the king, can hardly have been paid for out of profits.

In the fine wood-cut title-page, designed, it is said, by Holbein, for these Great Bibles, the king is shown seated while Cranmer and Cromwell stand distributing copies to the people, who receive them with shouts of 'Vivat Rex'. For the 1539 Bible Cranmer had done nothing, and it is accordingly called Cromwell's. That of April 1540 and the subsequent issues are enriched 'with a prologe thereinto, made by the reuerende father in God, Thomas archbysshop of Cantorbury', and these are

usually called Cranmer's.[1]   The April 1540 text shows
fairly numerous signs of further revision by Coverdale,
and that of July of a few further changes ; the remaining
editions were reprints.   The first, third, and fourth of the
seven editions bear the name of Grafton, the second and
fifth that of Whitchurch, the sixth mostly Whitchurch
with a few Grafton titles, the seventh mostly Grafton
with a few for Whitchurch.   The second, third, fifth, and
seventh bear only the notice, ' This is the Bible appoynted
to the vse of the churches ' ; the fourth and sixth bear
title-pages specially worded to comply with the proclamation, viz. :

> The Byble in Englyshe of the largest and greatest volume,
> auctorised and apoynted by the commaundement of oure moost
> redoubted prynce and soueraygne Lorde, Kynge Henry the VIII,
> supreme head of this his churche and realme of Englande : to
> be frequented and vsed in euery church w'in this his sayd
> realme, accordynge to the tenoure of hys former Iniunctions
> geuen in that behalfe.   Ouersene and perused at the comaunde-
> ment of the kinges hyghnes by the ryght reuerende fathers in
> God, Cuthbert, bysshop of Duresme, and Nicholas bisshop of
> Rochester.   Printed by Rycharde Grafton [*in other copies* by
> Edwarde Whitchurch].   Cum priuilegio ad imprimendum
> solum, 1541.

Diligent investigation has not yet discovered in what the
episcopal revision consisted.

A smaller folio edition was printed in 1540 by Petit
and Redman for Berthelet, who, from his presence at the
interview between Cranmer and Whitchurch as to the
price of the Great Bible, seems to have helped Whitchurch with funds.   It should be mentioned also that in
1539 an independent version by Richard Taverner, a
barrister with a considerable knowledge of Greek, was

[1] After Cromwell's execution in July, 1540, his arms were cut
out from this title-page.

printed by Petit for Berthelet, but this, as attaining little success at the time and having no influence on the version of 1611, need not detain us here.

After December, 1541, no more English Bibles were
xlv. printed during the reign of Henry VIII. Proposals were made for a more conservative rendering, with due retention of ecclesiastical phrases, but these came to nothing. During the short reign of Edward VI the idea was entertained of a new revision by Fagius and Bucer, but this also fell through. Reprints, however, were very numerous, Matthew's Bible, the Great Bible, and Tyndale's Testament (revised and unrevised) being the most favoured, but Coverdale's Bible was also reprinted, and even Taverner's version of the Old Testament was touched up and reissued with Tyndale's of the New.

The
Geneva
Bible.
Under the reign of Mary there was no Bible-printing in England, but the number of Protestant exiles, holding extreme views and interested in scholarship, who found themselves congregated at Geneva, led to a new revision of great importance in the history of the English Bible. The Geneva Bible itself did not appear until
xlvi. 1560, but it was preluded in 1557 by a New Testament, obviously the work of a single translator, identifiable with practical certainty as William Whittingham, a senior student of Christ Church, Oxford, who subsequently (1563) became Dean of Durham, although he had received no episcopal ordination. While working on his translation Whittingham was acting as a 'senior' or elder of the Church at Geneva, of which in 1559 he became deacon and the following year minister. He is said to have been connected by marriage with Calvin, who contributed to the New Testament of 1557 'The Epistle declaring that Christ is the end of the Lawe', and he

was undoubtedly the moving spirit of the Bible of 1560, which he stayed at Geneva to complete when other exiles were hurrying home on the accession of Elizabeth. Moreover, while the 1557 translation of the New Testament was very thoroughly revised when reprinted in the Bible of 1560, the general lines of the earlier book were carefully followed in the later, and even some phrases were taken over from its preface. There is thus a very strong presumption that the new translation, destined to so great a popularity, originated with Whittingham, and that the trial New Testament was his individual work. The printing of this was completed at Geneva ' this x. of Iune ' 1557, by Conrad Badius, the book being a pretty little 32°, in the style at that time specially popular at Lyons, with ornamental capitals and headpieces, printed in a small clear roman type, with a still smaller type of the same class for the marginal notes, and italics as a subsidiary fount. The title of the book reads :

> The ‖ New Testa- ‖ ment of our Lord Ie ‖ sus Christ. ‖‖ Conferred diligently with the Greke, and best ap- ‖ proued translations. ‖‖ With the arguments, aswel before the Chapters, as for euery Boke ‖ & Epistle, also diuersities of readings, and moste proffitable ‖ annotations of all harde places : wherunto is added a copi- ‖ ous Table. [Woodcut illustrating the theme [1] : God by time restoreth Truth ‖ and maketh her victorious.] At Geneva ‖ Printed by Conrad Badius, ‖ M.D. LVII.

In the preface, quoted in full in the Records, Whittingham says that in his translation he has chiefly had respect to the ' simple lambes, which partely are already in the folde of Christ, and so willingly heare their Shepeheards

xlvi.

---

[1] It is evident that we have here the inspiration for the pageant of Time, Truth, and the Bible at ' the Little Conduit in Cheape ' which attracted so much attention at the progress of Queen Elizabeth from Westminster to the Tower the next year.

voyce, and partly wandering astray by ignorance, tary the tyme tyll the Shepeherde fynde them and bring them vnto his flocke ', being himself ' moued with zeale, counselled by the godly, and drawen by occasion, both of the place where God hath appointed vs to dwel, and also of the store of heauenly learning & iudgement, which so abundeth in this Citie of Geneua, that iustely it may be called the patron and mirrour of true religion and godlynes '.

> To these therfore which are of the flocke of Christ which knowe their Fathers wil, and are affectioned to the trueth, I rendre a reason of my doing in fewe lines. First as touching the perusing of the text, it was diligently reuised by the moste approued Greke examples, and conference of translations in other tonges as the learned may easiely iudge, both by the faithful rendering of the sentence, and also by the proprietie of the wordes and perspicuitie of the phrase. Forthermore that the Reader might be by all meanes proffited, I haue deuided the text into verses and sections, according to the best editions in other langages, and also, as to this day the ancient Greke copies mencion, it was wont to be vsed. And because the Hebrew and Greke phrases which are strange to rendre in other tongues, and also shorte, shulde not be so harde, I haue sometyme interpreted them without any whit diminishing the grace of the sense, as our langage doth vse them, and sometyme haue put to that worde, which lacking made the sentence obscure, but haue set it in such letters as may easely be discerned from the commun texte.

He goes on to explain his system of annotation, and the critical marks by which he drew attention to differences in the Greek manuscripts, either in single words or ' in the sentence ', and finally expatiates at some length on the value of the Arguments ' aswel they which conteyne the summe of euery chapter, as the other which are placed before the bookes and epistles, wherof the commoditie is so great that they may serue in stede of a Commentarie to the Reader.'

Space forbids more quotation, but it will be evident from these extracts that it is to Whittingham's New Testament that the Version of 1611 owes two of its prominent features, its division into verses (taken by Whittingham from Étienne's Greek-Latin Testament of 1551) and the use of italics for explanatory and connective words and phrases (taken from Beza's New Testament of 1556). Whittingham's chapter-summaries, moreover, were much fuller than those of the Great Bible.

All the features in the New Testament of 1557 are repeated in the Bible of 1560, in preparing which Whit- xlvii. tingham had the help of Anthony Gilby and Thomas Sampson, afterwards (from 1561 till his deprivation in 1565) Dean of Christ Church. The funds for this were apparently subscribed by the Protestant exiles or sent out by friends in England, since the translator speaks of ' being earnestly desired and by diuers, whose learning and godlynes we reuerence, exhorted and also incouraged by the ready willes of suche, whose heartes God likewise touched, not to spare any charges for the fortherance of suche a benefite and fauour of God toward his Churche'. One of these helpers was John Bodley (father of Sir Thomas), who in January, 1561, received an exclusive patent from Elizabeth for printing this Bible under xlviii. episcopal supervision for seven years, a grant which in March, 1565 (? 1566), Parker and Grindal recommended should be extended for another twelve, but still subject to xlix. implied conditions which apparently Bodley could not accept. By the help of these funds the translators were able to borrow or buy woodcuts to illustrate the descriptions of the tabernacles, &c., in Exodus, 1 Kings, and Ezekiel from Antoine Rebul, the publisher of the French Bible printed at Geneva in the same year. They allude

to these cuts in their preface and also to the addition of
verse-numbers in the chapter-summaries, by which these
were brought into the form used in 1611.

As regards the literary influences which affected the
Geneva version, it is clear that increased use was made
of the Latin translation of Pagninus, the revised Bible
of Leo Juda, and that of Sebastian Münster, also of the
French revisions of Olivetan. For the New Testament
Whittingham had constant recourse to the French version
of Beza (Théodore de Bèze), published in 1556 ; further
use was made of this in 1560, while in 1576 Laurence
Tomson (a Fellow of Magdalen College, Oxford, who sat
for fourteen years, 1575–89, in the House of Commons)
used the Geneva version as the basis of a direct
translation from the French of Beza, and editions
of this were often bound up with the Geneva Old
Testament.

After Elizabeth's accession the Great Bible was once
again, by the Injunctions of 1559, ordered to be set up
in churches, and new editions were printed by R. Harrison
at London in 1562, and at Rouen in 1566 by Cardin
Hamillon, at the expense of Richard Carmarden (an
Englishman connected with the customs), this foreign
edition disarming suspicion by stating on its title-page
that it was ' According to the translation apoynted by
the Queenes Majesties Iniunctions to be read in all
Churches with in her Majesties Realme '. Archbishop
Parker had shown no ill-will to the Geneva version, was
even, indeed, subject to conditions, ready to support
John Bodley's application for an extension of his privilege for it, but the use of a translation with bitterly controversial notes in the public services of the Church was
contrary both to Tudor ideals of uniformity and to
1 A, B. Parker's own preference for the *via media*. In or before

1566, therefore, perhaps at the instigation of Richard The
Cox, Bishop of Ely, he revived the project, which had Bishops'
Bible.
come to naught in Cranmer's day, of a new revision to
be mainly the work of the Anglican bishops. Beyond
two or three quotations in Strype's Life of Parker from l c.
letters of prelates engaged in the task we know curiously
little about its progress until October 5, 1568, when
Parker was able to send to Sir William Cecil a bound li, lii.
copy for presentation to the Queen, and enclosed with it
a dedicatory letter, and (for Cecil's information) a list
of the revisers and a copy of the ' Observations respected '
by them. The observations tell us that the revisers were
to follow the Great Bible ' and not to recede from it but
where it varyeth manifestly from the Greek or Hebrew
original ', to make use of the versions of Pagninus and
Münster, to abstain from bitter or controversial notes, to
mark sections not edifying for public reading, and to
substitute more convenient terms and phrases for ' all
such words as sound [tend] in the old translation to any
offence of lightnes or obscenity '.

As regards the personality of the revisers, Parker tells
Cecil ' bicause I wold yow knewe all, I here send yow
a note to signifie who first traveiled in the diverse bookes,
though after them sum other perusing was had ; the
lettres of their names be partlie affixed in the ende of their
bookes ; which I thought a polecie to showe them, to make
them more diligent, as awnswerable for their doinges '.
When we turn to the Bible itself we find initials such as
Parker thus leads us to expect not only at the end of
certain books, but also in certain cases printed in or
under the ornamental capital with which a book or
chapter begins. We may thus construct the following
table :

	Parker's Note.	Indications in the Bible.	Author.
The sum of the Scripture . The Tables of Christ's Line . The Arguments of the Scripture The first Preface unto the Whole Bible . . The Preface unto the Psalter . The Preface unto the New Testament	M. Cant. .	The Archbishop's arms quartered with those of Christ Church, Canterbury, in the capital before the Table of Christ's Line ; his personal arms in the capital before the general preface or prologue.	Matthew Parker, Archbishop of Canterbury.
Genesis . . Exodus . .	M. Cant. .	Initials M. C. under capitals	Matthew Parker.
Leviticus . . Numbers . .	Cantuariae	Andrew Pierson, Prebend. of Canterbury.
Deuteronomy .	W. Exon. .	W. E. at end .	William Alley, Bishop of Exeter.
Joshua . . Judges . . Ruth . . Kings (Samuel) I, II . .	R. Meneven	R. M. at end .	Richard Davies, Bishop of St Davids.
Kings III, IV (I, II) . Chronicles I, II .	Ed. Wigorn	E. W. under capital and at end	Edwin Sandys, Bishop of Worcester.
Job . . . Proverbs . .	Cantuariae	A. P C at end of each book	Andrew Pierson Prebend. of Canterbury.
Ecclesiastes . Cantica . . Ecclesiasticus .	Cantabrigiae	A P E at end . .	Andrew Perne, Dean of Ely.
Susanna . . Baruch . . Maccabees .	J. Norwic	J. N. . . .	John Parkhurst Bishop of Norwich
Esdras . . Judith . . Tobias . . Wisdom . .	W. Cicestren.	W. C. (in some copies) at end of Wisdom	William Barlow Bishop of Chichester.
Isaiah . . Jeremiah . Lamentations .	R. Winton	R. W. at end . .	Robert Horne Bishop of Winchester.

	Parker's Note.	Indications in the Bible.	Author.
zekiel . . . aniel . . .	J. Lich. and Covent.	T. C. L. at end .	Thomas Bentham, Bishop of Coventry and Lichfield.
inor Prophets .	Ed. London .	E. L. at end .	Edmund Grindal, Bishop of London.
atthew . . ark . . .	M. Cant. .	M. C. under first capital	Matthew Parker.
ake . . . •hn . . .	Ed. Peterb.		Edmund Scambler, Bishop of Peter-borough.
cts . . . omans . .	R. Eliensis	R. E. at end of both	Richard Cox, Bishop of Ely.
Corinthians .	D. West-mon.	G. G. at end . .	Gabriel Goodman, Dean of Westmins-ter.
Corinthians . alatians . . phesians . hilippians . olossians . nessalonians . imothy . . tus . . . hilemon . . ebrews . .	M. Cant. .	M. C. under capitals beginning 2 Corinth., Galatians (in some copies), Ephesians, Philipp., 1, 2 Coloss., 1, 2 Thessal., Titus, Philemon, Hebrews	Matthew Parker.
anonical Epis-les pocalypse .	N. Lincoln	H. L. under capitals beginning 1 Peter v, 2 Peter iii, 1 John v, 3 John, Jude and Apocalypse xxii	NicholasBullingham, Bishop of Lincoln (? completed by Hugh Jones, Bishop of Llandaff).

It will be noticed that in the above list (the books in which are given in Parker's order, but with English instead of Latin names) there is no mention of the Psalms. These had originally been assigned to Guest, Bishop of Rochester, but the intention he expressed in a letter quoted by Strype of bringing his translation into violent l c. conformity with the New Testament quotations had apparently alarmed Parker, and the initials at the end of the book are T. B. These Strype interpreted as stand-ing for Thomas Becon, a prebendary of Canterbury, but a very unlikely man. Dr. Aldis Wright, in his revision of Westcott's *General View of the History of the English Bible* assigns them, no doubt rightly, to Thomas Bickley, one of Parker's chaplains, afterwards Bishop of Chichester. The only other difficulty is as to the responsibility for the Canonical Epistles and the Apocalypse. Until Dr. Wright drew attention to them, the initials beneath the capitals in such seemingly haphazard positions had escaped notice. His conjecture that the revision was begun by the Bishop of Lincoln and completed by his brother of Llandaff meets the case, though it is strange that the first worker should have left so many of his books unfinished.

Portioned out, as it was, among a number of individual revisers who, as far as we know, never checked each other's work, the Bishops' Bible, as it came to be called from the number of prelates who collaborated in it, while an improvement on the Great Bible, more especially in the New Testament, can hardly be regarded as much more than a makeshift. In form, on the other hand, it is a handsome book,[1] and Parker highly com-
ii A mended Richard Jugge, the printer, to Cecil for the pains
iii c he had taken with it, even to the point of printing the New Testament on thicker paper to withstand the extra amount of wear it was likely to receive. The Bible is embellished with numerous woodcuts, and also with a fine engraved title-page, attributed to Franciscus Hogenberg, bearing in the centre a rather pleasing portrait of the Queen. Before the Book of Judges there is another engraved portrait, representing the Earl of Leicester, in whom the bishops apparently found some resemblance to Joshua, and at the beginning of the Psalms a third

---

[1] Messrs. Darlow and Moule note that 27s. 8d. was paid for a copy by St. John's College, Cambridge, in 1571.

portrait, of Lord Burghley holding a B, which thus at once does duty for a capital and helps to identify its holder Punning capitals, of which this may claim to be one of the least pleasing, had been for some time in vogue, but in the second folio edition, published in 1572, the B was taken out of the plate and Burleigh divorced from his immediate connexion with the Psalter. A little further revision was bestowed on the New Testament in this reprint, and the Psalter is printed twice over, once as revised, and once in the text of the Great Bible, still familiar to all churchgoers as the ' Prayer-book version '.

The struggle for supremacy between the Geneva and the Bishops' version leads so directly to the undertaking of that of 1611 that we must leave the discussion of it to our next chapter. Meanwhile there is still another translation to be noticed here.

The years which followed the publication of the Bishops' Bible witnessed a devoted attempt by the Jesuits to win back England to the faith. It appears to have been in connexion with this attempt that the New Testament was rendered into English by members of the English College at Douay early in their temporary exile to Rheims, which began in 1578. In a Latin letter written by Cardinal Allen to Dr. Vendeville, September 16 in that year,[1] we find this interesting passage, in a description of the life of the college : *The Rheims New Testament liii.*

> On every Sunday and festival English sermons are preached by the more advanced students on the gospel, epistle or subject proper to the day. . . . We preach in English, in order to acquire greater power and grace in the use of the vulgar tongue. . . . In this respect the heretics, however ignorant they may be in

[1] The text is given on pp. 52–67 of *Letters and Memorials of William Cardinal Allen* by T. F. Knox (1882) the translation on p. xl. sq. of the *First and Second Diaries of the English College at Douay* by the same editor (1878).

other points, have the advantage over many of the more learned Catholics, who having been educated in the universities and the schools do not commonly have at command the text of Scripture or quote it except in Latin. Hence when they are preaching to the unlearned and are obliged on the spur of the moment to translate some passage which they have quoted into the vulgar tongue, they often do it inaccurately and with unpleasant hesitation, because either there is no English version of the words or it does not then and there occur to them. Our adversaries on the other hand have at their fingers' ends all those passages of Scripture which seem to make for them and by a certain deceptive adaptation and alteration of the sacred words produce the effect of appearing to say nothing but what comes from the bible. This evil might be remedied if we too had some catholic version of the bible, for all the English versions are most corrupt. I do not know what kind you have in Belgium. But certainly we on our part, if his Holiness shall think proper, will undertake to produce a faithful, pure and genuine version of the bible in accordance with the edition approved by the Church, for we already have men most fitted for the work.

The man of all others most fitted for the work in Allen's eyes was Gregory Martin, one of the original scholars (1557) of St. John's College, Oxford, when Edmund Campion was a Fellow, now, in 1578, lecturer in Hebrew and Holy Scripture at the Douay-Rheims College. According to the entry in the College Diaries he began to translate the Bible on or about October 16 (i. e. just a month after Allen's letter), and in order to get on with it rapidly, made a practice of translating two chapters daily, his version being corrected by Allen himself and by Richard Bristow, Moderator of the College. His work occupied him altogether three years and a half, the entry, ' Hoc ipso mense extrema manus Nouo Testamento Anglice edito imposita est ' occurring in the Diary under March, 1582, and in the same year the New Testament was published with the title :

The New Testament of Iesus Christ, translated faithfully into English, out of the authentical Latin, according to the best corrected copies of the same, diligently conferred with the Greeke and other editions in diuers languages : With Arguments of bookes and chapters, Annotations, and other necessarie helpes, for the better vnderstanding of the text, and specially for the discouerie of the corruptions of diuers late translations, and for cleering the controuersies in religion of these daies : in the English College of Rhemes. [Quotations[1] in Latin and English]. Printed at Rhemes by Iohn Fogny. 1582. Cum priuilegio.

On the back of the title is ' The Censure and Approbation ' signed by four licensers, and this is followed by twenty-two pages of small print containing ' The Preface to the Reader treating of these three points: of the translation of Holy Scriptures into the vulgar tongues, and namely into English ; of the causes why this new Testament is translated according to the auncient vulgar Latin text : & of the maner of translating the same.' Quotations liv. from this interesting preface will be found in our Records ; here it may be well to remind any reader struck with the superficial absurdity of translating from a translation instead of an original, that if St. Jerome worked from better Greek manuscripts than any which were known in the sixteenth century, his Latin translation might, at least theoretically, represent the original Greek better than any manuscript used by Erasmus. Practically, of course, the question would be one of the balance between loss and gain, and in striking this balance

[1] The first from Psalm 118 ' Give me vnderstanding, and I wil searche thy law, and wil keepe it with my whole hart ', the second from St. Augustine, tract 2, on the Epistles of St. John ' al things that are readde in holy Scriptures we must heare with great attention, to our instruction and saluation : but those things specially must be commended to memorie, which make most against Heretikes : whose deceites cease not to circumuent and beguile al the weaker sort and the more negligent persons.'

Gregory Martin, or whoever wrote the preface, was probably very insufficiently conscious that if the available Greek texts were corrupt the available Latin texts were very corrupt also, and far from representing what St. Jerome really wrote. Thus from the point of view of scholarship the decision to translate from the Vulgate was doubtless wrong, but it was not absurd, and there is ample evidence that Martin and his supervisors were good Graecists, and on any point, such as the use of the article, on which they felt free to interpret the Latin by the Greek, did so with conspicuous success.

Another point which must be made is that the translation is much simpler than popular accounts of it make out. It is quite true that the translators acted up to their declaration, ' we presume not in hard places to mollifie the speaches or phrases, but religiously keepe them word for word, and point for point, for feare of missing or restraining the sense of the holy Ghost to our phantasie,' and it is possible to quote verses, especially from the Epistles, which remain utterly unintelligible until we know the original. In this the translators seem to have forgotten the needs of popular preaching which Cardinal Allen made the main ground for setting Gregory Martin to work. But ' hard places ' do not occur on every page of the New Testament, and it is easy to find long passages in the Gospels without a difficult word in them, and which a good reader could make all the more dramatic because of the abruptness of some of the constructions and transitions.

The Jesuit New Testament was reprinted at Antwerp in 1600. In 1593 the College returned from Rheims to Douai, and in 1609–10, a press having been set up in the town, the Old Testament was printed there. This had liv. been mentioned in the Introduction of 1582 as ' lying by us for lacke of good meanes to publish the whole in such sort as a worke of so great charge and importance requireth ', and it was doubtless the news of the forthcoming new Anglican version which at last brought it to the light. No use was made of the Old Testament by the Anglican revisers, but in his excellent study, *The Part of Rheims in the making of the English Bible* (1902), Dr. James G. Carleton has shown that the influence of the Rheims New Testament on the version of 1611 was very considerable. That it attained this influence was mainly due to the exertions of the Rev. William Fulke, D.D., who in 1589 published ' The Text of the New Testament of Iesus Christ, translated out of the vulgar Latine by the Papists of the traiterous Seminarie at Rhemes ', and very honestly reprinted the whole translation with its notes, parallel with the Bishops' version and alternated with his own confutations. Fulke's folio (reprinted in 1601, 1617, and 1633) was regarded for over forty years as a standard work on the Protestant side, and probably every reviser of the New Testament for the edition of 1611 possessed it. Along with Tyndale, Coverdale, Whittingham, and Parker, the exiled Jesuit, Gregory Martin, must be thus recognized as one of the builders of the version of the Bible which after three centuries is still in scarcely disturbed possession of the affections of the English people.

II. THE BIBLE OF 1611

IN his letter of October 5, 1568, to Cecil, forwarding a copy of the Bishop's Bible for presentation to the Queen, Archbishop Parker writes with obvious timidity :
' The printer hath honestly done his diligence ; if your lii.

honour would obtain of the Queen's Highness that this edition might be licensed and only[1] commended in public reading in churches, to draw to one uniformity, it were no great cost to the most parishes, and a relief to him for his great charges sustained.' That the adoption of the new version for use in churches should thus be urged mainly on the ground of an obligation to recoup the printer is certainly strange, but the very half-hearted canons on the subject passed by the Province of Canterbury in 1571 show that there was not much enthusiasm to be reckoned on. The passage usually quoted (Cardwell, *Synodalia*, 115) is indeed almost malicious, since it merely lays down that every archbishop and bishop is to have the book (' sacra Biblia in amplissimo volumine, uti nuperrime Londini excusa sunt ') in his own house along with Fox's *Book of Martyrs* and other similar works, and that deans were to see that it was bought and placed in their cathedrals in order that vicars, minor canons, the servants of the church, strangers, and wayfarers might read and hear it, and were also to buy it for their own households, i. e. the chief obligation imposed was on the bishops and other ' superior clergy ' to buy their own revision. In a later canon (Cardwell, *Synodalia*, 123) churchwardens are enjoined to see that a copy of the new edition is placed in every church,[2] but the proviso, ' if it can be done conveniently,' is in striking contrast with the royal order to provide a copy by a certain day under penalty of a fine of four times its cost for every month of delay, which had been issued by Proclamation in the case of the Great Bible.

---

[1] i. e. to the exclusion of any other.

[2] ' Curabunt etiam ut sacra Biblia sint in singulis ecclesiis in amplissimo volumine (si commode fieri possit) qualia nunc nuper Londini excusa sunt.'

With little backing, either from the State or from his own Convocation, Parker was left to deal with the question of the circulation of the Bible by means of his own resources, and these, it must be remembered, owing to the duties cast on him in connexion with the licensing of books for the press, were, for any negative purpose, very great. In March 1565 (? 1566) he and Grindal, who as Bishop of London shared these duties, had recommended Cecil to extend John Bodley's exclusive privilege xlix for printing the Geneva Bible for another twelve years on the ground that ' thoughe one other speciall Bible for the churches be meant by us to be set forthe, as convenient time and leysor hereafter will permytte : yet shall it nothing hindre, but rather do moch good to have diversitie of translations and readinges '.   They had added, however, ' and if his licence, hereafter to be made, goe simplye foorthe withowt proviso of owr oversight, as we thinke it maye so passe well ynoughe, yet shall we take suche ordre in writing withe the partie, that no impression shall passe but by our direction, consent and advise.'   In the face of this last sentence it is highly significant that during Parker's life no edition of the Geneva Bible was printed in England, although at Geneva itself one was published by John Crispin in 1570. At variance with the Privy Council over the question of ' prophesyings ' during 1574, Parker was unable during the last months of his life to attend its meeting owing to his rapidly failing health. He died on May 17, 1575, and the first Geneva New Testament printed in London is dated in this year without specifying the month ; we have, however, documentary evidence that Parker was dead before its publication, and there are excellent reasons for placing this in the latter half of the year.   It is impossible, therefore, to avoid the conviction that to the

very end of his life Parker used his control over the
Stationers' Company to prevent the Geneva version being
printed in England, and also to secure for Jugge the
monopoly of printing the Bishops' Bible.

According to the ideas of the day the exclusion of the
Geneva Bible was perhaps justified by the character of
a few of the notes. The monopoly secured for Jugge
might also have been defended from the Tudor stand-
point, if it had been accompanied by an insistence that
the Bishops' version should be effectively circulated ;
but, as far as the evidence before us shows, there was
no such insistence. Editions in large folio were printed
in 1568. 1572, and 1574 ; others in large quarto in 1569
and 1573. Evidence as to editions in octavo, either of
the whole Bible or of the New Testament, is much less
exact, owing on the one hand to the curious absence of
dates from the two or three editions probably of this
period of which copies remain, and on the other to the
possibility of one or more entire editions having perished.
But taking the most favourable view possible, it seems
certain that the Archbishop cared little for providing
Bibles for private reading. He saw and met the need
of suitable editions for the service of the church, but to
use a phrase which, though it has a ring of these present
times, is taken from the preface to the version of 1611
(where it is applied to the Roman Catholic position) he did
not ' trust the people ' with cheap editions of the Bible,
and his lack of confidence sealed the fate of the Bishops'
Bible.

Immediately after the death of Archbishop Parker,
the other printers of London, who had previously
acquiesced in Jugge's monopoly of Bible-printing, took
courage to urge their right to share it. A compromise was
lvi. A. patched up by which Jugge was left with the exclusive

right of printing editions of the Bible in quarto, and of the
New Testament in sextodecimo, while the other sizes
were left free, subject (presumably to secure responsi- lvi. B.
bility for accuracy) to a licence from the Stationers'
Company. Licences were obtained, and on November 24,
1575, there appeared a folio edition of the Bishops'
Bible, printed by Jugge, but on behalf of William Norton,
Luke Harrison, and other stationers, each of whom put
his name on a portion of the edition. This was apparently
the beginning of the ' Bible Stock ' of the Stationers'
Company, a company within a company, the subsequent
history of which is very obscure, but which is said to
have earnt profits and possessed funds which enabled it,
on occasion, to lend money at interest to the Stationers'
Company itself. If, as is usually said, the revisers of
1611 received any payment from the Company, it must
have been from this separate Bible Stock that it was
derived. The existence of this Stock also offers a strong
ground for believing that the compromise of 1575 continued to affect the business of Bible-printing in ways
of which we have no knowledge. But for this we should
be bound to believe that it had no other result than
the folio edition of the Bishops' Bible already mentioned.
In this same year, 1575, under the powerful patronage lvi. C.
of Sir Francis Walsingham, Christopher Barker, who had
been in Walsingham's service, and was himself a man
of some means, employed Thomas Vautrollier to print
for him an edition in duodecimo of the Geneva Bible,
hitherto unprinted in England, and printed another
edition himself in octavo. Barker advertised his connexion with Walsingham by taking the latter's crest,
a tiger's head, as the sign of his house, and used a cut
of it as an ornament in his books. He also printed in
1576 the already mentioned translation of Beza's French

New Testament, on the basis of the Geneva version, made by Laurence Tomson, who was in Walsingham's service. He further printed two folio editions of the Geneva Bible in 1576 and another in 1577. In that year Richard Jugge made his will, on August 17 and 18, and died. From subsequent allusions we know that his patent as Queen's printer must immediately have been obtained (if the reversion had not already been secured) by Thomas Wilkes, a diplomatist of some ability. The new patent extended to all editions of the Bible, and Wilkes must have tried at first to work it through John Jugge, the son of Richard, since John, who had begun business for himself the previous May by copyrighting two insignificant books, is actually called Queen's Printer about this time in a largely signed petition against monopolies. He disappears, however, possibly by death, possibly because Wilkes learnt that he was receiving under his father's will the inconsiderable sum of 10s., and was thus not a person to be dealt with. On September 28, at Wilkes's instance, a new patent conferring lvii. c. complete monopoly of Bible-printing was granted to Christopher Barker. Five years later, in 1582, when monopolies were again challenged, Barker wrote as follows :

> The whole bible together requireth so great somme of a money to be employed in the imprinting thereof : as Master Iugge kept the Realme twelue yere withoute, before he Durst aduenture to print one[1] impression[1] ; but I considering the great somme I paide to Master Wilkes, Did (as some haue termed it since) gyue a Desperate aduenture to imprint fower sundry impressions for all ages, wherein I employed to the value of three thowsande pounde in the terme of one yere and an halfe, or thereaboute : in which tyme if I had died, my wife and children had ben vtterlie vndone, and many of my frendes

---

[1] This must refer to the period before 1568.

greatlie hindered by disbursing round sommes of money for me, by suertiship and other meanes : as my late good master Master Secretary for one, so that nowe this gappe being stopped, I haue little or nothing to doe, but aduenture a needlesse charge ; to keepe many Journemen in worke, most of them seruauntes to my predicessours.

The ' fower sundry impressions ' to which Barker here alludes, comprised a small folio and octavo in 1577, and two large folios in 1578. One of the large folios was of the Bishops' version but of this we find him writing to the City Companies as ' another Bible, which was begon lviii. before I had authoritie, as it is affirmed, which could not be finished but by my consent and therefore hath the name to be printed by the assignement of Christopher Barker '. All the other three impressions were of the Geneva version, and the large folio is a very notable volume since it was clearly intended for use in churches and was accompanied by a prayer-book in which the word ' minister ' was throughout substituted for ' priest ', and references to the books from which they come printed instead of the text of the Gospels and Epistles. All this surely shows that, despite the suspension of Grindal, the extremer Protestant party were very strong, and that behind these printing ventures, for which Walsingham helped to find money, there was something more than ordinary trading. Numerous other editions of the Geneva version were printed during the next five years, but I can find no single Bishops' Bible to balance them. When, however, Whitgift succeeded Grindal as Archbishop, Barker was awakened from his dream that the ' gappe ' was stopped, and ordered to put in hand a smaller and larger edition of the Bishops' Bible, as to which when they were both ready (the quarto in 1584, the folio in 1585), and apparently had not sold very quickly, Whitgift wrote (July 16, 1587) to the Bishop of Lincoln :

> Whereas I am credibly informed that divers, as well parish churches, as chapels of ease, are not sufficiently furnished with Bibles, but some have either none at all, or such as be torn and defaced, and yet not of the translation authorized by the synods of bishops : these are therefore to require you strictly in your visitations, or otherwise, to see that all and every the said churches and chapels in your diocese be provided of one Bible, or more, at your discretion, of the translation allowed as aforesaid, and one book of Common Prayer, as by the laws of this realm is appointed. And for the performance thereof, I have caused her highness's printer to imprint two volumes of the said translation of the Bible aforesaid, a bigger and a less, the largest for such parishes as are of ability, and the lesser for chapels and very small parishes ; both which are now extant and ready.

One other folio of the Bishops' Bible was printed by Christopher Barker himself in 1588. In August 1589 he secured a fresh patent from the queen for his own life and that of his son Robert, and thenceforth entrusted his Bible-printing to deputies, until his death in 1599. During the fourteen years 1589–1603 three more folio editions of the Bishops' Bible appeared, no quarto, and three or four octavos. Against this, during the entire period from 1575 onwards, on an average three editions of the Geneva version were produced each year, the majority of them in small sizes for private reading. How far this superiority was the result of demand, how far it was produced by a control of the supply, is a question which, difficult as it is to answer, deserves more attention than it has received. It is clear, on the one hand, that during Parker's life the circulation of the Geneva version was artificially barred, and nothing was done to popularize its rival. It is clear, I think, also, that from the death of Parker to the appointment of Whitgift, the positions were reversed, and that in these eight years the Geneva version, which was not only favoured, but pushed, by the aid of Walsingham and his friends, with a zeal in which politics, religion, and desire or gain (closely allied in those days) were all combined, was put on the market in such quantities as to give it a real hold on the English people. After Whitgift's accession it is possible that, as the scales were more evenly held, the editions of each version came gradually to be issued mainly in accordance with the demand, although until nearly the end of the century the rarity of octavo editions of the Bishops' version is very noticeable. But taking the period as a whole it is obvious that other influences than those of publishers merely anxious to make money were contending over the fortunes of the two versions, and that the short-sighted policy of Parker gave Walsingham and his friends a chance of which they availed themselves to the full. Interpret the evidence as we may, the fact must steadily be borne in mind that throughout the reign of Elizabeth, the production of editions of the Bible was always a controlled production, and when we come to consider the fortunes of the version of 1611 it will be well to remember that the control still went on.

The lack of agreement between the Bible which men read in their houses and that which they heard in church must have caused annoyance to both parties. It is creditable to the scholarship, and perhaps also to the foresight, of the Puritan party, that at the Conference at Hampton Court, which James I called together (quite informally) in January 1604 to ascertain how far the Puritan complaints could be met, the demand for a new translation, which would command the assent of the whole church, came from their spokesman, Dr. John Reynolds, President of Corpus Christi College, Oxford. According to the fullest account of the Con-

ference which has come down to us, Reynolds began by
raising questions about the Catechism, &c.

After that, he moued his Maiestie, that there might bee a
newe *translation* of the *Bible*, because, those which were allowed
in the raignes of *Henrie* the eight, and *Edward* the sixt, were
corrupt and not aunswerable to the truth of the Originall.
For example, first, *Galathians*, 4, 25, the Greeke word συστοιχεῖ
is not well translated, as nowe it is, *Bordreth*, neither expressing
the force of the worde, nor the Apostles sense, nor the situation
of the place.

Secondly, *Psalme*, 105, 28, *they were not obedient*; the Originall beeing, *They were not disobedient*.

Thirdly, *Psalme*, 106, verse 30. Then stood up *Phinees*
and *prayed*, the Hebrew hath *Executed iudgement*. To which
motion, there was, at the present, no gainsaying, the obiections
beeing triuiall and old, and alreadie, in print, often aunswered ;
onely, my Lord of *London* well added, that if euery mans humour
should be followed, there would be no ende of translating.
Whereupon his Highnesse wished that some especiall paines
should be taken in that behalfe for one vniforme translation
(professing that hee could neuer yet, see a Bible well translated
in English ; but the worst of all, his Maiestie thought the
Geneua to bee) and this to bee done by the best learned in
both the Vniuersities, after them to be reuiewed by the Bishops,
and the chiefe learned of the Church ; from them to bee
presented to the *Priuie-Councell* ; and lastly to bee ratified by
his *Royall authoritie* ; and so this whole Church to be bound
vnto it, and none other ; Marry, withall, hee gaue this caueat
(vpon a word cast out by my Lord of London) that no marginall
notes should be added, hauing found in them which are annexed
to the *Geneua* translation (which he sawe in a Bible giuen him
by an English Lady) some notes very partiall, vntrue, seditious,
and sauouring too much of daungerous, and trayterous con-
ceites. As for example, *Exod.* 1, 19, where the marginal note
alloweth *disobedience to Kings*. And 2. *Chron.* 15, 16, the note
taxeth *Asa* for deposing his mother, *onely*, and *not killing* her :
And so concludeth this point, as all the rest with a graue and
iudicious aduise. First, that errours in matters of faith might
bee rectified and amended. Secondly, that matters indifferent
might rather be interrupted and a glosse added ; alleaging
from *Bartolus de regno*, that as better a King with some weak-
nesse, then still a chaunge ; so rather, a Church with some

faultes, then an *Innouation*. And surely, sayth his Maiestie,
if these bee the greatest matters you be grieued with, I neede
not haue beene troubled with such importunities and com-
plaintes, as haue beene made vnto me ; some other more
priuate course might haue bene taken for your satisfaction,
and withall looking vppon the Lords, he shooke his head,
smiling.[1]

It is evident from every page in the narrative that the
writer of it, William Barlow, had no love for the Puritans,
and that his report is highly prejudiced. We cannot,
therefore, feel sure that Reynolds ignored the Bishops'
Bible by referring only to the versions allowed in the
reigns of Henry VIII and Edward VI, in the rather
insulting way that the text represents. The renderings
to which he objected are found also in the Bishops'
Bible, and if Reynolds passed over this, either as a mere
reprint, or as not formally ' allowed ' (i. e. approved),
he was needlessly provocative. But the genuine interest
which the king at once took in the proposal swept away
any difficulty which might have been raised by its form.
Nor was that interest transient. The Dean of Westminster and the Regius Professors of Hebrew at the
Universities of Oxford and Cambridge must have been
instructed ·with little delay to suggest the names of
revisers, and by June 30 Bancroft, Bishop of London,

---

[1] ' The Summe and Substance of the Conference, which it
pleased his Excellent Maiestie to haue with the Lords, Bishops
and other of his Clergie, (at which the most of the Lordes of the
Councell were present) in his Maiesties Priuy-Chamber, at
Hampton Court, Ianuary 14, 1603. Contracted by William
Barlow, Doctor of Diuinity, and Deane of Chester. Whereunto
are added, some Copies, (scattered abroad), vnsauory, and vntrue.
London, Printed by Iohn Windet, for Matthew Law and are to
be sold at his shop in Paules Churchyeard, neare S. Austens Gate.
1604.' It should be noted that a different turn is given to the
Puritan complaint in the preface to the 1611 Bible.

with whom (in the vacancy of the see of Canterbury) the King communicated, was able to write :

> His Majesty being made acquainted with the choice of all them to be employed in the translating of the Bible, in such sort as Mr. Lively can inform you, doth greatly approve of the said choice. And for as much as his Highness is very anxious that the same so religious a work should admit of no delay, he has commanded me to signify unto you in his name that his pleasure is, you should with all possible speed meet together in your University and begin the same.

The Mr. Lively here named was the Professor of Hebrew at Cambridge, and must have specially attracted the notice of the king, by whom he was presented to the rectory of Purleigh, Essex, in September 1604. His death the following May was a great blow to the work. The interest taken by James is further shown by a circular sent out by Bancroft to the other Bishops on July 31 enclosing a letter from the king of the 22nd, lx. A. stating that he had appointed ' certain learned men to the number of four and fifty [1] for the translating of the Bible, and that in this number divers of them have either no ecclesiastical preferment at all, or else so very small, as the same is far unmeet for men of their deserts '. The king himself being unable to remedy this ' in any convenient time ', enjoins all patrons of parsonages or prebends, of the value of twenty pounds at least, to certify him of the next vacancy in order that he may commend to them ' some such of the learned men as we shall think fit to be preferred unto it '. In another lx. B. circular of the same date Bancroft asks each bishop ' not only to think yourself what is meet for you to give for this purpose, but likewise to acquaint your dean and

---

[1] Only about fifty names in all have come down to us, and only forty-seven in any one list. It may have been intended at first that there should be nine revisers on each board.

chapter ' that they might subscribe also.   The response
to the first of these circulars seems to have been very
slight ; that to the second *nil*.

Of the lists of the translators which have come down
to us, the most trustworthy is that printed by Bishop
Burnet in his *History of the Reformation*,[1] which is here
given together with the Rules by which the revisers were
to be guided, and brief biographical notes, based on those
by Cardwell, supplemented from the *Dictionary of
National Biography* and other sources :

An Order set down for the Translating of the Bible, by
King James.

*The Places and Persons agreed upon for the Hebrew, with
the particular Books by them undertaken.*

Westminster.

Mr. Dean of *Westminster*
Mr. Dean of *Paul's*
Mr. Doctor *Saravia*
Mr. Doctor *Clark*
Mr. Doctor *Leifield*
Mr. Doctor *Teigh*
Mr. *Burleigh*
Mr. *King*
Mr. *Thompson*
Mr. *Beadwell*

Penteteuchon.
The Story from *Joshua*
to the first Book of
Chronicles, exclusive.

Mr. Dean of Westminster : Lancelot Andrewes, made Bishop of
    Chichester in 1605.
Mr. Dean of Pauls : John Overall, made Bishop of Coventry,
    1614.

---

[1] *The History of the Reformation of the Church of England.*   By
Gilbert Burnett.   The Fourth Edition, with Additions, &c.
London, 1715.   Part II.   A Collection of Records, p. 333 sqq.
The document has the side-note ' Ex MS. D. Borlase ', i.e. Edmund Borlase, the physician and historian.   There are several
similar lists in MS. in the British Museum, with unimportant
variants.   One of these (Add. 34218) is dated ' Anno secundi
regis Iacobi 1604 ', and there is no doubt that the lists refer to
that year, although Cardwell, from a mistake as to the date of
Barlow being made Dean of Chester, thought otherwise.

Cambridge.	Mr. Lively Mr. Richardson Mr. Chatterton Mr. Dillingham Mr. Harrison Mr. Andrews Mr. Spalding Mr. Binge	From the First of the *Chronicles*, with the rest of the Story, and the *Hagiographi*, viz. *Job*, *Psalms*, *Proverbs*, *Canticles*, Ecclesiastes.
Orford.	Doctor *Harding* Dr. *Reynolds* Dr. *Holland* Dr. *Kilbye* Mr. *Smith* Mr. *Brett* Mr. *Fairclough*	The four, or greater Prophets, with the *Lamentations*, and the twelve lesser Prophets.
Cambridge.	Doctor *Dewport* Dr. *Branthwait* Dr. *Radclife* Mr. *Warde*, Eman. Mr. *Downs* Mr. *Boyes* Mr. *Warde*, Reg.	The Prayer of *Manasses* and the rest of the *Apocrypha*.

Mr. Dr. Saravia : born at Hesdin in Artois in 1531, Professor of Divinity at Leyden, 1582 ; Rector of Tattenhill, Staffs, 1588 ; Prebendary of Canterbury and Vicar of Lewisham, 1595 ; Prebendary of Worcester and Westminster, 1601 ; died, 1612.

Mr. Dr. Clark : Dr. Richard Clark, Fellow of Christ's College, Cambridge.

Mr. Dr. Leifield : Dr. John Layfield, Fellow of Trinity College Cambridge (resigned 1603), Rector of St. Clement Danes London, 1601.

Mr. Dr. Teigh : Robert Tighe, Vicar of All Hallows, Barking, and Archdeacon of Middlesex.

Mr. Burleigh, probably the Dr. Francis Burley, who was one of the first Fellows of Chelsea College.

Mr. King : Geoffrey King, Fellow of King's College, Cambridge, and Regius Professor of Hebrew (1607–8) in succession to Spalding.

Mr. Thompson : Richard Tomson, of Clare Hall, Cambridge, B.D. 1593.

Mr. Beadwell : William Bedwell, Arabic Scholar, Rector of St. Ethelburga's, Bishopsgate Street, 1601.

Mr. Lively : Edward Lively, appointed Regius Professor of Hebrew at Cambridge, 1580 ; presented by the king to the rectory of Purleigh, Essex, September 20, 1604 ; died, May 1605.

Mr. Richardson : Dr. John Richardson, Fellow of Emmanuel College, Regius Professor of Divinity, 1607 ; Master of Peterhouse, 1609–15 ; then of Trinity.

Mr. Chatterton : Laurence Chaderton, Master of Emmanuel College, 1584–1622. Took part as a Puritan in the Hampton Court Conference.

Mr. Dillingham : Francis Dillingham, Fellow of Christ's, author of numerous books, 1599–1609 (or later) ; Incumbent of Wilden, Beds.

Mr. Harrison : Thomas Harrison, a noted Hebraist, Vice-Master of Trinity College, Cambridge.

Mr. Andrews : Roger Andrewes, brother of Lancelot, Fellow of Pembroke, Master of Jesus College, Cambridge.

Mr. Spalding : Robert Spalding, Fellow of St. John's College, Cambridge, Regius Professor of Hebrew in succession to Lively (1605–7).

Mr. Binge : Andrew Byng, Regius Professor of Hebrew at Cambridge in succession to King, 1608. ' About 1605 we find a decree of the Chapter of York to keep a residentiary's place for him.' [*D.N.B.*]

Dr. Harding: John Harding, Regius Professor of Hebrew (1591–8, 1604–10) and President of Magdalen College, Oxford.

Dr. Reynolds : John Reynolds or Rainolds, President of Corpus Christi College, Oxford, from 1598. Died, 1607.

Dr. Holland : Thomas Holland, Regius Professor Divinity, 1589 ; Rector of Exeter College, 1592. Died, 1612.

Dr. Kilbye : Richard Kilbye, Rector of Lincoln College, 1590 ; Regius Professor of Hebrew, 1610–21.

Mr. Smith : Miles Smith, of Brasenose, Prebendary of Hereford and Exeter Cathedrals, a noted Orientalist, one of the two final revisers of the version of 1611, and the writer of the preface ; made Bishop of Gloucester, 1612.

Mr. Brett : Richard Brett, Fellow of Lincoln College, Rector of Quainton, Bucks, 1595.

Mr. Fairclough : Richard Fairclough, Fellow of New College, Rector of Bucknell, Oxford, 1593.

Dr. Dewport : John Duport, Master of Jesus College, Cambridge, 1590 ; Prebendary of Ely, 1609.

Dr. Branthwait: William Branthwait, Fellow of Emmanuel College, 1584 ; Master of Gonville and Caius, 1607.

The Places and Persons agreed upon for the Greek, with the particular Books by them undertaken.

Oxford.

Mr. Dean of *Christchurch*
Mr. Dean of *Winchester*
Mr. Dean of *Worcester*
Mr. Dean of *Windsor*
Mr. *Savile*
Dr. *Perne*
Dr. *Ravens*
Mr. *Harmer*

The four Gospels. *Acts of the Apostles. Apocalyps.*

Westminster.

Dean of *Chester*
Dr. *Hutchinson*
Dr. *Spencer*
Mr. *Fenton*
Mr. *Rabbett*
Mr. *Sanderson*
Mr. *Dakins*

The Epistles of St. *Paul.* The Canonical Epistles.

- *Dr. Radcliffe* : Jeremiah Radcliffe, Fellow of Trinity College, Cambridge.
- *Mr. Warde* : Samuel Ward, Fellow of Sidney Sussex, 1599; master, 1610; King's Chaplain, 1611.
- *Mr. Downes* : Andrew Downes, Fellow of St. John's College, Cambridge, 1581 ; Regius Professor of Greek, 1585–1624.
- *Mr. Boyes* : John Boys, Fellow of Clare Hall, 1593 ; Dean of Canterbury, 1619.
- *Mr. Dean of Christchurch* : Thomas Ravis, Dean of Christ Church, 1596 ; Bishop of Gloucester, 1605 ; Bishop of London, 1607 ; died, 1609.
- *Mr. Dean of Winchester* : George Abbot, Master of University College, 1597 ; Dean of Winchester, 1600 ; Bishop of Coventry and Lichfield, 1609 ; of London, 1610 ; Archbishop of Canterbury, 1611.
- *Mr. Dean of Worcester* : Richard Edes, Dean of Worcester, 1597 ; Chaplain to James I. ; died, November 19, 1604. Edes was succeeded by James Montague, afterwards (1608) Bishop of Bath and Wells, &c. Fuller is the authority for identifying Edes as the (intended) reviser.
- *Mr. Dean of Windsor* : Giles Thompson, or Tomson, Fellow of All Souls, Bishop of Gloucester, 1611 ; died, 1612.
- *Mr. Savile* : Sir Henry Savile, Warden of Merton, 1585–1622 ; Provost of Eton, 1596 ; knighted, 1604 ; edited works of Chrysostom, 1610–13.

Dr. Perne : John Perin, Fellow of St. John's, Oxford ; Regius
Professor of Greek, 1597–1615 ; Canon of Christ Church,
November 24, 1604.

Dr. Ravens : apparently an error. See below.

Mr. Harmer : John Harmer, Fellow of New College, 1582 ;
Regius Professor of Greek, 1585 ; Head Master of Winchester, 1588 ; Warden of St. Mary's College, 1596 ; died, 1613.

Dean of Chester : William Barlow, Fellow of Trinity Hall, Dean,
1602 ; Bishop of Rochester, 1605 ; died, 1613.

Dr. Hutchinson : Ralph Hutchinson, President of St. John's
College, Oxford.

Dr. Spencer : John Spenser, Editor of Hooker, 1604 ; President
of Corpus Christi College, Oxford, 1607.

Mr. Fenton : Roger Fenton, Fellow of Pembroke Hall, Cambridge, Vicar of Chigwell, 1606 ; Prebendary of St. Paul's,
1609.

Mr. Rabbett : Michael Rabbett, Rector of St. Vedast Foster, 1603.

Mr. Sanderson : Thomas Sanderson, Rector of All Hallows the
Great, Thames Street, 1603 ; Archdeacon of Rochester, 1606.

Mr. Dakins : William Dakins, Fellow of Trinity College, Cambridge, Professor of Divinity, Gresham College, London, 1604;
died in 1607.

In other lists the name of J. Aglionby, Principal of St. Edmund
Hall, is substituted for that of the Dean of Worcester, and that
of L. Hutten, Canon of Christ Church, for the mysterious Dr.
Ravens. The choice of the revisers seems to have been determined solely by their fitness, and both parties in the Church were
represented by some of their best men.

The Rules to be observed in the Translation of the Bible.

1. THE ordinary Bible read in the Church, commonly called
the *Bishops Bible*, to be followed, and as little altered as the
Truth of the original will permit.

2. The Names of the Prophets, and the Holy Writers, with
the other Names of the Text, to be retained, as nigh as may be,
accordingly as they were vulgarly used.

3. The old Ecclesiastical Words to be kept, *viz.* the Word
Church not to be translated *Congregation* &c.

4. When a Word hath divers Significations, that to be kept
which hath been most commonly used by the most of the
Ancient Fathers, being agreeable to the Propriety of the Place
and the Analogy of the Faith.

5. The Division of the Chapters to be altered, either not at all, or as little as may be, if Necessity so require.

6. No Marginal Notes at all to be affixed, but only for the Explanation of the *Hebrew* or *Greek* Words, which cannot without some circumlocution, so briefly and fitly be express'd in the Text.

7. Such Quotations of Places to be marginally set down as shall serve for the fit Reference of one Scripture to another.

8. Every particular Man of each Company, to take the same Chapter, or Chapters, and having translated or amended them severally by himself, where he thinketh good, all to meet together, confer what they have done, and agree for their Parts what shall stand.

9. As any one Company hath dispatched any one Book in this Manner they shall send it to the rest, to be consider'd of seriously and judiciously, for His Majesty is very careful in this Point.

10. If any Company, upon the Review of the Book so sent, doubt or differ upon any Place, to send them Word thereof ; note the Place, and withal send the Reasons, to which if they consent not, the Difference to be compounded at the General Meeting, which is to be of the chief Persons of each Company, at the end of the Work.

11. When any Place of special Obscurity is doubted of Letters to be directed, by Authority, to send to any Learned Man in the Land, for his Judgement of such a Place.

12. Letters to be sent from every Bishop to the rest of his Clergy, admonishing them of this Translation in hand ; and to move and charge as many as being skilful in the Tongues ; and having taken Pains in that kind, to send his particular Observations to the Company, either at *Westminster*, *Cambridge* or *Oxford*.

13. The Directors in each Company, to be the Deans of *Westminster* and *Chester* for that Place ; and the King's Professors in the *Hebrew* or *Greek* in either University.

14. These translations to be used when they agree better with the Text than the Bishops Bible.
$\left\{ \begin{array}{l} \textit{Tindoll's.} \\ \textit{Matthews.} \\ \textit{Coverdale's.} \\ \textit{Whitchurch's.} \\ \textit{Geneva.} \end{array} \right.$

15. Besides the said Directors before mentioned, three or four of the most Ancient and Grave Divines, in either of the Universities, not employed in Translating, to be assigned by

the Vice-Chancellor, upon Conference with the rest of the Heads, to be Overseers of the Translations as well *Hebrew* as *Greek*, for the better Observation of the 4th Rule above specified.

In contrast with all these preparatory arrangements and rules, we may now quote the only nearly contemporary account of the experiences of one of the revisers which has come down to us. This relates to one of the second Cambridge group, to whom was committed the translation of the Apocrypha, Dr. John Boys, afterwards (1619) Dean of Canterbury, but at this time the holder of a living at Boxworth, which, it is to be feared, he rather neglected during his work as a translator. His biographer, Dr. Anthony Walker, writes :

When it pleased God to move King James to that excellent work, the translation of the Bible ; when the translators were to be chosen for Cambridge, he was sent for thither by those therein employed, & was chosen one ; some university men thereat repining (it may be not more able, yet more ambitious to have born [a] share in that service) disdaining that it should be thought they needed any help from the country.—Forgetting that Tully was the same man at Tusculan[um] as he was at Rome.   Sure I am, that part of the Apocrypha was alotted to him (for he hath shewed me the very copy he translated by), but to my grief I know not which part.

All the time he was about his own part, his commons were given him at St. John's ; where he abode all the week, till Saturday night ; & then went home to discharge his cure : returning thence on Monday morning.   When he had finished his own part, at the earnest request of him to whom it was assigned, he undertook a second ; and then he was in commons in another college : but I forbear to name both the person and the house.

Four years were spent in this first service ; at the end whereof the whole work being finished, & three copies of the whole Bible sent from Cambridge, Oxford & Westminster, to London ; a new choice was to be made of six in all, two out of every company, to review the whole work ; & extract one [copy] out of all three, to be committed to the presse.

For the dispatch of which business Mr. Downes & Mr. Bois

were sent for up to London. Where meeting (though Mr. Downes would not go till he was either fetcht or threatned with a pursivant) their four fellow labourers, they went dayly to Stationers Hall, & in three quarters of a year, finished their task. All which time they had from the Company of Stationers xxx[s] [each] per week, duly paid them : tho' they had nothing before but the self-rewarding, ingenious industry. Whilst they were imployed in this last businesse, he & he only, took notes of their proceedings : which notes he kept till his dying day.[1]

Dr. Boys's biographer seems ignorant of the fact that alike at Oxford, Cambridge, and Westminster, there were two companies, making six in all, so that if two revisers went to Stationers' Hall from each company, this final board of revision must have had twelve members instead of the six of which he speaks. We know this indeed as a fact from the report of the English delegates to the Synod of Dort, among whom was Samuel Ward, one of the revisers.[2] On the basis of a board of twelve, paid 30s. each a week for 39 weeks, the sum disbursed would be £702. That this sum was paid by the Company is incredible ; it is just possible, however, that it was the contribution of the proprietors of the ' Bible Stock ' already mentioned, which can only have continued in existence all these years if its owners were admitted by the holder of the royal patent to share a portion of the expenses and profits either of all editions or of those

[1] From *Desiderata Curiosa* : or a collection of divers scarce and curious pieces. By Francis Peck. New ed., 1779. Part viii. p. 325 sqq. ' The life of that famous Grecian, Mr. John Bois, S.T.B. one of the translators of the Bible, temp. Jac. I. . . By Anthony Walker, M.A., of St. John's College, Cambridge. From a 4° MS. in the hands of the publisher. The gift of the Rev. Mr. Thomas Baker.'

[2] ' Post peractum a singulis pensum, ex hisce omnibus duodecim selecti viri in unum locum convocati integrum opus recognoverunt ac recensuerunt.'

in particular sizes. Even, however, if this were so it is evident that such a payment would only be made in pursuance of a private agreement with Robert Barker, and forty years after the Bible was published we meet with a definite statement [1] that Barker had, in fact, ' paid for the amended or corrected Translation of the Bible £3,500 : by reason whereof the translated copy did of right belong to him and his assignes.' If, as the statement should mean, this sum was actually paid to the translators, it would have represented between £50 and £60 apiece for the work done during the sittings of the six companies. Now the preface to the Bible says of the translation that it ' hath cost the workemen, as light as it seemeth, the paines of twise seven times seventy-two dayes and more ', or about two years and nine months. On the basis of the prebend of the value of £20 at least which the King desired to secure for the translators, this would mean a payment of just £55, either to the translators direct or to the colleges which boarded them. But neatly as these figures work out, the hypothesis thus suggested is quite uncorroborated, and we have really no sound basis even for guessing how the £3,500 was paid. The sessions of the six companies, it may be noted, are usually supposed to have begun (although doubtless there were preliminary meetings) in 1607, the years 1605, 1606 being thus allotted to private research, 1607-9 to the

---

[1] In William Ball's *Briefe treatise concerning the regulating of printing*, 1651. On May 10, 1612, Robert Barker obtained an extended patent, and on February 11, 1617, this was re-granted to him for his own life and for thirty years after his death to his son, Robert II. In 1635 the reversion was re-granted to Charles and Matthew Barker. Robert died in 1646, and in 1664 a moiety of these rights was valued at £1,300. See the article by H. R. Plomer, ' The King's Printing House under the Stuarts,' in *The Library*, 2nd Series, vol. 8 (1901).

work of the six boards, part of 1610 to that of the twelve
revisers at Stationers' Hall, and the rest of 1610 and part
of 1611 to printing.   From the Report of the Synod of
lxii. Dort (November 16, 1618) already mentioned, we learn
that the final touches to the translation were given by
Bilson, Bishop of Winchester, and Miles Smith, afterwards Bishop of Gloucester.[1]   The former was not
a member of any of the boards of revisers, but that the
work of the revisers should subsequently be ' reviewed
by the Bishops and the chiefe learned of the Church ' was
part of the scheme which the King had sketched out at
the Hampton Court Conference, and another Bishop,
Bancroft of London, is said to have insisted on fourteen
afterations.   Whether in further pursuance of the King's
programme the version was presented by the bishops to
the Privy Council, and lastly ratified by his Royal
authority, we cannot say.   As is well known no authority
has ever been discovered for the words ' Appointed to be
read in Churches ' which appear on the title-page of all
editions, nor for the phrase, the ' Authorized Version ',
by which the Bible is usually known.   When, however,
this point was raised at the time of the Revision of 1881,
Lord Chancellor Selborne wrote to the *Times* (June 3,
1881), giving it as his opinion that if the version

> was ' appointed to be read in churches ' (as is expressly stated
> on the title-page of 1611), at the time of its first publication,
> nothing is more probable than that this may have been done
> by Order in Council.   If so, the authentic record of that order
> would now be lost, because all the Council books and registers
> from the year 1600 to 1613 inclusive were destroyed by a fire

[1] ' Postremo Reverendissimus Episcopus Wintoniensis Bilsonus
una cum Doctore Smitho nunc Episcopo Glocestriensi, viro
eximio, et ab initio in toto hoc opere versatissimo, omnibus mature
pensitatis et examinatis, extremam manum huic versioni imposuerunt.'

at Whitehall, on the 12th of January, 1618 (O.S.).   Nothing
in my opinion, is less likely than that the King's printer should
have taken upon himself (whether with a view to his own profit
or otherwise) to issue the book) being what it was, a translation
unquestionably made by the King's commandment to correct
defects in earlier versions of which the use had been authorized
by Royal injunctions, &c. in preceding reigns) with a title-page
asserting that it was ' Appointed to be read in Churches ' if the
fact were not really so.

Lord Selborne proceeds to speak of the terrors of the
Court of High Commission and the Star Chamber as
making it ' incredible ' that Barker should have taken
any risks.   But he does not seem sufficiently to have
distinguished between what may be done when authorities
are amiable and when they are the reverse.   The Version
of 1611 was produced to take the place of the Bishops'
Bible, on the title-pages of which, in the editions from
1585 to 1602 (the last) inclusive, had been printed the
words 'Authorised and Appointed to be read in Churches'.
In the small folio edition of 1584 the phrase runs, ' Of
that Translation authorised to be read in Churches.'
Previously to this (1574–8) we find only ' Set foorth by
aucthoritie '.   In 1568, 1569, and 1572, there are no
words to this effect of any sort or kind, although we
know that Parker would have liked to use them.   Parker
had even had to endure the sight of an edition following
the text of the Great Bible, which was published in 1569
by Cawood, and advertised itself as ' According to the
translation that is appointed to be read in the Churches ',
a phrase which he might not use of his own.   None the
less, the Bishops' Bible superseded the Great Bible, and
as the need for distinguishing it from the Geneva version
made itself felt we find Jugge (and the assigns of Christopher Barker in the folio of 1578) using the words, ' Set
foorth by aucthoritie '.   When Whitgift became Arch-

bishop we get first the phrase of 1584 and then the fuller 'Authorised and Appointed to be read in Churches' of 1585–1602. As far as I know it has never been contended that there was any Order in Council passed in 1584 or 1585 to justify this, and it seems therefore far from safe to postulate the existence of such an Order in 1611. There is indeed negative evidence that there was no such order, for the word 'Appointed', is considerably weaker than the 'Authorised and Appointed' which it replaced. By itself 'Appointed' means little more than 'assigned' or 'provided', and the words 'Appointed to be read in Churches' literally expressed the facts that this Bible was printed by the King's printer with the approval of the King and the Bishops for use in churches, and that no competing edition 'of the largest volume' was allowed to be published. Theoretically this justification by facts may have been insufficient; but when all the parties are agreed, legal formalities are often omitted.

If the notes which Dr. Boys treasured so carefully to the end of his life had been preserved, it might be possible to trace, if only for a single section, the work done at the different stages of the revision. As it is we have nothing but the finished result and a few remarks on it in the preface. As far as ecclesiastical politics were concerned the task of the revisers was with the smallest possible amount of disturbance to harmonize the Bishop's version with the Geneva wherever the latter was more correct, and the desire to do this accounts for the vast majority of the changes which in any way affect the sense. The revisers were concerned also, although pride prevented any reference to the fact, to meet the objections which had been urged in the preface and notes to the Rheims New Testament, and it is to their credit that they not only did this, but took from that version much that was good, though with no other acknowledgement than a gibe. Other changes were due to the study of two new Latin versions, that by Arias Montanus of the Old Testament printed in the Antwerp Polyglott, and that by Tremellius of the Old and New Testament, with the Apocrypha by his son-in-law, Franciscus Junius ; yet others from the Geneva French version (1587–8), Diodati's Italian (1607), and the Spanish (1602) of Cipriano de Valera. These three foreign translations seem to have attracted considerable attention, as they are mentioned not only in the Preface, but by Selden, in whose *Table-Talk* we read (clearly of the meetings of the final board of twelve) that :

> The translators in king James's time took an excellent way. That part of the Bible was given to him who was most excellent in such a tongue (as the Apocrypha to Andrew Downs) and then they met together, and one read the translation, the rest holding in their hands some Bible, either of the learned tongues, or French, Spanish, Italian, etc. If they found any fault they spoke ; if not, he read on.

Whether the wonderful felicity of phrasing should be attributed to the dexterity with which, after meanings had been settled and the important words in each passage chosen, either the board of twelve or the two final revisers put their touches to the work, or whether, as seems more likely, the rhythm, first called into being by Tyndale and Coverdale, reasserted itself after every change, only gathering strength and melody from the increasing richness of the language, none can tell. All that is certain is that the rhythm and the strength and the melody are there.

The Bible of 1611, being only a revised edition, was not entered on the Stationers' Registers, nor have we any information as to the month in which it was issued. In its original form it is a handsome, well-printed book, set up apparently with newly cast type yielding a clean and sharp impression, and on excellent paper. It begins with an engraved title-page signed ' C. Boel fecit in Richmont ', i.e. by Cornelis Boel, an Antwerp artist, who about this time produced portraits of the Queen, the Princess Elizabeth, and Prince Henry. In the upper panel SS. Peter and James sit, holding between them an oval frame within which is a representation of the Lamb, at the sides are SS. Matthew and Mark. On the two sides of the title stand Moses and Aaron in niches. At the foot are seated SS. Luke and John, while between them is another oval frame containing a picture of a pelican feeding her young. The title reads :

> ' The Holy Bible, conteyning the Old Testament and the New. Newly Translated out of the Originall tongues : & with the former Translations diligently compared and reuised by his Maiesties speciall Comandement. Appointed to be read in Churches. Imprinted at London by Robert Barker, Printer to the Kings most Excellent Maiestie. Anno Dom. 1611.'

Leaves 2 and 3ª are occupied with the Dedication : ' To the most High and Mightie Prince, Iames by the grace of God King of Great Britaine, France and Ireland, Defender of the Faith, &c.' ; 3b–8, by the preface headed ' The Translators to the Reader ', 9–14 by a Calendar ; 15ª, by ' An Almanacke for xxxix. yeeres ', 1603–1641 ; 15b, by Directions ' To finde Easter for euer ' ; 16–18ª by ' The Table and Kalendes, expressing the order of Psalmes and Lessons to be said at Morning and Euening prayer ', and a table headed, ' These to be obserued for Holy dayes, and none other ; ' 18b, by ' The names and order of all the Bookes of the Olde and New Testament, with the Number of their Chapters '. Inserted at the binder's pleasure after the preface, after leaf 18 or elsewhere, are usually eighteen leaves of the Genealogies of Holy Scripture and a sheet containing a Map of Canaan with a table of the places named printed on the reverse. In October 1610 John Speed had obtained a privilege from the king enabling him for ten years to saddle every edition of the Scriptures with his decoratively printed but useless Genealogies, and so the cost of the book was needlessly increased by from sixpence to two shillings a copy, according to the size. In some copies, it may be mentioned, the Genealogies begin with a blank page ; in others this is occupied by a fine cut of the royal arms, subscribed Cum Priuilegio Regiæ Maiestatis.

The text of the Bible is printed in black-letter with the inserted words (now printed in italics) in small roman, and roman type is also used for the summaries at the head of each chapter, for the subject headlines at the top of each page, and for the references to parallel passages in the margin ; the alternative renderings in the margins are in italics.[1] The text is printed in double columns enclosed within rules, with ornamental head-pieces and a few tailpieces and capitals at the beginning of each chapter and psalm. At the outset it was clearly intended that the capital at the beginning of a book should occupy the depth of nine lines of text, that at the beginning of each chapter after the first the depth of five ; but the run on capitals in the Psalter caused four- and six-line blocks to be used, and after this the arrange-

[1] The alternative renderings and references to parallels are probably the work of the six companies ; the chapter summaries and subject headlines are usually attributed to the two final revisers. In later editions the subject headlines, which are based on the chapter summaries, have usually been left to the printer's reader.

ment is more frequently disturbed,[1] though it still remains the normal one. In order to begin the Psalter (one of the old five sections into which Bibles used to be divided), on a right-hand page, the page before it is left blank, but there is no typographical break throughout the Old Testament. The New Testament has a separate title-page, with a woodcut previously used in editions of the Bishops' Bible. It was also taken as a new typographical starting-point. The book consists in all of 366 sheets of two leaves, or four pages each, grouped in 123 quires or gatherings signed as follows :

Preliminaries : A-D.

Old Testament : A-Z, Aa-Zz, Aaa-Zzz, Aaaa-Zzzz, Aaaaa-Ccccc.

New Testament : A-Z, Aa.

With the exception of B and D, in the preliminaries, of which the former has only one sheet, the latter only two, every quire is regularly made up of three sheets or six leaves. The whole book is homogeneous, and was almost certainly set up and printed in its own sequence, not in different sections worked simultaneously. Of the Bible thus set up only a single issue was printed. The so-called second issue is an entirely distinct and separate edition, save that a few leaves of the original edition, of which an excessive number had been printed by some mistake, are sometimes found used in it.

---

[1] In the New Testament two of the mythological ten-line set, the use of which in the Bishops' Bible had justly been censured, reappear at the beginning of Matthew and Romans ; and small pictorial capitals of an evangelist writing, at the beginning of the gospels according to S. Luke and S. John.

III. THE LATER HISTORY OF THE BIBLE OF 1611

As we have seen, every parish in England had been obliged to provide itself with a Bible of the 'largest volume' in 1541 under penalty of a fine of 40s. for every month of delay, the book costing 10s. in sheets and 12s. bound. Beyond the words on the title-page, 'Appointed to be read in Churches,' which, as they stand, are purely affirmative, not exclusive (unlike, for instance, the 'These to be obserued for Holy dayes, and none other' of this very volume), there is no tittle of evidence for any Order in Council having enjoined parishes to buy copies with inconvenient haste. In the year of issue the Dean and Chapter of Worcester bought 'a Great Bible of the new translation' for £2 18s., which probably represents the cost of the book in a binding good enough for cathedral use. From a book printed in 1641 (Michael Sparke's *Scintilla*) we learn that the price of Church Bibles had then recently been raised from 30s. to 40s., and that 'in former times' these were sold in quires at 25s., to which must be added the cost of binding. It would have been highly unpopular to force an expenditure of this kind on every parish, however small. To do so, moreover, would have been alike impolitic and needless; impolitic, because any haste in the matter would have suggested that very slur on the Bishops' version which the Preface so earnestly disclaims[1]; needless, because the supply of

[1] 'Truly (good Christian Reader) wee neuer thought from the beginning, that we should neede to make a new Translation, nor yet to make of a bad one a good one, (for then the imputation of *Sixtus* had bene true in some sort, that our people had bene fed with gall of Dragons instead of wine, with whey instead of milke :) but to make a good one better.'

Bibles being, as we have pointed out, a regulated and controlled supply, whenever an old Church Bible was worn out, it was necessarily replaced by a new one of the version of 1611, because no other Bible in large folio was purchasable. In an interesting article on *The Authorisation of the English Bible,* contributed by the present Archbishop of Canterbury to *Macmillan's Magazine* for June 1881, we find it stated :

> Of twenty-four [25 ?] ' inquiries ' between 1612 and 1641 thirteen Bishops and Archdeacons, ask for ' a Bible of the latest edition ', or ' of the last translation,' while twelve ask only for ' a Bible of the largest volume ', in accordance with what had been the usual form of the question prior to 1611. Among the latter are Bishop Neile of Lincoln (1614) ; Bishop Williams of Lincoln (1631) ; Bishop Duppa of Chichester (1638) ; and the Archdeacons of London, York and Colchester (1640). Archbishop Abbot in his metropolitical visitation in 1616 asks only for ' the whole Bible of the largest volume ', though three years later, in a visitation of the Diocese of Canterbury, he carefully refers to ' the Bible of the New Translation, lately set forth by His Majesty's authority '. Archbishop Laud, however, in a Diocesan visitation in 1634, departing from the form adopted by his predecessor, asks only for ' the whole Bible of the largest volume '.

With the policy of patience and quiet penetration which the bishops as a body (some, no doubt, being more urgent than others) thus seem to have pursued, the bibliographical evidence is in entire agreement. Misapprehension of the ecclesiastical position has indeed caused some bibliographers to go astray, and to imagine the simultaneous printing of two issues in 1611 to meet a demand for 20,000 copies, such as Grafton and Whitchurch had to provide for in 1540 and 1541. But the demand for 20,000 copies and the double issue are equally imaginary. After the first edition, completed in 1611, an entirely new one was put in hand, the issue of the bulk of which belongs to 1613, and in this year there appeared also a folio reprint for church use in smaller type ;[1] a third edition in the largest type was published in 1617, a fourth in 1634, a fifth in 1640. It is clear that if every parish had acquired a copy in 1611, there could have been no demand for new editions in 1613 and 1617. It is also clear, from the seventeen years interval before a reprint, that the 1617 edition did substantially complete the necessary supply. If so, the editions may have been of as many as 5,000 copies apiece.

To understand the trouble which has arisen it must be remembered that in the case of Bibles all editions of the same size were so printed that, the contents of each sheet being precisely the same, the sheets should be interchangeable. This probably made for correctness in reprinting, and the reprints follow each other so closely, mostly line for line, and always leaf for leaf, that they can only be distinguished from the copy they follow by careful collation. But the printer's object in this arrangement was probably the lower one of being able to use up sheets which had been printed in excess of the requirements of one edition by printing fewer copies for the next, and also, when any sheets of a nearly exhausted edition had accidentally been spoilt, by printing these particular sheets in advance of the next edition, to make one setting serve for both purposes. In a well-managed printing-office, neither class of accident would recur with sufficient frequency to be worth providing against ; but Barker's office was not well managed, and from his plea in one of the interminable lawsuits which made him end his days in a debtor's prison, we learn that about 1616–18

[1] By printing 72 instead of 59 lines to a column, and a corresponding lateral saving, the number of leaves was reduced from 732 to 508.

he owed over £200 to various booksellers as compensation for having supplied imperfect books.[1]

Before the end of 1611 the stock of the first edition of the new Bible was sufficiently low to cause a second to be put in hand. The engraved plate from which the title had been printed must by this time have been much worn and (possibly after some hesitation) henceforth Barker preferred the woodcut border which appears in the New Testament for the general title as well. The easiest hypothesis to account for the peculiarities which we find in the edition which he now proceeded to print is that he first reprinted the sheet which bears the title, and a few other sheets at various points, to complete imperfect copies of the first edition, and then settled down to reprint the rest, completing this, if we are bound to press the date 1611 found on the New Testament, within the year, somewhat ahead of the demand. Before this became urgent a serious accident must have happened in his warehouse, which rendered unusable a large part of the stock (about 119 out of 138 sheets) in one part of the book, viz. the quires signed Aa–Zz and Aaa–Zzz. A few sheets,[2] which I conjecture to have been among those printed in advance of the rest and kept in a different place, escaped, but the stock of the rest had to be completed by a second reprinting, and the completed stock was then stored according to the exigencies of the warehouse. By 1613 the supply of the title-sheet, of which only a small number seems to have been printed in 1611 (possibly because Barker at first thought

---

[1] See Mr. H. R. Plomer's article in *The Library* (Second Series, vol. ii, pp. 353–375), on ' The King's Printing House under the Stuarts '.

[2] Viz. (probably) Aa_1, Ff_2, $Gg_{1,2}$, Kk_1, Tt_{1-3}, Aaa_2, Bbb_3, Iii_2, Lll_1, $Ooo_{2,3}$, Qqq_3, $Sssl_{1-2}$, Zzz_3.

of re-engraving the original copper-plate [1]) was exhausted, and this sheet was then reprinted and dated 1613. During the next three or four years the copies sold exhibit so many combinations of the two printings of the sheets bearing the double and treble signatures (Aa and Aaa, &c.), that with the exception of a group of about twenty hardly any two copies agree. The inference is that this score of copies represent the part of the edition sold to the booksellers when first it was ready, since these copies would all be made up at the same time, and the sheets required for them would be extracted from the same part of each bundle. On the other hand, copies made up at later dates in response to the casual daily demand would naturally differ according to the whim of the man who picked out the sheets for them.

The above explanation is based [2] on the very able paper by the Rev. Walter E. Smith, published in three numbers of *The Library* for 1890 under the title *The Great She-Bible*, and is intended to account for the following facts:

(i) While the great majority of the extant title-pages of the second edition are dated 1613, those in at least three copies are dated 1611, and this title with the woodcut border and the date 1611 has also been found on some copies of the editio princeps. The title-page of the New Testament in all copies is dated 1611.

---

[1] I may note that the engraved title is said to be found in a ' very few ' copies of the cheaper Church folio (72 line) of 1613. In one at least of these it is clearly inserted. But as long as the plate existed it might be used on an emergency to complete copies.

[2] I use this word because Mr. Smith did not fully express his views on the significance of the 1611 printed title-page, as to which he obtained additional information after his text was printed, and in some points I think I interpret the evidence he collected a little differently. His paper settled the main question quite finally.

†

(ii) Out of a total of 357 sheets of text, four of those singly signed (E_3, $P_{2, 3}$, X_2), and 119 of those doubly and trebly signed (Aa, &c., Aaa, &c.) are found in two different forms, constituting different editions of these individual sheets, one of which can almost always be positively proved to have been set up from the other.

(iii) The sheets of these signatures first printed are not, as a rule, all found together in some copies, and the reprints of them in others, but the two printings are very much mixed together, and in very various ways.

The explanation is probably only a very rough approximation to the truth, and further investigation is rendered almost hopeless by the fact that collectors like Lea Wilson and Francis Fry (the latter of whom bought and sold an extraordinary number of copies), and many much more easily forgivable booksellers, have transferred sheets from one copy to another to bring them into accord with their own mistaken ideas of perfection, and the evidence has thus been hopelessly confused. Nor if, as I believe, the way in which copies of this second edition were made up depended mainly on the whim of Barker's storekeeper, is it possible as regards the bulk of the copies [1] to say with any probability that one is earlier than another. The important point is that we must repudiate altogether the misuse of bibliographical terms by which Mr. Fry constantly wrote of a certain type of copy of the second edition as the second ' issue ' of the first. A sheet of the first edition may here and there be found (for the reasons given) in a copy of the second, but the second edition as a whole, whether it bears a 1611 title or a 1613 title, was printed from a new

---

[1] Those with one or more 1611 sheets used in them may perhaps be set down as earlier, and those with 1617 sheets as later. But even this is not always certain.

setting up of the type, whereas the essence of a new
' issue ' is that it is printed from the same setting up,
but with additions, cancels, or other subordinate changes.
The only first edition is that which is here reprinted.

A still more serious error was committed by the distinguished scholar, Dr. F. H. A. Scrivener, who in 1884,
in his book entitled *The Authorised Edition of the English
Bible* (1611) : *its subsequent reprints and modern representatives* (an enlargement of his Introduction to the
Cambridge Paragraph Bible of 1873) argued strenuously,
but in entire ignorance of the customs of the book trade
in the seventeenth century, that copies of the (second)
edition with the woodcut title dated 1611 preceded the
(first) edition with the engraved title, here reprinted.
Dr. Scrivener was led to this conclusion by the idea,
natural to a modern scholar, that the opportunity of
a new edition would be used for making the text more
correct. So far from this being the case it is a practically
invariable experience that for every error corrected in
a seventeenth-century reprint, at least two are introduced. Dr. Scrivener allowed that the accepted editio
princeps was the finer and better, but did not see how
incredible it is that an eagerly expected book like the
version of 1611, of which copies would at once be given
to the king and other great persons, should have been
put on the market in the first instance in an inferior
form, have been then improved in almost every respect
in a second edition, and then have gone back to its
original state, or a little worse, in a third. The relations
of the copies with the 1611 and 1613 woodcut titles
constitute another insuperable difficulty to his theory,
but the priority of the true editio princeps can be proved
bibliographically in a dozen different ways. A few of
these may be indicated :

(i) Dr. Scrivener himself noted a blunder in the editio princeps by which three lines are repeated in Exodus xiv. 10. In the second edition we can see the printer, who could not ignore this particular error, bringing a couple of words on to another line, and leaving extra space at the head of chapter xv, in order to fill the gap created by omitting the three repeated lines.

(ii) The editio princeps, as we have seen, begins with a regular system of nine-line capitals at the beginning of the first chapter of each book, and five-line capitals at the beginning of other chapters, and only gradually departs from it. In the second edition the printer is careless all the way through, using additional capitals from other sets, and making changes in the line-arrangements obviously dictated by the different sizes of the new capitals.

(iii) In the editio princeps the word ' Lord ' is printed throughout the book of Genesis as LORD, afterwards as LORD. In the second edition it is always printed LORD.

All of these changes are intelligible if the second edition was printed from the first. None of them can be explained if the first edition was printed from the second. Add the fact that the type of the second edition is distinctly more worn, and the true sequence is obvious. This is now generally recognized, and it is only just to say that on this point Mr. Francis Fry was quite sound.

It remains to be added that the first edition of the new translation is frequently called the He-Bible and the second the She-Bible, from the fact that in Ruth iii. 15 the former reads ' He went into the city ', and the latter ' She '. All such nicknames for editions of the Bible are objectionable, and this, which suggests that the two editions form a pair, is mischievous. Their relation is not that of equality as between man and woman, but the second is derived from the first, as a child from its parents, an entirely new and distinct edition, reprinted from the original, and not a contemporaneous issue.

Turning now from the Church Bibles to those for private use we find that two quartos and two octavos were issued in 1612, one quarto and one octavo following the editio princeps, and the other quarto and octavo following the second edition. A quarto and octavo were printed at the turn of the years 1612–13, two other quartos and an octavo in 1613, two quartos in 1613–14, and two more quartos and an octavo in 1614, almost all of these following the text of the second edition. These fourteen editions (there may have been more) seem to have satisfied the immediate demand, and after this we find one, two, and three editions printed in different years. Very few editions of the New Testament seem at first to have been printed separately, and it is interesting to find Messrs. Darlow and Moule, in their catalogue of the treasures of the Bible Society, recording editions of the Bishops' version as being printed in 1613, 1614, 1615, and 1617. After this New Testaments of the new translation became more common.

As regards the Geneva Bible, of which a folio and quarto had been printed in 1611, we find another folio published in 1612, three quartos in 1614, two more quartos in 1615, and a folio in 1616. After this, although for another fifteen or twenty years eminent ecclesiastics, ordained before 1611, continued to take into the pulpit their old Geneva pocket editions, no doubt marked and familiar to their hands, and had no hesitation in using this version for their texts, the king's printers were encouraged to print no more Geneva Bibles, and the production of them was thus driven underground. It has long been a puzzle to bibliographers why there should be so many different editions (at least six), of the Geneva

Bible asserting themselves on their title-pages to have been 'Imprinted at London by the Deputies of Christopher Barker, Printer to the Queenes most excellent Maiestie. 1599.' One of these editions is found also bearing the much more truthful statement, 'By Iohn Fredericksz. Stam, dwelling by the South Churche at the signe of the Hope. 1633' (see Bible Society Catalogue, Nos. 191 and 364). Mr. N. Pocock, who wrote on the subject in the *Bibliographer*, vol. iii, stated as his conclusion that 'the whole investigation seems to show that these editions of the Geneva-Tomson [Bible] were published at different times at Amsterdam and Dort, and adopted afterwards by Barker, who affixed the date 1599, probably because this was a well-known and popular edition'. A still more probable reason for the selection of the date 1599 is surely that in 1600 Robert Barker took over his father's business, and the deputies vanished. Thus this particular imprint was the latest with which editions could circulate freely in England, without Robert Barker being personally implicated. Whether Robert himself was always in the position of having 'a few remaining copies' of one or other of these editions in stock we can only surmise. But the complete, or nearly complete, cessation of English-printed editions of the Geneva Bible after 1616, combined with the appearance of Dutch-printed editions, one at least of which belongs to the year 1633, disguised by spurious imprints, is fair proof that the Geneva Bible was now again subjected to the silent boycott by which Parker had repressed it until the year of his death. Fortunately, lethargy no longer accompanied repression, and the supply of Bibles of every size was abundant, although we hear murmurs that the king's printers were allowed to charge too much for them.

Although there can be no doubt that the price of Bibles gradually rose, in 1629 buyers of small folios and large quartos were for a short time able to obtain them cheap enough, as, on the Cambridge University Press for the first time exercising its right to print a Bible, and putting a small folio on the market at 10s. instead of 12s., the king's printers sold a specially printed folio edition and a thousand copies in quarto at 5s. apiece, ' to overthrow the Cambridge printing, and so to keep all in their own hands ' (Sparke's *Scintilla*, 1641). This Cambridge edition of 1629 is noteworthy also, not only as exceptionally well printed, but as bearing marks of careful revision, carried still further in an edition of 1638, which went so far as to improve the text (I quote from Dr. Scrivener) ' by inserting words or clauses, especially in the Old Testament, overlooked by the editors of 1611 ; by amending manifest errors ; by rendering the italic notation at once more self-consistent, and more agreeable to the design of the original translators.'   According to a contemporary note the revisers were Dr. Goad, of Hadley, Dr. Joseph Mede, Dean Boys, and Dr. Samuel Ward, of Sidney Sussex, of whom the last two were survivors of the original Cambridge board of 1611. Between these two Cambridge editions came one from the king's printers in 1631, for which the firm was fined £300 for omitting the word *not* in the seventh commandment.   After 1638 carelessness still continued, and the London market was also flooded with incorrect editions printed in Holland.   In the eighteenth century even Baskett, as a rule a careful printer, in aiming at sumptuousness could produce the Bible of 1716–17[1] with its ' basketfull ' of errors.   In 1762 a Bible revised by

[1] The so-called Vinegar Bible, from the misprint Vinegar for Vineyard in the headline to Luke xx.

Dr. Thomas Paris of Trinity College was printed at Cambridge, and seven years later a similar revision was carried through at Oxford by Dr. Benjamin Blayney, of Hertford College. It must be remembered that no copy of the version of 1611 had been ' sealed ' as a standard, as was done in the case of the Prayer-book, and these attempts to increase consistency and to remove errors were wholly laudable. On the other hand it is obvious that under cover of such minor revisions more serious changes might be introduced, and in 1831, in a pamphlet entitled *The Existing Monopoly an inadequate protection of the Authorised Version of the Scripture*, Thomas Curtis, of Islington, called public attention to a number of departures from the original text. The uneasiness thus created was effectually dispelled by the Oxford University Press producing, in 1833, a line for line reprint of the editio princeps, the extraordinary accuracy of which has been everywhere acknowledged.

ALFRED W. POLLARD.

RECORDS

I. PROHIBITION OF ENGLISH TRANSLATIONS OF THE BIBLE FROM THE TIME OF WYCLIF UNLESS AUTHORIZED BY A BISHOP OR A PROVINCIAL COUNCIL

The text of the Constitution adopted by the Provincial Council at Oxford, 1408, from Lyndewode's *Provinciale*, Antwerp, Christopher of Endhoven, December 20, 1525, fo. ccvi, compared with the same constitution as ratified by the Provincial Council which met at St. Paul's, London, January 14, 1408–9, from Wilkins's *Concilia*, 1737, vol. iii. 317.

[1] SCRIPTURA sacra non transferatur in linguam vulgarem nec translata interpretur donec rite fuerit examinata sub pena excommunicationis et nota hereseos.

Periculosa [quoque [2]] res est, testante beato Hyeronymo, textum sacre scripture de uno in aliud ydioma transferre, eo quod in ipsis translationibus non de facili idem sensus in omnibus [3] retinetur, prout idem beatus Hyeronymus, etsi inspiratus fuisset, se in hoc sepius fatetur errasse. Statuimus igitur et ordinamus, ut nemo deinceps textum aliquem [4] sacre scripture auctoritate sua in linguam Anglicanam, vel aliam transferat, per viam libri vel libelli aut tractatus, nec legatur aliquis huiusmodi liber, libellus, aut tractatus iam nouiter tempore dicti Iohannis

---

[1] The heading given by Wilkins is : ' Ne quis texta (*sic*) S. Scripturae transferat in linguam Anglicanam,' but he quotes from a Lambeth MS. the variant : ' Ne textus aliquis S. Scripturae in linguam Anglicanam de caetero transferatur per viam libri aut tractatus.'

[2] From Wilkins.   [3] Wilkins, ' in omnibus sensus.'

[4] Wilkins, ' aliquem textum.'

Wyklyff, siue citra, compositus, aut in posterum com-
ponendus, in parte vel in toto, publice vel occulte, sub
pena maioris excommunicationis, quousque per loci
diocesanum, seu, si res exegerit, per concilium prouinciale
ipsa translatio fuerit approbata. Qui vero [5] contra
fecerit, ut fautor heresis et erroris similiter puniatur.

TRANSLATION

The Holy Scripture not to be translated into the
vulgar tongue, nor a translation to be expounded, until
it shall have been duly examined, under pain of excommunication and the stigma of heresy.

Moreover it is a perilous thing, as the Blessed Jerome
testifies, to translate the text of Holy Scripture from
one idiom into another, inasmuch as in the translations
themselves it is no easy matter to keep the same meaning
in all cases, like as the Blessed Jerome, albeit inspired,
confesses that he often went astray in this respect. We
therefore enact and ordain that no one henceforth on
his own authority translate any text of Holy Scripture
into the English or other language, by way of a book,
pamphlet, or tract, and that no book, pamphlet, or tract
of this kind be read, either already recently composed
in the time of the said John Wyclif, or since then, or
that may in future be composed, in part or in whole,
publicly or privily, under pain of the greater excommunication, until the translation itself [6] shall have been
approved by the diocesan of the place or if need be by

[5] Wilkins omits ' vero '.

[6] It will be noted that it is the translation itself ('ipsa translatio')
which the Bishop or Provincial Council was to approve. In the
uncertainty which almost from the beginning surrounded the
origin of the Wyclifite versions it seems to have become the
practice to grant a licence to specified readers instead of to
a specified version.

a provincial council.   Whoever shall do the contrary to
be punished in like manner as a supporter of heresy and
error.

II. SIR THOMAS MORE ON THE PROHIBITION

From ' A dyaloge of syr Thomas More . . . Wherin be treatyd
dyuers maters, as of the . . . worshyp of ymagys . . . With many
othre thyngys touchyng the pestylent sect of Luther and Tyndale.
London, J. Rastell, 1529.   (fol. xciii verso.)

The thyrde boke.   The xvi. chapyter.

The messenger [1] reherseth som causys whych he hath
herd layd by som of the clergye, wherfore the scrypture
shold not be suffred in englysh.   And the author sheweth
hys mynde that yt were conuenyent to haue the byble in
englyshe.   And therwyth endeth the thyrd boke.

Syr quod your frende, yet for all thys can I se no
cawse why the clergye shold kepe the byble out of lay
mennys handys, that can no more but theyr mother
tonge.

I had wente quod I that I had proued you playnly,
that they kepe yt not from them.   For I haue shewed
you that they kepe none frome theym, but suche translacyon as be eyther not yet approued for good, or such
as be all redy reproued for naught, as Wyclyffys was
and Tyndals.   For as for other olde onys, that were
before Wyclyffys days, [these] remayn lawful, and be
in some folkys handys had and red.[2]

---

[1] More secures entire freedom of speech for his interlocutor by
making him merely the messenger of a friend, who reports everything he hears said without taking any responsibility for it.

[2] In ' An Answere vnto Sir Thomas Mores dialoge ' Tyndale (fol.
cv) thus comments on this section : ' What maye not Master More
saye by auctorite of his poetrie ? there is a lawfull translacion

Ye say well quod he. But yet as women say, somwhat yt was alway that the cat wynked whan her eye was oute. Surely so ys yt not for nought that the englysh byble is in so few mennys handys, whan so many wold so fayn haue yt.

That ys very trouth quod I. For I thynke that though the fauourers of a secte of heretyques be so feruent in the settynge forthe of theyr sect, that they let not to lay theyr money togyder and make a purse amonge them for the pryntyng of an euyll made or euyll translated boke, whych though yt happe to be forboden and burned yet som be solde ere they be spyed, and eche of theym lese but theyr parte, yet I thynk ther wyll no prynter lyghtely be so hote to put eny byble in prent at hys own charge, wherof the losse sholde lye hole in hys owne necke, and than hange vppon a doutfull tryall whyther the fyrst copy of hys translacyon was made before Wyclyffys dayes or synnys. For yf yt were made synnys, yt must be approued byfore the pryntynge. And surely howe yt hathe happed that in all thys whyle

that no man knoweth which is as moch as no lawfull translacion. Whi mighte not the bisshopes shew which were that lawfull translacion and lat it be printed ? Naye if that might haue bene obteyned of them with large money it had be printed ye maye besure longe yer this. But sir answere me here vnto, how happeneth that ye defendars translate not one youre selues, to cease the murmoure of the people, and put to youre awne gloses, to preuent [i.e. forestall] heretikes ? Ye wold no doute haue done it longe sens, if ye coude haue youre gloses agre with the texte in euery place. And what can you saye to this, how that besydes they haue done their best to disanull all translatynge by parlement, they haue disputed before the kinges grace that it is [*text* is it] perelous and not mete and so concluded that it shal not be, vnder a pretence of deferrynge it of certayne yeres. Where Master More was there speciall orator, to fayne lyes for their purpose.'

god hathe eyther not suffred or not prouyded that eny good vertuouse man hath had the mynde in faythfull wyse to translate yt, and thervppon eyther the clergye or at the lest wyse som one bysshop to approue yt, thys can [I] no thynge tell. But howe so euer yt be, I haue herd and here so myche spoken in the mater, and so mych dout made therin, that peraduenture yt wold let and wythdrawe eny one bishop from the admyttyng therof, wythout the assent of the remanaunt. And where as many thyngys be layd agaynst yt, yet ys there in my mynde not one thyng that more putteth good men of the clergye in dout to suffer yt, than thys that they se somtyme myche of the worst sort more feruent in the callyng for yt, than them whom we fynde far better. Whych maketh theym to fere lest such men desyre yt for no good, and lest yf yt were had in euery mannys hand, there wold gret parell aryse, and that sedycyouse people shold do more harme therwyth, than god and honest folke sholde take frute therby. Whyche fere I promyse you no thyng fereth me, but that who so euer wolde of theyre malyce or foly take harme of that thynge that ys of ytself ordeyned to do all men good, I wold neuer for thauoydyng of theyr harme, take frome other the profyte whyche they myght take, and no thyng deserue to lese. For ellys yf thabuse of a good thyng shold cause the takynge awaye therof frome other that wolde use yt well, Cryst shold hym selfe neuer haue ben borne, nor brought hys fayth in to the worlde, nor god sholde neuer haue made yt neyther, yf he shold for the losse of those that wold be dampned wreches, haue kepte away the occasyon of reward from theym that wold wyth helpe of hys grace endeuoure theym to deserue yt. . . .

III. MORE'S PLAN FOR A LIMITED CIRCULATION

From the same (fol. xcvii., recto.)

Fynally me thynketh that the constytucyon prouyn-
cyall of which we spake ryght now hath determyned
thys questyon all redy. For whan the clergye therin
agreed that the englysh bybles shold remayne whyche
were translated afore Wyclyffes dayes, they conse-
quentely dyd agre that to haue the byble in englysh was
none hurte. And in that they forbade eny new translacyon to be redde tyll yt were approued by the bishoppes,
yt appereth wel therby that theyre entent was that the
bysshoppe shold approue yt yf he founde yt fawtelesse,
& also of reason amend yt where yt were fawtye, but yf
the man were an heretyque that made yt, or the fawtis
suche and so many, as yt were more ethe[1] to make yt all
new than mend yt. As yt happed for bothe poyntys in
the translacyon of Tyndall.

Nowe yf yt so be that yt wold happely be thought not
a thyng metely to be aduentured, to set all on a flushe at
onys, & dash rashly out holy scrypture in euery lewde
felowys tethe, yet thynketh me there mighte suche a
moderacion be taken therin, as neyther good vertuous
lay folk shold lacke yt, nor rude and rashe braynes abuse
yt. For it might be with dylygence well and truly translated by som good catholyke and well lerned man, or by
dyuerse dyuydynge the laboure amonge theym, and
after conferryng theyr seuerall partys together eche
with other. And after that myght the work be allowed
and approued by the ordynaryes, and by theyre autho-
rytees so put vnto prent, as all the copyes shold come

[1] A misprint for ' easy ' ?

hole vnto the bysshoppys hande. Whyche he maye after hys dyscrecyon and wysedome delyver to suche as he perceyueth honest sad and vertuous, with a good monicyon & fatherly counsayl to vse yt reuerently wyth humble hart and lowly mynd, rather sekyng therin occasyon of deuocyon than of dyspycyon[2]. And prouydyng as mych as may be, that the boke be after the deceace of the partye brought agayn and reuerently restored vnto the ordynary. So that as nere as may be deuysed, no man haue yt but of the ordynaryes hande, and by hym thoughte and reputed for suche, as shall be lykely to vse yt to goddys honour and meryte of his own soule. Among whome yf eny be proued after to haue abused yt, than the vse therof to be forboden hym, eyther for euer, or tyll he be waxen wyser.

By our lady quod youre frende thys way myslyketh not me. But who sholde set the pryce of the boke ?

Forsothe quod I that reken I a thynge of lytell force.[3] For neyther were yt a grete mater for any man in maner to geue a grote or twayne aboue the meane pryce for a boke of so great profyte, nor for the byshop to gyue them al fre, wherin he myght serue hys dyocyse wyth the coste of .x. li. I thynke or xx. markys[4]. Whyche some I dare saye there is no bysshop but he wold be glad to bestowe about a thynge that myght do hys hole dyocyse so specyall a pleasure wyth suche a spyrytuall profyte.

By my trouth quod he yet wene I that the people wolde grudge to haue yt on thys wyse delyuered theym

---

[2] Discussion, disputation.   [3] Importance.
[4] The larger of these two sums is only twice as much as Bishop Nix contributed to the cost of buying up Tyndale's New Testaments (see no. xviii). It might have paid for thirty folio bibles or fifty in quarto.

at the bysshops hand, and had leuer paye for yt to the prenter than haue yt of the bysshop fre.

It myght so happen wyth some quod I. But yet in myne opinion there were in that maner more wylfulnesse, than wysedom or eny good mynd in such as wold not be content so to receyue them. And therfore I wolde thynke in good fayth that yt wold so fortune in fewe. But for god the more dowte wolde be, leste the[y] wolde grudge and holde them self sore greued, that wolde requyre yt and were happely denyed yt. Whych I suppose wolde not often happen vnto eny honest howse-holder to be by hys dyscrecyon reuerently red in hys howse. But though yt were not taken [5] to euery lewd ladde in hys awn handes to rede a lytel rudely whan he lyst, and than cast the boke at hys helys, or among other such as hym selfe to kepe a quodlibet [6] and a pot parlement vppon, I trowe there wyll no wyse man fynde a fawte therin.

IV. TYNDALE'S TRANSLATIONS

From Fox's 'Actes and Monuments of matters most speciall and memorable, happenyng in the Church. . . . Newly reuised and recognised, partly also augmented, and now the fourth time agayne published . . . by the Authour.[1] *J. Daye, London*, 1583. pp. 1076 sq.'

To be short, M. Tyndal being so molested and vexed in the countrey by the Priests, was constrained to leaue

---

[5] Entrusted.   [6] Argument on any subject.

[1] The fourth edition was the last which Fox revised. In the case of Tyndale Fox had inserted new information in the second edition of 1570, and this is here reprinted. The extract begins with Tyndale's leaving Gloucestershire, where he had acted as tutor in the house of Sir John Walsh at Little Sodbury, and had had controversies with the neighbouring clergy.

that country and to seke an other place : and so comming
to M. Welche, he desired him of hys good will that hee
myght depart from him, saying on this wise to him :
Syr, I perceiue I shall not be suffered to tary long heere
in this countrey, neither shall you be able though you
woulde, to keepe me out of the hands of the spiritualitie,
and also what displeasure might grow therby to you
by keeping me, God knoweth : for the which I shoulde
be right sorie. So that in fine, M. Tindall with the good
will of his maister, departed, and eftsoones came vp to
London, and there preached a while, according as he
had done in the country before, and specially about the
towne of Bristowe, and also in the sayde towne, in the
common place called S. Austines Greene. At length
he bethinking him selfe of Cutbert Tonstall, then Byshop
of London,[2] and especially for the great commendation
of Erasmus, who in his annotations so extolleth him for
his learning, thus cast with himselfe, that if hee might
attaine vnto his seruice hee were a happy man. And
so comming to Syr Henry Gilford the kings controller,[3]
and bringing with him an Oration of Isocrates, which he
had then translated out of Greeke into Englishe, he
desired him to speake to the sayde B. of London for him.
Which he also did, and willed him moreouer to wryte
an Epistle to the Byshop, and to go him self with him,
Which he did likewise and deliuered his Epistle to a
seruaunte of his, named William Hebilthwait, a man of
his olde acquaintaunce. But God who secretely dis-

[2] Cuthbert Tunstall or Tonstall (1474–1559), bishop of London,
1522–30 ; bishop of Durham, 1530 ; confined to his house, 1550,
deprived 1553, restored on Mary's accession the same year ;
deprived again, 1559. For Tyndale's own version of his relations
with Tunstall, see No. V.

[3] Sir Henry Guildford (1489–1532), Master of the Horse and
Comptroller of the King's Household.

poseth the course of things, saw that was not the best
for Tyndals purpose, nor for the profite of hys Churche,
and therefore gaue him to finde little fauor in the Bishops
sight. The answer of whom was thys, that hys house was
full, he had mo then he could wel finde, and aduised him
to seeke in London abroade, where hee saide hee coulde
lacke no seruice, &c. and so remained hee in London the
space almoste of a yeare, beholding and marking wyth
him selfe the course of the world, and especially the
demeanour of the preachers, howe they boasted them
selues and set vp their authoritie and kingdome : beholding also the pompe of the Prelates, wyth other
thynges moe whiche greatly misliked him : In so muche
that he understoode, not onely there to be no rowme in
the Bishops house for hym to translate the new Testament : but also that there was no place to do it in al
England. And therfore finding no place for his purpose
within the realme, and hauing some ayde and prouision,
by Gods prouidence ministred vnto hym by Humphrey
Mummouth aboue recited, as you may see before, pag.
1076.[4] and certain other good men, hee tooke hys leaue

---

[4] A wrong reference, 1076 being the page of the present text.
'The trouble of Humfrey Mummuth, Alderman of London,' is
told on p. 997. His story begins : 'Maister Humfrey Mummuth
was a right godly and sincere Alderman of London, who in the
dayes of Cardinall Woolsey, was troubled and put in the Tower,
for the Gospell of Christ, and for mainteyning them that fauoured
the same. Stokesley then Bishop of London, ministred Articles
unto him, to the number of xxiiij, as for adhereing to Luther and
his opinions : for hauing and reading heretical bookes and
treatises, for geuing exhibition [i.e. maintenance] to William
Tindall, Roy, and such other, for helping them ouer the sea to
Luther, for ministring priuie helpe to translate, as well the
Testament, as other bookes into English, for eating flesh in Lent
[&c.] . . . He being of these articles examined, and cast in the
Tower at last was compelled to make his sute or purgation, writing to the foresaid Cardinall, then Lord Chauncelor, and the whole

of the realme, and departed into Germanie.   Where the
good man being inflamed with a tender care and zeale of
his countrey, refused no trauell nor diligence howe by
all meanes possible, to reduce his brethren and countrey-
men of England to the same tast and vnderstandyng of
Gods holy word and veritie, which the Lord had endued
him withal.

Whereupon he considering in his minde, and partely
also conferring with Iohn Frith,[5] thought wyth him
selfe no way more to conduce therunto, then if the
Scripture were turned into the vulgar speach, that the

Counsayle out of the Tower.   In the contents whereof he answered
to the criminous accusation of them which charged him with
certayne bookes, receyued from beyond the sea :   Also for his
acquaintance wyth M. Tindall.   Whereunto he sayde, that he
denied not, but that foure yeares then past, he had heard the
said Tindal preach two or three sermons at S. Dunstons in the
west, and afterward meeting with the said Tindall, had certaine
communication with hym concerning his liuing, who then told
him that he had none at all, but trusted to be in the Bishop of
London his seruice :   for then he laboured to be his chaplayne.
But being refused of the Bishop, so came agayne to the sayd
Mummuth this examinate, and besought him to helpe hym.   Who
the same tyme tooke hym into hys house for halfe a yeare, where
the said Tindall liued (as he sayd) like a good priest, studieng
both night & day.   He would eat but sodden meate, by his good
will, nor drink but small single beere.   He was neuer seene in
that house to weare lynnen about him, al the space of his beyng
there.   Whereupon the sayd Mummuth had the better liking of
hym, so that he promised him ten pound (as he then sayd) for
his father and mothers soules, and all Christen soules, which money
afterward he sent him ouer to Hamborow, according to his promise.   And yet not to him alone he gaue this exhibition,' &c.

[5] John Frith (1503–33), of King's College, Cambridge, junior
canon of Wolsey's College, Oxford, imprisoned there in 1528 for
helping to circulate Tyndale's Testament, on his release went to
Marburg ;   returning to England, was imprisoned (1532) and
burnt.

poore people might also reade and see the simple plaine woord of God. For first hee wisely casting in hys minde, perceiued by experience, how that it was not possible to stablish the lay people in any truth, except the Scripture were so plainly layde before theyr eyes in theyr mother tongue, that they myght see the processe, order, and meaning of the text: For els what so euer truth shuld be taught them, these enemies of the truth would quenche it againe, either wyth apparant reasons of Sophistrie, and traditions of their own making, founded without all ground of Scripture : either els iuggling with the text, expounding it in such a sense, as impossible it were to gather of the text, if the right processe, order, and meaning thereof were seene . . .

For these and such other considerations, this good man was moued (and no doubt styrred vp of God) to translate the Scripture into his mother tongue, for the publicke vtility and profit of the simple vulgar people of the country : first, setting in hand with the newe Testament, whiche he first translated aboute the yeare of our Lord 1527.[6] After that he tooke in hand to translate the olde Testament, finishing the fiue bookes of Moyses, with sondry most learned and godly prologues prefixed before euery one, most worthy to be read and read againe of all good Christians : as the lyke also he did vpon the new Testament.

Hee wrote also diuers other woorkes vnder sundry titles, among the which is that most worthy monument of his, intituled : *The obedience of a Christian man* : wherin with singulare dexteritie he instructeth all men in the office and duetie of Christian obedience, wyth diuers other treatises : as *The wicked Mammon* : *The practise of Prelates*, wyth expositions vppon certaine partes of

[6] Fox's mistake for 1525.

the Scripture, and other Bookes also aunswearing to Syr Thom. More and other aduersaries of the truthe, no lesse delectable, then also most fruitfull to be read, which partly before beyng unknowen vnto many, partly also being almost abolished and worne out by time, the Printer heereof (good Reader) for conseruing and restoring such singulare treasures, hath collected and set foorth in Print the same in one generall volume,[7] all and whole together, as also the woorkes of John Frith, Barnes, and other, as are to be seene most special and profitable for thy reading.

These bookes of W. Tyndal being compiled, published and sent ouer into England, it cannot be spoken what a dore of light they opened to the eies of the whole English nation, which before were many yeres shut vp in darkenesse.

At his first departing out of the realme, he toke his iorny into the further parts of Germany, as into Saxony, where he had conference with Luther and other learned men in those quarters. Where, after that he had continued a certen season, he came down from thence into the netherlands, & had his most abiding in the town of Antwerp, vntil the time of hys apprehension : wherof more shalbe said god willing hereafter . . .

These godly bookes of Tindall, and specially the newe Testament of his translation, after that they began to come into mens handes, and to spread abroad, as they wroughte, great and singuler profite to the godly : so the vngodly enuying and disdaining that the people should be any thing wiser then they, and againe fearing least by the shining beames of truth, their false hypo-

[7] ' The whole workes of William Tyndall, John Frith and Doct. Barnes,' edited with biographical introductions by Fox and printed by John Day, 1573.

crisie & workes of darkenesse should be discerned :
began to stirre with no small ado, like as at the birth
of Christ, Herode & al Ierusalem was troubled with him.
But especially Sathan the prince of darkenes, maligning
the happy course and successe of the Gospel, set to his
might also, how to empeache and hinder the blessed
trauailes of that man : as by this, and also by sondry
other wayes may appeare. For at what time Tindall
had translated the fift booke of Moises called *Deutero-
nomium*, minding to Printe the same at Hamborough,
hee sailed thereward : where by the way vpon the coast
of Holland, he suffred shipwracke, by the which he loste
all his bookes, wrytings and copies, and so was compelled to begin al againe a new, to his hinderance and
doubling of his labors. Thus hauing lost by that ship,
both money, his copies and time, he came in an other
ship to Hamborough, where at his appoyntment M. Couerdale taried for him, and helped hym in the translating
the whole 5 bookes of Moises, from Easter till December,
in the house of a worshipfull widowe, Maistres Margaret
van Emmerson. Anno 1529. a greate sweating sicknesse
being the same time in the Towne. So hauing dispatched
his businesse at Hamborough, he returned afterward to
Antwerpe againe.[8]

[8] This paragraph first appeared in Fox's second edition (1570).
It is so precise in its statements that Fox would seem to have
written it from special information. It agrees with what we know
of the state of affairs at Antwerp, where Wolsey's agent, Hackett
(see No. XVI A–E.) made such a hue and cry after English-
Lutheran books in December, 1526, and January, 1527, that it
may well have seemed advisable to move a press and printing
materials elsewhere. The Pentateuch and other books of this
period profess to have been printed at ' Malborow [Marburg] in the
land of Hesse ' by Hans Lufft, Luther's printer.

V. TYNDALE'S STORY OF HIS TRANSLATION

This forms the preface to Tyndale's translation of Genesis in his version of the Pentateuch printed in 1530.[1]

W. T. To the Reader

WHEN I had translated the newe testament, I added a pistle vnto the latter ende,[2] In which I desyred them that were learned to amend [it] if ought were founde amysse. But oure malicious and wylye hypocrytes which are so stubburne and hard herted in their weked abhominacions that it is not possible for them to amend any thinge at all (as we see by dayly experience when their both lyvinges and doinges are rebuked with the trouth) saye, some of them that it is impossible to translate the scripture in to English, some that it is not lawfull for the laye people to have it in their mother tonge, some that it wold make them all heretykes, as it wold no doute from many thinges which they of longe tyme haue falsely taught, and that is the whole cause wherfore they forbyd it, though they other clokes pretende. And some or rather every one, saye that it wold make them ryse ageynst the kinge, whom they them selves (vnto their damnatyon) never yet obeyed. And leste the temporall rulars shuld see their falsehod, if the scripture cam to light, causeth them so to lye.

[1] This piece is given in this place because its interest lies chiefly in its narrative of Tyndale's experiences in London when he desired to translate the New Testament there. In this and the other English tracts printed abroad it should be noted that in the middle of words u and v are used indifferently.

[2] The Epilogue to the Worms octavo, printed in full below. See No. X.

And as for my translation in which they afferme vnto the laye people (as I haue hearde saye)[3] to be I wotte not how many thousande heresyes, so that it can not be mended or correcte, they haue yet taken so greate payne to examyne it, and to compare it vnto that they wold fayne haue it and to their awne imaginations and iugglinge termes, and to haue some what to rayle at, and vnder that cloke to blaspheme the treuth, that they myght with as little laboure (as I suppose) haue translated the moste parte of the bible. For they which in tymes paste were wont to loke on no more scripture then they founde in their duns [4] or soch like develysh doctryne, haue yet now so narowlye loked on my translatyon, that there is not so much as one I therin if it lacke a tytle over his hed, but they haue noted it, and nombre it vnto the ignorant people for an heresy. Fynallye in this they be all agreed, to dryve you from the knowlege of the scripture, and that ye shall not haue the texte therof in the mother tonge, and to kepe the world styll in darkenesse, to thentent they might sitt in the consciences of the people, thorow vayne superstition and false doctrine, to satisfye their fylthy lustes their proude ambition, and vnsatiable couetuousnes, and to exalte their awne honoure aboue kinge & emperoure, yee and aboue god him silfe.

A thousand bokes had they lever to be put forth agenste their abhominable doynges and doctrine, then that the scripture shulde come to light. For as longe as they may kepe that doune, they will so darken the ryght way with the miste of their sophistrye, and so tangle them that ether rebuke or despyse their abhominations with argumentes of philosophye and with

---

[3] The text omits the second bracket.
[4] i.e. the commentaries of Duns Scotus.

wordly⁵ symylitudes and apparent reasons of naturall
wisdom. And with wrestinge the scripture vnto their
awne purpose clene contrarye vnto the processe, order
and meaninge of the texte, and so delude them in des-
cantynge vppon it with alligoryes, and amase them
expoundinge it in manye senses⁶ before the vnlerned laye
people (when it hath but one symple litterall sense whose
light the owles can not abyde) that though thou feale
in thyne harte and arte sure how that all is false that
they saye, yet coudeste thou not solve their sotle rydles.

Which thinge onlye moved me to translate the new
testament. Because I had perceaved by experyence,
how that it was impossible to stablysh the laye people
in any truth, excepte the scripture were playnly layde
before their eyes in their mother tonge, that they might
se the processe, ordre and meaninge of the texte : for
els what so ever truth is taught them, these ennymyes
of all truth qwench it ageyne, partly with the smoke of
their bottomlesse pytte wherof thou readest apocalipsis ix.
that is, with apparent reasons of sophistrye and traditions
of their awne makynge, founded with out grounde of
scripture, and partely in iugglinge with the texte,
expoundinge it in soch a sense as is impossible to gether
of the texte, if thou see the processe ordre and meaninge
thereof.

And even in the bisshope of londons house I entended to
have done it. For when I was so turmoyled in the contre
where I was that I coude no lenger there dwell (the
processe wherof were to longe here to reherce) I this
wyse thought in my silfe, this I suffre because the
prestes of the contre be vnlerned, as god it knoweth

---

⁵ Worldly, the first l in which was often dropped.

⁶ The ' sensus mysticus ' was a distinct department of Biblical
exposition.

there are a full ignorant sorte which haue sene no more
latyn then that they read in their portesses[7] and missales
which yet many of them can scacely read (excepte it be
Albertus [8] de secretis mulierum in which yet, though
they be neuer so soryly lerned, they pore day and night
and make notes therin and all to teach the mydwyves
as they say, and linwood [9] a boke of constitutions to
gether tithes, mortuaryes [10], offeringes, customs, and
other pillage, which they calle, not theirs, but godes parte
and the deuty of holye chirch, to discharge their consciences with all : for they are bound that they shall
not dimynysh, but encreace all thinge vnto the vttmost
of their powers) and therfore (because they are thus
vnlerned thought I) when they come to gedder to the
alehouse, which is their preachinge place, they afferme
that my sainges are heresy. And besydes that they
adde to of thir awne heddes which I never spake, as the
maner is to prolonge the tale to shorte the tyme with all,
and accuse me secretly to the chauncelare [11] and other
the bishopes officers, And in deade when I cam before
the chauncelare, he thretened me grevously, and revyled
me and rated me as though I had bene a dogge, and
layd to my charge wherof there coude be none accuser
brought forth (as their maner is not to bringe forth the
accuser) and yet all the prestes of the contre were that
same day there. As I this thought the bishope of London
came to my remembrance whome Erasmus (whose tonge
maketh of litle gnattes greate elephantes and lifteth
vpp above the starres whosoever geveth him a litle

[7] Breviaries   [8] i. e. Albertus Magnus.

[9] William Lyndewode's *Prouinciale*, a digest of English canon
law written in 1433.   See above, No. I.

[10] Customary gifts claimed from the heirs of dead parishioners.

[11] i. e. the Bishop's Chancellor of the diocese.

exhibition) prayseth excedingly amonge other in his annotatyons on the new testament for his great learninge. Then thought I, if I might come to this mannes service, I were happye. And so I gate me to london, and thorow the accoyntaunce of my master came to sir harry gilford [12] the kinges graces countroller, and brought him an oration of Isocrates which I had translated out of greke in to English, and desyred him to speake vnto my lorde of london for me, which he also did as he shewed me, and willed me to write a pistle to my lorde, and to goo to him my silf which I also did, and delivered my pistle to a servant of his awne, one Wyllyam hebilthwayte, a man of myne old accoyntaunce. But god which knoweth what is within hypocrites, sawe that I was begyled, and that that councell was not the nexte way vnto my purpose. And therfore he gate me no favoure in my lordes sight.

Wherevppon my lorde answered me, his house was full, he had mo then he coude well finde, and advised me to seke in london, wher he sayd I coude not lacke a service. And so in london I abode almoste an yere, and marked the course of the worlde, and herde oure pratars, I wold say oure preachers how they bosted them selves and their hye authorite, and beheld the pompe of oure prelates and how besyed they were as they yet are, to set peace and vnite in the worlde (though it be not possible for them that walke in darkenesse to continue longe in peace, for they can not but ether stomble or dash them selves at one thinge or another that shall clene vnquyet all togedder) and sawe thinges wherof I deferre to speake at this tyme, and vnderstode at the laste not only that there was no rowme in my lorde of londons palace to translate the new testament, but

[12] See note 3 to No. IV.

H

also that there was no place to do it in all englonde, as experience doth now openly declare.

Vnder what maner therfore shuld I now submitte this boke to be corrected and amended of them, which can suffer nothinge to be well ? Or what protestacyon shuld I make in soch a matter vnto oure prelates those stubburne Nimrothes which so mightely fight agenste god and resiste his holy spirite, enforceynge with all crafte and sotelte to qwench the light of the everlastinge testament, promyses, and apoyntemente made betwene god and vs : and heapinge the firce wrath of god vppon all princes and rulars, mockinge them with false fayned names of hypocryse, and servinge their lustes at all poyntes, and dispensinge with them even of the very lawes of god, of which Christe him silf testifieth. Mathew v. that not so moch as one tittle therof maye perish or be broken. And of which the prophete sayth Psalme cxviij. Thou hast commaunded thy lawes to be kepte meod [13], that is in hebrew excedingly, with all diligence, mighte and power, and haue made them so mad with their iugglinge charmes and crafty persuasions that they thinke it full satisfaction for all their weked lyvinge, to torment soch as tell them trouth, and to borne the worde of their soules helth and sle whosoever beleve theron.

Not withstondinge yet I submytte this boke and all other that I have other made or translated, or shall in tyme to come (if it be goddes will that I shall further laboure in his hervest) vnto all them that submytte themselues vnto the worde of god, to be corrected of them, yee and moreover to be disalowed & also burnte, if it seme worthy when they have examyned it wyth the hebrue, so that they first put forth of their awne translatinge a nother that is more correcte.

[13] מְאֹד

VI. THE PRINTING OF THE FIRST NEW TESTAMENTS

From the ' Commentaria Ioannis Cochlaei, de Actis et Scriptis Martini Lutheri Saxonis chronographice ex ordine ab anno Domini 1517 usque ad annum 1546 inclusiue, fideliter conscripta. *Apud S. Victorem prope Moguntiam, ex officina Francisci Behem typographi.* 1549, pp. 132–135.' [1]

. . . Sed multo adhuc impudentiori audacia Lutherus aggressus est Regem Angliae, Henricum VIII. Quem publice prius tot probris lædoriis, sannis atque calumniis, ad populos & Nationes traduxerat. Ipse quidem affirmabat se illectum fuisse a Rege Daniae Christierno (qui e regnis suis profugus, exul, per Germaniam uagabatur) ut ad ipsum scriberet Regem Angliæ. Verum Duo Angli Apostatæ, qui aliquandiu fuerant Vuittenbergæ, non solum quærebant subuertere Mercatores suos, qui eos occulte in exilio fouebant & alebant : Verum etiam cunctos Angliæ populos, uolente nolente Rege, breui per nouum Lutheri Testamentum, quod in Anglicanam traduxerant linguam, Lutheranos fore sperabant. Venerant iam Coloniam Agrippinam, ut Testamentum sic traductum, per Typographos in multa Milia multiplicatum, occulte sub aliis mercibus deueherent inde in Angliam. Tanta enim eis erat rei bene gerendæ fiducia, ut primo aggressu peterent a Typographis, Sex Milia sub prælum dari. Illi autem subuerentes, ne grauissimo afficerentur damno, si quid aduersi accideret,

---

[1] Johann Dobneck, or as he called himself, Cochlaeus, born in 1479, proved himself next to Eck the keenest and most energetic controversialist on the Catholic side. He had already, in 1533 and 1538, given two brief accounts of his exploit in routing Tyndale out of Cologne, and now in the last year of his life narrated it in full. He starts his story with Luther's unlucky second letter to Henry VIII, in which he tried to make his peace for his previous attacks.

tantum Tria Milia sub prælum miserunt : Quae si
fœliciter uenderentur, facile possent imprimi denuo.
Iam literas ad Sanctos, qui sunt in Anglia, præmiserat
Pomeranus,[2] & ad Regem quoque scripserat ipse Lutherus.
Cunque nouum Testamentum mox subsequuturum
crederetur, tanta ex ea spe lætitia Lutheranos inuasit
ac uanæ fiduciæ uento inflauit, ut gaudio distenti, ante
diem ruperint secretum uanis iactationibus. Exulabat
eo tempore Coloniæ Ioannes Cochlæus, Decanus Ecclesiæ
B. Virginis Francofordiensis, Qui per hospitem suum,
Georgium Lauer, Canonicum ad Apostolos, Abbati
Tuitiensi redditus familiariter notus, ubi audisset opera
quædam Ruperti Tuitiensis quondam Abbatis, mittenda
esse Nurenbergam, ut a Lutheranis æderentur in publi-
cum : cœpit summo studio eam rem & dissuadere &
impedire. Nam Lutherani in eum usque diem, cum
omnes Bibliothecas antiquas diligentissime exquisiuissent
ac discussissent, nullum prorsus autorem ex cunctis tot
sæculorum Doctoribus Ecclesiæ inuenire potuerunt, qui
Lutheri dogmata comprobasset. Inuentum tandem
illius Ruperti, qui ante 400. annos uixerat, opusculum,
cui titulus erat, De Victoria uerbi Dei, mox Nurenbergae
a Lutheranis euulgatum est. Quod suo titulo ita mox
placuit omnibus Lutheranis, ut nihil uideretur eo autore
desiderabilius. Interim ex Tritemio [3] intelligebant, illum
complura scripsisse opuscula, sed duo tantum paruula
inuenerant. Quorum unum de potentia, alterum de
uoluntate Dei inscriptum erat. In eorum æditione
multa Lutherice apposuerat Osiander,[4] uxoratus pres-

[2] Johann Bugenhagen, of Pomerania, Protestant theologian,
1484–1558.

[3] i. e. from the *Catalogus Illustrium Virorum* of Johann Tritheim, abbot of the Benedictine monastery at Spanheim, which
enumerates the writings of many early German authors.

[4] Andreas Osiander, Protestant theologian, 1498–1552.

byter & prædicator, quibus pium autorem impiæ sectæ
patronum facere tentabat. Et iam dudum egerant
cum ipso Abbate Tuitiensi : ut reliqua Ruperti Opera
Nurenbergam excudenda, transmitteret. Ille uero, ut
à Cochlæo audiuit, quantum periculi foret ea in re, si
pium autorem traderet in manus impiorum, qui eum
non solum impiis præfationibus & annotationibus fœde
contaminaturi essent : Verum etiam integros & sanos
illius sensus deprauaturi, ex Catholico antiquo facturi
essent haereticum nouum, qui uideretur cuncta Lutheri
dogmata ante annos 400. approbasse. Abbas igitur ille,
uir bonus, mutata sententia, uolumina iam in grandem
fascem compacta, uelut Nurenbergam transmittenda,
apud se retinuit. In quo sane fasce erant xiiii. libri in
Euangelium Ioannis, xii. libri in Apocalypsim eiusdem,
& xii. libri, de Diuinis Officijs. Cum autem Monachi
quieturi non essent, nisi æderentur opera illa : Cochlæus
Petro Quentellio,[5] & Arnoldo Berckmanno sedulo
suasit, ut communibus inter se impensis & lucris ea
opera susciperent ædenda. Persuadere tamen non
potuit, donec tandem omnem suam operam ad æditionem
illam eis pollicitus esset. Cunque æditio illa satis
quaestuosa eis existeret, non egebant amplius impulsore
Cochlæo, sed ipsimet ultro plura illius opuscula desidera-
bant : rogantes nunc Abbatem, nunc Cochlæum, ut
undecunque plura conquirerent. Abbas itaque ex
uetustis S. Benedicti Monasteriis perquisiuit xxxii. libros
in xii. prophetas minores, & vii. libros in Canticum
Canticorum. Cochlæus uero inuenit Coloniæ in Biblio-
theca Maioris Ecclesiæ ix. libros, De glorificatione
Trinitatis, & processione Spiritus sancti. Et in scholis

---

[5] Peter Quentell was a prominent printer at Cologne, and
Arnold Birckmann a bookseller largely engaged in supplying
books to the English market.

Artium grande uolumen, quod de operibus Trinitatis inscriptum, XLII. complectebatur libros. E quibus in Genesim erant IX. In Exodum IIII. &c. Cunque sciret Rupertum olim Leodij ad S. Laurentium fuisse Monachum, scripsit Theodorico Hezio, Canonico Leodiensi, quem Romæ post obitum Adriani VI. (cuius ille à Secretis intimus extiterat) familiarius cognouerat, obsecrans, ut is in eo Monasterio perquireret, quidnam ex Ruperti libris extaret. Ille ergo repperit maxime desideratum opus, XIII. libros in Matthæum, de Gloria & honore filij hominis. Verum transmittere Coloniam non potuit Archetypum, nisi ipse cum duobus alijs Canonicis, pro restituendo exemplari, cuncta bona sua in hypothecam Monachis obligarent. Ea igitur uolumina uniuersa Cochlaeus, Moguntiam euocatus, secum detulit, atque ibi residens, ad æditionem praeparauit, Coloniamque aedenda remisit. Hinc Typographis Coloniensibus notior ac familiarior factus, audiuit eos aliquando inter pocula fiducialiter iactitare, Velint Nolint Rex & Cardinalis Angliæ, totam Angliam breui fore Lutheranam. Audiuit item, duos ibi latitare Anglos, eruditos linguarumque peritos et disertos, quos tamen uidere aut alloqui nunquam potuit. Vocatis itaque in hospitium suum quibusdam Typographis, postea quam mero incaluissent, unus eorum in secretiori colloquio reuelauit illi arcanum, quo ad Lutheri partes trahenda esset Anglia. Nempe uersari sub prælo Tria Milia Exemplarium Noui Testamenti Lutherani, in Anglicanam linguam translati, ac processum esse iam usque ad literam Alphabeti K. in ordine Quaternionum. Impensas abunde suppeti à Mercatoribus Anglicis, qui opus excusum clam inuecturi per totam Angliam latenter dispergere uellent, antequam Rex aut Cardinalis rescire aut prohibere possit. Cochlaeus intra se metu & admiratione uarie affectus, foris mirabundus mœrorem dissimulabat. Altero autem die, periculi magnitudinem tristis secum expendens, cogitabat, quo nam pacto possit commode pessimis illis conatibus obsistere. Abijt igitur clam ad Hermannum Rinck, Patricium Coloniensem, ac Militem Auratum, qui & Cæsari & Regi Angliæ familiaris erat & Consiliarius, eique rem omnem, ut acceperat uini beneficio, indicauit. Ille, ut certius omnia constarent, alium misit exploratum in eam domum, ubi opus excudebatur iuxta indicium Cochlæi. Cunque ab illo accepisset rem ita habere, & ingentem Papyri copiam ibi existere : adijt Senatum, atque effecit, ut Typographis interdiceretur, ne ultra progrederentur in eo opere. Duo Apostatae Angli, arreptis secum Quaternionibus impressis, aufugerunt, nauigio per Rhenum ascendentes Vuormaciam, ubi plebs pleno furore Lutherizabat, ut ibi per alium Typographum cœptum perficerent opus. Rincus uero & Cochlæus de his mox admonuerunt literis suis Regem, Cardinalemque & Episcopum Roffensem,[6] ut quàmdiligentissime præcauerent in omnibus Angliæ portubus, ne merx illa perniciosissima inueheretur. Ferunt Dominum Cuthebertum Tunstallum, uirum disertissimum, Episcopum tunc Londinensem, nunc Dunelmensem, cum adeptus fuisset unum ex illis exemplaribus, in maxima concione ad populum Londini publice affirmasse, supra duo Milia deprauationum atque peruersitatum se in uno opere illo depraehendisse. Dum hæc agerentur, peruenit tandem in manus Regis Angliæ epistola Lutheri,[7] quam is anno superiore scripserat Vuittenbergæ, prima die Septembris.

[6] Bishop Fisher.

[7] Epistola Martini Lutheri ad Henricum viii Angliæ ac Franciæ Regem, et in qua veniam petit eorum quae prius stultus in eundem regem effuderit.

Translation [8]

With a hardihood even still more impudent Luther approached the King of England, Henry VIII, whom he had previously traduced in public before peoples and nations with so many slanders, revilings, gibes, and calumnies. His own contention was that he had been enticed by King Christiern of Denmark (who was wandering about Germany as a fugitive exile from his realm) to write to the King of England. But two English apostates who had been sometime at Wittenberg were not only seeking to undo their own merchants, who were secretly supporting and maintaining them in exile, but were also hoping that all the peoples of England, whether the King liked it or not, would shortly become Lutherans by means of the New Testament of Luther which they had translated into English. They had already come to Cologne that thence they might convey to England, secretly, under cover of other goods, the Testament so translated after it had been multiplied by printers into many thousands. For they had so much confidence of managing the business well that at the first onset they asked of the printers that six thousand should be printed. The printers, however, fearing a very heavy loss if anything went wrong, sent only three thousand copies to press, on the ground that if these were successfully sold they could easily be printed afresh. Already Bugenhagen had sent forward letters addressed ' To the Saints who are in England ', and Luther himself had also written to the King. When it was believed that the New Testament would quickly follow, so great joy from that hope seized the Lutherans and inflated them with vain con-

[8] Partly based on that in Anderson's *Annals of the English Bible*.

fidence, that, swollen with delight, they prematurely broke their secret by their idle boasts.

At that time Johann Dobneck, Dean of the Church of the Blessed Virgin at Frankfort, was living in exile at Cologne, and through his host, Georg Lauer, Canon at [the church of] the Apostles, he was put on familiar terms with the Abbot of Deutz. On hearing, therefore, that certain works of Rupert, a former Abbot of Deutz, were to be sent to Nuremberg for publication by the Lutherans he began very zealously to dissuade from and hinder the business. For down to that time the Lutherans, although they had most diligently searched and ransacked all the old libraries, could find not a single author of all the Doctors of the Church for so many centuries whom they could quote as favouring the doctrines of Luther. At last there was discovered a little book of this Rupert, who had lived 400 years before, with the title *On the Victory of the Word of God*, and this was presently published by the Lutherans at Wittenberg, its title giving all the Lutherans so much pleasure that nothing could seem more delightful than the author. Meanwhile they learnt from Tritheim that he had written many small works, but they had only discovered two little ones, of which one was entitled *On the Power*, the other *On the Will of God*. In editing these, Osiander, a married priest and preacher, made many additions in the Lutheran manner in the endeavour to turn the pious author into the patron of an impious sect. They had now for some time been treating with the Abbot of Deutz to send the rest of the works of Rupert to Nuremberg to be printed. But the Abbot, as soon as he heard from Dobneck what danger there would be in delivering the pious author into the hands of impious editors, who would not only contaminate him foully with impious prefaces and notes, but would corrupt his upright and sound opinions and out of an ancient Catholic make a modern heretic who should seem to have approved all Luther's doctrines 400 years before,—the Abbot, I say, good man, changed his mind and kept in his own custody the volumes which had already been tied up in a bulky parcel to be sent to Nuremberg. In this parcel there were fourteen books on the Gospel of S. John, twelve books on the Apocalypse, and twelve on the Divine Offices. When, however, the monks were not to be quieted without these works being published, Dobneck put pressure on Peter Quentell and Arnold Birckmann to undertake their publication as a joint venture. But he could not persuade them to do this, until he had finally promised to give the edition all the help in his power. The venture proving profitable enough the publishers no longer needed Dobneck's incitement, but of their own accord began to look out for more of Rupert's little books, asking now the Abbot, now Dobneck, to hunt out more from wherever they could. The Abbot accordingly searched out from old Benedictine monasteries thirty-two books on the twelve Minor Prophets, and seven on the Song of Songs. Dobneck on his part discovered at Cologne, in the library of the greater Church, nine books on the Glorifying of the Trinity and the Procession of the Holy Spirit, and in the School of Arts a large volume entitled *On the Works of the Trinity* in forty-two books, of which nine were on Genesis, four on Exodus, &c. And when he learnt that Rupert had been formerly a monk at Liège he wrote to Dietrich Heze, Canon of Liège, whom he had known intimately at Rome after the death of Adrian VI, to whom he had been a privy councillor, and besought him to search in that monastery for any books of Rupert's that could be found. The Canon lighted upon a work much in request, the thirteen books on Matthew, *On the Glory and Honour of the Son of Man.*   But he could not send the original to Cologne until he himself and two other canons pawned all their property to the monks as a pledge for its return.   All these volumes, therefore, Dobneck, when he was called away to Mainz, took with him, and while he was living there prepared them for publication and sent them to Cologne to be published.

By all this business Dobneck had become pretty intimate and familiar with the Cologne printers, when one day he heard them boasting confidently over their wine that whether the King and Cardinal of England liked it or no, all England would soon be Lutheran.   He heard also that there were there in hiding two Englishmen, learned, skilled in languages and ready of speech, whom, however, he could never see nor speak to.   Dobneck therefore asked certain printers to his inn and, after he had warmed them with wine, one of them in confidential talk revealed to him the secret by which England was to be brought over to the side of Luther—namely that there were in the press three thousand copies of the Lutheran New Testament translated into English, and that in the order of the quires they had got as far as letter K ; funds were being freely supplied by English merchants who meant secretly to import the work when printed and disperse it surreptitiously through all England before King or Cardinal could discover or forbid it.

Alarmed and bewildered as he was, Dobneck disguised his grief under an appearance of admiration ; but the next day, weighing the greatness of the danger, he began to think by what means he could conveniently thwart the wicked project.   He went, therefore, secretly to Hermann Rinck, a patrician of Cologne, and military knight, intimate with the Emperor and the King of

England and of their counsel, and to him disclosed the whole business as, thanks to the wine, he had heard it. Rinck, to make more certain, sent another person to the house where, according to Dobneck's discovery, the work was being printed, to search. When this man reported that the facts were as stated, and that a great quantity of paper was lying there, Rinck approached the Senate and brought it about that the printers were forbidden to go on with the work. The two English heretics, hastily taking with them the printed quires, made their escape by boat up the Rhine to Worms, where the people were all mad on Luther, in order that there by another printer they might complete the work. Rinck and Dobneck, on their part, presently advised the King, Cardinal, and Bishop of Rochester of the affair by letters, so that they might take diligent precautions at all the English ports to prevent these pernicious wares being imported. It was while this affair was in progress that there reached the hands of the King of England the letter of Luther which he had written the year before at Wittenberg, on September 1st.

VII. THE NEWS SENT TO THE KING

From a letter to Henry VIII, written by Edward Lee, afterwards (1531) Archbishop of York, dated December 2.—Cotton MS. Vespasian, C. III, fol. 211.

Please it your highnesse morover to vnderstond, that I ame certainlie enformed as I passed in this contree, that an englishman your subiect at the sollicitacion and instaunce of Luther, with whome he is, hathe translated the newe testament in to Englishe, and within four dayes entendethe to arrive with the same emprinted in England. I nede not to aduertise your grace, what infection and

daunger maye ensue heerbie, if it bee not withstonded.
This is the next waye to fulfill your realme with luthe-
rians, for all Luthers peruerse opinions bee grownded
vpon bare wordes of scriptur not well taken ne vnder-
standed, wiche your grace hathe opened[1] in sondrie places
of your royall booke.   All our forfaders gouenors of the
chirche of England hathe with all diligence forbed
& exchued publicacion of englishe bibles, as appereth in
constitutions prouincall of the chirche of Englond.
Nowe sire as god hathe endued your grace with Christian
couraige to sett forthe the standard against thees
Philistees & to vanquish them, so I doubt not but that
he will assist your grace to prosecute & performe the
same, that is to vndertreade them that they shall not
nowe againe lift vppe their hedds, wiche they endevor
nowe by meanes of englyshe bibles.   They knowe what
hurte suche bookes hathe doone in your realme in tymes
passed.   Hidretoo blessed bee god, your realme is save
from infection of luthers sect, as for so mutche that
althowgh anye peradventure bee secretlie blotted within,
yet for feare of your royall maiestie, wiche hathe drawen
his swerd in godes cawse, they dare not openlie avowe.
Wherfor I can not doubte but that your noble grace wil
valiauntlie maynetaine that you have so noblie begonne.

This realme of fraunce hathe been somewhat tooched
with this sect, in so mutche that it hathe entred amongs
the doctors of parisse, wherof some bee in prison, some
fled, some called in Iudicium.   The bisshoppe also of
Meulx called Molday is summoned for that cause, for he
suffred luthers peruerse opinions to bee preached in his
diocese.   Faber[2] also a man hidretoo noted of excellent
good lief and lernyng is called among them, but some

[1] Expounded.
[2] Jacques Lefevre d' Etaples, the translator of the Bible.

saye heer for displeassure, wiche I can well thinke.   The
Parliament of Parisse hathe had mutche businesse to
represse this sect.   And yet blessed be god, your noble
realme is yet onblotted.   Wherfor lest anye daunger
myght ensue, if thees bookes secretlie shold bee browght
in, I thowght my duetie to advertise your grace therof,
considering that it toochethe your highe honor, & the
wealthe & intregrite of the christen fayth within your
realme wiche can not long endure, if thees bookes may
come in. . . .   At Burdeaulx the second Day of Decembre
[1525].

.   .   .   .

Your most humble preest, subiect & almesman
Edouardo lee.

[Endorsed : 'To the kinges higness p . . . th³ the
same thing.']

VIII.   THE SUPPOSED TRIAL VERSION OF
S. MATTHEW

From *The Life of Iohn Frith*, by Foxe, prefixed to Frith's
writings in Foxe's edition of *The Whole Workes of W. Tyndall,
Iohn Frith and Doct. Barnes.*   London, John Day, 1573.

Not long after the sayd William [Tyndale] & Iohn
Frith had many metinges and great conferences, and by
the sayd William he fyrst receaued into his hart the seede
of the Gospell and sencere godlines, & after with great
perill and Daunger they both being inquired & sought
for, fled.   William Tyndall first placed him selfe in
Germany, and there did first translate the Gospell of

³ The damaged word may be ' proveth '.   The king was warned
also by Dobneck, Rinck, and probably others.

S. Mathewe[1] into Englishe, and after the whole new
testament &c. And not long after the departure of
Tyndall, Iohn Frith escaped and fled into Flaunders, etc.

IX. THE BEGINNING OF TYNDALE'S PROLOGUE
TO THE FIRST NEW TESTAMENT

From the unique copy of the Cologne fragment of 1525
in the British Museum.

The Prologge

I haue here translated (brethren and susters moost
dere and tenderly beloued in Christ) the newe Testament
for youre spirituall edyfyinge, consolacion, and solas :

Exhortynge instantly and besechynge those that are
better sene in the tonges then y, and that have hyer
gyftes of grace to interpret the sence of the scripture, and
meanynge of the spyrite, then y, to consydre and pondre
my laboure, and that with the spyrite of mekenes. And

---

[1] Compare the reference of Robert Ridley (No. XIII) to the
' commentares and annotations in Mathew & Marcum in the
first print ', and that of Robert Necton (No. XIX) to 'the chapiters
of Matthew '.   In the Confession of John Tyball, a Lollard,
charged with heresy (printed by Strype, *Memorials*, I. ii. 50–56,
from Bishop Tunstall's Register), one paragraph reads : ' Furthermore, he saythe, that abowght ii. yeres agon he companyed with
Sir Richard Fox Curate of Bumstede, and shewid hym al his
bookys that he had : that is to say, the New Testamente in
Englishe, the Gospel of Matthew and Mark in Englishe : which
he had of John Pykas of Colchester, and a book expoundyng the
Pater Noster, etc.' All these references fall a little short of a
decisive proof that the gospels of Matthew and Mark in Tyndale's
version were printed separately, otherwise than in the ten quires
set up at Cologne for Tyndale in 1525.   Perhaps the easiest hypothesis is that Tyndale completed the Cologne fragment at Worms
to the end of Mark, and put this in circulation, subsequently
printing an entirely fresh quarto at Worms.

yf they perceyue in eny places that y have not attayned the very sence of the tonge, or meanynge of the scripture, or haue not given the right englysshe worde, that they put to there handes to amende it, remembrynge that so is there duetie to doo. For we have not receyved the gyftes of god for oureselues only, or forto hyde them: but forto bestowe them vnto the honouringe of god and christ, and edyfyinge of the congregacion, wchich is the body of christ.

The causes that moved me to translate, y thought better that other shulde ymagion, then that y shulde rehearce them.

More over y supposed yt superfluous, for who ys so blynde to axe why lyght shulde be shewed to them that walke in dercknes, where they cannot but stomble, and where to stomble ys the daunger of eternall dammacion, other so despyghtfull that he wolde envye eny man (y speake nott his brother) so necessary a thinge, or so bedlem madde to affyrme that good is the naturall cause of yuell, and derknes to procede oute of lyght, and that lyinge shulde be grounded in trougth and verytie, and nott rather clene contrary, that lyght destroyeth dercknes, and veritie reproveth all manner lyinge.

After hit had pleasyd god to put in my mynde, and also to ge[v]e me grace to translate this forerehearced newe testament in[t]o oure englysshe tonge, howesoever we have done it. I supposed yt very necessary to put you in remembraunce of certayne poyntes, which are : that ye well vnderstand what these wordes meane. ❡ The olde testament. ❡ The newe testament. ❡ The lawe. ❡ The gospell. ❡ Moses. ❡ Christ. ❡ Nature. ❡ Grace. ❡Workinge and belevynge. ❡Dedes and faythe, Lest we ascrybe[1], to the one that which belongeth to the

[1] Misprinted 'astrybe.'

other, and make of Christ Moses, of the gospell the Lawe,
despise grace and robbe faythe : and fall from meke
lernynge into ydle despicionns [2], braulinge and scold-
ynge aboute wordes.

The olde testament is a boke, where in is wrytten
the lawe and commaundmentes of god, and the dedes
of them which fulfill them, and of them also which fulfill
them nott.

The newe testament is a boke where in are coteyned
the promyses of god, and the dedes of them which beleue
them or beleue them nott.

Euangelion (that we cal the gospel) is a greke worde,
& signyfyth good, mery, glad and ioyfull tydinges, that
maketh a mannes hert glad, and maketh hym synge,
daunce and leepe for ioye As when Davyd had kylled
Golyath the geaunt, cam glad tydinges vnto the iewes,
that their fearfull and cruell enemy was slayne, and they
delyvered oute of all daunger : for gladnes were of, they
songe, daunsed, and wer ioyfull. In lyke manner is the
evangelion of god (which we call gospell, and the newe
testament) ioyfull tydinges, and as some saye : a good
hearing publisshed by the apostles through oute all the
worlde, of Christ the right Davyd howe that he hathe
fought with synne, with dethe, and the devill, and over
cume them. Whereby all men that were in Bondage to
synne, wounded with dethe, ouercum of the devill, are
with oute there awne merrittes or deservinges losed,
iustyfyed, restored to lyfe, and saved, brought to libertie,
and reconciled vnto the favour of god, and sett at one
with hym agayne : which tydinges as many as beleve
laude prayse and thancke god, are glad, synge and
daunce for ioye.

This evangelion or gospell (that is to saye, suche ioyfull

[2] Discussions.

I

tydinges) is called the newe testament. Because that as
a man when he shall dye apoynteth his gooddes to be
dealte and distributed after hys dethe amonge them
which he nameth to be his heyres. Even so Christ before
his dethe commaunded and appoynted that suche
evangelion, gospell, or tydynges shulde be declared
through oute all the worlde, and there with to geue vnto
all that beleve all his gooddes, that is to saye, his lyfe,
where with he swalowed and devoured vp dethe : his
rightewesnes, where with he bannyshed synne : his
salvacion, wherewith he overcam eternall damnacion [3].
Nowe can the wretched man (that is wrapped in synne,
and is in daunger to dethe and hell) heare no moare
ioyus a thynge, then suche glad and comfortable tydinges,
of Christ. So that he cannot but be glad and laugh from
the lowe bottom of his hert, if he beleve that the tydynges
are trewe. . . .

X. TYNDALE'S EPILOGUE TO THE SECOND
NEW TESTAMENT

From the Facsimile of the edition of Worms 1526, published
in 1862.

To the Reder

Geve diligence Reder (I exhorte the) that thou come
with a pure mynde, and as the scripture sayth with
a syngle eye, vnto the wordes of health, and of eternall
lyfe : by the which (if we repent and beleve them) we
are borne a newe, created a fresshe, and enioye the frutes
off the bloud of Christ. Whiche bloud cryeth not for
vengeance, as the bloud of Abel : but hath purchased,
lyfe, love, faveour, grace, blessynge, and whatsoever is

[3] Misprinted 'damancion.

promysed in the scriptures, to them that beleve and obeye
God : and stondeth bitwene vs and wrathe, vengeaunce,
cursse, and whatsoever the scripture threateneth agaynst
the vnbelevers and disobedient, which resist, and consent
not in their hertes to the lawe of god, that it is ryght,
wholy, iuste, and ought soo to be.

Marke the playne and manyfest places of the scriptures, and in doutfull places, se thou adde no interpretacion contrary to them : but (as Paul sayth) let all be
conformable and agreynge to the fayth.

Note the difference of the lawe, and of the gospell.
The one axeth and requyreth, the wother perdoneth and
forgeveth. The one threateneth, the wother promyseth
all good thynges, to them that sett their trust in Christ
only. The gospell signifieth gladde tydynges, and is
nothynge butt the promyses off good thynges. All is
not gospell that is written in the gospell boke : For if
the lawe were a waye, thou couldest not know what the
gospell meante. Even as thou couldest not se perdon,
favour, and grace, excepte the lawe rebuked the, and
declared vnto the thy sinne, mysdede, and treaspase.

Repent and beleve the gospell as sayth Christ in the
fyrst of Marke. Applye all waye the lawe to thy dedes,
whether thou finde luste in the bottom of thyne hert to
the lawe warde : and soo shalt thou no dout repent, and
feale in the silfe a certayne sorowe, payne, and grefe to
thyne herte : because thou canst nott with full luste do
the dedes off the lawe. Applye the gospell, that is to saye
the promyses, vnto the deservynge off Christ, and to the
mercye of god and his trouth, and soo shalt thou nott
despeare : butt shalt feale god as a kynde and a mercifull father. And his sprete[1] shall dwell in the, and shall
be stronge in the : and the promises shalbe geven the at

[1] Spirit.

I 2

the last (though not by and by[2], lest thou shuldest forgett
thysylfe, and be negligent) and all threatenynges shalbe
forgeven the for Christis blouddis sake, to whom commit
thy silfe all togedder, with out respect, other of thy good
dedes or of thy badde.

Them that are learned Christenly, I beseche : for as
moche as I am sure, and my conscience beareth me
recorde, that of a pure entent, singilly and faythfully
I have interpreted itt, as farre forth as god gave me
the gyfte of knowledge, and vnderstondynge : that the
rudnes off the worke nowe at the fyrst tyme, offende them
not : but that they consyder howe that I had no man to
counterfet, nether was holpe with englysshe of eny that
had interpreted the same, or soche lyke thinge in the
scripture before tyme. Moreover, even very necessitie
and combraunce (God is recorde) above strengthe, which
I will not rehearce, lest we shulde seme to bost ourselues,
caused that many thynges are lackinge, which neces-
saryly are requyred. Count it as a thynge not havynge
his full shape, but as it were borne afore hys tyme, even
as a thing begunne rather then fynnesshed. In tyme to
come (yf god have apoynted vs there vnto) we will geve
it his full shape : and putt out yf ought be added super-
fluusly : and adde to yff ought be oversene thorowe
negligence : and will enfoarce to brynge to compen-
deousnes, that which is nowe translated at the lengthe,
and to geve lyght where it is requyred, and to seke in
certayne places more proper englysshe, and with a table
to expounde the wordes which are nott commenly vsed,
and shewe howe the scripture vseth many wordes, which
are wother wyse vnderstonde of the commen people, and
to helpe with a declaracion where one tonge taketh nott
another. And will endever oureselves, as it were to sethe it

[2] Immediately.

better, and to make it more apte for the weake stomakes :
desyrynge them that are learned, and able, to remember
their duetie, and to helpe therevnto : and to bestowe
vnto the edyfyinge of Christis body (which is the congregacion of them that beleve,) those gyftes which they have
receaved of god for the same purpose. The grace that
commeth of Christ be with them that love hym. praye
for vs.

XI. HENRY VIII'S BELIEF THAT TYNDALE WAS INSTIGATED BY LUTHER[1]

Extract from ' A copy of the letters, wherin the most redouted
& mighty prince our souerayne lorde kyng Henry the eyght . . .
made answere vnto a certayne letter of Martyn Luther. *London,
Rycharde Pynson* [1526–27] (Sig. Av recto.)

So came it than to passe, that Luther at laste, par-
ceyuyng wyse men to espye hym, lerned men to leaue
hym, good men to abhorre hym, and his frantyke
fauourers to fall to wracke, the nobles and honest
people in Almaygne, beynge taught by the profe of his
vngratyous practyse, moche more hurt & myschefe to
folowe therof, than euer they loked after, deuysed a letter
to vs written, to abuse them and all other natyons, in
suche wyse, as ye by the contentes therof herafter shal
well perceyue. In whiche he fayneth hymselfe to be
enformed, that we be tourned to the fauour of his secte.
And with many flateryng wordes, he laboreth to haue vs
content that he myght be bolde to write to vs in the
mater, and cause of the gospell. And thervpon without

[1] Luther's letter was dated September 1, 1525. The King's
answer in the Latin edition, which differs from the English, is
dated 1526. This English edition probably belongs to March,
1527.

answere had from vs, nat onely publysshed the same
letter and put it in print, of purpose that his adherentes
shulde be the bolder, vnder the shadowe of our fauour,
but also fell in deuyce with one or two leude persons,
borne in this our realme, for the translatyng of the Newe
testament in to Englysshe, as well with many corruptions
of that holy text, as certayne prefaces, and other pestylent gloses in the margentes, for the aduauncement and
settyng forthe of his abhomynable heresyes, entendynge
to abuse the gode myndes and deuotion, that you oure
derely beloued people beare, towarde the holy scrypture,
& to enfect you with the deedly corruption and con-
tagious odour of his pestylent errours. In the aduoyd-
ynge wherof, we of our especiall tendre zele towardes
you, haue with the deliberate aduyse of the most reuerende father in god, Thomas lorde Cardynall, legate de
Latere of the see Apostolyke, Archebysshop of Yorke,
primate and our Chauncellour of this realme, and other
reuerende fathers of the spyritualtye, determyned the
sayde corrupte and vntrue translatyons to be brenned,
with further sharpe correction & punysshment against
the kepars and reders of the same, rekenyng of your
wisdomes very sure that ye wyll well and thankfully
parceyue our tendre and louyng mynde towarde you
therin, and that ye will neuer be so gredy vppon any
swete wyne, be the grape neuer so plesaunt, that ye wyll
desyre to taste it, beyng well aduertised that your enemy
before hath poysoned it.

XII. TYNDALE ON HIS FELLOW ' APOSTATE '
WILLIAM ROY [1]

The beginning and end of the preface to Tyndale's Parable of
the Wicked Mammon Printed at Malborowe in the londe oﬀ
Hesse by Hansluft the viij. day of May Anno M.D.xxviij.

William Tyndale otherwise called hychins to the reader.

Grace and peace with all maner spirituall fealinge and
livinge worthy of the kyndnes of Christ, be with the
reader and with all that thurst [2] the will of God Amen.
The cause why I sett my name before this little treatyse
and have not rather done it in the new testament is that
then I folowed the cownsell of Christ which exhorteth
men Matth. vj. to doo theyr good deades secretly and to
be content with the conscience of well doynge, and that
God seeth vs, and paciently to abyde the rewarde of the
last daye, which Christ hath purchased for vs and now
wold fayne have done lykewyse, but am compelled other
wyse to doo.

While I abode a faythfull companyon [3] which now hath
taken another vyage apon him to preach Christ where
(I suppose) he was never yet preached (God which putt in
his herte thither to goo sende his sprite with him, comforte
him and bringe his purpose to good effecte) one William

[1] Roy, who had studied at Cambridge, was a Franciscan, and
belonged to a convent at Greenwich. The sequence of Tyndale's
paragraphs suggests that Roy had been claiming some more
important part in the translation of the New Testament than
the facts justified. The passage is printed here because in several
of the hostile references the ' two apostates ' are treated as on an
equality, whereas, according to Tyndale, Roy was merely his
amanuensis.

[2] This is probably meant for ' trust ' rather than for ' thirst '.

[3] Presumably Frith.

Roye, a man somewhat craftye when he cometh vnto new accoyntaunce and before he be thorow knowen and namely when all is spent, came vnto me and offered his helpe. As longe as he had no money, somewhat I could ruele him, but as sone as he had goten him money, he became lyke him selfe agayne. Neuer the lesse I suffered all thinges till that was ended which I coulde not doo alone without one both to write and to helpe me to compare the textes together. When that was ended I toke my leve and bode him farewell for oure two lyves, and as men saye a daye longer. After we were departed [4] he went, and gate hym new frendes which thinge to doo he passeth all that ever I yet knewe. And there when he had stored him of money he gote him to Argentine [5] where he professeth wonderfull faculties and maketh bost of no small thinges. A yere after that and now xij. monethes before the printinge of this worke, came one Jerom a brother of Grenewich [6] also, thorow wormes to Argentine, saienge that he entended to be Christes disciple a nother while and to kepe (as nye as God wolde geve him grace) the profession of his baptim, and to gett his lyvinge with his handes, and to live no lenger ydely and of the swete and laboure of those captives which they had taught, not to beleve in Christ : but in cuttshowes [7] and russet coetes. Which Jerom wyth all diligence I warned of Royes boldnesse and exhorted him to bewarre of him and to walke quyetly and with all pacience and longe sofferinge acordinge as we have Christe & his Apostles for an ensample, which thinge he also promised me. Neverthelesse when he was comen to Argentine william

----

[4] Separated.   [5] Strassburg.

[6] Jerome Barlow, presumably of Roy's convent at Greenwich.

[7] I cannot explain this word. Russet coats are those of the Franciscans.

Roye (whos tonge is able not only to make foles sterke
madde, but also to disceave the wisest that is at the first
sight and accoyntaunce) gate him to him and sett him
a werke to make rimes,[8] while he him selfe translated
a dialoge[9] out of laten in to englisch, in whose prologe he
promyseth moare a greate deall than I fere me he will
ever paye. . . .

END.

They wolde devide you from Christe and his holy
testamente, and ioine you to the pope to beleve in his
testamente and promisses. Some men wil aske para-
uenture why I take the laboure to make this worke in as
moch as they will brunne it seinge they brunt the Gospel
I answare in brunninge the new testamente they did none
other thinge then that I loked for, no more shal they doo
if the[y] brunne me also if it be gods will it shall so be.
Neverthelesse in translatinge the new testamente I did
my dutye, and so doo I now, and will doo as moch more
as god hath ordened me to doo. And as I offered that to
all men to correcte it, whoso ever coulde even so doo
I this. Who so euer therfore readest thys, compare it
vnto the scripture. If gods worde beare recorde vnto it

---

[8] i.e. the tract in verse known as *Rede me and be not wroth*,
printed at Strassburg by Johann Schott in 1528.

[9] i.e. *The Dialogue between the Father and the Son*, also printed
in 1528 at Strassburg by Johann Schott. The authorities at
Strassburg were persuaded by Wolsey's agent, Hermann Rinck
(see No. IV, pp. 103 and 107), to order Schott to deliver the copies of
this tract to him on payment of his bill. It was believed that with
the exception of two they were all destroyed, but Mr. Robert Steele
has lately shown (Bibliographical Society's Newsheet, January,
1911) that they must have been brought to England and delivered
in Edward VI's reign to a printer named Walter Lynne, who
cancelled the preliminary half-sheet, and reissued the text in
1550, with a new introduction, under the title *The true belief in
Christ*.

and thou also felest in thine herte that it is so be of good comfort and geve god thankes. Iff gods worde condemne it, then hold it acursed, and so do all other doctrines. As Paul counseleth his galathiens. Beleve not every spyrite sodenly, but iudge them by the worde of god which is the triall of all doctrine and lasteth for ever Amen.

XIII. AN EXPERT CRITICISM OF TYNDALE'S VERSION

Letter from Robert Ridley, chaplain to the Bishop of London, to Henry Gold, chaplain to the Archbishop of Canterbury, dated February 24, almost certainly of the year 1527. From British Museum Cotton MS. Cleopatra E. v. 362[b].

Maister gold I hartly commaunde me vnto you, as concernyng this common & vulgare translation of the new testament in to englishe, doon by M. William hichyns, other wais called M. W. tyndale & frear William roy, manifest lutheranes heretikes & apostates, as doth opynly apeir not only by their daily & continuall company & familiarite with Luther & his disciples, but mych mor by their comentares & annotations in Mathew & Marcum, in the first print, also by their preface in the 2d prent,[1] & by their introduccion in to the epistle of paule ad romanes, al to gither most posoned & abhominable hereses that can be thowht, he is not filius ecclessiae

---

[1] See No. VIII. A few lines lower down Ridley writes of 'the first prent with annotationes in Matthew and Marcus & the preface' as if the annotations and preface came in the same book or fragment. If what he calls the '2d prent' contained the introduction to Romans it cannot have been the Cologne fragment. Despite some confusion it seems as if his 'first prent' must be the Cologne fragment, and his '2d prent' the Worms unannotated edition.

christi that wold receaue a godspell of such damned &
precised heretikes, thowh it wer trew lyk as paule & our
saviour christ, wold not take the trew testimonial of evil
spretes that prased christe treith (?) saying quod filius
dei erat, & quod ipse paulus seruus esset veri dei. As
for errors, if ye haue the first prent with annotationes in
Mathew and Marcus, & the preface al is mere frenesy, he
saith that euangelium nihil est aliud quam dulcis pro-
missio gratiae, so that by that meanes, penitentiam
agite [Matt. iii. 2][2], is no part of the evangelion, the
pater noster is no part of the godspell, ' ite maledicti in
ignem eternum ' [Matt. xxv. 41], no part of the evangelion, but only such appropinquavit regnum celorum
[Matt. iii. 2], inuenietis requiem animabus vestris
[Matt. xi. 29]. Also he writeth in that preface & annotationes that there is no difference between virginite & an
hoor of the stewes, if she cum to repentaunce, Also that
lyk as no man doth evil to the extent that he show[d]
be punyshed or hanged there for, so no man showd do
good to haue any rewarde therfor contra ad faciendas
iustificationes tuas propter retributionem [Ps. cxix. 112]
et ad Hebræos [xi. 26] de Mose aspiciebat enim in
remuneratorem alias remunerationem et illud facite
vobis amicos de mammona, ut cum defeceritis recipiant
eos in eterna tabernacula [Luke xvi. 9]. Also that by
good warkes we do no thyng merite, contra illud ad
Corinthos ut referat unusquisque prout gessit siue
bonum siue malum [2 Cor. v. 10] et illud genes. [xxii. 16]
ad Abram quia fecisti hanc rem etc. item illud Matthæi
quod sitiui et dedistis mihi potum [Matt. xxv. 35] &c.
et venite benedicti patris mei [Matt. xxv. 34]. Also
he saith that he that doth any thyng to haue hy place in
heven, he is satanice & luciferine supervius. I have none

[2] The references in brackets are all here added.

of thies bowkes but only I remembre such thynges
I redde in the prefaces & annotationes.   As for the texte
of the godspell, first the title is hereticall saying that it is
prent as it was writen by the evangelistes : cum neque
consentiat cum antiqua translatione neque cum erasmica
this is the bowk of generacion of ies[us] the son of
Abraham & also the son of david.   Cum in archetypo sit
nominatus absolutus et in illo filii Abraham filii Dauid &c.
[Matt. i. 1] fit sensus ipse unum solum affert eumque
minus germanum ; voluit clam ab ea diuertere he wold
have put hir away [Matt. i. 10] ; in quo omnes peccaue-
runt ad Romanos [iii. 12] in so mych that every man hath
synned, et homo stultissime poenitentiam agite [Matt.
iii. 2], repent.   By this translation shal we losse al thies
christian wordes, penance, charite, confession, grace,
prest, chirche, which he alway calleth a congregation,
quasi turcharum et brutorum nulla esset congregatio nisi
velit illorum etiam esse ecclesiam : Idololatria callith he
worshyppyng of images, I wold that ye showd have
seen my lordes bowkes.   As for the translation in franche
withowt any postille it is for certane condemned in
parys decreto publico thow it be trewly doon, condemned
I say that it shal not be lawfull to publishe it to every
layman, bot by prestes quorum labia custo[diunt]
sc[ientiam] so it was in the olde law & in the tyme of
the apostles.   Vide Sutorem de Translatione Bibliae.[3]

I certefy you if ye look well, ye shal not look iij lynes
withowt fawt in al the bowk, bot I haue not the bowk to
marke them owt, ye showd haue had lasure your selff to
have doon it, how be it, it becummyth the people of
truste to obey & folowe their rewellers which hath geven
study & is lerned in such matters as thys.   People showd

---

[3] Petrus Sutor's ' De tralatione Bibliæ et nouarum reprobatione
interpretationum ', Paris, J. Petit, 1525.

heir & beleve, thai showd not iudge the doctrine of paule
ne of paule vicares & successors bot be iudged by their
learnyng, as long as thai knaw no thyng contrary goddes
lawes as saynt bernard saith most goodly & clerkly in
libro de dispensatione & precepto.   Vale in al haist

Yo^r awn

Robert Ridley prest.

item idem pauli stultas questiones devita &c. [2 Tim.
ii. 23], bewarre of fowlishe problemes or questiones in
the scoles, Hoc procul dubio dictum in odium scolastice
theologie & universitatum.   Such a thyng is in the
translation, thowh it be not in the same wordes.   Ego
& pater unum sumus [John x. 30].   We are on quasi
diceret unus sumus & not on substance or on thyng.

Shew ye to the people that if any be of so prowde &
stuburne stomac that he will beleve ther is no fawt ne
error except it be declared to hym that he may se it, latt
hym cum hither to my lordes which hath profowndly
examined al & he shal heir & se errors except that he be
blynde & have no eys.

24 February.

Master Gold I pray you be good to this pore whoman
Gylbarttes whyff as yet your tenaunt.[4]

Ye shal not neede to accuse this translation, it is
accused & damned by the consent of the prelates &
learned men, and comanded to be brynt both heir &
beyonde the see, wher is many hundreth of theym
brynt.   So that it is to layt now to ask reson why thai
be condemned, & which be the fawtes & errores.   Luther
& his scoole teachith quod nos non cooperamus cum

---

[4] Added in a different handwriting at the foot of the first page.

gratia dei sed tantum patimur ut saxa et stipites, bycawse of that, this texte non ego sed gratia dei mecum [1 Cor. xv. 10], thus is translate not I bot the grace of god in me. Quam hoc heretice, maligne, sediciose et falso translatum sit, qui non perpendit stupidus est. My lorde your maister hath of thies bowkes geven & send to hym by my lorde my master.

Shew the people that ye be cum to declare vnto them, that certane bowkes be condemned by the cownsell and profownde examination of the prelates & fathers of the chirch.

[Addressed]: To Master henry golde chaplayne to my lorde of Canterbury, at Knolle.

XIV.   THE CRITICISMS OF SIR THOMAS MORE

From 'A dyaloge of syr Thomas More', 1529, as No. II. (fol. lxxix.)

The thyrd booke.—The viij chapyter.

The author shewethe why the new testament of Tyndales translacyon was burned, & shewith for a sample certain wordes euill & of euyll purpos changid.

But now I pray you let me kno your mynd concernyng the burning of the new testament in english, which Tindal lately translated, & (as men say) right wel, whiche makethe men mich meruayl of the burning.

It is, quod I, to me gret meruayl, that eny good cristen man hauing eny drop of wyt in hys hed, wold eny thing meruell or complayn of the burning of that boke if he knowe the mater which who so callith the new testament calleth it by a wrong name, except they wyl call yt Tyndals testament or Luthers testament. For so had tyndall after Luthers counsayle corrupted & chaunged yt from the good & holsom doctryne of Criste to the deuylysh heresyes of theyr own, that it was clene a contrary thing.

That were maruayle quod your frend that it shuld be so clene contrary, For to som that red it yt semed very lyke.

It ys quod I neuer the lesse contrary, and yet the more peryllous. For like as to a trew siluer grote a fals coper grote is neuer the lesse contrary thogh yt be quyk syluered ouer, but so mych the more false in how mich it is counterfeted the more lyke to the trouth, so was the translacion so mich the more contrary in how mich it was craftely deuysed like, and so mych the more peryllus in how miche it was to folke vnlernyd more hard to be dyssernid.

Why quod your frend what fautes wer ther in yt ?

To tell you all that quod I were in a maner to reherse you all the hole boke, wherin ther were founden and noted wrong & falsly translated a boue a thousand textes by tale.

I wolde quod he fayn here some one.

He that shuld quod I study for that, shuld study where to finde water in the see. But I wyll shewe you for ensample two or thre suche as euery one of the thre ys more than thryes thre in one.

That were quod he very straunge except ye mene more in weyght. For one can be but one in nomber.

Surely quod I as weyghty be they as eny lyghtly can be. But I mene that euery one of them is more than thryes thre in nomber.

That were quod he sumwhat lyke a rydel.

This rydell quod I wyl sone be red. For he hath mystranslated .iii. wordes of gret weyght & euery one of them is as I suppose more than thryes three tymes repeted and rehersed in the boke.

Ah that may well be quod he, but that was not well done. But I pray you what wordes be they ?

The tone ys quod I this word prestys. The tother, the chyrch. The thyrd charyte. For prestis wher so euer he speketh of the prestes of Crystis chirch he neuer calleth them prestes but alway senyours, the chyrch he calleth alway the congregacyon, and charyte he callyth all loue loue. Now do these names in our englysh tong neyther expresse the thyngis that be ment by them, and also there appereth (the circumstaunces well considered) that he had a mischeuous mind in the chaunge. For fyrst as for prestes and presthed though that of old they vsed comenly to chese wel elderly men to be prestes, & ther fore in the greke tong prestys wer called presbeteri, as we myght say elder men, yet nether were all prestes chosen old as apperyth by sainte Poule wryting to Timotheus, nemo iuuentutem tuam contempnat let no man contempne thy youth, nor euery elder man is not a prest. And in our englysh tonge thys word senyor sygnyfieth nothing at al, but is a french word vsed in englysh more than halfe in mockage, whan one wyll call a nother my lord in scorn. And if he mene to take the laten worde senyor, that word in the laten tong neuer sygnyfyed a prest but only an elder man. By whych name of elder men yf he wold call the prestes englishly, than shold he rather sygnify theyr age than theyr offyce. And yet the name doth in english plainly sygnify thaldermen of the cyties, and nothyng the prestys of the chyrch. And thus may we perceyue that rather than he wolde call a prest by the name of a prest, he wold seke a new word he neyther wyst nor cared what.

Now where he calleth the chyrch alway the congre-

gacyon, what reson had he therin ? For euery man well
seeth that though the chyrch be in dede a congregacion,
yet is not euery congregacion the chirch bu[t] a congregacion of cristen peple, whiche congregacion of crysten
peple hath ben in englond alway called & known by the
name of the chirch, which name what good cause or
colour could he find to torn into the name of congregacion,
whych worde is comen[1] to a company of cristen men or
a company of turkys ?[2] . . .

Ibid. fol. lxxx. col. 2.

For now yt ys to be consydered that at the tyme of
thys translacyon hychens was wyth Luther in wytten-
berge, and set certayne glosys in the mergent, framed
for the settyng forthe of that vngracious sect.

By saynt John quod your frende yf that be true that
Hychens were at that tyme with Luther, it is a playne
token that he wrought sumwhat after hys counsayle,
and was wyllynge to helpe hys maters forwarde here.
But whyther Luthers matters be so badde as they be
made for, that shall we see hereafter.

Very true quod I. But as touchyng the confederacye
betwene Luther and hym, is a thyng well knowen and
playnly confessed, by suche as haue ben taken and
conuycted here of herysye comyng from thense, and
some of them sente hyther to sowe that sede aboute
here, and to sende worde thyther fro tyme to tyme how
yt sprang.

But now the cause why he chaunged the name of
charyte and of the chyrche and of presthed, is no very
grete dyffyculte to perceyve. For sithe Luther and his
felowes amonge other theyre damnable heresyes haue
one, that all our saluacyon standyth in fayth alone, and

<hr>

[1] common.　　　　　　[2] Turks.

K

toward our saluacyon nothynge force of good workys, therfore yt semeth that he laboreth of purpose to mynyshe the reuerent mynd that men bere to charyte, and therfore he chaungeth that name of holy vertuous affeccyon, in to the bare name of loue comen[1] to the vertuouse loue that man berith to god, & to the lewd loue that is bytwene flekke & his make.[3] And for by cause that Luther vtterly denyeth the very catholyque chyrche in erthe, and sayth that the chyrch of Crist is but an vnknowen congregacyon of sum folke, here ii & there iii, no man wot where hauyng the ryght fayth, whych he calleth onely hys owne new forgede faythe, therfore Hichens in the new testament can not abyde the name of the chyrch, but turneth it into the name of congregacyon, wyllyng that yt shuld seme to englysh men, eyther that Cryste in the gospell had neuer spoken of the chirch, or ellys that the chyrche were but such a congregacyon as they myghte haue occasyon to say, that a congregacyon of some such heretyques were the chyrch that god spake of.

Now as towchinge the cause why he chaunged the name of prest into senior, ye muste vnderstand that luthere and his adherentys holde thys heresye, that all holy order ys nothyng. And that a prest is nothyng ellys, but a man chosen among the peple to preche, and that by that choyce to that offyce he is preste by and by wythoute eny more ado, and no preste agayne whan so euer the people chese a nother in hys place, and that a preestys offyce is no thynge but to preche. For as for saynge masse and herynge of confessyon and absolucyon theruppon to be geuen, all thys he sayethe that euery man woman and childe may do as well as eny preste.

[3] A contemptuous expression for a man and his paramour (*Oxf. Eng. Dict.*).

Now doth Hychen therfore to set forthe thys opynyon wythall after hys masters herysye putte awaye the name of preste in hys translacyone, as thoughe prestehede were nothyng, where so euer the scrypture speketh of the prestys that were amonge the Iewes, there dothe he in hys translacyon call theym styll by the name of prestis. But where so euer the scrypture spekith of the prestys of Christis chyrche, there doth he put away the name of prest in his translacyon, bycause he wold make hyt seme that the scrypture dyd neuer speke of eny prestys dyfferent from leymen amonge chrysten peple.

XV. EPISCOPAL PROHIBITION

Text and translation from Fox's *Acts and Monuments* (first edition). John Day, 1563, pp. 449, 450.

A prohibition sent out by Cuthberth Tunstall Byshop of London, to the Archedeacons of his dioces, for the calling in of the newe Testamentes translated into Englyshe.[1]

Cvtbertus permissione diuina Lond. Episcopus dilecto nobis in Christo Archidiacono nostro Londo.[2] seu eius officiali salutem gratiam & benedictionem, Ex pastoralis officij nostri debito ea quæ ad subiectorum nostrorum periculum et maxime ad internetionem animarum

[1] Fox adds here the words 'with diuers other bookes, the Cataloge whereof hereafter ensueth'. But the list of books which he mistakenly appends belongs to a later date than October 1526, when this prohibition was issued. In reprinting Fox's text a few obvious misprints have been corrected.

[2] Fox notes 'The like commission in like manner and forme was sent to the thre other Archdeacones, of Middlesexe, Essex, and Colchester, for the execution of the same matter, vnder the Byshoppes seale'.

earundem tendere dinoscuntur, salubriter propellere
& totis viribus extirpare astringimur, sane ex fide
dignorum relatione ipsaque rei euidentia, ad nostram
iamdudum peruenit noticiam, quod nonnulli iniquitatis
filij ac Lutheriane factionis ministri quos summa exce-
cauit malicia a via veritatis & orthodoxe fidei declinantes
sanctum dei euangelium in vulgare nostrum Anglicanum
subdola versutia transferentes ac nonnullos hereticæ
prauitatis articulos & opiniones erroneas perniciosas
pestiferas, scandalosas & simplicium mentium seductiuas
intermiscentes, illibatam hactenus sacre scripture maiestatem, suis nepharijs & tortuosis interpretationibus
prophanare, & verbo domini sacrosancto & recto sensu
eiusdem callide et peruerse abuti tentarint. Cuius
quidem translationis nonnulli libri impressi quidam
cum glosis, quidam sine glosis vt accepimus dictum
pestiferum et perniciosum virus in vulgari idiomate in
se continentes in promiscuam nostrarum dioc. et
iurisdictionis Lond. multitudine sunt dispersi, qui sane
gregem nobis commissum nisi citius prouideatur tam
pestifero veneno et mortifero prauitatis hereticæ morbo
proculdubio inficient et contaminabunt in animarum
nobis commissarum graue periculum et diuine maiestatis
grauissimam offensam.   Vnde nos Cutbertus episcopus
ante dictus de predictis magnopere dolentes et antiqui
hostis calliditati ire, quam suis satellitibus ad animarum
subditorum nostrorum interemptionem subministrat,
obuiam curaque pastorali super grege nobis commisso
diligenter inuigilare ac remedia oportuna premissis
adhibere cupientes, vobis coniunctim et diuisim comit-
timus ac firmiter in virtute sancte obediencie qua nobis
tenemini iniungendo, mandamus quatenus autoritate
nostra moneatis monerive faciatis omnes et singulos
tam exemptos quam non exemptos, infra vestrum

Archidiaconatum vbi libet commorantes, quatenus infra
xxx. dierum spacium quorum quidem dierum decem
pro primo, decem pro secundo, et decem pro tertio
et peremptorio termino sub excommunicationis poena
ac criminis, hereseos suspitionis incurrende eis assignamus
omnes et singulos huiusmodi libros translationem noui
testamenti in vulgarem linguam factam continentes ad
nos seu nostrum in spiritualibus vicarium generalem
inferant et realiter tradant. Et quid in premissis feceritis
nos aut vicarium nostrum huiusmodi infra duos menses
a die data presentium debite certificare personaliter vel
per literas vestras patentes vna cum presentibus autentice
sigillatas non omittatis sub poena contemptus. Dat.
sub sigillo nostro 24. die mensis Octobris An. M.D. 26.
nostræ cons. An. quinto.

Thus in Englyshe

Cutbert by the permission of god, byshop of London.
vnto our wellbeloued in christ the Archdeacon of London,
or to his officiall, helth grace and benediction. By the
deuty of our pastorall office, we are bounde diligently
with all our power to forsee, prouide for, roote out and
put away all those things, which seme to tende to the
perill and daunger of our subiectes and specialy the
distruction of ther soules, wherfor we hauing vnderstanding by the reporte of diuers credible persones, and also
by the euident apparaunce of the matter, that many
children of iniquitie mainteiners of Luthers sect, blinded
through extreame wickednes, wandring from the way of
truth and the catholike faith, craftely have translated
the new testament into our English tongue, enter-
medling there with many hereticall articles and erronious
opinions, pernicious and offensiue, seducing the simple
people, attempting by their wicked and peruerse inter-

pretations, to prophanate the maiestie of the scripture, whiche hetherto hath remayned vndefiled, and craftely to abuse the most holy word of God, and the true sence of the same, of the whiche translation there are many bokes imprinted, some with gloses and some without, conteining in the english tongue that pestiferous and moste pernicious poyson dispersed throughout all our dioces of London in great nomber, whiche truely without it be spedely forsene without doubt will contaminate and infect the flocke committed vnto vs, with moste deadly poyson and heresy. To the greuous perill and daunger of the soules committed to our charge, and the offence of gods diuine maiestie. Wherfore we Cuthbert, the byshop aforesaid, greuously sorowing for the premisses, willing to withstande the craft and subteltie of the auncient enemy and his ministers, which seke the destruction of my flock, and with a diligent care to take heade vnto the flocke committed to my charge, desiring to prouide spedy remedies for the premisses, we charg you iointly and seuerally, and by vertue of your obedience, straightly enjoyne & comaund you that by our autorytie you warne or cause to be warned, all and singuler aswell exempte as not exempt, dwelling with in your Archdeacons that with in xxx. daies space, wherof ten daies for the first, x for the second and x. for the third peremptory terme, vnder payne of excommunication, and incurring the suspicion of heresie, they do bring in and really deliuer vnto our vicar-generall, all and singular such books conteyning the translation of the new testament in the English tongue, and that you doo certyfie vs or our said comissary, within ii monthes, after the day of the date of these presents, dewly, personally or by your letters, together with these presentes, vnder your seales, what you haue done in the premisses, under paine of contempt, geuen vnder our seale the xxiii. of October, in the v. yeare of our consecration.

XVI.   THE   SEARCH   FOR   ENGLISH   NEW TESTAMENTS   AND   OTHER   HERETICAL BOOKS AT ANTWERP AND · ENDEAVOUR TO GET THEIR PRINTERS PUNISHED

Extract from a letter of John Hackett[1] to Wolsey, November 24, 1526 (*Letters and Papers of Hen. VIII*, vol. iv, 2652).   From the original in the Record Office.

Aftyr my comyng here to thys towne, I haue send prively to all places here to know surly, wher that thys nywe translatyd volumes be pryntyd In Inglishe, or to be sold, & as I haue fownd by Inquesission ther be tweyn[2]

[1] One of Wolsey's confidential agents.

[2] One of these two printers of English heretical books was Christopher van Endhouen, also known as Christopher van Ruremond, the printer of the first Antwerp New Testament, 1526 ; the name of the other is not known.   From the fact that only Christopher is subsequently mentioned it is possible that this other printer was Hans van Ruremond (presumably a kinsman of Christopher), who had been convicted by the town council on October 30, 1525, of printing Lutheran books, and ordered · to leave the town and go on a pilgrimage to the Holy Blood at Wilseraken in. Prussia (see Duff, *Westminster and London Printers*, p. 223).   Mr. Duff writes : ' Christopher left in Antwerp soon afterwards started on the very dangerous undertaking of printing English New Testaments, which were sent into England and sold there by Hans.   In 1528 in the table of certain persons abjured within the diocese of London we find " John Raimund a Dutchman for causing fifteen hundred of Tyndale's New Testaments to be printed at Antwerp and for bringing five hundred into England ".   John Raimond is clearly the English form of Jan Roemundt [otherwise Hans van Ruremond] and is probably identical with the Dutchman who earlier in the year was in the Fleet for having sold to Robert Necton some 200 or

In thys towne that pryntys & syllys the sayd bokes, wherfore I wrott sodenly to my lord of palermo [3] That he shold aduertyse my lady [4] & requyre hyr that she shold make comandment to the margrave of thys towne to se thys errurs Remedyyd, whych mediatly she has done, & I was thys day meselfe with the sayd margrave & have had long comm[un]ycasion to gyddyr, & showd me the sayd lady ys [5] letter. whych was wrytten In very good forme, & att a conclusion he promest me by hys faythe that he wyll do hys ottermust best to fulfyll my

300 copies of the New Testament. On a previous page (218) Mr. Duff recorded how a certain Jan Silverlink recovered April 4, 1531, from the heirs of Francis Birckmann (a member of the same family of book-agents as the Arnold Birckmann mentioned by Cochlaeus, cp. No. VI, p. 101) the balance of an account of £28 17s. 3d. for 700 New Testaments, obviously delivered on behalf of Hans or Jan van Ruremond, since the heirs were allowed to deduct a debt due from him to Birckmann. Mr. Duff identifies Christopher van Endhouen or Van Ruremond with the Antwerp bookseller named Christopher, of whom Fox writes, under the year 1531, that for selling certain New Testaments in English to John Row, bookbinder, he was thrown into prison at Westminster, and there died. This is confirmed by his business being found after this date in the hands of his widow (see No. xxvii, A. B.). Hans van Ruremond is further identified by Mr. Duff with the ' John Holibusche alias Holybusche of London, Stationer otherwise bookbinder, born in Ruremond under the obedience of the Emperor ' on a London list of denizens in 1535, and through this entry with the Johan Hollybushe whose name was put by John Nycholson of Southwark on the title-page of his second edition of the Latin-English New Testament in 1538 (' Faythfullye translated by Johan Hollybushe ') after his quarrel with Coverdale. This would not, of course, imply that the Dutch bookseller had really revised Coverdale's work, but merely that Nycholson desired to provide himself with a scapegoat.

[3] The Archbishop of Palermo.

[4] Margaret of Savoy, Archduchess of Austria, Regent of the Netherlands.

[5] Hackett's way of forming the possessive case.

lady ys commandment. the kynges hyghnes & yowr grace ys mynd & dessyr. In thys matner & all odyr wher he may do hys hyghnes or your grace any honor plessure or seruys convenient.

.   .   .   .

I send your grace here Inclosed ij of thys nywe translatyd volumes In Inglyshe. of the whych sorte I tryst or xiiij dayys cum to an end to se agrett meyne of them afyre, & as shortly as I can ther shalbe adefens [6] made to all the Inprimurs of thys contre that from hensforward They shall nott pryme neddyr by ne syll [7] non of syche lyke bokes & what ther shalbe don I wyll aduertysse your grace praynge the holy trynyte to preserwe your grace wher euer ye be, from andwerpe The xxiiij day of novembre. 1526.

per your humbyll Bedesman. John Hackett.

Addressed :—' Legat ys good grace.'

B

Extract from letter of John Hackett to Wolsey, December 22, 1526 (*Letters and Papers of Henry VIII*, vol. iv, 2721). Printed from Cotton MS. Galba B. IX. 37, which like many other Cotton MSS. has been damaged by fire.

. . . By my last lettris datyd the xvij[th] day of thys monythe I wrott to [Mr.] Bryan tuck [1] how that the lordes of the towne of andwerpe showyd [to] me that thei had submyttyd them selfs as towchynge the correccion o[f] thys nywe bokes In Inglyshe, to be ordryd aftyr the

[6] i. e. a prohibition.
[7] They shall not print, neither buy nor sell.
[1] This letter of December 17, 1526, to Sir Brian Tuke, has not been preserved.

dyscression [and] avyse of the lady margrett [2] and hyr
consell, And aftyr thys conclusion takyn, the forsayd
lordes came to the cowrte wher I was present, & [I]
showyd to the sayd consell. howe that I made grett
dylygence to se the for[sayd] bokes bowrnt & the
Inprimwrs to be crimynally punnyshyd acordyng to
the . . . merytees, & that they have had in party the
examinacion of the sayd impri[murs].

But consyderynge that syche byssynes as thys ys
towchys both lyfe [and goods] the sayd lordes of andwerp
declaryd vnto the forsayd consell that thei th[ought] nott
in no wysse to Juge apon the example of anothyr Juge
ys Ju[gement] wythowt thei hawe perfytt knowlege apon
the fowndment & reyson that [thei] may do hytt,
Desyrynge the sayd consell that thei myght haue the
sayd [bokes] translatyd in to lattyn or duche, so that
they myght wnderstand the [menin]ge. Where apon
that thei may gywe the sentence, to the whych the off [3] the
prive consell wold lyghtly consent, But I answeryd
apon [that] artycle that hytt were not convenyent to
permit that syche translac[ion] shold be don in thys syde
of the sees, for lafully I wold suspect [eny] that wolds
medyll In the same, They answeryd me that the [iuges]
Ought not to iuge without they knewe the fowndement
of the cawse. I answerd them that the kynge my
sowerayne lord & master ys lettris were sufficient Inoughe
for the defence of syche a cawse, and for the condemnacion of thys bookes & all syche othyr lyke erytycke
scriptours as has ben condemnyd & bowrnd In Ingland,
They answeryd me agayne that yf that the kynges
highnes or your grace had send them hyther of euery
booke one of syche lyke as ye haue bowrnd there, that

[2] Margaret of Savoy.
[3] 'the off must be read 'they of'.

fyndynge syche bookes here thei wold do syche lyke
Iustyce, Yea there has ben one of them that sayd that
euery contre hawe ther owne lawys & that the Juges
of thys contres ought as well to know where apon thei
shall Juge. as owr Juges knowys what they have
Jugyd, & apon what grownd hytt standes. But to cum
to a conclusion aftyr many arguments, nott as in fowrme
of consell, but mediatly to brynge owr matur to an
effecte, I toke apon me to wryte wnto yowr grace, & that
within short tyme. yow shall send to the lady margrett,
or to the forsayd lordes of andwerpe sufficient certy-
ficacion with one or tweyne or tre off syche lyke bokes,
whyche as were condemnyd & bowrnt In Ingland :
whych I supose ye have kept sum for syche an intent,
& here apon the lordes off the prive consell defferyd the
translacion of the forsayd bokes, & requyrd me to
wryte wnto yowr grace to have the same, & that thei
wold as fayne do the Justyce apon syche lyke cawsys,
as we to desyre ytt, & that as sone as your good answere
cumys, that thei wyll admynystre the Iustys In syche
fowrme & maner that ther shalbe suffycient correccion
don apon them that do offende, Whych surly I certefye
yor grace hytts very nessessary & tyme to be done,
afore the end of thys barro[4] markett, But the fyrst
begynynge & execusion must be done in the towne of
andwerpe whych ys the fowntayne of sych tynges,
& here with all othyr places shall take an ensample,
& consyderynge that thys byssynes requyres dylygence,
I send thys paper post purposely vnto yowr grace to
have yowr gracious answere & Instruccions when ye
tynke the tyme.

And yf hapent that yowr grace had nott ressewit sum

[4] Barro or Barrow, the English form of Berghen op Zoom,
a port in North Brabant.

othyr bookes of thys translacions, as I have send yow her before, now att all aventures, I yow with thys inclosyd one of syche lyke, as has ben impryntyd in the sayd towne of andwerpe, of the whyche be arestyd in the Justyce their handes ny a iii abydyng sentence, & yf yowr grace haue any othyr of syche lyke bookes, hytt were nessessary to send one of euery sorte hydyr to the condemnasion of all syche othyrs as we can fynd in thys partyys . . . mechlyn the xxijth day of dessember. 1526.

per yowr hummyl Bedesman

John Hackett.

C

Extract from letter of John Hackett to Brian Tuke, January 4, 152⁶₇ (*Letters and Papers of Henry VIII*, vol. iv, 2778). Printed from Cotton MS. Galba B. IX. 38.

My last wrytyng vnto your grace was datyd the 22 day of dessember which letter derecktyd I post to my lord legattes grace, only for the recoveryng of sych bokes as ye have send me now with yowr wrytyng datyd the xjth day of the forsayd monyth which be cum too my handes a monday last was at after dynner, And sodenly the same day betwx four & fyve of clock I came to audyence in the preve counsell, & aftir I schowd them aparty of the substance of your wrytyngs vnto me, be my [lord] legattes comandment, & schowyng them the forsayd bookes awant syngnyd[1] with my lord of london ys hand wrytyng, the lord of hooghestrat[2] & monsieur de Palermo[3] ordynyt & concludyd that my lady schold wryt to the margr[ave] & consell of

[1] avant [?] signed, signed at the beginning.
[2] Antoine de la Lalaing, Count of Hochstrate.
[3] The Archbishop of Palermo.

the towne of andwerp to do Ju[stice] & corexion apon
all sych lycke bookes as the[y] can fynd in ther lemyttes
or Juredyctyons, & so hyt has ben don, & I delyuyrd
me self the sayd lady ys lettrys to the forsayd mar-
[grave] in pressens of the hole consell of the sayd towne
of andwerp & aftir that they had the redy[ng] of the sayd
letters, they answered me in good maner that they schold
do ther dewoy acordyng to ryght & raysson & that
within fo[wer] days I shall knowe howe they sall procede
in th[ys] byssenys, my trust ys that they sall do well.

.   .   .   .

From andwerp the iiijth day of Ienne . . . 1526

per yowr own   John Hackett.

D

Extract from Letter of John Hackett to Wolsey, January 12,
152⁶⁄₇ (*Letters and Papers of Henry VIII*, vol. iv. 2797).   Printed
from Cotton MS. Galba B. IX. 40.

Plesse yowr grace to vnderstand that my last lettris
vnto yowr grace was datyd xxij^{ti} day of December. &
synnes I hawe ressewt[1] a lettyr fro Mr. bryan tuke
d[atyd] the xith day off the sayd monyth & with the
sayd lettyr I ressewyth syche . . . Bookes as I dessyred
by my last wrytyng vnto your grace, the whych bookes
lyke . . . I hawe wrytten to the sayd Mr. tuke the fowrthe
day of thys present monyth.   Trywe hytt ys that by the
avysse off thees lordes of the prive consell, I del[yuered]
them with the lady margrett ys lettris wnto the lorde margrave off andwerpe in presens of all the lordes that
admynystris the lawys nowe in the sayd to[wne] off
andwerpe.   And aftyr that they had red the sayd lady
ys lettris, & visityd [my] lorde off london ys veryficacion

[1] received.

in the fyrst levys of the forsayd bookes, w[ith] grett
honor & reuerence they made answere wnto me that
they wold gladl[y] do ther devoyre, and that within iij or
iiij dayes ther aftyr that I sh[old] know ther resolute
answere

Where apon I desyred them in the kyng my souerayne
lorde & maisteris na[me] for the incressynge & preseruacion of owr crysten feythe & for the anychil[atyon] &
extyrpacion off the malycious sept lutherianen that in
as muche as h[yt] apers by one off syche orygynall bookes
as were condemnyd & bowrnt in Ingland whyche was
ther present afore them, & that hytt apers playnly that
ther [ys] no defference nethyr defuculte, but that in the
text of ther bookes that [were] imprynted in thys towne,
ther conteynes all syche errures & herissees as conteyne[d]
in the text of the forsayd condemnyd & bownt bookes,
requirenge them that they showld do apon the sayd
bookes that be here, syche correccion & punission as ye
& dayly ys done apon syche lyke & semblabell heretyke
bookes in Ingland.

The sayd lordes answeryd me agayne that within the
space aforesaid I showlde know ther intere resolucion.

In the space of the whyche tyme the margrave aforsayd
as the Emperor is officer d[esyred] Justyce to be done,
declarynge to the sayd lordes how that hytt aperyd by
the v[erification] off my lorde the byshope off london
that in the text off the bookes that be inp[rinted] in thys
towne, conteynes all the same errures & heresees as has
conteyned . . . the text off the orygynall bookes that were
condemnyd & bownt in Ingland [as] hytt may apere by
one of the sayd orygynall bookes whych ys nowe h[ere]
present, & ought to be sufficient profe & certifycacon to
collacion the tone by the todyr. Wherfore & consyderynge that the Emperor had commandyd apon peyne off

bany[shment] & to lese the tyrd part off hys goodes that showld inprime syche errures or . . . as thys be, that the Inprimer of the sayd bokes namyd Christofer endhowe . . .[2] ought to be banyshyd owte off all the Emperor is landes & contres & that t[he] tyrd part off all hys goodes showld be confyskyd in the Emperor is han[dis] & all the forsayd Englyshe bookes bowrnt to the fyre acordynge to the Emperor is last mandment apon syche lyke eryssees.

And ther beynge present the Inprimure of the forsayd bookes, hys atorney or procuror spake . . . spal for hym, sayenge that he had nott offendyd the Emperor ys mandment nedyr that he had nott inprymed no bookes with heryssees.   And more sayd forthe that the Emperor is subiectes beynge in the Emperor is contres and in land of Justyce, ought nott to be Jugyd nedyr condemnyd by the sentence or condemnacion of the lawys or Iuges off eny othyr contres concludynge by the lawe that the Iuges of thys contres ought nott to gyve no blynd sentence to banyshe dishonor or confyske eny man or hys goodes with owt that they knew ryght well them selfs the very fowndment & cawse, sustenyng lyke wyse that with owt that the lord margrave as the Emperor is officer can showe or do show sum particuler articlyes in the sayd bookes wher that theis forsayd errures & herissees ben fownd, that the forsayd Christofer inprimure ought to be eslargyd owt off prisone & to do hys plessure with the forsayd bookes.

And for a conclusion aftyr many othyr replikes & duplikes done on bothe sides betwix the margrave & the sayd malefactor & hys procuror, nott withstandynge the promesses that the lordes of the prive consell made vnto me when I send yow my last post, whyche promesses

---

[2] Christopher of Endhoven, the printer of the Antwerp New Testament of 1526.   See No. XVI, note 2.

was, that with condicion that I myght showe them here
eny of syche lyke bookes as has ben condemnyd &
bownrt in Ingland, that they as ther, showld orthyn [3]
& comand all othyr syche lyke bokes or with syche lyke
heressees as myght be fownd in thys contres to be
condemnyd & bowrnt in lyke wyse. But yett for all
thys, nethyr for my lady ys fyrst second nethyr tyrd
lettyr whyche were wrytten in metly good fowrme, the
lordes of andwerpe has gyven for ther sentence that afore
the banyshment of the sayd Inprimure the confeskacion
of hys goodes or the burnynge off hys bookes that the
margrave aforesayd as officer for the Emperor shall show
and declare sum articles conteynyge in the sayd bookes
wher thys errures & heryssees ben fownd, And in thys
maner the margrave told me that he cowd procede no
ferdyr in thys byssines. Wherfore I have turned to the
cowrte agayne fro the sayd towne of andwerpe to showe
my lady & the lordes of hyr pryve consell, the denegacion
off Justyce that they off the towne of andwerpe has done
vnto me att thys tyme. there apon I have had grett
comunycacion with the forsayd lordes of the pryve consell.
Showyng them with fayre wordis that I had grett
marvell of the fyrst denegacion off Justyce that they of
andwerpe dyd vnto me I showynge them the efecte &
substance off the kyng my souerayne lorde ys lettris with
presentynge them the lettris of my lady margrett con-
fowrmynge to my comyssion, & now that acordynge to the
presentacion that they made vnto me whych was lyke
as aforsayd ys, that yff I had here to showe any syche
boke or bokes as has ben bowrnt in Inglande, & fyndynge
any syche lyke bokes, in thys contres, that they sholde
do syche lyke Justyce off them.

And lyke as hytt aperes off trowte that they have had

[3] ordain ?

the vysytacion of the sayd bookes, & hawe seyne my
lord the byshope off london is verificacion, in the fyrst
levys of thos same. whych books with the lady margrett
is second & tyrd lettrys to them of Andwerpe I dyd
deliuer, & for eny reyson that I myght show besydes
nethyr for no lettyr that the sayd lady cowd wryte
nethyr for none . . . off Justyce that the margrave off
andwerpe dyd desyre, yett cowd I have none othyr
Justyce off them but lyke as afore sayd ys.

Wher apon sum off the sayd lordes answeryd me that
hytt ys as gr[eat] Reyson that the Iuges of thys contres
ought as well to know what they shall Juge here as the
Juges off owr contre knowys what thei juge there.

I answeryd agayne that hytt was very hard to make
a man vnders[tand] the Inglyshe tunge in generall, that
can nott speke hytt nethyr neuer has lernyd hytt in
particuler, & that I cowd fynd no defference in yewynge
off correccion to hym that has fyrst forgyd or cownyd
[false] mone [4] by hym that secondly has forgyd or inynyd
syche lyke.

They answeryd me that hytt ys becawse that they have
nott the perfytt knowlege whyther the fyrst or second
be false or not & that they wyll do ther best to know the
veryte in thys contre & that they w[yll] as feyne do
good Justyce in thys contres as we can or may desyre
hytt.

I answeryd them that I knowe nott. nethyr I am
assuryd, that ther [ys] nott in all the Emperor is lands, in
thys syde the sees no susi . . . ne bettyr lernyd men to
kan determe the Englyshe tunge fro the latten, & latten
fro Inglishe then syche prelates doctours & lerny[d] men
off the kynges consell that has fownd the errures &
heressee[s] off siche bookes as has ben condemnyd &

---

[4] Money; 'inynyd' in the same line awaits explanation.

bowrnt In Ingland. A[nd] here apon my lorde of palermo, presens my lorde off hoghestrate & othyrs off the sayd lordes, required me to be plesyd that thy[se] maturs myght be spoken of yett onys agayne, amonges them, & that aftyr that they may know the lordes of andwerpe is [ex]cusacions. Whyche be here cum to cowrte for syche an intent [and] that as then by my lady ys advyse, & delyberacion of consell [they] trustyd to gywe me sysh answere that resonably, I showld [have] no caw[s]e to cumplayne. but what hytt shalbe I can nott [tell] and knowynge the resolucion I wyll send yowr grace the hole [of the] declaracion, sertyfyenge yowr grace that I was onys so dysplesyd with them [of] Andwerpe that I was purposed to a bought vp all the forsayd bookes [5] & to a send them to yowr grace there to burne & destrue there att home lyke as all syche maliciowse bookes meritably & wordy ar to be done. but aftyrward that my colora was descendyd & by consell off a good frend of myne I thought hytt was bettyr to antyse my lady & hyr consell, fyrst to knowe & see fynally what remedy that they showld do apon my complayntes & yff ther resolucions lykyd me nott that as then I wold by all the forsayd bookes or as many as I cowde fynd & send ham yow there to do yowr grace ys plessure lyke as I wyll in deyd yff they do nott here bettyr Justyce.

Hytt shall plese yowr grace to wnderstand that where ther was two inprimurs taken prisoners, there ys but one off them that was fownd gylty in the inprimynge off the Englyshe bookes, whych ys namyd Christofer endhowen as afore wryten ys.

. . . .

I hawe wryten to my lorde of barro requyrynge hym

───

[5] This suggestion was subsequently carried out by Tunstall and Warham. See Nos. XVII and XVIII.

in the kynges ys hyghnes & yowr grace hys name, that
for the preseruacion off the cristen feythe & the extyrpacion off the abhomynable secte luterian that he wold
se Justyce to be done in hys towne, apon all syche
Inglyshe bookes entytled the nywe testment, & all syche
lyke bookes as I have infowrmyd to the gouuenor off owr
nasion whych shall show hys lordshype the efecte of all
syche byssynes.

My lorde of Valleyne came yesternyght to thys towne
& showyd me by mowthe that my sayd lorde hys fadyr
recomandyd hym unto me & that he has promest surly
that he wyll se syche Justyce to be done, that the kynges
hyghnes nethyr yowr grace shall have no cawse to be,
but well plesyd with hym, desyrynge me that I myght
cum me selfe to barro as sone as I cowde to awans [6] the
sayd bysynes lyke as I wyll as sone as I shall know how
that the maturs betux me & the lordes of andwerpe shalbe
determyned.

I haue begon the wrytynge off thys letyr att andwerpe
and fynshyd hytt here att maghlynge.[7]   The xij[th] day
of Jenner, 1526.

.   .   .   .

Afftyr this letter wryten I hawe spocken with my lady
margret touchyng thes Inglis bookes, & sche promest
me suyrly that afore fywe dayys to a nend that ther
salbe sych justyce don of them that I salbe plessyd,
then as then,

per yowr hummyll Bedesman John Hackett.

[6] Advance.   [7] Mechlin.

E

Extract from letter of John Hackett to Wolsey, February 20, 152⅞ (*Letters and Papers of Henry VIII*, vol. iv, No. 2903). Printed from Cotton MS. Galba, B. VI. 4.

Plesse yowr grace to wnderstand that synnes my last wrytyngs [to your] g[race] I hawe ressewyth none of yowrys. I trust by this tyme that yowr [grace has] ample infowrmacion off syche execucion & Justyce as has bene done in [these] townes of Andwerpe & barrow apon all syche Inglyshe bookes as we [could] fynd in thys contres. semblablys to trye syche othyr bookes as yowr g[race shall] send wnto me, with my lorde the byshope off london is sygnature, And b[y my] last wrytyngs wnto M^r bryan tuke I aduertyssyd hym that there [were] dyvers marchands off scottland that bought many off syche lyke bookes [to take]Them in to scottland, aparty to edenbowrghe & the most party to the tow[ne of] sent androys for the whyche cawse when I was at barro beyng a . . . the skottyshe shyppes were in se land thare the sayd bookes were ladyn . . . sodenly thedyrwarde thynkynge yff that I had fownd syche stuffe th[at] I wold cawse to make as good a fyer off them as there has bene [made] off the remenaunt in brabant, but fortune wold nott that I showld [this] tyme, for the forsayd shyppes were departyd a day afore my cummyng so I must atakyn pacience for all my labowre, with levyng my lady is lettris & good instruccion with my lorde off beveris & the rent m[aste]r off . . . concernyng the forsayd byssynes.

The margraw off andwerpe & drossard of barghys requyred & pray[ed] yff hytt were possibell to cawse them to gett qute off Ingland a [notyfy]cacion off sum partyculer artyclys off erryssees conteynynge in the say[d bokes] by the whyche notyfycacion, they may lafully nott only to bowrne syche . . . bookes, but also to correcte & punnyshe the inprymurs byers & syllers of [them] bothe in body & in goodes, for els acordynge to the lawys off thys [land] They may nott punnyshe nethyr make correcion apon the forsayd [imprimurs] nethyr apon there goodes, as they say.

.   .   .   .

. . . att maglyne the . . . day off Februer.

per yowr ryght hummyll Bedes man]

John hackett.

[Addressed : ' My Lorde Legate.']

F

Extract from postscript to previous letter (*Letters and Papers of Henry VIII*, vol. iv, No. 2904). Printed from Cotton MS., Galba B, IX, 235.

And as for the xl mark that I ressewt here at y[owr] grace ys comandment. I tynke ye wyll alowe me the same for the expenssis extra ordenary that I have done in comyng & goyng & abyddyng at andwerpe at Barow selomd (?) & elswher. with the prewe[1] Inquesissiones that I have don at gant at bruges at Brussellis, and lowayn and els wher touchyng the recoverans & execussyons to be don apon all syche heretyk bokes as I myght fynd in this contres acordyng vnto your grace ys mynd instruxions & wryghtyngs sobmytyng me self all ways to be ordyrt acordyng vnto your gracious comandment goodwyll & plessure.

[The postscript is dated ' fro machlyng the xx[th] day of fewrer å 1526.]

Privy.

XVII. THE BISHOP OF LONDON BUYS NEW TESTAMENTS

Extract from Halle's *Chronicle*, or ' Union of the two noble and illustrious famelies of Lancastre and Yorke ', London, R. Grafton, 1548, fol. clxxxvi.

Here is to be remembred, that at this present tyme, Willyam Tyndale had newly translated and imprinted the Newe Testament in Englishe, and the Bishop of London, not pleased with the translacion thereof, debated with hymself, how he might compasse and deuise, to destroye that false and erronious translacion (as he saied). And so it happened that one Augustine Packyngton, a Mercer and Merchant of London, and of a greate honestie, the same tyme was in Andwarp, where the Bishope then was,[1] and this Packyngton was a man that highly fauored William Tindale, but to the bishop vtterly shewed hymself to the contrary. The bishop desirous to haue his purpose brought to passe, commoned of the New Testamentes, and how gladly he would bye them. Packyngton then hearyng that he wished for, saied vnto the bishop, my Lorde, if it bee your pleasure I can in this matter dooe more I dare saie, then moste of the Merchauntes of Englande that are here, for I knowe the Dutchemen and straungiers, that haue bought theim of Tyndale, and haue theim here to sell, so that if it be your lordshippes pleasure, to paye for theim, for otherwise I cannot come by them, but I must disburse money for theim, I will then assure you, to haue every boke of them, that is

Marginal note: Cutbard Tonstall bishop of London bought Newe Testamentes to burne.

[1] Presumably in connexion with the negotiations closed by the Treaty of Cambrai, between France and Spain, August 1529.

imprinted and is here vnsolde. The Bishop thinkyng
that he had God by the too,[2] when in deede he had (as
after he thought) the Deuell by the fiste, saied, gentle
Master Packyngton, do your diligence and get them and
with all my harte I will paie for them, whatsoeuer thei
cost you, for the bokes are erronious and naughtes and
I entende surely to destroy theim all, and to burne
theim at Paules Crosse. Agustine Packyngton came to
Willyam Tyndale and saied, Willyam
I knowe thou arte a poore man, and
hast a hepe of newe Testamentes, and
bokes by thee, for the whiche thou

Augustyne Pack-
yngton the Bishop
of Londons mer-
chaunt.

hast bothe indaungered thy frendes, and beggered
thy self, and I haue now gotten thee a Merchaunt,
whiche with ready money shall dispatche thee of all
that thou hast, if you thynke it so proffitable for
your self. Who is the Merchant said Tyndale ? The
bishoppe of London, saied Packyngton, O that is
because he will burne them saied Tyndale, ye Mary quod
Packyngton, I am the gladder said Tyndale for these
two benefites shall come therof, I shall get money of
hym for these bokes, to bryng myself out of debt (and
the whole world shall crie out vpon the burnynge of
Goddes worde.) And the ouerplus[3] of the money, that
shall remain to me, shall make me more studious, to
correct the said Newe Testament, and so newly to Imprint the same once again, and I trust the second will
muche better like you, then euer did the first : And so
forward went the bargain, the bishop had the bokes,
Packyngton had the thankes, and Tyndale had the
money.

[2] Toe.
[3] Tyndale had first to repay the merchants who advanced
money to print his Testaments.

Afterward when mo newe Testamentes were Imprinted, thei came thicke and threfolde into Englande, the bishop of London hearyng that still there were so many Newe Testamentes abrode, sent for Augustyne Packyngton and saied vnto him : Sir how commeth this, that there are so many Newe Testamentes abrode, and you promised and assured me that you had bought al ? then saied Packyngton, I promes you I bought all that then was to bee had : but I perceiue thei haue made more sence, and it will neuer bee better, as long as thei haue the letters and stampes, therefore it wer best for your lordshippe to bye the stampes to, and then are you sure : the bishop smiled at hym and saied, well Packyngton well, and so ended this matter.

Shortly after it fortuned one George Constantine,[4] to be apprehended by Sir Thomas More, whiche then was lorde Chauncellor of England of suspicion of certain heresies. And this Constantine beyng with More, after diuerse examinacions of diuerse thynges, emong other, Master More saied in this wise to Constantine. Constantine I would haue thee plain with me in one thyng that I will aske of thee, and I promes thee I will shewe thee fauor, in all the other thynges, whereof thou art accused to me. There is beyond the sea Tyndale, Ioye, and a great many mo of you. I knowe thei cannot liue without helpe, some sendeth theim money and succoureth theim, and thy self beyng one of them, haddest parte thereof, and therefore knowest from whence it came. I praie thee who be thei that thus helpe them ? My lorde quod Constantine, will you that I shal tell you the

---

[4] George Constantine, a Cambridge graduate. When under examination by More he gave information as to the method of shipping the Lutheran books. For his activity before his arrest, see No. XIX.

truthe ? Yea I praie thee quod my Lorde. Mary I will quod Constantine, truly quod he it is the Bishoppe of London that hath holpen vs, for he hath bestowed emong vs, a greate deale of money in New Testamentes to burne theim, and that hath and yet is our onely succoure and comfort. Now by my trothe quod More, I thynke euen the same, and I said so muche to the bishop, when he went about to bye them.

XVIII. THE BISHOP OF NORWICH REFUNDS THE ARCHBISHOP PART OF HIS OUTLAY ON NEW TESTAMENTS

Letter of Richard Nix, Bishop of Norwich, to the Archbishop of Canterbury, June 14, 1527. Printed from Cotton MS. Vitellius B, IX, 117.

In right humble maner I commende me vnto your goode Lordeshippe, Doynge the same tundrestand, that I lately receyued your letters dated at your manor of Lambethe, the xxvj daie of the moneth of Maij. by the whiche I do perceyue that youre grace hath lately goten into your handes all the bokes of the newe testamente translated into Englesshe and pryented beyonde the see aswele those with the gloses ioyned vnto theym as thoder without the gloses,[1] by meanes of exchaunge by you made therfore to the somme of lxij*l*. ix*s*. iiij*d*.[2]

[1] The books purchased must have been the 8° and 4° printed at Worms.

[2] Large as this sum is, about £700 of modern value, if the average retail price of a New Testament was six groats (five for the 8° and seven for the 4°, see No. XIX) or 2*s*., the number purchased would only be about 663, and even if 50 per cent be added to this to represent the allowance made to a wholesale buyer, it would amount to about one thousand, or one-sixth of the total number printed.

Surely in myne opynion you have done therin a graciouse and a blessed dede, and god I doubt not shall highly rewarde you therfore, And where in your said letters ye write, that in so moche as this matur and the daunger therof if remedie had not be prouyded shulde not only haue towched you but all the Busshoppes within your province, and that it is no reason that the holle charge and coste therof shulde reste only in you, but that thei and euery of theym for their parte shulde avaunce and contribute certain sommes of money towarde the same. And for that entente desire me to certifie you what conuenyent somme I for my part wulbe contented to avaunce in this behalue, and to make pay-mente therof vnto Maister William Potkyn your ser-uaunte. Pleaseth it you tundrestande that I am right wele contented to geue and avaunce in this behalue ten markes,[3] and shall cause the same to be delyúered vnto the said maister Potkyn shortely the which somme I thinke sufficient for my parte if euery Busshopp within your said provynce make like contribution & avaunce-mente after the Rate and substance of their benefices. Neuer the lesse if your grace thinke this somme of ten markes not sufficient for my parte in this mater, (the nombre and substance of thoder your suffragans con-sidered) your furdre pleasure knowen I shalbe as gladde to conforme my self therunto in this or any other mater concernynge the churche, as any your subgiet within your provynce. As knowes Almyghty god, who longe preserue you to his moste pleasure and your hertes desire. At hoxne in Suff. the xiiij daie of Junii 1527.

Your humble obediencur and baidman

R. Norvich.

[3] i.e. £6 13s. 4d., about one-tenth of the whole sum.

I wolde be as gladde to wayte vpon your lordeshipp
and do my duetie vnto you as any man lyvinge, but
I thynke that I can not so do this somer, I praye god
I may haue some tyme for to do it.

[Addressed : To my Lorde of Canterbury is goode
lordeshippe.]

XIX. THE CONFESSION OF ROBERT NECTON[1]
THAT BOUGHT AND SOLD NEW TESTAMENTS
IN ENGLISH

From Strype, *Ecclesiastical Memorials*, 1822, vol. i, Pt. II,
pp. 63–5. Reference given to MSS. Fox. Regist. Cuthb., i. e. to
the Register of Cuthbert Tonstall, Bishop of London.

He bowght at sondry tymes of Mr. Fyshe [2] dwellyng
by the Whight Frears in London, many of the New
Testaments in English ; that is to say, now V. and
now X. And sometyme mo, and sometyme less, to the
nombre of XX. or XXX. in the gret volume. The
which New Testaments the said Mr. Fyshe had of one
Harmond, an English man, beyng beyond see. But
how many he had this respondent cannot tell. And
this respondent saith, that about a yere and half agon he
fell in a quaintaunce with Vicar Constantyne [3] here in
London. Which shewed this respondent first, that the
said Mr Fyshe had New Testaments to sell ; and caused
this respondent to by some of the said New Testaments
of Mr Fyshe. And the said Mr Fyshe, at the desire and
instance of Vicar Constantine, browghte the said New

---

[1] Probably a kinsman of Thomas Necton, sheriff of Norwich
(1531), whose sympathies were with the Protestants.

[2] Simon Fish, a student of Gray's Inn, who subsequently wrote
the *Supplication of the Beggars*.

[3] See No. XVII note 4.

Testaments home to this respondents house. And before that Vicar Constantine caused this respondent to by some of the said New Testaments, he had none, nor no other books, except the chapiters of Matthew.[4]

And moreover, this respondent saith, that about the same tyme he sold fyve of the said New Testaments to Sir [5] William Furboshore synging man, in Stowmarket, in Suffolk, for vii or viii grotes a pece. Also, two of the same New Testaments in Bury St. Edmunds : that is to say, to Raymond Wodelesse one ; and Thomas Horfan another, for the same price.

Also, he saith, that about Cristmas last, he sold one New Testament to a Priste ; whose name he cannot tell, dwellynge at Pycknam Wade in Northfolke ; and two Latin books, the one Oeconomica Christiana ; and the other Unio Dissidentium. Also, one Testament to William Gibson merchant man, of the parish of S. Margaret Patens.

Also, Vicar Constantyne at dyvers tymes had of this respondent a XV. or XVI. of the New Testaments of the biggest.[6] And this respondent saith, that the sayd Vicar Constantyne dyvers tymes bowght of him certayne of the sayd New Testaments : and this respondent lykewise, of hym. Also, he sold Sir Richard Bayfell two New Testaments unbound about Cristmas last : for the which he payd iiis iiiid.

Farthermore, he saith, that he hath sold V or VI of the said N. Testaments to diverse persons of the cite of London : whose namys, or dwellyng places, he doth not remember.

----

[4] This reference may equally well be to the Cologne fragment of the New Testament, or to a separate edition.

[5] Here and elsewhere ' Sir ' denotes a priest.

[6] i.e. of the quarto edition with marginal notes.

Moreover, he saith, that since Easter last, he bowght of Geffray Usher of Saynct Antonyes, with whom he hath byn aqueynted by the space of a yere, or thereabout (by reason he was Mr Forman, the person of Hony Lane his servant, and for that this respondent did moche resort to the said persons sermons) XVIII N. Testaments in English of the smal volume, and XXVI. books, al of one sort, called Oeconomica Christiani in Latin ; and two other books in Latin called Unio Dissidentium. For which he payed hym xl*s*. Of the which Oeconomica Christiana Vicar Constantyne had XIII. at one tyme.

And of which N. Testaments since Easter this respondent caryed XV of them, and thother XXIII Oeconomica Christiana, to Lynne, to sell. Which he wold have sold to a young man, callid William . . . merchant man, dwellyng by one Mr Burde of the same towne. Which young man wold not medle with them, because they were prohibite. And so this respondent left the said books at Lynne with the said William, untyll his retornyng thider ayen. And so the said bookes do remayne ther still, as yet. And two of the said N. Testaments he hath in his own custodie, with another of the great volume. Also, another Testament of the smal volume [7] he sold since Easter to young Elderton, merchant man, of Saynct Mary Hill parishe.

Howbeit he saith, that he knew not that any of thies bookes were of Luthers sect.

To the xviiJ[th], That he hath byn a receptor, he saith, that he twice or thryese hath byn in Thomas Mathews [8]

---

[7] Presumably the octavo Worms edition.

[8] The name is worth noting, as it is possible that this Thomas Matthew was used in connexion with the Bible of 1537 as a scapegoat, on whom, after he had been got out of the way, any blame could be laid. Compare the part possibly played by Hans van

house of Colchestre. Wheras he hath red diverse tymes in the N. Testament in English, before the said Thomas Matthew, his wif, William Dykes, and other servantes ther. And there, and then have herd old Father Hacker speke of prophesies ; and have had communications of diverse articles : which he doth not now remember.

To the XIXth, so begynnyng, That he went about to by a great nombre of N. Testaments, he saith, that about Cristmas last, there came a Duche man,[9] beyng now in the Flete, which wold have sold this respondent ii or iii hundreth of the said N. Testaments in English : which this respondent did not by ; but sent him to Mr Fyshe to by them : and said to the Duche man, Look what Mr Fyshe doth, I wil do the same. But whether Mr Fyshe bowght any of them, he cannot tell : for the which iii hundreth he shold have paid XVI *l* V *sh*. after IX *d*. a pece.[10]

To the XX article, That he is inframed ; he saith, that since Easter last, he was at Norwiche at his brothers house, wher as one had complayned of this respondent to my Lord of Norwiche,[11] because he had a N. Testa-

Ruremond as the ' Johan Hollybushe ' of the second Latin-English New Testament printed by Nicholson in 1538 (see note to No. XVI. A).

[9] Probably Hans van Ruremond acting for Christoffel van Endhoven or van Ruremond, who brought out an edition at Antwerp in 1526 (see note to No. XVI. A). This was apparently a little 16mo, and sold consequently wholesale at either 9*d*. or 1*s*. 1*d*., according to which emendation of the faulty reckoning made at the end of the paragraph is adopted. The 700 copies sold to F. Birckmann for £28 17*s*. 3*d*. work out at just under 10*d*. each. But in the case of copies sold in England the price would naturally be higher.

[10] Three hundred copies at 9*d*. each come to £11 5*s*., not £16 5*s*.

[11] See Nos. XVII and XIX.

ment. Wherfor his brother counceled this respondent
to send or delyver his said N. Testament, and said to
him, If he wold not delyver it, my Lord of Norwiche
wold send him to my Lord of London, his Ordinary·
And so afterwards he sent it to London by the caryer.

To the XXI. article, so begynnyng, That contrary to
the prohibition, he hath kept the N. Testament, he con-
fessith, that after he had knowledge of the condempna-
tion of the said N. Testament, by the space of a yere, or
more, he hath had in his custodie, kept, and studyed
the same Testament, and have red it thoroughly many
tymes.   And also have red in it as wel within the citie
and diocess of London, as within the citie and diocesse
of Norwiche.   And not onely red it to himself, but redd
and tawght it to diverse other.

To the XXII. he awnsweryth and denyeth, that he had
Wycliefs Wycket or the Apocalips at any tyme.

Per me Robert Necton.

XX.   BISHOP NIX IMPLORES THE KING'S HELP

From a letter of Richard Nix, bishop of Norwich, to the Archbishop of Canterbury, May 14, 1530 (Cotton MS. Cleopatra E. V.
360).

After moste humbill recomendation, I do your grace
tvndrestande that I am accombered with suche as
kepith and redethe these Arronious bokes in engleshe
and beleve and gif credence to the same and teacheth
other that they shuld so doo, My Lorde I have done
that lieth in me for the suppression of suche parsons,
but it passith my power, or any spirituall manne for
to do it, for dyuerse saith openly in my diocesse, that the
kinges grace wolde that they shulde have the saide

Arronious bokes, and so maynteynith them self of the kinge, wherupon, I desired my lorde Abbot of Hide to shew this to the kinges grace, besechinge him to sende his honorabill lettres vndre his seall downe to whome he please in my diocesse that they may shew and publiche that it is not his pleasure that suche bokes shuld be had or red. And also punyshe suche as saith soo, I truste before this lettre shall come vnto you, my saide lorde Abbot hath donne soo, the saide Abbot hath the names of some that crakith in the kinges name that ther false opinions shuld goo furth, and will dye in the quarell that ther vngracious opinions be true, And trustith by michalmas daye ther shalbe more that shall beleve of ther opinions than they that beleveth the contrary. If I had knowen that your grace had bene at london, I wolde have commanded the saide Abbot to have spoke with you, but your grace may sende for him whan ye please, and he shall shew you my holl mynde in that mater, and how I thought best for the suppression of suche as holdeth these Arronious opinions, for if they contynue any tyme I thinke they shall vndoe vs all, The said Abbot departed from me on monday laste and sith that tyme I have had moche trobill and busynes with other, in like mater, And they say that where somever they go they here say that the kinges pleasure is the new testament in inglishe shulde go forth, and men shuld have it, and rede it, and from that opynion I canne no wise induce them, but I had gretter auctorite to punyshe them, thanne I haue, Wherfor I besiche your good lordeshippe to advertise the kinges grace, as I trust the saide abbot hath done before thes lettre shall come vnto your grace that a remedy may be had, for now it maye be done well in my diocesse, for the gentilmen and the commentye be not greatly inseth, but marchantes and suche that hath ther abyding not ferre from the see, the saide Abbot of Hide canne shew you of a curat and well lerned in my diocesse, that exorted his parishioners to beleve contrary to the Catholicall faith.

Ther is a collage in Cambrige called gunwell haule [1] of the foundacion of a Bishoppe of Norwiche. I here of no clerke that hath come ought lately of that collage but saverith of the friainge panne thoughe he speke never so holely, I beseche your grace to pardon me of my rude and tedious writinge to you, the zele and love that I ough to almighty god cause me this to do, And thus almighty god longe preserue your grace in good prosperite and helth. At hoxne the xiiij[th] Day of Maii 1530.

Your obediensary and

Daily orator

Ri Norwich.

XXI. THE KING CONSULTS HIS COUNCIL AND THE BISHOPS

May 25, 1530

Extract from Halle's *Chronicle, The Union of the two Noble Houses*, &c. Grafton, 1548, fol. 192.

The xxii yere

In the begynnyng of this two and twentie yere, the kyng like a politike and prudent prince, perceiued that his subiectes and other persons had diuers times within

---

[1] Gonville Hall was founded in 1348 by Edmond Gonville, rector of Terrington in Norfolk, but William Bateman, Bishop of Norwich, whom Gonville left his executor, changed both the site and the statutes of the Hall, and added to its endowments in 1353, and is thus reckoned as its second founder. The Hall became Gonville and Caius College by the benefactions of Dr. John Caius, its third founder, in 1558.

foure yeres last past, brought into his realme, greate
nombre of printed bokes, of the new Testament, translated into the English tongue by Tyndall, Joy, and
other, which bokes the common people vsed and dayly
red priuely, which the clargie would not admit, for thei
punnished suche persones as had red studied or taught
the same with greate extremitie, but bycause the multitude was so greate, it was not in their power to redresse
there grefe : wherefore they made complaint to the
Chauncelor [1] (which leaned much to the spirituall mennes
part, in all causes) where vpon he imprisoned and
punished a greate nomber so that for this cause a great
rumor and controuersie rose daily emongst the people :
wherfore the kyng consideryng what good might come
of readyng of the new Testament with reuerence and
folowyng the same, and what euell mighte come of the
readyng of the same if it were euil translated, and not
folowed : came into the starre chambre the fiue and
twentie day of May,[2] and there commoned with his
counsaile and the prelates concernyng this cause, and
after long debatyng, it was alleged that the translacion[s]
of Tyndall and Joy were not truely translated, and also
that in theim were prologues and prefaces which sounded
to heresie, and rayled against the bishopes vncharitably,
wherefore all such bokes were prohibited and commaundement geven by the kyng to the bishoppes, that

[1] Sir Thomas More.

[2] Of the proceedings of May 24 (see XXII, note 1) the ' Bill
in English to be published by the prechours ' says that ' his
gracious highnes, being in parson in the chapell called the " Old
Chapell ", which sometime was called Saint Edwards chambre,
sett on the est side of the parliament chambre, within his gracis
palace at Westminster, then and there in the presence of all the
parsonages there assembled and gathered ' caused three notaries
to record the decisions arrived at.

thei callyng to theim the best learned men of the vniuersities should cause a new translacion to be made, so that
the people should not be ignoraunte in the law of god :
And notwithstandyng this commaundement the bishopes
did nothing at all to set furth a new translacion, which
caused the people to stody Tindalles translacion, by
reason where of many thinges cam to light, as you shall
here after.

In this yere in Maye,[3] the bishop of London caused al
his newe Testamentes which he had bought with many
other bokes, to be brought into Paules churcheyarde in
London and there was openly burned.

XXII. THE KING'S PROCLAMATION, JUNE, 1530

From the copy in the British Museum, printed by Thomas
Berthelet.

Mense Junii, Anno regni metuendissimi domini nostri
regis Henrici octaui. xxii.

A proclamation made and diuysed by the kyngis
highnes, with the aduise of his honorable counsaile, for
dampning of erronious bokes and heresies, and prohibit-
inge the hauinge of holy scripture, translated into the
vulgar tonges of englisshe, frenche, or duche, in suche
maner, as within this proclamation is expressed.

The kinge our most dradde soueraigne lorde, studienge
and prouidynge dayly for the weale, benefite, and honour
of this his most noble realme, well and euidently per-

[3] Tunstall succeeded Wolsey as Bishop of Durham in February,
1530, and John Stokesley, his successor, was nominated July,
1530, and consecrated the following November. There can be no
doubt that Tunstall is meant.

ceiueth, that partly through the malicious suggestion of
our gostly enemy, partly by the yuell and peruerse inclination and sedicious disposition of sundry persons,
diuers heresies and erronious opinions haue ben late
sowen and spredde amonge his subiectes of this his said
realme, by blasphemous and pestiferous englisshe bokes,
printed in other regions, and sent in to this realme, to
the entent as well to peruerte and withdrawe the people
from the catholike and true fayth of Christe, as also to
stirre and incense them to sedition, and disobedience
agaynst their princes, soueraignes, and heedes, as also
to cause them to contempne and neglect all good lawes,
customes, and vertuous maners, to the final subuersion
and desolation of this noble realme, if they myght haue
preuayled (whiche god forbyd) in theyr most cursed
persuasions and malicious purposes. Where vpon the
kynges hignes, by his incomparable wysedome, forseinge
and most prudently considerynge, hath inuited and called
to hym the primates of this his gracis realme, and also
a sufficient nombre of discrete vertuous and well lerned
personages in diuinite, as well of either of the vniuersites,
Oxforde and Cambrige, as also hath chosen and taken
out of other parties of his realme : gyuinge vnto them
libertie, to speke and declare playnly their aduises,
iudgementes, and determinations, concernynge as well
the approbation or reiectynge of suche bokes as be in
any parte suspected, as also the admission and diuulga-
tion of the olde and newe testament, translated in to
englisshe. Wher vpon his highnes, in his owne royall
person, callynge to hym the said primates and diuines,
hath seriously and depely, with great leisure and longe
deliberation, consulted, debated, inserched, and discussed
the premisses : and finally, by all their free assentes,
consentes, and agrementes, concluded, resolued, and

determined, that these bokes ensuynge, That is to say,[1]
the boke entitled the wicked Mammona, the boke named
the Obedience of a Christen man, the Supplication of
beggars, and the boke called the Reuelation of Antichrist,
the Summary of scripture, and diuers other bokes made
in the englisshe tonge, and imprinted beyonde the see,
do conteyne in them pestiferous errours and blasphemies :
and for that cause, shall from hensforth be reputed and
taken of all men, for bokes of heresie, and worthy to be
dampned, and put in perpetuall obliuion. The kynges
said highnes therfore straitly chargeth and commaundeth,
all and euery his subiectes, of what astate or condition
so euer he or they be, as they wyll auoyde his high
indignacion and most greuous displeasure, that they from
hensforth, do not bye, receyue, or haue, any of the bokes
before named, or any other boke, beinge in the englisshe
tonge, and printed beyonde the see, of what matter so
euer it be, or any copie written, drawen out of the same,
or the same bokes in the frenche or duche tonge.   And
to the entent that his highnes wylbe asserteyned, what
nombre of the sayd erronious bokes shalbe founde from
tyme to tyme within this his realme, his highnes therfore

<hr />

[1] These works, by Tyndale, Simon Fish, and Frith, form the
first five of the seven books, a list of the ' heresies and errours ' in
which was set forth in the ' Publick Instrument made A.C.
M.D.xxx. May 24 in an assembly of the Archbishop of Canterbury, the Bishop of Durham, and others, by order of King
Henry VIII containing divers heretical and erroneous opinions,
considered and condemned.' Printed ' Ex reg. Warham, fol. 188. a.
in Wilkins, *Concilia*, iii. 728 sqq.   There is reference in this to
' the translation also of Scripture corrupted by William Tyndall,
as well in the Olde Testamente as in the Newe ', and again in
' the bill in Englisshe to be published by the prechours ' to ' the
Newe Testament in Englisshe of the translation which is nowe
prynted ', but the Instrument was mainly concerned with the
controversial books.

chargeth and commaundeth, that all and euery person
or persones, whiche hath or herafter shall haue, any boke
or bokes in the englisshe tonge, printed beyonde the see,
as is afore written, or any of the sayde erronious bokes
in the frenche or duche tonge : that he or they, within
fyftene dayes nexte after the publisshynge of this present
proclamation, do actually delyuer or sende the same
bokes and euery of them, to the bisshop of the diocese,
wherin he or they dwelleth, or to his commissary, or els
before good testimonie, to theyr curate or parisshe preest,
to be presented by the same curate or parisshe preest, to
the sayd bisshop or his commissary. And so doynge, his
highnes frely pardoneth and acquiteth them, and euery
of them, of all penalities, forfaitures, and paynes, wherin
they haue incurred or fallen, by reason of any statute,
acte, ordinaunce, or proclamation before this tyme made,
concernynge any offence or transgression by them commytted or done, by or for the kepynge or holdynge of the
sayde bokes.

Forseen and prouided alwayes, that they from hensforth truely do obserue, kepe, and obey this his present
gracis proclamation and commaundement. Also his
highnes commaundeth all mayres, sheriffes, bailliffes,
constables, bursholders[2], and other officers and ministers
within this his realme, that if they shall happen by any
meanes or wayes to knowe that any person or persons
do herafter bye, receyue, haue, or deteyne any of the
sayde erronyous bokes, printed or written any where, or
any other bokes in englisshe tonge printed beyonde the
see, or the sayd erronious bokes printed or written in the
frenche or duche tonge, contrarye to this present proclamation, that they beinge therof well assured, do
immediatly attache the saide person or persons, and

[2] I cannot explain this word.

brynge hym or them to the kynges highnes and his most
honorable counsayle : where they shalbe corrected and
punisshed for theyr contempte and disobedience, to the
terrible example of other lyke transgressours.

More ouer his highnes commaundeth, that no maner
of person or persons take vpon hym or them to printe
any boke or bokes in englisshe tong, concernynge holy
scripture, not before this tyme printed within this his
realme, vntyll suche tyme as the same boke or bokes be
examyned and approued by the ordinary of the diocese,
where the said bokes shalbe printed : And that the
prynter therof, vpon euery of the sayde bokes beinge so
examyned, do sette the name of the examynour or
examynours, with also his owne name vpon the sayde
bokes, as he wyll answere to the kynges highnes, at his
vttermoste peryll.

And farthermore, for as moche as it is come to the
herynge of our saide soueraigne lorde the kynge, that
report is made by diuers and many of his subiectes, that
as it were to all men not onely expedyent, but also neces-
sarye, to haue in the englisshe tonge bothe the newe
testament and the olde : and that his highnes, his noble
men, and prelates were bounden to suffre them so to
haue it : His highnes hath therfore semblably there vpon
consulted with the sayd primates and vertuous, discrete,
and well lerned personages in diuinite forsayde, and by
them all it is thought, that it is not necessary, the sayde
scripture to be in the englisshe tonge, and in the handes
of the commen people : but that the distribution of the
sayd scripture, and the permyttyng or denyenge therof,
dependeth onely vpon the discretion of the superiours,
as they shall thynke it conuenyent.   And that hauing
respecte to the malignite of this present tyme, with the
inclination of people to erronious opinions, the translation

of the newe testament and the olde in to the vulgare tonge
of englysshe, shulde rather be the occasion of contynuance
or increace of errours amonge the sayd people, than any
benefyte or commodite towarde the weale of their soules.
And that it shall nowe be more conuenient that the same
people haue the holy scripture expouned to them, by
preachers in their sermons, accordynge as it hath ben
of olde tyme accustomed before this tyme. All be it if
it shall here after appere to the kynges highnes, that his
saide people do vtterly abandon and forsake all peruerse,
erronious, and sedicious opinyons, with the newe testament and the olde, corruptly translated in to the englisshe
tonge nowe beinge in print : And that the same bokes
and all other bokes of heresy, as well in the frenche tonge
as in the duche tonge, be clerely extermynate and exiled
out of this realme of Englande for euer : his highnes
entendeth to prouyde, that the holy scripture shalbe by
great lerned and catholyke persones, translated in to the
englisshe tonge, if it shall then seme to his grace conuenient so to be. Wherfore his highnes at this tyme,
by the hoole aduise and full determination of all the
sayde primates and other discrete and substanciall lerned
personages, of both vniuersites, and other before expressed, and by the assent of his nobles and others of
his moste honorable Counsayle, wylleth and straytly
commaundeth, that all and euery persone and persones,
of what astate, degree or condicion so euer he or they be,
whiche hath the newe testament or the olde translated
into englisshe, or any other boke of holy scripture so
translated, beinge in printe, or copied out of the bokes
nowe beinge in printe, that he or they do immediatly
brynge the same boke or bokes, or cause the same to be
brought to the bysshop of the dyocese, where he dwelleth,
or to the handes of other the sayde persones, at the daye

afore limytted, in fourme afore expressed and mencioned, as he wyll auoyde the kynges high indignation and displeasure. And that no person or persons from hensforth do bie, receyue, kepe or haue the newe testament or the olde, in the englisshe tonge, or in the frenche or duche tonge, except suche persones as be appoynted by the kinges highnes and the bishops of this his realme, for the correction or amendinge of the sayd translacion, as they wyll answere to the kinges highnes at their vttermost perils, and wyll auoyde such punysshement, as they doinge contrary to the purport of this proclamacion shall suffer, to the dredefull example of all other lyke offenders.

And his highnes further commandeth, that all suche statutes, actes, and ordinances, as before this tyme haue be made & enacted, as well in the tyme of his moste gracious reigne, as also in the tyme of his noble progenitours, concernynge heresies, and hauynge and deteynynge erronyous bokes, contrary and agaynst the faith catholyke, shall immediatly be put in effectuall and due execution ouer and besyde this present proclamation.

And god saue the kynge.   Thomas Bertheletus regius impressor excusit. Cum priuilegio.

XXIII. TYNDALE'S TERMS OF SUBMISSION

From a letter written by Stephen Vaughan to Henry VIII.[1] Printed from Cotton MS. Galba B. X, 5 (a corrected draught) completed from the letter itself in the Record Office.

I have agayne byn in hande to perswade Tyndall and to draw him the rather to fauour my perswasions and not to thinke the same fayned, I shewed hym a clause

[1] Stephen Vaughan, who in 1534 became Governor of the English Merchant Adventurers at Antwerp, was charged by Henry VIII in 1531 to persuade Tyndale to retract and return

conteyned in Maister Crumwells lettre conteynynge these
wordes followinge, And not withstanding other the premisses in this my lettre conteyned if it were possible by
good and holsom exhortacions to reconsile and convert
the sayde tyndall, from the trayne and affection whiche
he now is in, and to excerpte and take away the opynyons
and fantasies sorely rooted in hym, I doubte not, but
the kynges highnes wolde be muche ioyous of his con-
version and amendement, And so beinge converted, if
then he wolde returne into his realme, vndoubtidly, the
kinges royall magestie is so inclined to mercie, pitie and
compassion, that he refusethe none, whiche he seyth[2], to
submyt them self to the obedyence and good order of
the worlde.

In these wordes I thought to be suche swetnes and
vertue, as were able to perse the hardest harte of the
worlde, And as I thought so it cam to passe. For after
sight therof I perceyued the man to be excidinge altered,
and [moued] to take the same very nere vnto his harte, in
suche wise that water stode in his yees[3], And answered,
what gracious wordes are these, I ass[ure] youe, sayed
he, if it wolde stande withe the kinges most gracious
pleas[ure] to graunte only a bare text of the scriptures[4]

---

to England. On January 26 he reported to the king that he had
written letters to Tyndale addressed to Frankfort, Hamburg, and
Marburg, not knowing in which place he was, and encloses his
answer (State Papers, v. 65); on March 25 he reports to Cromwell
his negotiations with Tyndale (ib., 153); in a mutilated letter
assigned to April he reports to the king an interview with Tyndale
outside Antwerp (ib., 201). The present letter begins with secular
politics, then refers to Frith, and finally to Tyndale. Besides
the draft here printed it exists also in the Record Office, ib., vii.
301.   It must have been crossed by an answer to No. 153 from
Cromwell commanding Vaughan to break off all negotiations with
Tyndale.   [2] Sees.   [3] Eyes.

[4] This expression has sometimes been twisted so as to denote

to be put forthe emonge h[is] people, like as is put forthe
emonge the subgectes of the emperour in th[ese] parties,
and of other cristen princes be it of the translation of
what perso[n] soeuer shall please his magestie, I shall
ymedyatly make faithful[l] promyse, neuer to wryte
more, ne abide ij. dayes in these parties after th[e] same,
but ymedyatly to repayre into his realme, and there
most humbly submytt my selfe at the fete of his roiall
magestie, offerynge my bodye, to suffer what payne or
torture, ye what dethe his grac[e] will, so this be obteyned,
And till that time, I will abide thasper[itie] of all chaunses
what so euer shalle come, and indure my lyfe, in asm[any]
paynes, as it is able to bere and suffer, And as concernynge m[y] reconsiliacion, his grace maye be assured that
what soeuer I haue sayd or written, in alle my lyfe
agenste thonour of goddes worde, and so proued, the
same shall I before his magestie and all the worlde
v[tterlie] renownce and forsake, and with most humble
and meke mynde im[brace] the truthe, abhorringe all
errour, soner at the most gracious and benygne req[uest]
of his royall magestie, of whose wisdome, prudence, and
learnynge, I [here] so greate prayse and commendation, then of any other creature, ly[uyng].   But if those
thinges whiche I haue written, be true, and stande w[ith]
goddes worde, why shulde his magestie hauynge so
excellent a gu[yfte] of knowlege in the scriptures, moue
me to do any thinge agenst m[y] conscience, with many
other wordes whiche were to longe to writte, Fyn[ally]
I haue some good hope in the man, and wolde not
doubte to bringe [hym] to some good poynt, were it that
some thing now and then myght pro[ceede] from your

a preference on Tyndale's part for unannotated texts. It is
clear that he preferred annotated ones, but would have accepted
the circulation of the bare text of the scriptures as a compromise.

magestie towardes me, wherby the man myght take the better comforte of my perswasions.

[I] aduertised the same tyndall, that he shulde not put forthe [t]he same booke[5], tyll your most gracious pleasure were knowen, wherunto he answered, myne aduertisement cam to late, for he feared lest one that had his copie wolde put it very shortly in prynte, whiche he wolde lett if he coulde, if not there is no remedy, I shall staye it asmuche as I can, as yet it is not come forthe, ne will not in a while by that I perceyue.

Luther hathe lately, put forthe a worke agenst themperour in the German tongue, whiche I wold cause to be translated into laten, and send it to your magestie, if I knew your gracious pleasure, in it were many thinges to be seen.

. . . .

from Barroughe [the xx Daye of Maye an° M.D. XXXI]

the most humble subgect of your Royall

Magestie

S[tephen] V[aughan].

XXIV. FRITH'S DEFENCE OF TYNDALE AND HIS WORK

From 'An answer to the preface of master mores boke ',[1] part of ' A Boke made by John Frith prisoner in the Tower of London, answeringe unto M. more's lettur which he wrote agenst the first litle treatyse that John Frith made concerninge the sacramente of the body and bloud of Christ. Monster. C. Willems, 1533.'

It ys not possyble for hym that hathe hys eyen and seth hys brother which lackyth sight in Ieoperdye of peryshynge at a perylous pyt, but that he must com to

[5] Presumably Tyndale's Answer to Sir Thomas More's 'Dialoge'.
[1] Frith answers More paragraph by paragraph. He here replies

hym and guyde hym tyll he be past that Ieoperdye, and
at the lest wise, yf he can not come to hym, yet wyll he
calle a crye vnto hym to cause hym chose the better
waye, excepte hys herte be cankered with the contagion
of suche hatered that he can reioyse in hys neighbours
distructyon.   And euyn so ys yt not possyble for vs
whiche haue receyuyd the knowelege of goddes worde,
but that we moste crye and call to other, that they leue
the perillous pathys of ther owyn folishe phantasyes.
And do that only to the lorde, that he comandeth them,
nether addinge any thinge nor diminishyng.   And therfor
vntyll we se som meanes founde, by the which a reasonable reformacyon may be had on the on partye, And
suffecyent instructyon for the pore comens I insure yow,
I nether wyll nor can cease to speake, for the worde of
God boylyth in my bodye, lyke a feruent fyere, and wyll
nedes haue an issue and breakyth oute, whan occasyon
ys geuyn. But this hath ben offered yow, ys offered, and
shall be offered ?   Graunt that that the worde of God,
I meane the text of scrypture, may goo abrode in oure
ynglyshe tonge, as other nacyons haue yt in ther tonges,
and my brother Wyllyam tendale, and I haue don, and
wyll promisse you to wryte no more. Yf yow wyll not
graunt this condicyon then wyll we be doynge whyle
we haue brethe and shewe in fewe wordes that the scrypture doth in many : and so at the lest saue some. . . .

[Sig. B 8 recto :[2]] And Tyndale I truste leuyth, well

to More's wish as to the reformers, ' sith there can nothing re-
frayne their studie from deuising and compassyng of euill and
ungracious writyng, that they would and could kepe it so
secretly, that neuer man should see it, but such as are so farre
corrupted, as neuer would be cured of their canker.'
    [2] More had accused Frith of ' teaching in a few leaues shortly
al the poyson that Wickleff, Oecolampius, Tyndall, and Zwinglius

content with suche a poore apostylis lyffe, as god gaue
his son christe, and hys faythfull ministers in this worlde
which ys not sure of so many mites, as ye be yerly of
poundes, allthough I am sure that for hys lernynge and
Iudgement in scrypture, he were more worthye to be
promoted, then all the bushoppes in england. I receyuyd
a letter from hym, which was wrytyn syns crystmas
wherin amonge other maters he wrytyth thus. I calle
God to record agaynst the day we shall apere before our
lorde Iesus to geue a reconynge of our doynges, that
I never altered one sillable of goddes worde, agaynst my
conscyence nor wolde do this daye, yf all that ys in
yerth, whether yt be honour, pleasure or rychis, mighte
be geuyn me. Moreouer I take God to record to my conscience that I desyre of God to my sellf in this world no
more then that with oute which I can not kepe his lawes,
&c., Iudge Christen reader whether thes wordes be not
spoken of a faythfull, clere innocent harte. And as for
hys behauyour ys suche that I am sure no man can
reproue hym of, any synne, howbeyt no man ys innocent
before god which beholdeth the harte.

XXV. GEORGE JOYE'S LETTER TO THE KING
AND QUEEN

From *A Letter of M. W. Tyndall to Iohn Frith*, in Foxe's edition
of *The Whole Workes of W. Tyndall, Iohn Frith and Doct. Barnes*
(London, John Day, 1573), p. 454.

George Ioye[1] at Candlemasse being at Barrow, Printed
two leaues of Genesis in a greate forme, and sent one

haue taught in all their bookes before '. Frith eulogizes each in
succession.

[1] George Joye was a Cambridge graduate, and fellow of Peterhouse (1517). On being denounced as a heretic to the Bishop of
Lincoln in 1527, he fled to Strassburg. Four years later (May 10,

Copy to the King, and an other to the newe Queene,
with a letter to N. for to deliuer them : and to purchase
licence, that he might so goe through all the Bible.
Out of that is sprong the noyse of the new Bible : and
out of that is the greate seeking for Englishe bookes at all
Printers & Booke bynders in Antwarpe, and for an
English Priest that shoulde Printe. This chaunced the
ix. day of May [1533].

XXVI. THE BISHOPS PETITION FOR AN ENGLISH BIBLE

Petitio synodi Cantuariensis provinciae de libris suspectis
exhibendis, et de transferendis Bibliis in linguam Anglicanam.
19 Dec., 1534 (From Wilkins's *Concilia* iii, compared with the
Cotton MS. Cleopatra E. v. 339 b.)

Decimo nono die Decembris, anno Domini Millesimo
Quingentesimo tricesimo quarto, Episcopi, Abbates et
Priores superioris domus conuocationis, siue sacre synodi
Cantuariensis provincie, In domo Capitulari Ecclesie
Cathedralis diui Pauli London. in presentia Reueren-
dissimi in Christo patris et domini, domini Thome, permissione diuina Cant. archiepiscopi, totius Anglie Pri-
matis, et Metropolitani legitime congregati, unanimi
eorum consensu pariter et assensu consentiebant, quod
dictus Reuerendissimus pater apud Illustrissimum in
Christo Principem et dominum nostrum, dominum

1531) he published there a translation of ' the prophet Isaye '.
Of these two leaves of Genesis, copies of which Joye sent from
Barrow (i. e. Bergen-op-Zoom), Humphrey Wanley, Harley's
librarian, is said to have possessed an example.   Joye aided
Tyndale in his controversy with More, but the tone of Tyndale's
reference here printed suggests that the latter thought his action
ill considered, and the two men came into violent collision the
next year (see No. XXVII).

Henricum, Dei gratia Anglie et Francie regem, fidei de-
fensorem, et dominum Hiberniae, Ecclesiaeque Angli-
cane (sub Deo) caput supremum, instantiam faceret,
quatenus sua regia maiestas dignaretur pro augmento
fidei subditorum suorum decernere et mandare, Quod
omnes et singuli subditi sui, penes quos aut in quorum
possessione aliqui libri suspecte doctrine existunt, pre-
sertim in lingua vulgari, citra aut ultra mare impressi,
moneantur et cogantur eosdem suspecte doctrine libros
infra tres menses a tempore monitionis in ea parte
facte, coram personis per regiam majestatem nominandis
presentare, et realiter exhibere, sub certa pena per regiam
maiestatem moderanda, et limitanda. Et quod ulterius
sua regia maiestas dignaretur decernere, quod sacra
Scriptura in vulgarem linguam Anglicanam, per quos-
dam probos et doctos viros per dictum illustrissimum
regem nominandos transferatur, et populo pro eorum
eruditione deliberetur et tradatur. Ac insuper quatinus
sua Regia maiestas dignaretur prohibere et mandare,
etiam Indicta et imposita pena, ne quisquam laicorum
aut secularum subditorum suorum de fide catholica aut
articulis fidei, sacrave scriptura, aut eiusdem intellectu
publice disputare, aut aliquo modo rixose contendere
presumat infuturum.

TRANSLATION

The petition of the synod of the province of Canterbury concerning the declaring suspected books and the
translation of the Bible into English.

On the 19th day of December, in the year of the Lord
one thousand five hundred and thirty four, the Bishops,
Abbots and Priors of the upper house of convocation,
otherwise the sacred synod of the province of Canterbury in the chapter house of the Cathedral Church of

S. Paul, London, in the presence of the most reverend
father in Christ and lord, the lord Thomas, by divine permission archbishop of Canterbury, Primate of all England
and Metropolitan, lawfully assembled, unanimously alike
by consent and assent agreed that the said most reverend
father should make instance to the most illustrious prince
in Christ and our lord, the lord Henry, by the grace of
God, King of England and France, defender of the faith,
and lord of Ireland, and (under God) supreme head of the
English Church, that his royal majesty should think fit
for the increase of the faith of his subjects to decree and
command that all and singular his subjects, in whose
keeping or possession are any books of suspected doctrine, more especially in the vulgar tongue, whether
printed here or beyond the sea, be admonished and compelled to show and actually declare [1] those books of suspected doctrine within three months from the date of
the admonishment being published in that district, before
persons to be named by the king's majesty, under
a fixed penalty to be controlled and limited by the
king's majesty. And that furthermore the king's majesty
should think fit to decree that the holy scripture shall be
translated into the vulgar English tongue by certain
upright and learned men to be named by the said most
illustrious king [2] and be meted out and delivered to the
people for their instruction. And moreover that his
royal majesty should think fit to forbid and command,
with a penalty assigned and imposed, that no layman or
secular person among his subjects should for the future
presume publicly to dispute or in any manner to wrangle
concerning the catholic faith, or the articles of the faith,
the Holy Scripture or its meaning.

[1] 'realiter exhibere,' they were to produce the books.
[2] Compare No. XXIX and note.

XXVII. GEORGE JOYE'S UNAUTHORIZED REVISION OF TYNDALE'S NEW TESTAMENT

A. Tyndale's Complaint

From a supplementary preface to Tyndale's revised New Testament, Antwerp, Martin Keysere, November 1534.

Willyam Tindale, yet once more to the christen reader

THou shalt vnderstonde moost dere reader, when I had taken in hande to looke ouer the new testament agayne and to compare it with the greke, and to mende whatsoeuer I coulde fynde amysse and had almost fynesshed the laboure : George Ioye secretly toke in hand to correct it also by what occasyon his conscyence knoweth : and preuented[1] me, in so moche, that his correccyon was prynted in great nombre, yer[2] myne. beganne. When it was spyed and worde brought me ; though it semed to dyuers other that George Joye had not vsed the offyce of an honest man, seinge he knewe that I was in correctynge it myselfe : nether dyd walke after the rules of that loue and softenes which christ, and his disciples teache vs, how that we shuld do nothynge of stryfe to moue debate, or of vayne glorie or of couetousnes. Yet I toke the thinge in worth as I have done dyuers other in tyme past, as one that have moare experyence of the nature and dysposicion of the mannes conplexion, and supposed that a lytle spyse of couetousnes and vayne glorie (two blynde gydes) had bene the onlye cause that moued him so to do, aboute which thynges I stryue with no man : and so folowed after and corrected forth & caused this

---

[1] Forestalled. Joye's edition appeared in August, Tyndale's in November.   [2] before.

to be prynted, without surmyse or lokynge on his correctyon.

But when the pryntynge of myne was almost fynesshed, one brought me a copie and shewed me so manye places, insoche wyse altered that I was astonyd and wondered not a lytle what furye had dryuen him to make soche chaunge and to call it a diligent correction. For thorow oute Mat. Mark & Luke perpetually : and ofte in the actes, and some-tyme in John and also in the hebrues, where he fyndeth this worde Resurreccion, he chaungeth it into the lyfe after this lyfe, or verie lyfe, and soche lyke, as one that abhorred the name of the resurreccion.

If that chaunge, to turne resurreccion into lyfe after this lyfe, be a dylygent correccion, then must my trans-lacion be fautie in those places, and saynt Jeromes, and all the translatours that euer I heard of in what tonge so euer it be, from the apostles vnto this his dylygent cor-reccyon (as he calleth it) which whither it be so or no, I permyt it to other mennes iudgementes.

But of this I chalenge George Joye, that he dyd not put his awne name thereto and call it rather his awne translacion : and that he playeth boo pepe, and in some of his bookes putteth in his name and tytle, and in some kepeth it oute. It is lawfull for who will, to translate and shew his mynde, though a thousand had translated before him. But it is not lawfull (thynketh me) ner yet expedyent for the edifienge of the vnitie of the fayth of christ, that whosoeuer will shall by his awne auctorite, take another mannes translacion and put oute and in and chaunge at pleasure, and call it a correccion.

Moreover, ye shall vnderstonde that George Joye hath had of a longe tyme marvelouse ymaginacions aboute this worde resurreccion, that it shuld be taken for the state of the soules after their departinge from their

bodyes, and hath also (though he hath been reasoned with
thereof and desyred to cease) yet sowen his doctryne by
secret lettres on that syde the see, and caused great
division amonge the brethren.   In so moche that John
Fryth beynge in preson in the toure of London, a lytle
before his death, wrote that we shuld warne him and
desyer him to cease, and wolde have then wrytten agaynst
him, had I not withstonde him.   Therto I have been
sence informed that no small nomber thorow his
curiositie,[3] vtterly denye the resurreccion of the fleshe
and bodye, affirminge that the soule when she is departed,
is the spirituall bodye of the resurreccion, & other resurreccion shall there none be.   And I have talked with
some of them myselfe, so doted in that folye, that it
were as good perswade a post, as to plucke that madnes
oute of their braynes.   And of this all is George Joyes
vnquyet curiosite the hole occasion, whether he be of
the sayde faccion also, or not, to that let him answere
him selfe.

If George Joye wyll saye (as I wot well he will) that
his chaunge, is the sence and meaninge of those scriptures.
I answer it is soner seyde then proved :   howbeit let
other men iudge :   But though it were the verie meaninge
of the scripture :   yet if it were lawfull after his ensample
to every man to playe boo pepe with the translacions
that are before him, and to put oute the wordes of the text
at his pleasure and to put in everywhere his meaninge ;
or what he thought the meaninge were, that were the
next waye to stablyshe all heresyes and to destroye the
grounde wherewith we shuld improve them.   As for an
ensample, when Christ sayeth Jo : v. The tyme shall
come in the which all that are in the graves shall heare
his voyce and shall come forth ; they that have done good

[3] Fancifulness.

vnto resurreccion of lyfe, or with the resurreccion of lyfe,
and they have done evell, vnto the [resu]reccion or with
the resurreccion of damnacion ; George Joyes correccion
is, they that have done good shall come forth into the
verie lyfe, and they that have done evell into the life of
damnacion, thrustinge cleane oute this worde resurreccion.
Now by the same auctorite, and with as good reason
shall another come and saye of the rest of the text, they
that are in sepulchres, shall heare his voyce, that the
sence is, the soules of them that are in the sepulchres
shall heare his voyce, and so put in his diligent correccion
and mocke oute the text, that it shall not make for the
resurreccion of the flesshe, whiche thinge also George
Joyes correccion doth manyfestlye affirme.   If the text
be lefte vncorrupt, it will pourge hir selfe of all maner
false gloses, how sotle soever they be fayned, as a sethinge
pot casteth vp hir scome.   But yf the false glose be made
the text, diligentlye oversene and correct,[4] wherewith then
shall we correcte false doctrine and defende Christes flocke
from false opinions, and from the wycked heresyes of raven-
inge of wolves ;   In my mynde therfore a lytle vnfayned
love after the rules of Christ, is worth moche hie learninge,
and single and sleyght vnderstondinge that edifieth in
vnitie, is moche better then sotle curiosite, and mekenes
better then bolde arrogancye and stondinge over moche
in a mannes awne consayte.

Wherfore, concernynge the resurreccion, I protest
before god and oure savioure Jesus Christ, and before
the vniversall congregacion that beleveth in him, that
I beleve accordynge to the open and manyfest scriptures
and catholyck fayth, that Christ is rysen agayne in the
flesshe which he receaved of his mother the blessed

---

[4] The words 'diligentlye oversene and correct' should be read
as a sarcastic quotation.   These sentences sum up Tyndale's case.

virgin marie, and bodye wherin he dyed. And that we shall all both good and bad ryse both flesshe and bodye, and apere together before the iudgement seat of christ, to receave every man accordynge to his dedes. And that the bodyes of all that beleve and contynew in the true fayth of christ, shalbe endewed with lyke immortalyte and glorie as is the bodye of christ.

And I protest before God and oure savioure Christ and all that beleve in him, that I holde of the soules that are departed as moche as maye be proved by manifest and open scripture, and thinke the soules departed in the fayth of Christ and love of the lawe of God, to be in no worse case then the soule of Christ was, from ye tyme that he delivered his sprite into the handes of his father, vntyll the resurreccion of his bodye in glorie and immortalite. Neverthelater, I confesse openly, that I am not persuaded that they be all readie in the full glorie that Christ is in, or the elect angels of god are in. Nether is it anye article of my fayth : for if it so were, I se not but then the preachinge of the resurreccion of the flesshe were a thinge in vayne. Notwithstondinge yet I am readie to beleve it, if it maye be proved with open scripture. And I have desyred George Joye to take open textes that seme to make for that purpose, as this is, To daye thou shalt be with me in Paradise, to make therof what he coulde, and to let his dreames aboute this worde resurreccion goo. For I receave not in the scripture the pryvat interpretacion of any mannes brayne, without open testimony of eny scriptures agreinge thereto.

Moreover I take God (which alone seeth the heart) to recorde to my conscience, beschinge him that my parte be not in the bloude of Christ, if I wrote of all that I have wrytten thorow oute all my boke, ought of an evell purpose, of envie or malice to anye man, or to stere vp any false doctrine or opinion in the churche of Christ, or to be auctor of any secte, or to drawe disciples after me, or that I wolde be estemed or had in pryce above the least chylde that is borne, save onlye of pitie and compassion I had and yet have on the blindnes of my brethren, and to bringe them vnto the knowledge of Christ, and to make every one of them, if it were possible as perfect as an angell of heaven, and to wede oute all that is not planted of oure hevenly father, and to bringe doune all that lyfteth vp it selfe agaynst the knowledge of the salvacion that is in the bloude of Christ. Also, my parte be not in Christ, if myne heart be not to folowe and lyve accordinge as I teache, and also if myne heart wepe not nyght and daye for myne awne synne and other mennes indifferentlye, beseching God to convert vs all, and to take his wrath from vs, and to be mercifull as well to all other men, as to myne awne soule, caringe for the welth of the realme I was borne in, for the kinge and all that are therof, as a tender hearted mother wolde do for hir only sonne.

As concerninge all I have translated or other wise written, I beseche all men to reade it for that purpose I wrote it : even to bringe them to the knowledge of the scripture. And as farre as the scripture approveth it, so farre to alowe it, and if in anye place the worde of God dysalow it, there to refuse it, as I do before oure savyour Christ and his congregacion. And where they fynde fautes let them shew it me, if they be nye, or wryte to me, if they be farre of : or wryte openly agaynst it and improve it, and I promyse them, if I shall perceave that there reasons conclude I will confesse myne ignoraunce openly.

Wherfore I beseche George Joye, ye and all other to, for to translate the scripture for them selves, whether oute of Greke, Latyn or Hebrue. Or (if they wyll nedes) as the foxe when he hath pyssed in the grayes [5] hole chalengeth it for his awne, so let them take my translacions and laboures, and chaunge and alter, and correcte and corrupte at their pleasures, and call it their awne translacions, and put to their awne names, and not to playe boo pepe after George Joyes maner. Which whether he have done faythfully and truly, with soche reverence and feare as becommeth the worde of God, and with soche love and mekenes and affeccion to vnite and circumspexcion that the vngodlye have none occasion to rayle on the verite, as becommeth the servauntes of Christ, I referre it to the iudgmentes of them that knowe and love the trouth. For this I protest, that I provoke not Joye ner any other man (but am prouoked, and that after the spytfullest maner of provokynge) to do sore agaynst my will and with sorow of harte that I now do. But I nether can ner will soffre of anye man, that he shall goo take my translacion and correct it without name, and make soche chaungynge as I my selfe durst not do, as I hope to have my parte in Christ, though the hole worlde shuld be geven me for my laboure.

Finally that new Testament thus dyligently corrected, besyde this so ofte puttinge oute this worde resurreccion, and I wote not what other chaunge, for I have not yet reede it over, hath in the ende before the Table of the Epistles and Gospelles this tytle :

(Here endeth the new Testament dylygentlye ouersene and correct and printed now agayne at Andwarp, by me wydow of Christophell of Endhouen. In the yere of oure Lorde. A.M.D. xxxiiii in August) Which tytle (reader) I have here put in because by this thou shalt knowe the booke the better. Vale.

[5] A badger.

B. George Joye's Answer

From Joy's second edition. Antwerp, by Catharyn (wydow of Christoffel of Endhouen), January 9, 1535,[1] sigs. C 7–C 8 recto.

Vnto the Reader

Thus endeth the new Testament prynted after the copye corrected by George Joye : wherin for englisshyng thys worde Resurrectio, the lyfe after this. W. Tindale was so sore offended that he wrote hys vncharitable

[1] As this edition has only recently come to light I append a collation.

Title missing.—Colophon : ❧ The ende of the hole new Testamēt | with the Pistles taken out of the olde | Testament/ to be red in the chirche | certayn dayes thorowt the year. | Prynted now agayne at Ant- | werpe by me Catharyn wy- | dowe [of Christoffel of Endhouen] in the yere of oure | lorde. M.CCCCC, and | xxxv, the ix. daye of | Januarye.

472 leaves. Sigs. : + a–z, A–H, Aa–Xx, Aaa–Ccc, A–C in eights. 32 lines to a page. 16°.

[Title ✠ 1ᵃ ; Almanacke ✠ 1ᵇ ;] Kalendar [✠ 2ᵃ]–✠ 7ᵇ ; The Gospell of S. Matthew &c. to end of the Actes ✠ 8ᵇ–Xx8ᵇ ; title to the Epistles of the Apostle of S. Paul, within a border containing the mark c | E Aa1ᵃ, verso blank ; The Epistles &c. Aa 2ᵃ–[Bbb 1ᵇ] ; Table/ wherein you shall fynde/ the Pistelys to the Gospellys after the vse/ of Sarysbuery. Bbb ii–[Ccc 6ᵇ], followed by Ccc 7 and 8, which may have been both blank ; [? Title to the Pistles taken out of the olde Testament] A1 ; heading to the Pistles and text A2ᵃ–C6ᵇ ; Vnto the Reader, C7ᵃ–C8ᵃ ; Colophon, C8ᵇ.

The heading to the Epistles reads as follows :

❧ Here folow the pistles | taken out of the olde Testament/ to be | red in the chyrche certayn dayes tho : | rowt the year : trāslated by George Jo- | ye/ ɀ cōpared with the Pistles pointed | forth ād red in the messe boke/ and also | withe the chapiters alleged in the By- | ble : so that nowe here they maye be fo- | unde easlyer then euer before. Whiche | thys my laboure in translatyng these | pistles in correcking ɀ redressing them | to make them correspondent wyth the chapters alleged in the byble/ ād with | the pistles red in the chirche/ whe- | ther yt be

pistle agenst me prefixed [to] his newe corrected testament, prynted 1534. in Nouember, entytled. W. T.
yet once more to the Christen redere.   Which pistle
W. T. hath promysed before certayne men and me (or els
I wolde my selfe haue defended my name and clered
myselfe of those lyes and sclaunders there writen of me)
that he wolde calle agene his Pystle and so correcte
yt, redresse yt, and reforme yt accordinge to my mynde
that I shulde be therewyth contented, and vs bothe
(as agreed) to salute the readers withe one salutacion in
the same reformed pistle to be set before his testament
now in printing.   And that I, for my parte shulde
(a rekeninge and reson firste geuen of my translacion of
the worde) permyt yt vnto the iudgement of the lerned
in christis chirche.   Which thynge, verely I do not onely
gladly consent there to, vpon the condicion on his parte,
but desyer them all to iuge expende and trye all that
euer I haue or shall wryte, by the scriptures.

Let yt not therfore in the mean ceason offende the
(good indifferent reder) nor yet auerte thy mynde nether
from W. Tindale nor fro me : nor yet from redyng our
bokis whiche teche and declare the very doctryne and
Gospel of Christe, because yt thus chaunceth vs to varye
and contende for the trewe englisshing of this one worde
Resurrectio in certayne places of the newe Testament.
For I doubt not but that God hathe so prouyded yt,
that our stryfe and dyssent shalbe vnto hys chirche the
cause of a perfayter concorde and consent in thys mater,
Noman to thinke hence forth that the soulis departed
slepe with out heauen feling nether payne nor ioye vntill

more diligent then | hathe ben shewd hitherto/ | let the indifferent
re- | ders be iuges.

The unique copy in the British Museum wants sigs+ 1, 2, Ee 1
Bbb 1, Bbb 8–Ccc 2, Ccc 6–8, A 1.

domes daye as the Anabaptistis dreame but to be a lyue
in that lyfe after thys whithe, and in Christe in blysse
and ioye in heuen, as the scriptures clerely testifye.
Whych verite and true doctrine off Christe and his
apostles, as yt is a swete and present consolacion vnto the
pore afflicte persecuted and trowbled in thys worlde for
Christis sake when they shall dye, so doeth the tother
false opinion and erroneouse doctryne, that is to weit,
that they sleap out of heauen nether feling payn nor
ioye, minyster and geue perellous audacite and bolde
suernes to the vngodly here to lyue styl and continew in
their wickednes, sith they se and be so taught that after
their departing there is no punysshment but sleap and
reste as wel as do the soulis of the good and ryghteous
tyll domes daye. Which daye as some of them beleue
it to be very longe ere yt come, so do many of them
beleue that yt shal neuer come. Also to stryue for the
knowlege of the trowth with a meke and godly contencion
hathe happened vnto farre perfayter men then we be
bothe, Nether haue there bene euer any felowship so
fewe and smal, but some tyme syche breache and imper-
feccion hath hapened emonge them for a lytle ceason
(as I trust in god this shal not continew longe betwene
vs two) ye and that euen emonge the apostles as betwene
Paule and Peter, and Paule and Bernabas. This thing
(I saye) may fall vpon vs also to lerne men that all men
be but lyers and maye erre, and to warne vs that we
depende not wholl vpon any mannis translacion nor hys
doctryne nether to be sworne nor addicte to any mannis
lerning, make he neuer so holye and deuoute protestacions and prologs, but to mesure all mennis wrytingis,
workis and wordis wyth the infallible worde off God
to whom be prayse and glory for euer.

Amen.

C. The Reconciliation breaks down

Extracts from An Apologye made by George Joye to satisfye
(if it may be) W. Tindale of hys new Testament, 1535. (Unique
copy at the University Library, Cambridge, Sayle 568.)

How we were once agreed.

After that w. Tyndale had putforth in prynt and
thrusted his vncharitable pystle into many mennis
handis, his frendis and myne vnderstanding that I had
prepared my defence to pourge and clere my name
whyche he had defamed and defiled, called vs togither
to moue vs to a concorde and peace, where I shewed
them my grete greif and sorowe, for that he shulde so
falsely belye and sclaunder me of syche crymes which
I neuer thought, spake, nor wrote, and of siche which
I knowe wel his owne conscience doth testifye the
contrarie, euen that I denied the Resureccion of the
bodie, but beleue it is constantly as himselfe : and this
with other haynous crymes whiche he impingeth vnto
me in his pistle, nether he nor no man els shall neuer
proue : wherfore except Tin. (sayd I) wil reuoke the
sclaunders fayned vpon me hym self, I wyl (as I am
bounde) defende my fame and name, whiche there is
nothyng to me more dere and leif And to be shorte
aftir many wordis : It was thus thorowe the mocion of
our frendis concluded for our agrement and peace :

That I shulde for my parte (a reason
and rekenyng firste geuen why I
translated this worde Resurrectio into
the lyfe after this) permyt and leaue my translacion vnto
the iugement of the lerned in christis chirche. And T.
on his parte shuld cal agein his pistle into his hand,
so to redresse it, reforme it, and correcke it from siche

The condycions
of oure agrement.

sclaunderous lyes as I was therwith offended and he
coude not iustifye them, that I shulde be therwith wel
contented, T. addyng with hys own mouthe that we
shulde with one accorde in his next testament then in
printing in the stede of this vncharitable pistle wherwith I was offended, salute the reders with one comon
salutacion to testifye our concorde : of these condicions we departed louyngly. Then after .v. or vj. dayes
I came to Tin. to se the correccion and reformacion of
hys pistle, and he sayd he neuer thought of it sence,
I prayd him to make yt redy shortely (for I longed sore
to se it) and came agene to him after .v. or .vj. dayes.
Then he sayd it was so wryten that I coude not rede it :
and I sayd I was wel aquainted with his hande and
shulde rede it wel ynough : but he
wolde not let me se it. I came agene   Tindal first
the thirde tyme desyring him to se it,   breaketh hys promyse.

but then had he bethought him of this cauyllacion contrary to the condicions of our agrement, that he wolde
firste se my reasons and wryte agenst them ere I shulde
se this his reformacion and reuocacion. Then thought I,
syth my parte and reasons be put into the iugement of
the lerned, T. ought not to write agenst them tyl their
iugement be done, no nor yet then nether, syth he is
content before these men to stonde to their iugement,
and not to contende any more of thys mater withe me.
yet I came agene the fourthe tyme, and to be shorte :
he persisted in his laste purpose and wolde fyrste se my
reasons and wryte agenst them and then leaue the
mater to the iugement of Doctour Barnes [1] and of his
felowe called Hijpinus pastour of s. nicholas parisshe in
Hambourg, adding that he wolde reuoke that euer he

----

[1] Robert Barnes, formerly Prior of the Cambridge Augustinians,
burnt in 1540.

wrote that I shulde denye the resurreccion. Then I tolde
one of the men that was present at the condicions of
our agrement all this mater : and wrote vnto the other
these answers that I had : so ofte seking vpon T. to be
at peace and to stande to hys promyse, desyering them
al to moue him and aduyse him to holde his promyse,
or els, if he wolde not, them not to blame me thoughe
I defende my selfe and clere my fame whiche he hath
thus falsely and vncharitably denigrated, deformed, and
hurte. But in conclusion I perceyued that T. was half
ashamed to reuoke according to his promyse al that he
coude not iustifye by me, and with whiche I was so
offended. wherfore sythe he wolde not kepe promyse,
I am compelled to answere here now for my selfe :
which I desier euery indifferent reder to iuge indifferently.

D. JOYE'S NARRATIVE

From the same, ff. 19–23.

Lo good Reder, here mayst thou se of what nature
and complexion T. is so sodenly fyercely and boldely

to choppe in to any mannis conscience

*Nolite iudicare
vt non iudicemini.*

and so to vsurpe and preuent the
office of god in iugment which is onely
the enseer and sercher of herte and mynde. Thys
godly man, iugeth and noteth me vayngloriouse curiouse
and couetouse, and al for correcking a false copie of
the testament that thei mought be the trwelyer printed
agen, and so not so many false bokis solde into the
realme to the hurt and deceyt of the byers and reders of
them. I correcked but the false copye wherby and aftir
whyche the printer dyd sette his boke and correcked
the same himself in the presse.

But I shall now playnly and sengly (for the trowth knoweth no fucated polesshed and paynted oracion) declare vnto euery man, wherof, howe, and by whom I was moued and desyered to correcke this false copie that shulde els haue brought forth mo then two thousand falser bokes more then euer englond had before.

First, thou shalt knowe that Tindal aboute .viij. or .ix. yere a goo translated and printed the new testament in a mean great volume,[1] but yet wyth oute Kalender, concordances in the margent, and table in thende. And a non aftir the dwche men [2] gote a copye and printed it agen in a small volume adding the kalendare in the begynning, concordances in the margent, and the table in thende. But yet, for that they had no englisshe man to correcke the setting, thei themselue hauyng not the knowlege of our tongue, were compelled to make many mo fautes then were in the copye, and so corrupted the boke that the simple reder might ofte tymes be taryed and steek. Aftir this thei printed it agein also without a correctour in a greatter letter and volume with the figures in thapocalipse whiche were therfore miche falser then their firste.[3] when these two pryntes (there were of them bothe aboute v. thousand bokis printed) were al soulde more then a twelue moneth a goo, Tind. was pricked forthe to take the testament in hande, to print it and correcke it as he professeth and promyseth to do in the later ende of his first translacion.[4] But T. pro-

---

[1] A mean great volume, apparently the Worms octavo of 1526.

[2] Christoffel and Hans van Endhoven in their Antwerp edition of 1526.

[3] This may be the edition of 1532 of which Dr. Angus possessed a mutilated title-page, a tracing from which was reproduced by Mr. Demaus in his *Life of Tyndale*.

[4] i. e. in the Epilogue to the Worms octavo. See No. X.

longed and differred so necessary a thing and so iust desyers of many men. In so miche that in the mean season, the dewch men prynted it agen the thyrde tyme in a small volume lyke their firste prynt, but miche more false than euer it was before. And yet was T. here called vpon agen, seyng there were so many false printed bokis stil putforth and bought vp so fast (for now was ther geuen thanked be god a lytel space to breath and reste vnto christis chirche aftir so longe and greuouse persecucion for reading the bokes) But yet before this thyrd tyme of printing the boke, the printer desiered me to correcke it: And I sayd It were wel done (if ye printed them agene) to make them truer, and not to deceiue our nacion with any mo false bokis, neuertheles I suppose that T. himself wil put it forth more perfait and newly corrected, which if he do, yours shalbe naught set by nor neuer solde. This not with-standing yet thei printed them and that most false and aboute .ij. M. bokis, and had shortly solde them all. Al this longe while T. slept, for nothing came from him as farre as I coude perceiue. Then the dewche began to printe them the fowrth tyme because thei sawe noman els goyng aboute them, and aftir thei had printed the first leif which copye a nother englissh man had correcked to them, thei came to me and desiered me to correcke them their copie, whom I answered as before, that if T. amende it with so gret diligence as he promysethe, yours wilbe neuer solde. Yisse quod thei, for if he prynte .ij. m. and we as many, what is so litle a noumber for all englond? and we wil sel ours beter cheape,[5] and therfore we doubt not of the sale: so that I perceyued well and was suer, that whether I had correcked theyr copye or

[5] Joye apparently saw nothing objectionable in this intention to undersell Tyndale's own revision.

not, thei had gone forth with their worke and had geuen
vs .ij.m. mo bokis falselyer printed then euer we had before. Then I thus considred with myself : englond hath
ynowe and to many false testaments and is now likely
to haue many mo : ye and that whether T. correck his
or no, yet shal these now in hand goforth vncorrecked
to, except some body correck them : And what T. dothe
I wote not, he maketh me nothing of his counsel, I se
nothyng come from him all this longe whyle. wherin
with the helpe that he hathe, that is to saye one bothe
to wryte yt and to correcke it in the presse, he myght
haue done it thryse sence he was first moued to do
it. For T. I know wel was not able to do yt with out
siche an helper which he hathe euer had hitherto.
Aftir this (I saye) consydered, the printer came to me
agen and offred me .ij. stuuers and an halfe for the
correcking of euery sheet of the copye, which folden
contayneth .xvj. leaues, and for thre stuuers which is
.iiij. pense halpeny starling, I promised to do it, so that
in al I had for my labour but .xiiij. shylyngis flemesshe,
which labour, had not the goodnes of the deede and
comon profyte and helpe to the readers compelled
me more then the money, I wolde not haue done yt
for .v. tymes so miche, the copie was so corrupt and
especially the table : and yet saith T. I did it of couetousnes : If this be couetousnes, then was Tindal moche more
covetouse, for he (as I her say) toke .x. ponde for his
correccion. I dyd it also, sayth he, of curiositie and
vaynglory, ye and that secretly : and did not put to
my name, whiche, I saye, be two euydent tokens that
I sought no vaynglory, for he that doth a thing secretly
and putteth out hys name, how seketh he vaynglory?
and yet is not the man ashamed to wryte that vaynglory
and couetousnes where my two blynde goides, but I tell

o

Tin. agen, that if malyce and enuy (for all his holy protestacions) had not bene his two blynde goidis, he wold neuer haue thus falsely, vncharitably, and so spightfully belyed and sclaundred me with so perpetual an infamie. Tin. saith I walked not aftir the rules of loue and softenes, but let men read how maliciously he belyeth and sclaundereth me for wel doing : and iuge what rule of loue and softnes he obseruethe. It is greate shame to the teacher when his owne deedis and wordis reproue and condempne himself : He hath grete experience of my natural disposicion and complexion saith he. But I wyll not be his Phisicion and decerne his water at this tyme. And as for his two disciplis that gaped so longe for their masters morsel that thei might haue the aduauntage of the sale of his bokis of which one sayd vnto me. It were almose [6] he were hanged that correcketh the testament for the dewch, and the tother harped on his masters vntwned string, saying that because I englissh Resurreccion the lyfe aftir this, men gatherd that I denied the general resurreccion : which errour (by their own sayng) was gathred longe before this boke was printed, vnto which ether of theis disciples I semed no honest man for correcking the copye, I wil not now name them, nor yet shew how one of them, neuer I dare say seyng s. Ierome de optimo genere interpretandi, yet toke vpon him to teche me how I shuld translat the scripturis, where I shuld geue worde for worde, and when I shulde make scholias, notis, and gloses in the mergent as himself and hys master doith. But in good faithe as for me I had as lief put the trwthe in the text as in the margent and excepte the glose expowne the text (as many of theirs do not) or where the text is playn ynough : I had as

* Almose, alms, a mercy.

lief leue sich fryuole gloses clene out. I wolde the scripture were so purely and playnly translated that it neded
nether note, glose nor scholia,[7] so that the reder might
once swimme without a corke. But this testament was
printed or T. was begun, and that not by my preuencion,
but by the printers quicke expedicion and T. own longe
sleaping, for as for me I had nothing to do with the
printing ther of, but correcked their copie only, as where
I founde a worde falsely printed, I mended it : and when
I came to some derke sentencis that no reason coude
be gathered of them whether it was by the ignorance
of the first translatour or of the prynter, I had the latyne
text by me and made yt playn : and where any sentence
was vnperfite or clene left oute I restored it agene : and
gaue many wordis their pure and natiue significacion
in their places which thei had not before. For my
conscience so compelled me to do, and not willingly and
wetingly to slip ouer siche fautis into the hurte of the
text or hinderance of the reder.

XXVIII. TYNDALE'S WORK AS A TRANSLATOR

From Halle's Chronicle, ' The Union of the two noble and
illustre families of Lancastre & Yorke.' London, R. Grafton,
1548, reign of Henry VIII, fol. CC.xxvii.

This yere in the moneth of September Wyllyam
Tyndale otherwyse called Hichyns was by the crueltie
of the clergie of Louayn condempned and burned in
a toune besyde Bruxelles in Braband called Vylford.
This man translated the New testament into Englishe
and fyrst put it in Prynt, and likewise he translated

[7] It is Joye who writes this, not Tyndale (cp. note to XXIII),
and he desired to make it possible by manipulating the text
according to his views. The text reads ' puerly and plyanly '.

O 2

the v. bookes of Moses, Iosua, Iudicum, Ruth, the bookes of the Kynges and the bookes of Paralipomenon, Nehemias or the fyrst of Esdras, the Prophet Ionas, and no more of the holy scripture. He made also diuers treatises, which of many were well lyked and highly praysed, and of many vtterly dispised and abhorred, and especially of the moste part of the bishoppes of this realme, who often by their great labours caused Proclamacions to be made against his bookes, and gatte them condempned and brent, aswell the Newe testament as other woorkes of his doynges . . .

XXIX. THE PROJECTED BISHOPS' VERSION

From Harley MS. 422, fol. 87. One of Fox's manuscripts.

The lyke fyne answer he[1] [Mr. Thomas Lawney] made of Bisshopp Stokeleys answer made to my Lorde of Cant. his letters requiryng his part of the translation of the new Testament.

My Lorde Cromwell mynding to haue the New Testament thoroughlie corrected, deuided the same into ix or x partes and caused yt to be written at large in paper bokes and sent vnto the best lernyd Bisshopps, and other lernyd men, tothintent thei sholde make a perfectt correccion thereof, and when thei hadd don to sende them vnto hym at Lambethe by a day lymyted for that purpose. It chanced that the Actes of the Apostells were sent to Bisshopp stokisley to ouersee and correcte than Bisshopp of London, When the day came euerymanne hadd sentt to Lambeth thair partes correcte,[2]

---

[1] Thomas Lawney was chaplain to the Duke of Norfolk.

[2] This seems highly improbable (cp. No. XXXIII). One bishop, however, Stephen Gardiner, performed his task, as on June 10, 1535, he wrote to Cromwell : ' I haue as gret cause as

onlie Stokisley's portion wanted, My Lorde of Cant. wrote to the Bisshopp lettres for his parte. requiring to delyuer them vnto the bringer this his Secretary. Bisshopp Stokesley being at Fulham receyued the lettres, vnto the whiche he made this answer, I maruaile what my Lorde of Canterbury meaneth, that thus abuseth the people in gyving them libertie to reade the scriptures, which doith nothing els but infect them with heryses, I haue bestowed neuer an howre apon my portion nor neuer will. And therfore, my lorde shall haue his boke againe, for I will neuer be gyltie to bring the simple people into error.

My Lorde of Cant. servaunte toke the boke, and brought the same to Lambeth vnto my Lorde, declaring my Lorde of London's answer. When my l. had perceyued that the Bisshopp hadd don nothing therein, I marvaile quod my Lorde of Cant. that my Lorde of London ys so frowarde, that he will not do as other men do. Mr Lawney stode by hearyng my lorde speake somoche of the Bisshopps vntowardnes, saied, I can tell your grace whie my Lorde will not bestowe any labor or payne this way. Your grace knoweth well (quod Lawney) that his portion ys a pece of Newe Testament, And than he being persuaded that Christe had bequeth hym nothing in his Testament, thoughte it were madnes to bestowe any labour or payne where no gayne was to be gotten, And besides this It ys the Actes of the Apostells, whiche were symple poore felowes, and ther-

---

any man to desire rest and quiet for the helth of my body; wherunto I thought to haue entended and to absteyne from bookes and wryting, hauing finished the translation of Saynt Luke and Saynt John, wherin I have spent a gret labour. (*State Papers of Henry VIII*, vol. i, p. 430. Printed ' From Crumwell's Correspondence in the Chapter House. Bundle W.')

fore my lord of London disdayned to haue to do with any of thair Actes.

My Lorde of Cant. and other that stode by coulde not forbere from lawghter to here Mr Lawney's accute invensyon in answeryng to the Bisshopp of London's frowarde answer to my lorde of Cant. lettres.

XXX.   FINANCIAL HELP GIVEN TO COVERDALE BY JACOB VAN METEREN

A

Part of a deposition of Jacob's son Emanuel in 1609, as to the Dutch Church in London, quoted from the transcript in 'The Marriage, Baptismal and Burials Registers of the Dutch Reformed Church, Austin Friars, London; edited by W. J. C. Moens.' Lymington, 1884.

Emanuel Demetrius, marchant of Andwarp, aged about 74 yeares, doth witnes and can depose. That he was brought in England Anno 1550 in King Edward's the 6 dayes, by his Father, a furtherer of reformed religion, and he that caused the first Bible at his costes to be Englisshed by Mr. Myles Coverdal in Andwarp, the which his father, with Mr. Edward Whytchurch, printed both in Paris and London,[1] by which meanes he, wel acquaynted, was one of the Suters for the erection of a Dutche Church at the Augustin Fryers and made this Deponent a member of the same Anno 1552.

And he doth wel remember that the Churchyeard and houses on bothe sydes of the West dore of the Church were inhabited and possessed by the Members of the

[1] There is an obvious confusion here between the 'first Bible' of 1535, which was certainly not printed at Paris and London, and the first Great Bible, which was begun at Paris and finished at London.

Church. And harde his sayd father and others of the
Elders of the Church often tymes consel of buylding
there [&c.] . . . Thus much I can depose, in London,
28 of May, 1609.   Emanuel Demetrius.

B

Part of ' Het leven ende sterven vanden eerweerden, vromen
ende vermaerden, Emanuel van Meteren, cortelijck beschreven
door sijnen ghetrouwen Vriendt, Simeon Ruytinck,' forming
an appendix to ' Emanuels van Meteren Historie der Neder-
landscher ende haerder Naburen Oorlogen ende geschiedenissen.'
In 's Graven-Haghe, 1614.

Emanuel van Meteren, die met grooten vlijt ende
vernuft desen Boeck by een versamelt was heeft, t'Antwerpen gheboren den 9. Iulij 1535.

Sijn Vader hiet Iacob van Meteren van Breda, Sone
van Cornelius van Meteren. Sijn Moeder hiet Ottilia
Ortels, docter van Willem Ortels van Ausborch, die
Groot-vader was, van den wijdt-beroemden Werelt
beschrijver, Abrahamus Ortelius.

Sijn Vader in sijn Ieucht hadde ghelurt die edele
Conste van't Letter setten, hy was begaeft met de
kennisse van veelderley talen ende andere goede weten-
schappen, wist van in die tijden t'licht t'onderscheyden
van dysternisse, ende bethoonde sijnen bysonderen yver
in't becostighen vande oversettinghe ende Druck vanden
Engelschen Bijbel binnen Antwerpen, daer toe ghe-
bruyckende den dienst van een gheleert Student met
namen Miles Couerdal, tot groote bevoorderinghe van het
Rijcke Iesu Christi in Enghelandt.

Translation

Emanuel van Meteren, who with great industry and
intelligence brought together the present book, was born
at Antwerp, 9 July, 1535.

His father, named Jacob van Meteren of Breda, was son of Cornelius van Meteren. His mother, named Ottilia Ortels, was daughter of Willem Ortels of Augsburg, the grandfather of the far-famed Cosmographer, Abraham Ortelius.

His father had taught him in his youth the noble art of letter-setting, and he was endowed with a knowledge of several languages and other useful sciences. He knew how to distinguish light from darkness, and showed his zeal more especially in bearing the cost of the translating and printing of the English Bible at Antwerp,[1] using for this purpose the services of a learned student named Miles Couerdale, to the great advancement of the kingdom of Jesus Christ in England.

XXXI. COVERDALE'S BIBLE, 1535

A

[END OF DEDICATION]

Considerynge now (most gracyous prynce) the inestimable treasure, frute & prosperite euerlastynge, that God geueth with his worde, and trustynge in his infynite goodnes that he wolde brynge my symple and rude laboure herin to good effecte, therfore as the holy goost moued other men to do the cost herof,[1] so was I boldened

---

[1] If this version of the Van Meteren legend were not at third hand, Ruytinck's version of Emanuel's recollections of what his father had told him, it would be entitled to some weight as evidence as to where the Bible of 1535 was printed. As it stands it can hardly be adduced as evidence of more than some general support of Coverdale.

[1] The plural here seems to negative any theory that Jacob van Meteren bore the whole expense, as has been contended. It is probable that Cromwell was one of Coverdale's instigators; whether he helped him with funds is much more doubtful.

in God, to laboure in the same.   Agayne, consyderynge
youre Imperiall maiestye not onely to be my naturall
soueraigne liege Lorde & chefe heade of the church of
Englonde, but also the true defender and maynteyner of
Gods lawes, I thought it my dutye, and to belonge vnto
my allegiaunce, whan I had translated this Bible, not
onely to dedicate this translacyon vnto youre highnesse,
but wholy to commytte it vnto the same : to the intent
that yf any thynge therin be translated amysse (for in
many thynges we fayle, euen whan we thynke to be sure)
it may stonde in youre graces handes, to correcte it, to
amende it, to improue it, yee and cleane to reiecte it, yf
youre godly wysdome shall thynke it necessary.   And
as I do with all humblenes submitte myne vnderstondynge, and my poore translacyon vnto the spirite of
trueth in your grace, so make I this protestacyon (hauyng
God to recorde in my conscience) that I haue nether
wrested nor altered so moch as one worde for the mayntenaunce of any maner of secte : but haue with a cleare
conscience purely and faythfully translated this out of
fyue sundry interpreters,[2] hauyng onely the manyfest
trueth of the scripture before myne eyes : Trustynge in
the goodnes of God, that it shalbe vnto his worshippe :
quietnes and tranquilite vnto your highnes : a perfecte
stablyshment of all Gods ordynaunces within youre
graces domynion : a generall comforte to all Christen
hertes, and a continuall thankfulnesse both of olde and
yonge vnto god, and to youre grace, for beynge oure
Moses, and for bringynge vs out of this olde Egypte from
the cruell handes of our spirituall Pharao.   For where
were the Iewes (by ten thousande partes) so moch bounde
vnto Kynge Dauid, for subduynge of greate Goliath, and
all theyr enemyes, as we are to your grace, for delyuerynge

[2] See Introduction, p. 12.

vs out of oure olde Babylonycall captiuyte ?[3] For the
whiche delyueraunce and victory I beseke oure onely
medyatoure Iesus Christ, to make soch meanes for vs
vnto his heauenly father, that we neuer be vnthankfull
vnto him, ner vnto youre grace : but that we euer
increace in the feare of him, in obedience vnto your
hyghnesse, in loue vnfayned vnto oure neghbours : and
in all vertue that commeth of God. To whom for the
defendynge of his blessed worde (by your graces most
rightfull administracyon) be honoure and thankes, glory
and dominyon, worlde without ende, Amen.

Youre graces humble sub-

iecte and daylye oratour,

Myles Couerdale.

B

[BEGINNING OF THE ADDRESS TO THE READER]

A prologe

Myles Couerdale Vnto the Christen reader

COnsiderynge how excellent knowlege and lernynge an
interpreter of scripture oughte to haue in the tongues,
and ponderyng also myne owne insufficiency therin, and
how weake I am to perfourme the office of translatoure,
I was the more lothe to medle with this worke. Notwith-
stondynge whan I consydered how great pytie it was
that we shulde wante it so longe, and called to my remembraunce the aduersite of them, which were not onely
of rype knowlege, but wolde also with all theyr hertes
haue perfourmed that they beganne, yf they had not had

---

[3] The phrase is from Luther's tract, *De Captiuitate Baby-
lonica Ecclesiae.*

impediment [1] : considerynge (I saye) that by reason of
theyr aduersyte it coulde not so soone haue bene broughte
to an ende, as oure most prosperous nacyon wolde fayne
haue had it : these and other reasonable causes consydered, I was the more bolde to take it in hande.   And
to helpe me herin, I haue had sondrye translacions, not
onely in latyn, but also of the Douche interpreters [2] :
whom (because of theyr synguler gyftes and speciall
diligence in the Bible) I haue ben the more glad to folowe
for the most parte, accordynge as I was requyred.[3]
But to saye the trueth before God, it was nether my
laboure ner desyre, to haue this worke put in my hande :
neuertheles it greued me that other nacyons shulde be
more plenteously prouyded for with the scripture in theyr
mother tongue, then we : therfore whan I was instantly
requyred, though I coulde not do so well as I wolde, I
thought it yet my dewtye to do my best, and that with
a good wyll.

where as some men thynke now that many translacyons make diuisyon in the fayth and in the people of
God, that is no[t] so : for it was neuer better with the
congregacion of god, then whan euery church allmost
had the Byble of a sondrye translacyon.   Amonge the
Grekes had not Origen a specyall translacyon ?   Had
not Vulgarius one peculyar, and lykewyse Chrysostom ?
Besyde the seuentye interpreters, is there not the translacyon of Aquila, of Theodotio, of Symachus, and of
sondrye other ?   Agayne amonge the Latyn men, thou
findest that euery one allmost vsed a specyall and sondrye
translacyon : for in so moch as euery bysshoppe had the

---

[1] The reference seems to be clearly to Tyndale, but Coverdale
must have begun his task long before Tyndale's arrest.

[2] See Introduction, p. 12.

   Compare the first note to the preceding section.

knowlege of the tongues, he gaue his diligence to haue
the Byble of his awne translacion. The doctours, as
Hireneus, Cyprianus, S. Iherome, S. Augustine, Hylarius
and S. Ambrose vpon dyuerse places of the scripture reade
not the texte all alyke.

Therfore oughte it not to be taken as euel, that soche
men as haue vnderstondynge now in our tyme, exercyse
them selues in the tongues, and geue their diligence to
translate out of one language in to another. Yee we
ought rather to geue god hye thankes therfore, which
thorow his sprete stereth vp mens myndes, so to exercise
them selues therin. wolde god it had neuer bene left of after
the tyme of S. Augustine, then shulde we neuer haue come
in to soch blindnes and ignoraunce, in to soch erroures
and delusyons. For as soone as the Byble was cast asyde,
and nomore put in exercyse, then beganne euery one of his
awne heade to wryte what so euer came in to his brayne
and that semed to be good in his awne eyes : and so
grewe the darknes of mens tradicions. And this same is
the cause that we haue had so many wryters, which
seldome made mencyon of the scripture of the Byble :
and though they some tyme aleged it, yet was it done so
farre out of season and so wyde from the purpose, that
a man maye well perceaue, how that they neuer sawe
the oryginall.

Seynge then that this diligent exercyse of translatynge
doth so moch good and edifyeth in other languages, why
shulde it do so euell in oures ? Doutles lyke as all
nacyons in the dyuersite of speaches maye knowe one
God in the vnyte of faith, and be one in loue : euen so
maye dyuerse translacyons vnderstonde one another,
and that in the head articles and grounde of oure most
blessed faith, though they vse sondrye wordes. wherfore
me thynke we haue greate occasyon to geue thankes

vnto God, that he hath opened vnto his church the gyfte
of interpretacyon and of pryntyng, and that there are
at this tyme so many, which with soch diligence and
faithfulnes interprete the scripture to the honoure of god
and edifyenge of his people, where as (lyke as whan many
are shutynge together) euery one doth his best to be
nyest the marke. And though they can not all attayne
therto, yet shuteth one nyer then another, and hytteth
it better then another, yee one can do it better then
another. who is now then so vnreasonable, so despytefull,
or enuyous, asto abhorre him that doth all his diligence
to hytte the prycke,[4] and to shute nyest it, though he
mysse and come not nyest the mark ? Ought not soch
one rather to be commended, and to be helped forwarde,
that he maye exercyse himselfe the more therin ?

For the which cause (acordyng as I was desyred)
I toke the more vpon me to set forth this speciall translacyon, not as a checker, not as a reprouer, or despyser
of other mens translacyons (for amonge many as yet
I haue founde none without occasyon of greate thankes-
geuynge vnto god) but lowly and faythfully haue I folowed
myne interpreters, and that vnder correccyon. And
though I haue fayled eny where (as there is noman but
he mysseth in some thynge) loue shall constyrre[5] all to
the best without eny peruerse iudgment. There is noman
lyuynge that can se all thynges, nether hath god geuen
eny man to knowe euery thynge. One seyth more
clearly then another, one hath more vnderstondyng then
another, one can vtter a thynge better then another,
but noman oughte to enuye, or dispyse another. He
that can do better then another, shulde not set him at
naught that vnderstondeth lesse : Yee he that hath the
more vnderstondyng, ought to remembre that the same

---

[4] The bull's eye.   [5] Construe, interpret.

gyfte is not his but Gods, and that God hath geuen it him to teach & enfourme the ignoraunt. Yf thou hast knowlege therfore to iudge where eny faute is made, I doute not but thou wilt helpe to amende it, yf loue be ioyned with thy knowlege. Howbeit wherin so euer I can perceaue by my selfe, or by the informacyon of other, that I haue fayled (as it is no wonder) I shall now by the helpe of God ouerloke it better and amende it.

XXXII. COVERDALE'S LATIN–ENGLISH NEW TESTAMENT FOLLOWING THE VULGATE TEXT

A. Dedication[1] to the First Edition Printed by J. Nycholson at Southwark

To the moost noble, moost gracious, and oure moost dradde soueraigne lord kynge Henry the eyght, kynge of Englande and of Fraunce, &c. Defender of Christes true fayth, and vnder God the chefe and supreme heade of the churche of Englande, Irelande, &c.

COnsyderynge (moost gracious Soueraigne) how louyngly, how fauourably, and how tenderly your hyghnesse hath taken myne infancy & rudenesse in dedicatynge the whole bible in Englysh to your moost noble grace. And hauyng sure experience also how benygne and gracious a mynde your hyghnes doth euer beare

---

[1] From the edition which Coverdale caused to be printed at Paris we learn that he supplied James Nycholson of Southwark with copy, but was obliged to leave the correction of the press in his hands. The result was an edition so incorrect that Coverdale repudiated it and printed a new edition, which he dedicated to Cromwell. Nothing daunted, Nycholson printed it a second time as ' Faythfully translated by Johan Hollybushe ' (cp. No. XVI A, note 2).

to all them that in theyr callyng are wyllynge to do theyr beste : It doth euen animate and encorage me now lyke-wyse to use the same audacite towarde your grace : Neuer intendyng nor purposynge to haue ben thus bold, yf your most noble kyndnes and princely benygnite had not forced me here vnto. This (doutles) is one of the chefest causes why I do now with moost humble obed-ience dedicate and offre this translacion of the new Testa-ment vnto your moost royall maiestye. And to saye the truth : I can not perceaue the contrary, but as many of vs as intende the glory of god haue all nede to commytte vnto your gracious protection and defence aswell our good doynges as our selues : Oure good doynges I meane, and not our euel workes. For yf we went aboute euel, god forbyd that we shuld seke defence at your grace. But euen our weldoynges, our good wylles and godly purposes, those with all humble obedience must we and do submytte to your graces moost sure protection. For as our aduer-sary the deuell walketh about lyke a roarynge lyon, and seketh whom he may deuoure. And as the enemies of Christ went aboute to tangle hymselfe in his wordes, and to hunt somwhat out of his owne mouth : Euen so do not the enemies of gods word ceasse yet to pycke quarels, and to seke out new occasions, how they may depraue and synistrally interprete our wel doynges. And where as with all faythfulnes we go about to make our brethren (youre graces louynge subiectes) participante of the frutes of oure good wylles, they yet not regardynge what profite we wolde be glad to do them, reporte euell of vs, sklaunder vs, and saye the worste of vs : Yee they are not ashamed to affirme, that we intende to peruerte the scripture, and to condemne the commune translacion in Latyn, whych costumably is red in the church : where as we purpose the cleane contrary. And because it greueth them that

your subiectes be growen so farre in knowlege of theyr
dewtye to God, to youre grace, and to theyr neghboures,
theyr inwarde malyce doth breake oute in to blasphemous
and vncomlye wordes, in so much that they cal your
louynge and faythfull people, heretikes, new fangled
fellowes, English biblers, coblers of diuinite, fellowes of
the new fayth &c, with such other vngodly sayenges.

How nedefull a thynge is it then for us to resorte vnto
the moost lawfull protection of God in youre graces
suppreme and imperiall authorite vnder hym ?   Without
the which moost lawfull defence now in these turbulent
and stormy assaultes of the wycked, we shuld be, but euen
Orphanes, and vtterly desolate of comforte.   But God
whom the scripture [2] calleth a father of the comfortles and
defender of wedowes, dyd otherwyse prouyde for us,
whan he made youre grace his hye supreme mynister
ouer vs.

To come now to the original and fyrst occasion of this
my moost humble laboure, and to declare howe lytle
I haue or do intende to despyse this present translation
in Latyn (or ony other in what language so euer it be)
I haue here set it forth and the Englysh also therof, I
mean the text which communely is called S. Hieroms, and
is costumably red in the church.   And thys (my moost
gracious Soueraigne) haue I done not so much for the
clamorous importunyte of euell speakers, as to satisfye
the iust request of certayne youre graces faythfull
subiectes.   And specially to induce and instructe such
as can but Englishe, and are not learned in the Latin, that
in comparynge these two textes together, they maye the
better vnderstonde the one by the other.   And I doute
not but such ignoraunt bodies as (hauynge cure and
charge of soules) are very vnlearned in the Latyn tunge,

[2] Marginal note : Ps. lxvii.

shall trough thys smal laboure be occasioned to atteyn
vnto more knowlege, and at the leest be constrayned to
saye well of the thynge, whyche here tofore they haue
blasphemed. The ignoraunce of which men yf it were
not so exceadyng great, a man wolde wonder what
shulde moue them to make such importune cauillacions
agaynst vs. It is to be feared, that frowardnesse and
malice is myxte with theyr ignoraunce. For in as much
as in our other translacions we do not followe thys olde
Latyn texte word for word they crye out vpon vs : As
though al were not as nye the truth to translate the
scripture out of other languages, as to turne it out of the
Latyn. Or as though the holy goost were not the
authoure of his scripture aswell in the Hebrue, Greke,
French, Dutche, and in Englysh, as in Latyn. The
scripture and worde of God is truly to euery Christen man
of lyke worthynesse and authorite, in what language so
euer the holy goost speaketh it. And therfore am I, and
wyl be whyle I lyue (vnder youre moost gracious fauoure
and correction) alwaye wyllynge and ready to do my best
aswell in one translation, as in another.

Now as concernynge thys present text in Latyn, for
asmuch as it hath bene and is yet so greatly corrupt, as
I thynke none other translacion is, it were a godly and
gracious dede, yf they that haue authorite, knowlege, and
tyme, wolde (vnder youre graces correction) examen it
better after the moost auncient interpreters and moost
true textes of other languages. For certaynly, in
comparynge dyuerse examplers together, we se, that in
many places one copye hath eyther more or lesse then
a nother, orels the texte is altered from other languages.

To geue other men occasion now to do theyr best, and
to expresse my good wyll, yf I could do better, I haue
for the causes aboue rehearsed, attempted this smal

P

laboure, submyttynge (with all humblenesse and sub-
iection) it and all other my lyke doinges, to your graces
moost noble Maiestye. Not onely because I am bounde
so to do, but to the intent also that through youre moost
gracious defence, it maye haue the more fredome amonge
your obedient subiectes, to the glory of the euerlastynge
God: To whom onely for your grace, for youre mooste
noble and deare sonne Prynce Edward, for youre moost
honourable counsell, and for all other hys syngular
gyftes that we daylye receaue in youre grace. To hym
I saye, which is the onely geuer and graunter of all thys
oure welth, be honoure and prayse for euermore. To
youre grace, continual thankfulnesse, and due obedience
with longe lyfe and prosperite : Fynally to vs the
receauers of gods good gyftes, be daylye increace of grace
and vertue more and more. Amen.

Youre graces humble
and faythfull subiecte

Myles Couerdale.

B. Preface to the same Edition
To the Reader

I Must nedes aduertise the (moost gentle Reader,) that
this present text in Latyn which thou seist set here
with the Englyshe, is the same that costumably is red
in the church, and communly is called S. Hieroms
translacion. Wherin though in some places I vse the
honest and iust libertye of a grammaryan (as nedeful is for
thy better vnderstondynge,) yet because I am lothe to
swarue from the texte, I so tempre my penne, that yf
thou wylt, thou mayest make playne construction of it,
by the Englyshe that standeth on the other syde. Thys
is done now for the that art not exactly learned in the

latyn tunge and woldest fayne vnderstonde it. As for
those that be learned in the latyn already, thys oure
small laboure is not taken for them, saue onely to moue
and exhorte them, that they lykewyse knowynge of
whome they haue receaued theyr talent of learnynge,
wyll be no lesse greued in theyr callyng to serue theyr
brethren therwith, than we are ashamed here with thys
oure small mynistracion to do them good. I besech
the therfore take it in good worth ; for so well done as
it shulde and myght be, it is not : But as it is, thou
hast it with a good wyll.

Where as by the authorite of the text I somtyme make
it cleare for thy more vnderstondyng, there shalt thou
fynde thys mark [   ] whych we haue set for thy
warnynge, the texte neuerthelesse nother wrested nor
peruerted. The cause wherof is partely the figure
called Eclipsis diuerse tymes vsed in the scriptures, the
which though she do garnysh the sentence in latyn, yet
wyll not so be admitted in other tunges : wherfore of
necessite we are constrayned to enclose suche wordes in
thys marke. Partely because that sundery, and sometyme to rash wryters out of bokes, haue not geuen so
greate diligence, as is due in the holy scripture, and haue
lefte out, and sometyme altered some word or wordes
and another vsynge thesame boke for a copy, hath
commytted lyke faut. Let not therfore thys oure
diligence seme more temerarious vnto the (gentle reader,)
than was the diligence of S. Ierome and Origene vnto
learned men of theyr tyme, which vsynge sundery
markes in theyr bokes, shewed theyr iudgmente what
were to be abated or added vnto the bokes of scripture,
that so they myghte be restored to the pure and very
originall texte. Thy knowlege and vnderstondynge in
the worde of God shall iudge thesame of vs also, yf it be

ioyned with loue to the truth.   And though I seme to be
al to scrupulous callyng it in one place penaunce, that
in another I call repentaunce :   and gelded, that another
calleth chaist, thys me thynk ought not to offende the
seynge that the holy goost (I trust) is the authoure of
both our doynges.   Yf I of myne owne heade had put
in to the new Testament these wordes : Nisi pœnitueritis
Pœnitemini, Sunt enim eunuchi, Pœnitentiam agite. &c.
then as I were worthy to be reproued, so shulde it be
ryght necessary to redresse thesame.   But it is the holy
gooste that hath put them in, and therfore I hartely
requyre the thynke nomore harm in me for callyng it in
one place penaunce, that in another I call repentaunce,
then I thynk harme in hym that calleth it chaist, which
I by the nature of thys worde *Eunuchus* cal gelded.
Let euery man be glad to submytte his vnderstondyng
to the holy goost in them that be learned and no doute
we shall thynk the best one by another, and fynde no
lesse occasion to prayse god in another man, then in our
selues.   As the holy goost then is one, workynge in the
and me as he wyl, so let us not swarue from that vnite,
but be one in him.   And for my parte I ensure the I am
indifferent to call it aswell with the one terme as with the
other, so longe as I knowe that it is no preiudice nor
iniury to the meanynge of the holy goost : Neuerthelesse
I am very scrupulous to go from the vocable of the text.

And of truth so had we all nede to be : For the worlde
is capcious, and many ther be that had rather fynde
xx fautes, then to amende one.   And ofte tymes the
more laboure a man taketh for theyr commodite, the
lesse thanke he hath.   But yf they that be learned and
haue wherwith to maynteyne the charges dyd theyr
dewty, they themselues shulde perfourme these thynges,
and not onely to loke for it at other mens handes.   At the

leest yf they wolde nother take the payne of translatynge
themselues, nor to beare the expenses therof, nor of the
pryntyng, they shulde yet haue a good tunge, and helpe
one waye, that they can not do another. God graunt
thys worlde once to spye theyr vnthankfulnesse. Thys
do not I saye for onye lucre or vauntage that I loke for
at your handes ye rych & welthy bellyes of the worlde :
for he that neuer fayled me at my nede, hath taught
me to be content with such prouision as he hath and
wyll make for me. Of you therfore that be seruauntes
to your owne ryches, requyre I nothynge at all, saue
onely that which S. Iames sayeth vnto you in the
begynnynge of hys fyfth chapter : Namely, that ye wepe
and howle on your wrechednesse that shall come vpon
you. For certaynly ye haue great cause so to do,
nother is it vnlyke but great misery shal come vpon
you, consyderynge the gorgious fare and apparell that
ye haue euery daye for the proude pompe and appetite
of your stynkynge carcases, and yet be not ashamed to
suffre youre owne fleshe and bloude to dye at youre dore
for lacke of your helpe. O synfull belly Gods. O vnthankfull wretches. O vncharitable Idolatrers. Wyth
what conscience darre ye put one morsell of meate in
to youre mouthes ? O abhominable helhoundes, what
shall be worth[1] of you ? I speake to you, ye ryche
nyggardes of the worlde, whych as ye haue no fauoure to
gods holy worde, so loue ye to do nothynge that it commaundeth. Our LORDE sende you worthy repentaunce.

But now wyll I turne my penne vnto you that be
lordes and rulers of youre ryches. For of you whom God
hath made stewardes of these worldly goodes. Of you
whom God hath made plenteous aswell in hys knowl[e]ge,
and in other ryches, of you (I saye) wolde I fayne

Become.

requyre and begge (euen for his sake that is the geuer
of all good thynges) that at the last ye wolde do but
youre dewty, and helpe aswell with youre good counsell
as with youre temperall substaunce, that a perfyte prouision maye be made for the poore, and for the vertuous
bryngynge vp of youth : That as we now already haue
cause plentyfull to geue God thankes for his worde and
for sendynge vs a prynce (with thousandes of other
benefytes) Euen so we seynge the poore, aged, lame,
sore, and syck prouided for, and oure youth brought vp
aswell in gods knowlege as in other vertuous occupations
maye haue lykewyse occasion sufficient to prayse God
for the same. Our LORD graunt that this oure longe
beggyng and moost nedeful request, may once be herde.
In the meane tyme tyll God brynge it to passe by his
ministers let not thy counsel nor helpe be behynde
(moost gentle Reader) for the furtheraunce of the same.
And for that thou hast receaued at the mercifull hande
of god already, be thankful alway vnto hym, louynge
and obedient vnto thy Prynce. And lyue so continually
in helpynge and edifyenge of thy neghbours, that it may
redounde to the prayse and glory of God for euer : **AMEN**.

XXXIII. THE LICENSING OF MATTHEW'S BIBLE

A LETTER FROM CRANMER TO CROMWELL, 4 AUGUST [1537]

From the original in the Record Office. (*Letters and Papers of the reign of Henry VIII*, 1537, vol. xii, pt. 2, 434.)

My especial good Lorde after moost hartie commendacions unto your Lordeship. Theis shalbe to signifie vnto
the same, that you shall receyue by the bringer herof,
a Bible in Englishe, both of a new translacion and of a

new prynte, dedicated vnto the Kinges Majestie, as farther apperith by a pistle vnto his grace in the begynnyng of the boke, which, in myn opinion is very well done, and therefore I pray your Lordeship to rede the same. And as for the translacion, so farre as I haue redde therof I like it better than any other translacion hertofore made ; yet not doubting but that ther may, and wilbe founde some fawtes therin, as you know no man euer did or can do so well, but it may be from tyme to tyme amendid. And forasmoche as the boke is dedicated vnto the kinges grace, and also great paynes and labour taken in setting forth the same, I pray you my Lorde, that you woll exhibite the boke unto the kinges highnes; and to obteign of his Grace, if you can, a license that the same may be sold and redde of euery person, withoute danger of any acte, proclamacion, or ordinaunce hertofore graunted to the contrary, vntill such tyme that we, the Bishops shall set forth a better translacion,[1] which I thinke will not be till a day after domesday. And if you con-tynew to take such paynes for the setting forth of goddes wourde, as you do, although in the meane season you suffre some snubbes, many sclandres, lyes, and reproches for the same, yet one day he will requite altogether ; and the same wourde (as Saincte John saieth) Whiche shall judge every man at the last daye must nedes shewe favour to theym, that now do favour it. Thus my Lorde, right hartely faire you well.

At Forde the 4th of August,

Your assured ever,

T. Cantuarien.

To the Right Honourable
and my especiall good Lorde
my Lorde Pryvye Seale.

[1] Cp. No. XXIX, note 2.

B. Cranmer to Cromwell, 13 August [1537]

From Cotton MS. Cleopatra E. v. 329 b. [348.]

My verey singuler good Lorde, in my moost hartie wise I commend me unto your Lordeship And whereas I vnderstande, that your Lordeship at my requeste hath not only exhibited the Bible which I sent vnto you, to the Kinges majestie, but also hath obteigned of his grace, that the same shalbe alowed by his auctoritie to be bowght and redde within this realme. My Lorde for this your payne, taken in this bihalf, I give vnto you my moost hartie thanks, assuryng your Lordeship for the contentacion of my mynde, you have shewed me more pleasour herin than yf you had given me a thowsande pownde ; and I doubt not but that herby such fruicte of good knowledge shall ensewe, that it shall well appere herafter, what high and acceptable service you have don unto godde and the King, whiche shall somoche redown to your honour, that, besides goddes reward you shall opteyn perpetuall memorye for the same within this Realme. And as for me, you may recken me your bonde-man for the same, and I dare be bold to say so may ye do my lorde of Wurcester. Thus my Lorde, right hartely faire you well. Att Forde the xiii day of Auguste.

Your own Bowndman ever

T. Cantuarien.

C. Cranmer to Cromwell. 28 August [1537]

From Cotton MS. Cleopatra E. v. 292.

My very singuler and especiall good Lorde in my most hartie wise I comend me to your Lordeship. Theis shalbe to give to you most hartie thanks that any harte can thinke, and that in the name of theym all which favoreth goddes wourde, for your Diligence at this tyme in procuring the Kinges highnes to set forth the said goddes wourd and his gospell by his graces auctoritie. For the whiche acte not only the Kinges maiestie, but also you shall have a perpetuall Lawde and memorye of all theym that be now or hereafter shalbe goddes faithfull people and the favorers of his wourde. And this dede you shall here of at the greate daye, whan all thinges shalbe opened and made manifest. For our Saviour Christ saieth in the said gospell, that whosoeuer shrynketh from hym and his wourde, and is abasshed to professe and sett it forth bifore men in this worlde, he will refuse hym at that day. And contrarye, whosoeuer constantly doth professe hym and his wourde, and studeth to sett that forwarde in this worlde, Christe will declare the same at the laste daye bifore hys father and all his Angells, and take upon hym the defence of those men. Theis shalbe farder to aduertise youre Lordeship that syns my last commyng frome London into Kent I have founde the people of my dioces very obstinately given to observe and kepe with solempnitie the halidayes lately abrogated.[1] Whereupon I have punisshed diuers of the offenders, and to diuers I have given gentill monition to amende . . . Whan shal we perswade the people to ceasse from kepynge theym. For the Kyngs own howse shalbe an example vnto all the realme to breake his own ordinances . . .

Thus my Lorde right hartely faire you well

At Forde the xxviij day of Auguste.

Your Lordeshipps own euer

T. Cantuarien.

[1] By the Injunctions of 1536, which were specially directed against ' holydayes in haruest time '.

D. RICHARD GRAFTON TO CROMWELL.
AUGUST 28, 1537

From Cotton MS. Cleopatra E. v. 330.

Moost humbly besechynge your lordship to vnderstand
that accordynge to your request, I haue sent your lordship vj bybles, which gladly I wolde haue brought my
selfe, but because of the sycknes which remayneth in the
cytie. And therfore I haue sent them by my servaunt
which this daye came out of Flaundyrs, requyrynge your
lordship yf I maye be so bolde as to desyer you to accept
them as my symple gyfte, geuen to you for those most
godly paynes,˙ for which the heuenly father is bounde
euen of his Justice to rewarde you with the euerlastynge
kyngdom of god. For your lordship mouynge our moost
gracyous prynce to the alowance and lycensynge of soche
a worke, hath worought soche an acte worthy of prayse,
as neuer was mencyoned in any cronycle in this realme.
And as my lorde of Cantorbury sayde The tydynges
therof dyd hym more good then the gyfte of ten thousand
pounde. Yet certen there are which beleue not that
yt pleased the kynges grace to lycence yt to go forth.
Wherfore yf your lordshippes pleasour were soche that
we myght have yt lycensed vnder your preuy seale.
Yt shuld be a defence at this present and in tyme to
come for all enemyes and aduersaryes of the same.
And for as moche as this request is for the mayneten-
aunce of the lordes worde, which is to mayntayne the
lorde him selfe. I feare not but that your lordship
wilbe ernest therin. And I am assewred that my lorde
of Cantorbury, Worsetter and Salsbury, will geue your
lordship soche thankes as in them lyeth and sewre ye

maye be that the heuenly lorde will rewarde you for
the establysshynge of his gloryous truthe. And what
youre lordshipes pleasor is in this request, yf it maye
please your lordship to enforme my seruaunt, I and
all that loue god hartely are bound to praye for your
preseruacyon all the dayes of our lyfe. At london
the xxviij daye of this present moneth of August 1537,

Your Orator whyle he lyueth

Rychard grafton grocer.

To the honorable lorde pryvayé Seale.

E. RICHARD GRAFTON TO CROMWELL, AFTER
AUGUST 28, 1537

From Cotton MS. Cleopatra E. v. 325.

Moost humbly besechynge your lordshippe to vnderstand that accordynge as your comyssyon was by my
seruaunt to sende you certen bybles, so have I now done,
desyrynge your lordship to accept them as though they
were well done. And where as I wryt vnto your lordship
for a preuye seale to be a defence vnto the enemyes of
this byble I vnderstonde that your lordshipes mynde is
that I shall not nede it. But now moost gracyous lorde,
for as moche as this worke hath bene brought forthe
to our moost great and costly laboures and charges, which
charges amount aboue the some of v c li., and I haue
caused of these same to be prynted to the some of xv c
bookes complete. Which now by reason that of many
this worke is commended, there are that will and dothe
go aboute the pryntynge of thesame worke againe in

a lesser letter,[1] to the entent that they maye sell their lytle bookes better chepe then I can sell these gret, and so to make that I shall sell none at all, or elles verye fewe, to the vtter vndoynge of me your orator and of all those my credytors that hath bene my comforters and helpers therin. And now this worke thus set forthe with great stodye and laboures shall soche persons (moued with a lytle couetousnes to the vndoynge of other for their owne pryuate welthe) take as a thynge don to their handes, in which halffe the charges shall not come to them that hath done to your poore orator. And yet shall they not do yt as they fynde yt, but falsefye the texte, that I dare saye, looke how many sentences are in the byble, euen [as] many fautes and errours shalbe made therin. For their sekyn [g] is not to set it out to goddes glorie and to the edefyenge of christ congregacyon (but for couetousnes) and that maye apere by the former bybles that they have set forthe, which hath nether good paper, letter, ynke ner correccyon,[2] Sir euyn so shall they corrupt this worke and wrapp yt vp after their fassyons, and then maye they sell yt for naught at their pleasor. Ye and to make yt more trewer then yt is, therfore douchemen [3] dwellynge within this realme go about the pryntyng of ytt, which can nether speke good englyshe, ner yet wryte none, and they wilbe bothe the prynters & correctors therof, because of a lytle couetousnes that wyll not bestow xx or xl li to a learned man to take payne in yt to haue yt well done. It were therfore (as your lordship

---

[1] Grafton probably feared competition from Nycholson.

[2] The reference is to Nycholson's quarto editions of Coverdale's Bible.

[3] This supports Mr. Gordon Duff's identification of Johan Hollybushe with Hans van Ruremond. See No. XVI A, note 2, and XXXII, note 1.

dothe euydently perceaue) a thynge vnreasonable to permyt or soffer them (which now hath no suche busynes) to enter into the laboures of them that hath had bothe sore trouble and vnreasonable charges. And the truthe is this that if yt be prynted by any other before these be solde (whiche I thynke shall not be this iij yere at the least) that then am I your poore Orator vtterly vndone.

Therfore by your moost godly fauor if I maye obtayne the kynges moost gracyous priuiledge that none shall prynt them tyll these be solde, which at the least shall not be this iij yere, your lordship shall not fynde me vnthankfull, but that to the vtter most of my power I wyll consyder yt, and I dare saye that so will my lorde of Cantorbury with other my moost speciall frendes. And at the least, god will loke vpon your mercifull heart that consydereth the vndoynge of a pore yonge man. For truly my whole lyuynge lyeth hervpon, which if I maye have sale of them, not beynge hyndered by any other man, yt shalbe my makyng and welthe, and the contrary is my vndoynge. Therfore most humbly I beseche your lordship to be my helper herin that I maye obtayne this my request. Or elles yf by no meanes this pryuyledge maye be had (as I have no dout thorow your helpe yt shall) and seinge men are so desyrous to be pryntynge of yt agayne to my vtter vndoynge as afor-sayde. That yet for as moche as it hath pleased the kynges highnes to lycence this worke to go abroade and that it is the moost pure worde of god which teacheth all true obedyence and reproueth all scismes and con-tencyons. And the lacke of this worde of the allmightie god is the cause of all blyndenes and supersticion, yt maye therfore be commaunded by your lordship in the name of our most gracyous prynce that euery curat haue one of them that they maye learne to knowe god and to instruct their parysshens. Ye and that euery abbaye shuld have vj to be layde in vj seuerall places that the whole covent and the resorters thervnto maye have occasyon to looke on the lordes lawe. Ye I wold none other but they of the papisticall sorte shuld be compelled to haue them, and then I knowe there shuld be ynow founde in my lorde of londons dyocesse to spende away a great part of them, and so shuld this be a godly acte worthy to be had in remembrance whyle the world doth stande, Sir I know that a small comyssyon wyll cause my lorde of Cantorbury, Salsbury & Worscetter to cause yt to be done thorow their dyocesse, Ye and this shuld cease the whole scisme and contencyon that is in the realme, which is, some callyng them of the olde and some of the new, now shuld we all folow one god, one boke and one learnynge, and this is hurtfull to no man but proffyte to all men. I will trouble your lordship no lenger for I am sory I have troubled you so moche. But to make an ende I desyer your moost gracyous answer by my servaunt, for the sycknes is bryme [4] aboute vs or elles wolde I wayte vpon your lordship, and because of comynge to your lordship, I have not soffred my servaunt with me sence he came ouer. Thus for your contynuall preseruacyon I with all that truly loue god do most hartely praye that you maye ouercome all your aduersaryes of the papisticall sorte.

> Your Orator Rychard grafton.

[4] Furious.

XXXIV. FOX'S ACCOUNT OF THE PRINTING OF THE GREAT BIBLE OF 1539.

From Fox's *Actes and Monumentes*, Fourth Edition. London, 1583, p. 1191.

¶ Of the Bible in English printed in the large volume, and of Edmund Boner preferred to the Bishoprike of London, by the meanes of the Lord Cromwell.

ABout the time and yere, when Edmund Boner bishop of Hereford, and ambassadour resident in Fraunce, began first to be nominate and preferred by the meanes of the lord Cromwel to the bishoprike of London : which was, anno 1540,[1] it happened that the said Thomas, Lord Cromwell and Erle of Essex,[2] procured of the king of england his gracious letters to the French king to permitte and licence[3] a subiect of his to imprint the Bible in English within the vniuersitie of Paris[4] because paper was there more meete and apt to be had for the doing therof, then in the realme of England, and also that there were more store of good workmen for the readie dispatch of the same. And in like maner at the same time the said king wrote vnto his ambassadour, who then was Edmund

The Bibles of the greatest volume printed in Paris.

The doers hereof were Rich: Grafton and Whytchurch.

---

[1] This is a year too late for the beginning of the Great Bible. Bonner was elected Bishop of London October 20, 1539, confirmed November 11, consecrated April 4, 1540.

[2] Cromwell was only made Earl of Essex on April 17, 1540, less than four months before his execution (July 28).

[3] See No. XXXV.

[4] The University had the supervision of all printing in Paris, and the chief printers were *libraires jurés* of it.

Boner Bishop of Herford lying in Paris, that he should
ayde and assist the doers thereof in all their reasonable
sutes. The which Bishop outwardly shewed great friendship to the merchants that were the imprinters of the
same, and moreouer did diuers and sundrie times call

Edmund Boner
a great furtherer in
printing the Bibles
in Englishe.

and commande the said persons, to
be in maner daily at his table both
dinner and supper, and so much re-
joyced in the workemanship of the
said Bible, that he himselfe would visite the imprinter's
house, where the same bibles were printed, and also would
take part of such dinners as the Englishmen there had,
and that to his cost, which, as it seemed he little wayed.
And further the sayd Boner was so feruent that he

The new testa-
ment in Englishe
and Latine put in
print by Boner.

caused the said Englishmen to put in
print a new testament in english &
latine,[5] and himselfe took, a great many
of them and payd for them and gaue
them to his friends. And it chaunced the meane time,
while the said Bible was in printing, the king Henry

Edmund Boner
made Byshop of
London.

the 8. preferred the said Boner from
the said bishoprike of Herford, to
be bishop of London, at which time [6]
the said Boner according to the statute law of England, tooke his othe to the king, knowledging his supremacie, and called one of the aforesaid Englishmen that
printed the bible, whom he then loued, although after-

[5] This is the Paris edition of Coverdale's Latin and English
New Testament printed to supersede the faulty edition published
by Nycholson ; see No. XXXII A, note 1, and No. XXXVIII.
Inasmuch as it was translated from the Vulgate this would be regarded as more likely to be orthodox than those which followed
the Greek or German. But there is no reason to think that
Bonner 'caused' it to be printed.

[6] i. e. in October or November, 1538.

ward vppon the change of the worlde he did hate him as much, whose name was Richard Grafton : to whom the said Boner saide when he tooke his othe, maister Grafton, so it is, that the kings most excellent maiestie hath by his gracious gift presented me to the Bishoprike of London, for the which I am sory, for   Boners wordes
if it would haue pleased his grace,   to Grafton, when
I could haue bene well content to haue   he toocke his othe
kept mine old bishopricke of Herford.   to the king.

Then said Grafton I am right glad to heare of it, and so I am sure will bee a great number of the Citie of London : for though they yet know you not, yet they haue heard so much goodnes of you from hence, as no doubt they will hartily reioyce of your placing, Then said Boner, I pray God I may doe that may content them, and to tel you M. Grafton, Before god (for that was commonly his othe) the greatest fault that I euer found in Stokesley, was for   Boner reproueth
vexing and troubling of poore men, as   Stokesley for his
Lobley the bookebinder [7] and other,   persecuting.
for hauing the scripture in english, and God willing he did not so much hinder it, but I wil as much further it, and I wil haue of your Bibles set vp in the Church of Paules, at the least in   Boners promise
sundrie places sixe of them, and I will   to set forth the
pay you honestly for them and giue   Scripture in Eng-
you hartie thankes.[8] Which wordes   lishe.
hee then spake in the hearing of diuers credible persons, as Edmund Stile Grocer and other. But now M. Grafton at this time I haue specially called

[7] Michael Lobley was indicted in 1531 for buying heretical books at Antwerp and speaking against images and purgatory. He lived, however, to be a warden of the Stationers' Company in 1560.

[8] Bonner carried out this promise, and on the occasion of his doing so issued the exhortation mentioned in No. XLIV, B.

you to be a witnes with me that vpon this translation of Bishops Sees, I must according to the statute
take an othe vnto the kings maiestie knowledging his

Boner sweareth hartely to the kinges supremacy. Supremacie, which before God I take
with my heart and so thinke him to
be, and beseech almightie God to
saue him, and long to prosper his grace : holde the
booke sirah, and reade you the oth (said he) to one of
his chapleins, and he layd his hand on the booke and
so he tooke his othe. And after this he shewed great
friendship to the saide Grafton and to his partener

Myles Couerdale corrector in print- ing the Bible of the large volume. Edward Whitchurch, but specially to
Myles Couerdall, who was the cor-
rector of the great Bible.

Now after that the foresaid letters
were delivered, the French kyng gaue very good
wordes, and was well content to permit the doing
therof. And so the printer went forward and
printed forth the booke euen to the last part, and
then was the quarrell picked to the printer, and he

The printing of the Bible stayed at Paris thorough the practise of Eng- lishe Bishops. was sent for to the inquisitors of
the fayth, and there charged with cer-
taine articles of heresie. Then were
sent for the Englishmen that were
at the cost and charge thereof, and
also such as had the correction of the same, which
was Myles Couerdale, but hauing some warning what
would folow the said Englishmen posted away as fast
as they could to saue themselues, leauing behynd
them all their Bibles, which were to the number of
2500,[9] called the Bibles of the great volume, and neuer

[9] The true number was 2,000, as stated by Grafton in his
'Abridgement of the Chronicles of England . . . 1564. In ædibus
Richardi Tothyl,' fol. 135[b] : ' In this yere the Great Bible in

recouered any of them, sauing that the Lieftenaunt
criminal hauing them deliuered vnto   English Bibles
hym to burne in a place at Paris (like   burnt at Paris.
Smithfield) called Maulbert place, was somewhat mooued
with couetousnes, and sold 4. great dry fattes of them to
a Haberdasher to lap in caps, and those were bought
againe, but the rest were burned, to the great and importunate losse of those that bare the charge of them.
But notwithstandyng the sayd losse after they had
recouered some part of the foresayde bookes, and were
comforted and encouraged by the Lord Cromwell, the
said Englishmen went agayne to Paris,[10] & there got the
presses, letters, and seruaunts of the aforesayd Printer,
and brought them to London, and there they became
printers themselues (which before they   How Grafton and
neuer entended) and printed out the   Whitchurch be-
said Bible in London, and after that·   came printers.
printed sundry impressions of them: but yet not without
great trouble and losse, for the hatred of the bishops
namely, Steven Gardiner, and his fellowes, who mightily
did stomacke and maligne the printing thereof.

  Here, by the way, for the more direction of the story,
thou hast louying Reader, to note and vnderstand that
in those daies there were ii sundry Bibles in English,
printed and set forth, bearing diuers titles, and printed

English in the Great Volume was printed in Paris in as privy
a manner as might bee, but when it was knowne, not only the
same Bible beeing XXC in nomber was seased and made con-
friscat, but also both the printer, marchants, and correctors in
great jeopardy of their lyves eskaped.' There is not the smallest
reason to attribute the interference of the Inquisition to 'the practise of the Englishe Bishops'. It was a political move, suggested
by the French ambassador in London, see No. XXXIX C.

  [10] It was presumably during this visit to Paris that Grafton
witnessed the taking by Bonner of the Oath acknowledging the
king's supremacy in October or November 1538.

in diuers places. The first was called Thomas Mathews

Tho: Mathewes Bible, by whom and how.

Bible, printed at Hambrough,[11] about the yeare of our Lord, 1532.[12] the corrector of which print was then John Rogers, of whom ye shall heare more Christ willing hereafter. The Printers were Richard Grafton, and Whitchurch. In the translation of this Bible, the greatest doer was in deede William Tyndall, who with the helpe of Miles Couerdale had translated all the bookes thereof, except onely the Apocrypha,[13] and certaine notes in the margent which were added after. But because the said William Tyndall in the meane tyme was apprehended before this Bible was fully perfected, it was thought good to them which had the doing therof, to chaunge the name of William Tyndall, because that name then was odious, and to father[14] it by a strange name of Thomas Mathew, John Rogers the same time beyng corrector to the print, who had then translated the residue of the Apocrypha, and added also certaine notes thereto in the margent, and thereof came it to be called Thomas Mathewes Bible. Which Bible of Thomas Mathew, after it was imprinted and pre-

The Bible presented to the king by the Lord Cromwell.

The Byble put forth with the kings priuiledge.

sented to the Lord Cromwell, and the Lord Cranmer, Archbishop of Canterbury, who liked very well of it, the sayd Cromwell presented it to the kyng, and obteined that the same might freely passe to be read of hys subiectes with hys graces licence : So that there was Printed

---

[11] No one believes that the Bible was printed at Hamburg.

[12] Fox's mistake for 1537 (reading MDXXXVII as MDXXXII).

[13] This exaggerates Tyndale's share. None of the Old Testament after 2 Chronicles is believed to be his. See No. XXVIII.

[14] Misprinted 'farther'.

upon the same booke, one lyne in red letters with these wordes : *Set forth with the kings most gracious licence.*

The setting forth of this booke did not a little offend the Clergy, namely, the Bishop aforesayd, both for the Prologues and specially because in the same booke was one special table collected of the common places in the Bible, and the scriptures for the approbation of the same, and chiefly about the supper of the lord and mariage of priests, and the masse, which there was said not to be found in Scripture.

Furthermore, after the restraint of this foresayde Bible of Mathew, another Bible began to be printed at Paris, an. 1540. which was called the Bible of the large Volume. The Printers whereof were the foresayde   *An other Byble of the great volume printed at Paris.* Richard Grafton, and Whitchurche which bare the charges. A great helper thereto was the lord Cromwell. The chiefest ouerseer was Myles Couerdale, who taking the translation of Tyndall, conferred the same with the Hebrue, and amended many things.

In this Bible, although the former notes of Thomas Mathew was omitted, yet sondry markes and handes were annexed in the sides, which   *The Byshops offended at the Byble translated into Englishe.* ment that in those places shuld be made certeine notes,[15] wherwith also the clergy was offended, though the notes were not made.

After this, the bishops bringing their purpose to passe, brought the Lord Cromwell out of fauour, and shortly to his death : and not long after, great complaint was made to the king of the translation of the Bible, and of the preface of the same, and then was the sale of

[15] See Nos. XXXVI C., XXXVIII B.

the Bible commaunded to be stayed, the B[ishop] promis-

The sale of the Bible stayd by the king, throug[h] the Byshops meanes.

ing to amend and correct it, but neuer performing the same : [16] Then Grafton was called, and first charged with the printing of Mathewes Bible, but he being feareful of trouble, made excuses for himselfe in all things. Then was he examined of the great Bible, and what notes he was purposed to make. To the which he aunswered, that he knewc none. For his purpose was to haue retayned learned men to have made the notes, but when he per-ceyued the kynges maiestie, and his Clergye not willing

Rich. Grafton imprisoned for printing the Bible.

to haue any, he proceded no further. But for al these excuses, Grafton was sent to the Fleet, and there remayned vi weekes, and before he came out, was bound in CCC li that he should neither sell nor imprint, or cause to be imprinted any moe Bibles, vntill the king and the clergy should agree vpon a translation. And thus was the Bible at that tyme stayed, during the raigne of Kyng Henry the viii.

But yet one thing more is to be noted, that after the imprinters had lost their Bibles, they continued suiters to Boner, as is aforesaid, to be a meane for to obteyne of the French king their bookes againe : but so long they continued suters, and Boner euer fed them with faire wordes, promising them much, but did nothing for them [17], till at the last Boner was discharged of his ambassade, and returned home, where he was right ioyfully welcomed home by the lord Crom-well, who loued him dearely, and had maruelous good

[16] See No. XLV.

[17] This is contradicted by XXXIX B (last paragraph but one).

opinion of him. And so long as Cromwell remained in autoritie, so long was Boner at his beck and friend to his friends and enimy to his enimies ; as namely, at that tyme to Gardiner B[ishop] of Winchester, who neuer fauoured Cromwell, and

Edm. Boner a great frend to L. Cromwell, al the tyme of his prosperitye.

therefore Boner could not fauour him, but that he and Winchester were the greatest enemies that might be. But so soone as Cromwell fel, immediately Boner and Winchester pretended to be the

Steph. Gardiner and Boner of enemyes made frendes.

greatest men that liued, and no good word could Boner speake of Cromwell, but the lewdest, vilest, and bitterest that he could speake, calling him the rankest heretike that euer liued : and then such as the sayd Boner knew to be

Doct. Boner altereth his frendship and religion.

in good fauour with Cromwell, he could neuer abide theii sight. Insomuch, as the next day after that Cromwell was apprehended, the abouenamed Grafton, who before had bene very familiar with Boner, met with the sayd Boner sodenly, and sayd vnto hym, that he was sory to heare of the newes that then was abroad. What are they, sayd he ? Of the apprehension of the L. Cromwell sayd Grafton. Are ye sory for that (sayd he ?) It had bene good that he had bene dispatched long ago. With that Grafton looked vpon hym and knew not what to say, but came no more to Boner. Howbeit afterward the sayd Grafton beyng charged for the imprinting of a ballet made in the fauour of Cromwel was called before the Councel, where Boner was present and there Boner

Doctor Boner agaynst the L. Cromwell.

charged hym with the wordes that hee spake to hym of Cromwell, and told out a great long tale. But the lord Awdeley, who then was Lord Chauncellor, right discretly and honourably, cut of the matter, and entered into other talke.

XXXV. THE FRENCH KING'S LICENCE[1]

Printed from an early transcript, Cotton MS. Cleopatra, E. v. 326.

Franciscus etc. dilectis nobis Richardo Grafton et Edwardo Whitchurch Anglis et civibus londini salutem, Quia fide digno testimonio accepimus quod charissimus frater noster anglorum Rex vobis cuius subditi estis sacram bibliam tam latine quam britannice sive anglice imprimendi ac imprimi curandi et in suum Regnum apportandi et transferendi libertatem sufficientem et

[1] The date of this document being in dispute it is here placed immediately after Fox's narrative. It is, however, fairly obvious, since it mentions Latin as well as English printing, that it must be placed after the appearance of the faulty edition of Coverdale's Latin-English Testament at Southwark, which caused him to desire to print a more perfect one in Paris, and as it was his absence which obliged him to leave the correction of the proofs to Nycholson, this licence cannot have been obtained until after he had been some time at Paris. On the other hand, as the Latin-English New Testament was safely printed in 1538 it seems impossible to agree with Dr. Kingdon, who in his monograph on Poyntz and Grafton contends that this licence was only granted on the return of Grafton to Paris late in 1539 (see No. XXXIV, note 10). That theory is also negatived by the fact that ample facilities then existed for printing Bibles in England, and Grafton only wanted to get back the stock. The true date appears to be some time after the letter of June 23 (see next document), in which the printers ask Cromwell to write letters on their behalf to the English ambassadors, who would supply the ' fide dignum testimonium ' alluded to in the opening paragraph of the licence. While, however, issuing the licence in accordance with Cromwell's request, the French king, by the vague stipulation that the translation should avoid all private and unlawful opinions, made it valueless.

legittimam, concesserit, et vos tum propter chartam
tum propter alias honestas considerationes animos vestros
in hac parte iuste moventes dictam bibliam sic impri-
mendam Parisiis infra hoc nostrum Regnum curaveritis
ac in Angliam quam primum transmittere intenderitis,
Nos ut hec vobis facere liceat potestatem facientes, vobis
coniunctim et deuisim ac procuratoribus factoribus et
agentibus vestris et cuiuslibet vestrum, vt in Regno
nostro apud calchographum quemcumque dictam sacram
bibliam tam latine quam anglicana lingua tuto imprimere
et excudere possitis et possint, necnon excussam et impressam in Angliam dumtaxat sine ulla perturbacione
aut molestia vel impedimento quocumque transmittere et
apportare, dummodo quod sic imprimentes et excudentes
sincere et pure quantum in vobis erit citra vllas privatas
aut illigittimas opiniones impressum et excussum fuerit,
et onera ac officia mercatoria nobis et ministris nostris
debite in hac parte extiterint prosoluta licentiam nostram
impartimur et concedimus specialem per presentes, Datis
et ceteris.

Translation

Francis, etc. to our well beloved Richard Grafton and
Edward Whitchurch Englishmen and citizens of London
greeting. Whereas by trustworthy testimony we have been
informed that our most dear brother the King of the English, whose subjects ye are, hath granted you sufficient and
lawful liberty of printing and getting printed the Holy
Bible both in Latin and in British or English and of bringing and transporting it into his kingdom, and that ye,
alike for the sake of the paper and for other honourable
reasons rightfully influencing you in this matter, have
taken steps for thus printing the said Bible at Paris
within this our kingdom and intend as soon as may be

to send it over to England. We therefore, that you may
be able to do this, empowering you jointly and severally,
and also the representatives, factors and agents of both
or either of you, that within our kingdom in the house
of any printer you and they may safely impress and print
the said Holy Bible alike in Latin and in the English
tongue and when it is printed and impressed may transport it into England without any interference, annoyance, or hindrance, provided always that ye shall so
print and impress it sincerely and purely so far as in
you lies, avoiding any private or unlawful opinions, and
when it is so printed and impressed all imposts and
custom duties have been duly paid to us and to our
officers, grant and concede our special licence by these
presents. Dated, etc.

XXXVI. REPORTS OF PROGRESS

A. Letter of Coverdale and Grafton to Crom-
well, June 23, 1538 [1]

From the original in the Record Office, (*Letters and Papers of
the reign of Henry VIII*, vol. xiii, pt. 1, 1249).

After moost humble and hartie commendacions to
your good lordship. Pleaseth the same to vnderstand,
that we be entred into your worke of the byble, wherof
(accordynge to our moost bounden dutie) we haue here
sent vnto your lordship ij ensamples, one in parchement,
wherin we entende to prynt one for the kynges grace,
and another for your lordship : and the seconde in

---

[1] [*Docketed*] Myles Coverdale and Rychard Grafton letter cer-
tefyinge that the byble is almost prynted at Parys.

paper, wherof all the rest shalbe made, trustynge that
it shalbe, not onlye to the glorye of god, but a synguler
pleasure also to your good lordship the causer therof, and
a generall edefyenge of the kinges subiectes, accordynge
to your lordshipes moost godlye request.   For we
folowe not only a standynge text of the hebrue, with the
interpretacion of the Caldee, and the greke, but we set
also in a pryuate table the dyuersite of redinges of all
textes, with soche annotacions in another table, as shall
douteles delucidate and cleare thesame, as well without
any singularyte of opinions as all checkinges and re-
profes. The prynt no dout shall please your good lordship. The paper is of the best sorte in Fraunce. The
charge certaynly is great, wherin as we moost humbly
requyer your fauourable helpe at this present, with
whatsoeuer yt shall please your good lordship to let vs
haue,[2] so trust we, (yf nede requyer) in our iust busynes,
to be defended from the papistes by your lordshipes
fauourable letters, which we moost humbly desyer to
haue, (by this berer, Wyllyam Graye) ether to the
bysshop of Wynchester,[3] or to some other whome your
lordship shall thinke moost expedyent. We be daylye
threatened, and look euer to be spoken withall, as this
berer can farther enforme your lordship, but how they
will vse vs, as yet, we knowe not. Neuerthelesse for our
farther assewraunce where thorough we maye be the
abler to performe this your lordshipes work, we are so
moche the bolder of your good lordship, for other refuge
haue we none vnder god and our kynge, whom with
noble prynce Edward and all you their most honorable

[2] Cromwell informed the French ambassador that he had himself spent on the work £400. See No. XXXIX, B and C.

[3] Stephen Gardiner, the English ambassador, superseded by
Bonner in July of this year.

councell, god allmightie preserue now and euer, Amen.
Wrytten at Parys the xxiij daye of Juyn by your lordshipes assured and daylye oratours,

Myles Couerdale

Rychard Grafton grocer

To the right honorable and their syngular good lorde,
the lorde Cromewell and lorde preuaye Seale.

B. LETTER OF EDWARD WHITCHURCH TO CROMWELL, UNDATED [1]

From the original in the Record Office (*Letters and Papers of the reign of Henry VIII*, vol. xiii, pt. 2, 1086).

Pleas it your lordship to be advertysed, that your
lordships certyfying me, that you wold not wryt your
lettres, nor medle at all, with owr purposed worke, Lately
taken in hand for your lordship, so greatly dyscomforted
me your poore Orator, that it almost brought me vtterly
into dispeire, but that I hadd sum hope of comfort, when
I Rem[em]bryd your godly Intent euer in preferyng of
all thyngs wyche were for goddes glory trustyng that your
sayd lordship woll styll contenew in the same. And ayde
& defend vs in thys our iust besynes. Havyng non other
refuge vnder god and the Kynges highnes but of your
lordship. Wherfor I most humbly besche your lordship
not to refuse vs now, but wythe your goodnes to helpe vs
in the furtherans of our sayd worke, And when yt shall
pleas your lordship to command me I shall informe your
lordship of those people, and moste chieffly of our contrey-

---

[1] This letter being undated its place is uncertain. It is inserted
here on the supposition that Cromwell at first replied unfavour-
ably to the letter of Coverdale and Grafton of June 23, but was
moved by the appeal from Whitchurch to instruct the English
ambassador to take action.

men, wyche doo compleyn on vs vnto the vniuersitye, & most shamfully vsethe their toungs toward the Kynges grace, & his most honorable counsaill.

Your bound Orator

Edward Whitchurche.

C. LETTER OF COVERDALE, GRAFTON, AND W. GRAY TO CROMWELL, AUGUST 9, 1538[1]

From the original in the Record Office (*Letters and Papers of the reign of Henry VIII*, vol. xiii, pt. 2, 58).

After moost humble and due salutacion to your good lordship. Pleaseth the same to vnderstand, that your worke going forward, we thought it oure moost bounden dutie to sende vnto your lordship certayne leaues therof, specially, seynge we had so good occasyon, by the returnynge of your beloued seruant Sebastian. And as they are done, so will we sende your lordship the residue from tyme to tyme. As touchynge the maner and order that we kepe in thesame worke, Pleaseth your goode lordship to be aduertised that this merke ☞ in the text, signifieth, that vpon the same (in the later ende of the booke) there is some notable annotacion, which we haue writen, without any pryuate opinion,[2] onlye after the best interpreters of the hebrues for the more clearenesse of the texte. This marke ♣ betokeneth, that vpon the same texte there is diuersite of redynge amonge the hebrues, Caldees and Grekes and latenystes, as in a table

[1] Endorsed : ' Myles couerdale Ric. Grafton Wm. Gray certefying the maner howe they are in hand to translate the Byble. At Parys. ix Aug.'

[2] This reads like a translation of the ' citra vllas priuatas opiniones ' of the licence which had almost certainly been granted by this time.

at the ende of the booke shalbe declared. This marke ⸾ sheweth that the sentence written in small letters is not in the hebrue or Caldee, but in the latyn, and seldome in the Greke, and that we neuerthelesse wolde not haue it extinct, but hig[h]lye accept yt for the more explanation of the text. This token † in the olde testament geueth to vnderstand, that thesame texte which foloweth it, is also alledged of christ or of some apostle in the newe testament.[3] This (amonge other oure necessarie laboures) is the waye that we take in this worke, trustynge verely, that as God allmightie moued youre lordship to set vs vnto yt : so shall it be to his glorie, and right welcome to all them that loue to serue him and their prynce in true faithfull obedyence. As is onlye knowen to the lorde of heauen, to whom we moost harteley praye for your lordshipes preseruacion. At parys the ix daye of August 1538 by your faithfull oratours.

Myles Couerdale
Richard grafton
William Grey.

To the right honorable and their synguler good lorde, lorde preuye seale be this delyuered.

D. Coverdale and Grafton to Cromwell September 12, 1538 [1]

From the original in the Record Office (*Letters and Papers of the reign of Henry VIII*, vol. xiii, pt. 2, 336).

After most humble and due salutacions to your mooste honorable lordshippe, pleaseth the same to vnderstand, that we are instantly desyred of oure hoste (whose name

---

[3] As to these marks see No. XXXIV on page 229.

[1] Endorsed : Miles Coverdale and Richard Grafton. The byble is in printing.

is Fraunces Reynold[2] a frenchman) to make supplicacion
for him vnto your lordshippe. Where as of long tyme
he hath bene an occupier in to England more then xl. yere,
he hath allwayes provyded soche bookes for England,
as they moost occupied, so that he hath a great nombre,
at this present in his handes, As prymers in Englishe,
Missales with other soche like : Whereof now (by the
company of the booksellers in London) he is vtterly
forbydden to make sale, to the vtter vndoyng of the man,
Wherfore moost humbly we beseke your lordshippe to be
gracious and fauourable vnto him, that he maye have
lycence to sell those which he hath done allready, so
that herafter he prynte nomoo in the english tong,
onlesse he have an english man that is lerned, to be his
corrector ; and that is the man well contented withall.
he is also contented and hath promised before my lord
elect of harfford, that yf there be founde anye notable
faute in his bookes, he will put the same out, and
prynte the leafe agayne. Thus are we bolde to wryte
vnto your lordshippe in his cause (as doth also my lord
elect of herfford) beseching your l. to pardon oure
boldnesse, and to be good lorde vnto this honest man,
whose servaunt shall geve attendaunce vpon your l.
most fauourable answere. Yf your l. shewe him this
benefyte, we shall not fare the worse, in the readynesse
and due expedicion of this your l. worke of the byble.

---

[2] i. e. Francois Regnault, the printer of the Bible, with whom
apparently Coverdale and Grafton were lodging. Regnault had
begun printing service-books for the use of Salisbury in 1519, and
from 1524 to 1535 his output had been large and uninterrupted.
He had already in 1536 himself written to Cromwell asking that the
Act of 1534 regulating the importation of foreign books might
not be used to exclude those he had printed, and he now procured
the aid of Grafton and Coverdale. He died some little time before
June 21, 1541.

Which goeth well forwarde, and within few monethes
will drawe to an ende, by the grace of allmightie god,
who preserue your good lordshippe now and euermore.

From Parys the xij[th] daye of Septembre.

> Myles Couerdale.
> Rychard Grafton.

To the right honorable and their singular good lorde,
the lord prevye seale.

E. BISHOP BONNER TO CROMWELL

Extract from the original letter in the Record Office (*Letters
and Papers of the reign of Henry VIII*, vol. xiii, pt. 2, 557).

Of late ther is a stay made att Parys towching the
printing of the bible in English, and sute made to the
great mayster [1] to prouide for remedie therin ; but as yet
it is not obteyned.   God send all to the best and preserue
your Lordeship so well as I can and am mooste bounden
to desire.   At St. Quyntyns 7° Octobris.

XXXVII. THE KING'S PROCLAMATION
NOVEMBER 16, 1538

From the British Museum facsimile of the copy in the library
of the Society of Antiquaries.

The Kynges Moste Royall maiestie beinge enfourmed,
that sondry contentious and sinyster opinyons, haue by
wronge teachynge and naughtye printed bokes, encreaced
and growen within this his realme of Englande. : . .

Fyrste for expellynge and aduoydinge the occasion
of the said errours and seditiouse opinions, by reason of
bokes imprinted in the englyshe tonge, brought and

[1] Anne de Montmorency, Grand Master and Constable of
France since February 10 of this year.

transported from outward parties, The kynges most royall maiestie straytely chargeth and commaundeth, that no person or persons, of what estate degree or condition so euer he be, shall from hensforth (without his maiesties speciall licence) transport or bringe from outwarde parties, into this his realme of England, or any other his gracis dominions, any maner bokes printed in the englyshe tonge, nor sell, gyue, vtter, or publishe any suche bokes from hensforthe to be broughte into this realme, or into any his highnes domynions, vpon the peynes that the offendours in that article shall nat onely incurre and runne into his gracis moste high displeasure and indignation, but also shall lose and forfaite vnto his maiestie, all his or theyr goodes and cattalles, and haue emprisonment at his gracis wyll.

Item that no persone or persons in this realme, shall from hensforth print any boke in the englyshe tonge, onles vpon examination made by some of his gracis priuie counsayle, or other suche as his highnes shall appoynte, they shall haue lycence so to do, and yet so hauynge, not to put these wordes *Cum priuilegio regali*, without addyng *ad imprimendum solum*,[1] and that the hole copie, or els at the least theffect of his licence and priuilege be therwith printed, and playnely declared and expressed in the Englyshe tonge vnderneth them: Nor from henseforth shall printe or bryng into this his realm any bokes of diuine scripture in the englishe tonge, with any annotations in the margyn, or any prologe or additions in the calender or table, excepte the same be firste viewed, examyned, and allowed by the kynges highnes, or suche of his maiesties counsayle, or other, as it shall

[1] i.e. they were not to make a mere permission to print appear as if any special favour or monopoly were being conferred on the edition.

R

please his grace to assigne therto, but onely the playne sentence and texte, with a table or repertorie, instructynge the reader to fynde redely the chapiters conteyned in the sayd boke, and the effectes therof. Nor shall from henseforthe prynte any boke of translations in the englyshe tonge, oneles the playne name of the translatour therof be conteyned in the saide boke, or elles that the prynter will answere for the same as for his owne priuie dede and acte, and otherwise to make the translatour the printer and the setter forthe of the same, to suffre punishment, and make a fyne at the kynges wyll and pleasure.

Item that no persone or persons, vsyng the occupation of pryntyng of bokes in this realme, shall prynt, vtter, sel, or cause to be published any bokes of scripture in the englishe tonge, vntyl suche time as the same bokes be fyrst viewed, examyned, and admitted by the kynges highnesse, or one of his priuie counsayle, or one byshoppe of this realme, whose name also his grace wylleth shall be therin expressed, vpon peyne not onely to incurre and runne into the kynges most hygh displeasure and indignation, but also to lose and forfayte al theyr goodes and catalles, and suffre emprisonement at his gracis wyll and pleasure. . . .

Westminster xvi. Nouembr. Anno regni regis Henrici octaui xxx.

Tho. Berthelet, regius impressor excudebat.

Cum priuilegio.

XXXVIII. MORE REPORTS FROM PARIS

A. Grafton to Cromwell [1]

From Cotton MS. Cleopatra E, v. 323.

After moost humble comendacions. Pleaseth it your lordship to vnderstand that it chaunsed sence oure comynge into these partes, that James Nycolson that dwelleth in Southwark put in prynt the newe testament both in latyn and englyshe,[2] which booke was delyuered vnto vs by a straunger And when Master Couerdale had aduysed and consydered thesame. he founde his name added thervnto as the translator, with thewhich he neuer had to do, nether sawe he it before it was full prynted and ended. And also founde the booke so folyshly done, ye and so corrupt, that yt did not only greue him that the prynter had so defamed him and his learnyng by addynge his name to so fonde a thinge, but also that the commen people was depryued of the true and syncere sence of godes true worde, and also that soche an occasyon was mynystred to the enemyes of Godes worde, that rather seke occasyons to rayle and sclaunder, then to be edefyed. And therfore at his moost honest and lawfull request (although I had ynough to do besyde) I haue prynted thesame agayne, translated and corrected by Master Couerdale him selfe. Of the which bookes now beynge fyneshed, I have here sent your lordship the fyrst (and so haue I also sent vnto my lorde of Cantorbury another and almoost to euery christen bysshop [3]

[1] Endorsed : ' To ye right honorable and their synguler good lorde, my lord preuaye seale. Rychard Grafton. the firste of Decembre from parys.'

[2] See above, No. XXXII, A, note 1.

[3] By 'christen bishop', here and in the final paragraph, Grafton seems to mean those favourable to the Protestant cause.

that is in the realme, My lorde of harfforde also hath
sent to Mr. Rychard Cromwell one of the same) thewhich
I moost humbly desyer your lordship to accept, hauyng
respecte rather vnto my harte, then to the gifte ; for
it is not so well done as my harte wolde wysshe it
to be : I haue also added, as your lordship maye
perceaue, these wordes, Cum gracia et priuilegio Regis.
And the day before this present came there a post
named Nycolas which brought your lordshipes letters
to my lorde of harfforde, with thewhich was bounde
a certen inhibicion for pryntynge of bookes, and for
addynge of these wordes Cum priuilegio.[4] Then assone
as my lorde of harfforde had receaued yt, he sent
ymedyatlye for Mr. Couerdale and me, readynge thesame
thynge vnto vs, in thewhich is expressed, that we shuld
adde these wordes (ad imprimendum solum) which
wordes we neuer heard of before. Nether do we take it
that those wordes shuld be added in the pryntynge of
the scripture (if yt be truly translated) for then shuld
yt be a great occasyon to the enemyes to saye that yt
is not the kynges acte or mynde to set yt forth, but only
lycence the prynters to sell soche as is put forth. Wherfore moost humbly we beseke your lordship to take no
dyspleasor for that we haue done, for rather then any
soche thynge shuld happen, we wolde do yt agayne, but
I trust the thynge yt selfe is so well done, that it shall not
only please your lordship, but also the Kynges highnes
and all the godly in the realme. And where as your
lordship hath added in thesayd inhibicions that your
lordship and all the Kynges most honorable councell
wylleth no booke from henceforth to be put in prynt,
but that fyrst yt be alowed at the least by one bysshop.
We moost humbly beseke your lordship to apoynt certen

<hr>

[4] See No. XXXVII.

therto,[5] that they maye be as readye to reade them, as other good men be to put them forth. For yt is now vij yere,[6] sence the bysshopes promysed to translate and set forth the byble, and as yet they haue no leasor, I praye god they maye haue. howbeyt, the christen bysshops in dede haue small leasor. Thus I commyt your lordship to the tuition of allmyghtie god, who euermore preserue your good lordship.

> your humble and faythfull
>
> seruytor Rychard grafton.

At Parys the first daye of December.

B. COVERDALE TO CROMWELL, DECEMBER 13, 1538[1]

From Harleian MS., No. 604, p. 98 (112).

Right honorable and my syngular good lorde (after all dew salutacions) I humbly beseche youre lordshippe, that by my lorde electe of Herdforde, I maye knowe youre pleasure, concernynge the Annotacions of this byble, whether I shall proceade therin, or no. Pitie it were, that the darck places of the text (vpon the which I haue allwaye set a hande ☞) shulde so passe vndeclared. As for anye pryuate opynion or contencious wordes, as I wyll utterly avoyde all soche, so wyll I offre the annotacions first to my sayde lord of Herdforde ; to the intent that he shall so examen the same, afore they be put in prynte, yf it be your lordshippes good pleasure, that I shall so do. As concernyng the new Testamentes in english & latyn, wherof your good lordshippe receaued

[5] This was not done in the case of this edition, nor of any of the Great Bibles, except the fourth and sixth. See text, p 23.

[6] The promises of 1530 were vague ; it was after December 1534 that an effort was made.

[1] Endorsed : Myles Coverdale about thexposycyon of darke places of the byble, &c.

lately a boke by your seruaunt Sebastian the Cooke,
I besech your l[ordship] to consydre the grenesse therof,
which (for lack of tyme) can not as yet be so apte to be
bounde as it shulde be : And where as my sayde lord of
Hardforde is so good vnto vs as to convaye thus moch
of the Byble to your good lordshippe, I humbly beseche
the same, to be the defender & keper therof : To the
intent that yf these men proceade in their cruelnesse
agaynst us & confiscate the rest, yet this at the leest
maye be safe by the meanes of your lordshippe, whom
god the allmightie euermore preserue to his good pleasure.
Amen. Written somwhat hastely at Parys the xiij daye
of Decembre.

> Your l[ordships] humble & faithfull seruitour

> > Myles Couerdale.

To my most syngular good lorde and master the lorde
Cromwell lorde prevye seale. this delyuer.

XXXIX. THE BIBLES CONFISCATED : CROM-
WELL'S EFFORTS TO OBTAIN THEIR
RELEASE

A. Citation of François Regnault for Printing
the Bible at Paris, December 17, 1538

From the copy transcribed in Cotton MS., Cleopatra E, v. 58,
fol. 326.[1]

Frater henricus Garuais in sacra theologia Doctor.
Regius Prior conventus fratrum predicatorum, paris.
necnon vicarius generalis venerabilis patris fratris
mathei ory eiusdem ordinis etiam sacre theologie doc-
toris, Inquisitoris generalis heretice prauitatis in toto

---

[1] Endorsed : ' The copie of the seconde citacion and inhibicion
made to the prynter.'

Regno francie apostolica et Regia auctoritatibus spe-
cialiter deputati.

Omnibus Presbiteris vicariis curatis et non curatis
notariis quoque et tabellionibus publicis vbilibet consti-
tutis salutem in domino. Quoniam ex traductione sacre
scripture tam veteris quam noui testamenti in vernacu-
lam linguam que ad simplicium manus pervenit com-
pertum est novissimis diebus nonnullos occasionem
sumpsisse erroris in fide, Et edicto supreme curie parliamenti cautum est ne quispiam vetus aut novum testamentum vernacula lingua imprimat aut impressa vendat
Nobis autem notum est quendam franciscum Regnault
bibliopolam huiusce ciuitatis parisiensis his diebus
imprimere bibliam in ydiomate vulgari britannice, Occa-
cione cuius possent oriri scandala et errores in ecclesia
hinc est quod nobis quibus ex officio incumbit nedum
ortos errores et hereses in fide extirpare sed etiam futuris
pro posse obuiare vobis omnibus et singulis supradictis
in virtute sancte obedientie districte percipiend. mandamus quatenus ad Requestam et Instantiam venerabilis
viri promotoris causarum officii dicte sancte Inquisitionis
Citetis peremptorie et personaliter apud dictum con-
ventum fratrum predicatorum coram nobis ad diem
primam post presentium nostrarum literarum executionem
hora secunda expectatem tertiam post meridiem eiusdem
diei franciscum Regnault et alios quos decebit nobis ex
officio nostro et dicti promotoris supra premissis respon-
suros, inhibentes eisdem sub pena canonica ne vltra ad
impressionem dicte biblie vernacula lingua procedant.
Nec folia impressa a se et sua possessione abdicent et
alienent donec utraque biblia [2] per nos visa aliter fuerit

[2] The information thus applied to the Latin-English New
Testament which Regnault was printing for Coverdale, as well
as to the English Bible.

ordinatum. Date parisius sub sigillo quo in talibus vtimur ac signo manuali notarii seu scribe dicte sancte Inquisitionis iurati. Anno domini millessimo quingentesimo tricesimo octavo die decima septima mensis decembris. Item et aliam bibliam in sermone gallico impressam passim vendere.[3] Date ut supra.

Le tellier.

TRANSLATION

Friar Henry Garvais, Regius Doctor in Sacred Theology, Prior of the Convent of Preaching Friars at Paris, Vicar-General also of the venerable father Friar Matthew Ory of the same order, also Doctor of Sacred Theology, Inquisitor general of heresy in all the Kingdom of France, specially deputed by the authority of the Apostolic See and the King, To all priests, vicars, with and without cures, notaries also and summoners, wherever they be, health in the Lord. Whereas from the translation of Holy Scripture alike of the Old and New Testament into the vernacular tongue which has come into the hands of the simple it has been found lately that some have taken occasion to err in the faith. And by an edict of the supreme court of parliament it has been provided that none shall print the Old or New Testament in the vernacular or sell printed copies. And it has become known to us that a certain François Regnault, bookseller of this city of Paris, at the present time is printing a bible in British in the vulgar tongue, by occasion of which scandals and errors might arise in the church, hence is it that we whose official duty it is not only to root out errors and heresies in faith when they have arisen but also as far as possible to obviate them, to you the aforesaid, one and all, in the virtue of holy obedience

[3] This sentence about a French Bible seems to have got into the transcript by mistake.

give command, at the request and instance of the venerable promoter of the office of the said holy Inquisition, to cite peremptorily and personally at the said convent of the Preaching Friars before us on the first day after the execution of our present letters, between the hours of two and three after noon, François Regnault and others whom it shall beseem to make answer to us in accordance with our office and the premises of the said promoter, prohibiting the aforesaid persons under the canonical penalty from proceeding further to the impression of the said Bible in the vernacular tongue and from surrendering and alienating the printed sheets from their possession until, after such bible has been examined by us, it be otherwise ordained. Given at Paris under the seal which we use in such matters and the sign manual of the sworn notary or scribe of the said holy Inquisition in the year of our Lord 1538 the seventeenth day of December. Also that another Bible printed in the French language is being sold everywhere. Given as before.

Le Tellier.

B. CASTILLON, THE FRENCH AMBASSADOR IN ENGLAND, TO THE CONSTABLE OF FRANCE, DECEMBER 31, 1538[1]

Extract from British Museum Additional MS. 33514, f. 9.

Monseigneur, depuis la lettre que ie vous escriuis hier, Milord Prive seel m'a ce matin enuoye prier que ie me trouuasse en son logis, pour vng peu deviser auec moy, Et m'a compte comme il auoir receu des lettres de

[1] This letter describing an interview with Cromwell is thus summarized in the *Letters and Papers of the Reign of Henry VIII*, vol. xiii, 2, No. 1163 : ' The substance of his discourse was that he himself had at his own cost got a Bible printed in English,

l'Ambassadeur du Roy son maistre devers le Roy ; lequel, comme il m'a dit, est modeste et veritable Ambassadeur, escrivant toutes choses pour la continuation de l'amitie d'entre nos deux Roys, Et selouant de l'audience et assez bonne chere qu'on luy faict. La substance de ses propos est que luy-mesmes, a ses propres cousts et despens, a faict imprimer vne Bible en vulgaire Angloys, Et que les Imprimeurs ont este citez et tourmentez par quelques-vns de l'Vniuersite de Paris, et les liures arrestez, Il vouldroit bien prier le Roy et vous, qu'on permist (attendu que ce n'est que le vray texte de la Bible, trans-late de mot a mot, pour la lecture des Angloys qui n'ont pas la langue latine, et que ladicte Bible ne peult seruir qu'aux Angloys) Il pleust au Roy permettre qu'elle fust imprime a Paris ; pource que les impressions y sont plus belles qu'en autre lieu, et pour le grand nombre des Imprimeurs, et la grande abondance de papier qui y est, les liures y sont plustost expediez qu'en nul autre pays. Et s'il plaist au Roy tant faire pour luy, il luy donnera a congnoistre (comme il espere faire en bref,) qu'il fera autant pour luy en quelqu'autre endroit ; comme celuy

and the printers have been cited and troubled by certain of the University of Paris, and the books arrested. He would pray the King and you (as it is the true text of the Bible, and could only be used by Englishmen) to permit its being printed in Paris ; because the printing is finer there than elsewhere, and with the great number of printers and abundance of paper, books are despatched sooner than in any other country. If the King will do this for him he hopes soon to do as much in return in some other way. If the King will not grant this, will he allow (as it seems he has already promised the ambassador) the books to be sent here as they are ? He told me they cost him 600 marks, that is 3600 livres tournois, and that his only object is to give them away. Moreover he wishes the King to forbid in his realm people to speak against this King, etc. . . . As to the first, I replied as I had done long before, and as you answered the English ambassador, etc.'

qui est du tout enclin a son seruice. Quelque opinion que i'ay autres-foys eu au contraire et dont certes il m'asseure, et me prie le croyre. Et au cas qu'il ne pleust au Roy ainsi luy octroyer, qu'il soit content (comme il me semble qu'il dict qu'on l'a desia accorde audict Ambassadeur) qu'ils soyent R'enuoyez ainsi qu'ils sont. Il m'a dict que les dicts liures luy coustent bien six cents marcs, qui sont troys mil six cens liures tournoys, et que le tout n'est, sinon pour les donner.

C. EXTRACT FROM LETTER OF THE IMPERIAL AMBAS-
SADOR IN ENGLAND TO THE EMPEROR CHARLES V,
JANUARY 9, 1539[1]

From *Correspondenz des Kaisers Karl V. aus dem Königlichen Archiv und der Bibliothek de Bourgogne zu Brüssel, mitgetheilt von Dr. Karl Lanz*, Band II, Leipzig, 1845, p. 299 sqq.

Sire, en oultre ledit Crumuel avertist icelluy ambassadeur, comme il avoit fait imprimer a Paris une libelle [?bible] en anglois que luy coustoit bien environ deux mille escuz, et que dez ce quelle avoit este achevee et payee ceulx de luniversite lavoient fait detenir, arrester et sequestrer, ce qu'il trouvait bien estrange ; parquoy prioit tresfort ledit ambassadeur vouloir escripre bien acertes pour la relaxacion di celle, et asseurer de sa part ledit roy treschrestien, que, sil faisait tant pour luy faire tout incontinent relaxer sadite bible, quil luy rendroit bien la pareille. Et sur ce, sire, ledit seigneur

---

[1] This letter summarizes the conversation between Cromwell and Castillon already recounted by Castillon himself. Its importance lies in the postcript, which implies that it was the French ambassador himself who had suggested that the Inquisition should be allowed to seize the Bibles. The cost of the Bibles to Cromwell is here given as 2,000 crowns.

Crumuel vint a prier ledit ambassadeur, vouloir penser,
imaginer et luy dire, sil y avoit chose en ce monde qui
puist ayder et seruir au laugmentement et confirmation
de lindissoluble amytie entre leurs maiestes, il se feroit
fort dy conduire cedit roy son maistre, comme aussi de
oster toutes les causes et occasions qui pourroient en
facon du monde engendrer quelque scrupule entre eulx,
pressant extremement ledit ambassadeur, luy vouloir
declairer, sil en scavoit ou suspeconnoit quelcune ; et
pense icelluy ambassadeur, que ledit seigneur Crumuel
desiroit, quil lui dit, quil serait bon dabolir la pension
que cedit roy pretendoit en France, pour abatre tous les
scrupules.

.   .   .   .

[Postscript [2]]

Sire, en cest instant veuillant serrer ceste, le secre-
taire de l'ambassadeur de France mest venu dire de la

[2] Summarized in *Letters and Papers, &c.*, vol. xiv, I. 37 :
' At this moment the secretary of the French ambassador has
come to tell me on his master's part that Cromwell returning late
from Court visited him and told him that within two hours the
King had received letters from his ambassador in France stating that the French King had imprisoned two Cordeliers who
had defamed the King in their sermons, and it was said they
would be severely punished ; and that Francis had on the first
day of the year given the English ambassador a good reception
and ordered that what was already printed of the Bible in English
should be delivered to his ministers ; at which the King had
showed himself wonderfully pleased and felt himself greatly
bound to Francis, and also to the said Ambassador, who did not
cease to do everything to preserve the amity. The Ambassador
informs me that all that was done in France was merely an
artifice to abuse those here, not to put them in mistrust, and that
he had advised it by his letters ; nevertheless those which he
wrote about the defamation of the King and the sequestration
of the Bible could scarcely have yet arrived at the French court.'

part de sondit maistre, comme hier sur le tard revenant
Crumuel de la court, saddressant son chemin par devant
le logis dicelluy ambassadeur, il entre dedans pour
ladvertir, que puis deux heures ce roy avoit receu lettres
bien freiches de son ambassadeur resident en court dudit
France, par lesquelles il ladvertissoit, que le roy treschrestien avoir fait mectre en prison deux cordeliers qua
voient voulu en leurs sermons diffamer cedit roy, et ce
parloit que lesdits cordeliers seroient tres aigrement
pugnis et chastoyez, et que ledit roy treschrestien avait
a ce premier jour de lan fait bon recueil et grosse chiere
a son ambassadeur, et si avoit commande, que ce questoit
desja imprime de la bible en anglais, il fut delivre a ses
ministres ; de quoy cedit roy sestoit monstre merveil-
leusement joyeulx et sen tenoit tres oblige audit seigneur
roy treschrestien et aussi a icelluy ambassadeur qui ne
cessoit de faire tout bon office pour conserver lamytie
entre ledit seigneur roy treschrestien et luy. Et ma mande
dire ledit ambassadeur, que tout ce quavoit este fait audit
France nestoit que artiffice pour abuser ceulx cy, pour
non les mectre en meffiance, et quil avoit cella sollicite
par ses lettres : toutefois celles quil a deu escripre sur le
cas de la diffamation de cedit roy et touchant le sequestre-
ment de la bible a payne pour lheure presente peuvent
estre arrivees a la court dudit France. Ledit ambassadeur ma aussi envoye demander, sil estoit vray, que ce
roy eust envoye presenter a la duchesse du Milan ung
dyamant de la valeur de seize mil ducatz, comme luy
avoit este dit ; a quoy luy envoyay dire nen avoit oncques
ouy parler, comme aussi en verite ne avoie.

Sire, atant &c. De Londres le 9e de janvier 1538 [1539].

D. Postscript of a Letter from the French Ambassador, Charles Marillac, to the Grand Constable of France, May 1, 1539

From British Museum Additional MS. 33514, f. 18.

Monsegneur le s^r Crumoil qui a le maniement de tous les affaires de ce Royaulme ma prie et Requis vous supplyer tresaffectueusement de sa part de luy faire deliurer certaines bibles en Angloys qui furent Imprimes a Paris soffrant en cas pareil a faire tout ce quil vous plaira luy commandey et soy disant votre treshumble seruiteur a quoy je nay fait aulcune Responce sinon que je te vous escrivois.[1]

E. Extract from a Letter from the Grand Constable of France to the French Ambassador in England, May 6, 1539 [1]

From the letter of M. Francisque Michel to the *Athenaeum*, May 20, 1871, compared with *Correspondance politique de MM. de Castillon et de Marillac, ambassadeurs de France en Angleterre*, 1537–1542, *publiée par M. Jean Kaulek*. Paris, 1885, No. 113.

Au demeurant, quant à ce que le sieur Cramoel vous a dict et prié touchant les bibles en vulgaire angloys imprimées à Paris, qu'il désire luy estre delivrez, je pense

[1] Marillac being newly appointed ambassador in succession to Castillon simply reports Cromwell's application, in ignorance of the part which his predecessor had played in the matter.

[1] This letter instructs Marillac to decline to give up the Bibles, on the ground that if they were unobjectionable they could as well be printed in England ; if objectionable, the French king did not wish to be responsible for them. The point of the better equipment of the French presses is not considered.

qu'à vostre partement d'icy il vous a esté communicqué
la responce que l'on a plusiers foys fecte là-dessous
à la continuelle instance que en faisoict lambassadeur
d'Angleterre estant icy, qui est en substance, que le roy,
apres avoir entendu plusiers choses falciffiées et erron-
nées estre dedans, s'est résolu de ne les faire délivrer : car
ce qui est bon se peult aussi bien imprimer en Angleterre
que en France ; mais ce qui est mauvais, ledict seigneur
ne permetra qu'il se imprime par deçà, où, soubz la
faculté de l'impression, il ne veult donner coulleur ne
auctorité aux maulvaises choses. Veez là ce que l'on
a respondu, comme ledict Cramoel a esté assez adverty,
sans ce que vous luy en réplicque aultre chose, &c. . . .

Escript a Chasteau Regnard, le vie jour de May, 1539.

F. Extract from a Letter of the French Ambassador to the Constable, July 5, 1539[1]

From the same sources as the preceding.

[Londres], 5 juillet.—Le dernier jour du passé arriva le
sieur d'Ampont, dépéché pour laffaire de monseigneur de
la Rochepot avec les lettres du roi de France au roi
d'Angleterre et celles du connétable à Cromwell et au duc
de Norfolk. Marillac a exposé l'affaire au long à Crom-

---

[1] Cromwell is here shown trying to use a case in which the
French were complainants as a lever to obtain the restoration
of the Bibles, but the tone of Marillac's report shows that not
much attention was then being paid to him. It has been suggested that the Bibles were ultimately given up early in November,
the dispute in which Monseigneur de Rochepot, i. e. François de
Montmorency, Governor of Picardy and brother of the Constable
of France, was involved eventually giving Cromwell a strong
enough card to play.

well. Celui-ci a fait si honnête réponse ' que s'il estoit si vaillant à tenir qu'il est hardy à promettre, sans difficulté ne m'en pourrois espérer que bien, combien qu'entre aultres propoz en discourant sur cest affaire et aultres qu'il avoit mis en avant, il se soit bien souvenu des bibles en vulgaire dont aultrefoys il me avoit pryé de vous escripre, alléguant le dommaige qu'il en avoit eu pour avoir esté aucteur et fait les fraiz de ce qui fust comencé à Paris, ne voulant prendre pour grand satis-faction les responces que je luy en ay faictes le plus dextrement qu'il m'estoit possible, pour l'entretenir le mieux que pourroie, d'aultant que l'on a affaire de luy et que l'yssue de cest affaire pend plus de sa voulenté que de celle du roy, son maistre ; lequel aussi, aprés que je luy ay remonstré les mesmes raisons du fait de mondit sieur vostre frère, nous a dict pour responce qu'il escriroit audict sieur Cramoil, à son chancellier et aultres de son conseil, qu'ilz eussent à regarder et examiner ceste cause, en laquelle s'ilz y voyent apparance pour nous, encores que la justice en fust doubteuse, qu'ilz nous eussent gratifiez en tout ce qu'ilz verroyent que la raison de justice ne seroict directement au contraire, pour l'amour du roy, son frère, que luy en rescripvoit si affecteusement ; et sur ceste responce, Monseigneur, je suys retourné des champs, où jestoys allé, trouver ce roy en ceste ville pour solliciter vifvement ledict affaire pour en tirer briefve résolution et responce par escript, ainsi que ledict seigneur roy m'a promis, &c. . . .

De Londres, ce v^e de juillet.

XL. THE PRICE AND COPYRIGHT OF THE GREAT BIBLE

LETTER FROM CRANMER TO CROMWELL, NOVEMBER 14 [1539][1]

From the original in the Record Office (*Letters and Papers of Henry VIII*, vol. xiv, pt. 2, 517).

My veray singuler good Lorde,—After my moste hartie commendations theis shalbe to signifie unto your Lordeship that Bartelett and Edward Whitecherche hath ben with me, and have, by thair accomptes, declared thexpensis and charges of the pryntyng of the great bibles ; and by thadvise of Bartelett I haue appoynted theym to be soulde for xiij s. iiij d. a pece, and not aboue. Howbeit Whitechurche enformeth me, that your lordeship thinketh it a moore convenient price to haue theym solde at x s a pece[2], which, in respecte of the greate chargis, both of the papar (which in very dede is substanciall and good) and other great hinderaunces, Whitechurche and his felowe thinketh it a small price, Nevertheles they ar right well contented to sell theym for x s., so that you wolbe so good lorde unto theym, as to graunte hensforth none other Lycence to any other printer, saving to theym, for the printyng of the said bible. For els thei thinke that thei shalbe greately hindered therbye ; yf any other should printe, they susteynyng suche charges as they al redie have don. Wherefore I shall beseche your Lordeshipe, in consideration of

---

[1] Endorsed : The bishopp of Cant. the xiiij[th] of November.

[2] This was presumably the price at which the early Great Bibles were issued, although, since Cromwell kept the matter in his own hands (see next document), it was not until April 1541 (see No. XLII), that it was fixed by the Privy Council.

their travaile in this behalf, to tender thair requestes, and thei have promysed me to prynte in thende of their bibles the price therof, to thente the Kinges lege people shall not hensforth be deceyvid of thair price.

Farther, yf your Lordeship hath known the kinges highnes pleasure concernyng the preface of the Bible, whiche I sent to you to oversee, so that his grace doth alowe the same, I pray you that the same may be delyvered unto the said Whitechurch, unto printyng : trusting that it shall both encorage many slowe readers, and also stay the rash judgementes of theym that reade therin. Thus our Lorde have your good Lordeship in his blessed tuition. Att Lambeth the xiiijth Day of Nouember.

Yor own ever assured,

T. Cantuarien.

To my singuler good Lorde my Lorde Privie Seale.

XLI. PATENT FOR BIBLE PRINTING GRANTED TO CROMWELL [1]

From the original Patent Roll, 31 Henry VIII, part 4, November 14, 1539.

For the Bible to be pryntyd by the ouersight of the lord Crumwell

Henry the eight &c. To all and singular Prynters and sellers of bookes within this oure realme and to all other officers mynistres and subiectes theise oure lettres

---

[1] As this patent is dated on the same day as Cranmer's letter, it is evident that immediately on hearing from the archbishop of the need for protecting the printers, Cromwell must have obtained a patent from the king, not for them, but for himself. He was thus enabled to keep the whole matter in his own hands.

heryng or seyng, gretyng. We late you witt that beyng desirous to haue oure people at tymes conuenyent geue theym selfes to thatteynyng of the knowlege of goddes worde Wherby they shall the better honour hym and obserue and kepe his commaundementes and also do their duties the better to vs beyng their Prince and soueraigne lorde. And consideryng that as this oure zeale and desire cannot by any meane take so good effecte as by the grauntyng to theym the free and lyberall use of the bible in oure oune maternall english tonge so onles it be forseen that the same passe at the begynnyng by one translation to be perusid and considered, the frailtie of menne is suche that the diuersitie therof maye brede and brynge forthe manyfolde inconuenyences as when wilfull and hedy folkes shall conferre upon the diuersitie of the said translacions, We have therfore appoynted oure right trusty and welbeloued counsellour the lorde Crumwell keper of oure pryvye seale to take for vs and in oure name speciall cure and charge that no manner of persone or persones within this oure realme shall enterprise attempte or sett in hande to print any bible in the english tonge of any maner of volume duryng the space of fyue yeres next ensuyng after the date hereof, but only all suche as shalbe deputid assignid and admytted by the said lorde Crumwell, Willyng and commaundyng all maires Shrifes Bailyffes constables and all other oure officers ministres and subiectes to be aydyng to oure said counsailour in thexecution of this oure pleasure and to be conformable in the accomplishment of the same as shall apperteigne. In Witnes wherof &c, Witnes oure self at Westm. the xiiij days of Nouembre. per ipsum Regem & de dat. predicta, &c.

XLII. ANTHONY MARLER AND THE PRIVY COUNCIL

From *Proceedings and Ordinances of the Privy Council of England*. Edited by Sir Harris Nicolas, vol. vii, pp. 181-6.

A. At Greenwich, April 25, 33 Hen. VIII, 1541

At Grenewiche the xxv^ty of April beyng present the Counsail which was present the daye before.

It was agreed that Anthony Marler of London, merchant, might sell the bibles of the gret volume unbounde for x s. sterl. and bounde being trymmed with bullyons for xij s. sterling.

B. At Greenwich, May 1, 33 Hen. VIII, 1541

At Grenewich the furst daye of Maye being present the Archebishop of Cantorbury, the Chauncelor of Englande, the Duke of Norffolk, the Lord Pryvey Seale, the Gret Chambrelain, of Englande, the Erle of Hertforde, the Gret Admiral of Englande, the Bisshop of Duresme, the Treasurer of Household, the Comptroller of Household, Sir Thomas Wriothesley Secretary, Sir Rauff Sadleir Secretary. . . .

Wheras Antony Marler of London marchaunt put up a supplicacion unto the forsaid Counsaill in maner & forme folowing. Wheras it hath pleased you for the comon wealth to take no small peynes in the furtheraunce of the price of my bookes, moost humbly I beseche the same to have in consideracion that onles I have by the meane of proclamacion sum charge or commission that every church not redy provided of one bible, shall according to the Kinges highnes former injunctions gyven in that behalf, provide them of a Bible of the largest volume, by a day to be prefixed and appointed, as shalbe thought moost convenient by your wisdomes, my grete sute, that I have made herin is not only frustrate and voyde, but also being charged as I am with an importune somme of the said bookes now lying on my hande, am undone for ever. And therfor trusting to the merciful consideracions of your high wisedomes, I humbly desire tobteyn the same commission, or sum other commaundement, and I with all myne during our lifes ar and shalbe bounde to pray contynually for your prosperous felicites long tendure.

It was agreed by the Lordes and others of the Kinges Maiesties Consaill that there shalbe a proclamacion made according to his request, and that the day to be limited for the havyng of the saide bookes shall be Hallowmasse.

XLIII. THE KING'S PROCLAMATION FOR THE ENGLISH BIBLE TO BE SET UP IN CHURCHES

MAY 6, 1541

From the original edition in the British Museum.

A proclamacion, ordeyned by the Kynges maiestie, with the aduice of his honourable counsayle for the Byble of the largest and greatest volume, to be had in euery churche. Deuised the vi day of May the xxxiii. yeare of the kynges moste gracious reygne.

Where, by Iniunctions [1] heretofore set forth by the

---

[1] The third and fourth of the Injunctions issued by Cromwell as Vicar-General were : ' Item, that ye shall provyde on this side the feast of . . . next commyng, one boke of the whole Bible

auctorite of the kynges royall maiestye, Supreme head
of the churche of this his realme of Englande. It was
ordeyned and commaunded amongest other thynges,
that in al and synguler paryshe churches, there shuld be
prouyded by a certen day nowe expyred, at the costes of
the curates and paryshioners, Bybles conteynynge the
olde and newe Testament, in the Englyshe tounge, to be
fyxed and set vp openlye in euery of the sayd paryshe
churches. The whiche Godlye commaundement and
iniuntion was to the onlye intent that euery of the
kynges maiesties louynge subiectes, myndynge to reade
therin, myght by occasyon thereof, not only consyder
and perceyue the great and ineffable omnipotent power,

of the largest volume in Englyshe, and the same sett up in summe
convenyent place within the said churche that ye have cure of,
whereas your parishners may most commodiouslye resort to the
same, and rede yt ; the charges of which boke shal be ratablie
born between you the parson, and the parishners aforsaid, that
ys to say, the one half by yowe, and th'other half by them.

'Item, that ye discorage no man pryuely or apertly from the
readinge or hearing of the same Bible, but shall expresslye provoke, stere, and exhorte every parsone to rede the same, as that
whyche ys the verye lively worde of God, that every christen
man ys bownde to embrace, beleve, and followe, yf he loke to
be saved ; admonyshinge them neverthelesse, to avoid all contention, altercation therin, and to use an honest sobrietye in the
inquisition of the true sense of the same, and referre th'explica-
tion of obscure places, to men of higher jugement in Scripture.'
(Printed from Reg. Cranmer, fol. 99b, in Wilkins's *Concilia*, iii.
815, under the date 1536, which is probably two years too early.)

In 1537 Latimer, Bishop of Worcester, had laid as his second
and third Injunctions on the prior and convent of St. Mary's
House in Worcester : 'Item, that the prior shall provide of the
monasteries charge, a whole Bible in English to be laid, fast
chained, in some open place, either in their church or cloister.
Item, that every religious person have at the least a New Testament in English, by the feast of the nativity of our Lord next
ensuing ' (Wilkins, iii. 832).

promyse, iustice, mercy and goodnes of Almyghtie God,
But also to learne thereby to obserue Gods commaundementes, and to obeye theyr soueraygne Lorde
and hyghe powers, and to exercyse Godlye charite, and
to vse themselues, accordynge to theyr vocations : in
a pure and syncere christen lyfe without murmure or
grudgynges. By the which Iniunctions the Kynges
royall maiestye intended, that his louynge subiectes
shulde haue and vse the commoditie of the readyng of
the sayd Bybles, for the purpose aboue rehersed, humbly,
mekely, reuerently and obediently ; and not that any
of them shulde reade the sayde Bybles, wyth lowde and
hyghe voyces, in tyme of the celebracion of the holye
Masse and other dyuyne seruyces vsed in the churche,
nor that any hys lay subiectes redynge the same, shulde
presume to take vpon them, any common dysputacyon,
argumente or exposicyon of the mysteries therein conteyned, but that euery suche laye man shulde humbly,
mekely and reuerentlye reade the same, for his owne
instruction, edificacion, and amendement of hys lyfe,
accordynge to goddes holy worde therin mencioned.
And notwythstandynge the kynges sayde moost godlye
and gracious commaundement and Iniunction in forme
as is aforesayde, Hys royall maiestye is informed that
dyuers and many Townes and paryshes wythin thys hys
realme haue negligently omytted theyr dueties in the
accomplishement therof wherof his highnes maruayleth
not a lytle.   And myndynge the execucion of his sayde
former, moost godly and gracyous Iniunctions : doeth
straytlye charge and commaunde that the Curates and
paryshioners of euerye towne and paryshe wythin thys
hys realme of Englande, not hauynge already Bybles
prouyded wythin theyr paryshe churches, shall on thys
syde the feaste of Alsayntes next commynge, bye and

prouyde Bybles of the largest and greatest volume, and cause the same to be set and fyxed in euery of the sayde paryshe churches, there to be vsed as is aforesayd : accordynge to the sayde former Iniunctions ; vpon payne that the Curate and inhabitauntes of the paryshes and townes, shal lose and forfayte to the Kynges maiestye for euery moneth that they shall lacke and want the sayde Bybles, after the same feast of Alsayntes fourty shyllynges, the one halfe of the same forefayt to be to the kynges maiesty, and the other halfe to hym or them whyche shall fyrste fynde and present the same to the Kynges maiestyes counsayle. And fynally, the kynges royall maiestie doeth declare and sygnifye to all and syngular his louynge subiectes, that to thentent they maye haue the sayde Bybles of the greatest volume at equall and reasonable pryces, His hyghnes by the aduyse of hys counsayle hath ordeyned and taxed : that the sellers therof, shall not take for any of the sayde Bybles vnbounde, aboue the pryce of ten shyllynges. And for euery of the sayde Bybles well and sufficientlye, bounde, trymmed and clasped, not aboue twelue shyllynges, vpon payne, the seller to lose for euerye Byble solde contrary to this his hyghnes proclamacion fourty shyllynges, the one moyte therof to the kynges maiestie : & the other moyte, to the fynder and presenter of the defaulte, as is afore sayde. And his hyghnes streyghtly chargeth and commaundeth that all and syngular ordinaries hauynge ecclesiasticall iurysdiction within this his churche and realme of Englande and the dominion of Wales, that they and euery of them shall put theyr effectuall endeuours, that the Curates and parishioners shall obeye and accomplyshe, thys his maiestyes proclamacion and commaundement, as they tendre the aduauncement of the kynges moost gracious and godly purpose in that behalfe, and as they wyll answer to his hyghnes for the same.

GOD SAVE THE KYNGE

Excussum per Richardum Grafton & Eduardum Whitchurch.   Cum priuilegio ad imprimendum solum.

XLIV. THE READING OF THE BIBLE

A.   Draft for a Proclamation

From Cotton MS. Cleopatra E. v. 327.[1]

Where it hathe pleased the kinges maiestie oure most dradde souereigne lor[d] and supreme hed vnder god of this Churche of England for a declaratyon of the greate zeale he bereth to the setting furthe of goddes woorde and to the vertuouse mayntenaunce of his commenwealthe to permy[t] and commaunde the Bible being translated in to our mother tongue to be synceiely taught and declared by vs the curates, And to bee openly[e] layed furthe in every parrishe churche ; to thintent that all his good subiectes aswel by reading thereof as by hering the true explanacion of the same may First lerne their dieuties to allmightie god and his maiestie and euery of vs charitably to vse other And thenne applying themselfes to doo according to that they shall here and lerne, may bothe speke and doo Christienly and in al thinges as it beseamethe Christien men, Because his highnes very muche desireth that this thing being by him most godly begonne And sett forward maye of all you be Receyued as is aforesaide His maiestie hathe willed and commaunded this to be declared vnto youe that his graces pleasure and hiegh commaundement is that in the reading and hering thereof, first most humbly and Reuerently vsing and addressing yourselfes vnto it, you

[1] Endorsed : Towchinge the reading of the Byble.

shall haue allwayes in your Rememberaunce and
memoryes that all thinges conteyned in this booke is
the vndoubted wylle, lawe and commaundement of
almightie god thonely and streight meane to knowe the
goodnes and benefytes of god towardes vs and the true
dieutye of euery christien manne to serue him accordingly,
And that therefore reading this booke with suche mynde
and firme feythe as is aforesaid, you shall first endevor
yourselfes to conforme your owne lyvinges and conuer-
sacion to the contentes of the same And so by your good
and vertuouse exemple to encourage your wifes childerne
and seruauntes to lyue wel and christienly according to
the rule thereof. And if at any tyme by reading any
doubt shall comme to any of youe touching the sense and
meanyng of any parte thereof, that thenne not geving
to moche to your owne mynde, fantazies and opinions
nor having thereof any open reasonyng in your open
Tauernes or Alehowses, ye shall haue Recourse to suche
lerned menne as be or shalbe auctorised to preache and
declare the same, soo that avoyding all contentions and
disputacions in suche Alehowses and other places
vnmete for suche conferences and submytting your
opinions to the Iudgementes of suche lerned menne as
shalbe appoynted in this behaulf, his grace may wel
perceyue that you vse this most hiegh benefyte quietly
and charitably euery of you to the edefying of himself his
wief and famylye in al thinges aunswering to his hieghnes
good opinion conceyued of you in thaduauncement of
vertue and suppressing of vice without failing to vse suche
discrete quietnes and sober moderatyon in the premisses as
is aforesaid   As ye tender his graces pleasure and intend
to avoyde his hiegh indignacion and the perill and daunger
that may ensue to you and euery of you for the contrary

And god saue the King

B. An admonition and advertisement given by the
bishop of London to all readers of the Bible
in the English tongue.   1542.

From Wilkins's *Concilia*, vol. iii, p. 863 sq. : ' Ex reg. Bonner,
et Burnet Hist. Reform. vol. i, App. p. 251.'

To the intent, that a good and wholesom thing, godly
and virtuously for honest intents and purposes set forth
for many, be not hindered or maligned at, for the abuse,
default, and evil behaviour of a few, who for lack of
discretion and good advisement commonly without
respect of time or other due circumstances, proceed
rashly and unadvisedly therein, and by reason thereof
rather hinder than set forward the thing, that is good
of itself : it shall therefore be very expedient, that
whosoever repaireth hither to read this book, or any
such like in any other place, he prepare himself chiefly
and principally with all devotion humility and quietnes,
to be edified and made the better thereby, adjoining
thereto his perfect and most bounden duty of obedience
to the king's majesty, our most gracious and dread
sovereign lord, and supreme head, especially in accomplishing his grace's most honourable injunctions and
commandment, given and made in that behalf ; and
right expedient, yea necessary it shall be also, that
leaving behind him vain glory, hypocrisy, and all other
carnal and corrupt affections, he bring with him discretion, honest intent, charity, reverence, and quiet behaviour to and for the edification of his own soul, without
the hinderance, let, or disturbance of any other his
christian brother ; evermore foreseeing, that no number
of people be especially congregate therefore to make
a multitude, and that no exposition be made thereupon
otherwise than is declared in the book itself ; and that

especial regard be had, no reading thereof be used, allowed, and with noise in the time of any divine service or sermon, or that in the same be used any disputation, contention, or any other misdemeanour ; or, finally, that any man justly may reckon himself to be offended thereby, or take occasion to grudge or malign thereat.

God save the King.

C. The Narrative of William Maldon of Newington, written for Fox's *Actes and Monuments*.[1]

From British Museum, Harley MS. 590, fol. 77.

A young man inhumanly persecuted by his Father for reading ye scripture, in K Henries time.

Grace peace and mercy from god our father, & from our lorde Jesus chryste be with all them that love the gospell of Jesus chryst vnfaynedly, so be it, Not vnto vs lord not vnto vs but vnto thy name be all honour & glory.

Jentyll reder vnderstand that I do not take in hande to wryte this lytyll tratyse as followeth, of myne anone provokyng but I with another chavnced to goo in the coumpany of Mr. Foxe the gather[er] together of this grete boke & he desyred vs to tell hym yf we knewe of any man that had suffered persecvcyon for the gospell of Jesus Chryst, to that end he myght adde it vnto the boke of martres, then sayd I that I knewe one that was whipped in kyng henryes tyme for it of his father, then he enquired of me his name, then I bwrayed & sayd it was I myselfe & tould hym a pece of it then was he desyrous to have the whole svrcomstavnes of it, then

---

[1] Endorsed : receaued of W. Maldon of Newyngton. With some misgivings this ingenuous document is printed exactly as it stands.

I promysed hym to wryght it, & as I sayd to hym not
for any vayne glory I will speke, but vnto the prayse
& honour of our god that worketh all in all, men of all
good gyftes that cometh from aboue, vnto whom be all
honour & glory for euer, in this life & for euer in the lyfe
to come so be it, As I fynde by the brefe crovnakill that
the bibill of the sacred chrypetvres was set forthe to bee
rede in all chvrches in ingelonde, by   then was I
the late worthy kynge henry the   about a xv yeres
viijth, & Imedyately after dyueres   of age.
poore men in the towne of chelmysford in the county
of Essyx where my father dwellyd & I borne & with
hym brovght vp, the sayd poore men bought the
newe testament of Jesus chryst & on svndayes dyd syt
redyng in lower ende of chvrche, &
manye wolde floke abovte them to   no man can
here theyr redyng then I cam amonge   comme vnto me
the sayd reders to here them, redyng   hym of my father.
of that glade & swete tydynges   John vi.
of the gospell, then my father seyng this that I
lestened vnto them euery svndaye, then cam he &
sovght me amonge them, & brovght me awaye from
the heryng of them, and wold have me to saye the lattyn
mattyns with hym, the which greued me very myche
& thvs did fete[2] me awaye dyueres tymes, then I see
I covlde not be in reste, then thovghte I I will learne to
read engelyshe, & then will I haue the newe testament
& read ther on myselfe, and then had I larned of an
engelyshe prymmer as fare as patrissapyentia & then
on svndayes I plyed my engelysshe prymmer, the mayetyd
follovyng I & my fathers prentys, thomas Jeffary layed
our mony to gether, & bought the newe testament in
engelyshe, & hydde it in our bedstrawe & so exersysed

[2] Fetched.

it at convenyent tymes, then shortly after my father set
me to the kepyng of habardashe[ry] & grossary(?) . . .
wares beyng a shott from his howse, & then I plyed my
boke, then shortly after I wold begyn to speke of the
schryptores, & on a nyght aboute eyght acloke my father
sate slepyng in a chayr & my mother & I fyll on reson-
yng of the crvsyfyx, & of the knelyng downe to it,
knokeynge on the breste, & hovldyng vp our handes to
it, when it cam by on precessyon, then sayd I it was
playne Idolatry & playnely agayneste the comavnde-
ment of god, wher he sayeth, thou shalt not make to thy
selfe anye graven Image thou shalt not bow downe to it
nor worshyp it, then sayed she a thou thefe yf thy father
knewe this he wolde hang the, wilte not thou worshyppe
the crosse & it was aboute the when thou were crystened,
& mvste be layed on the when thou art deade, with other
tavlke, then I went & hyde frythes boke on the sacarment
then I went to bede, &, then my father awakyd, & my
mother,tovlde hym of our commvyncatyon, then came he
vp in to our chamber with a greate rodde, & as I harde
hym comyng vp, I blessyd me, saying in the name of
the father & of the sonne & of the holy goste so be it,
then sayd my father to me serra who is your scholmaster
tell me, for sovthe father sayd I, I have no scholmaster
but god wher he sayth in his commaundement thou shant
not make to thyselfe anye graven Image you shavlt not
bow downe to it nor worshypp it, then he toke me by
the heare of my heade with bothe his handes & pvllyd
me out of the bed behynd Thomas Jeffary bake he sytt-
yng vp in his bedde, then he bestowed his rodd on my
bodye & styll wolde knowe my scholmaster & other
master then I sayd before he had none of me & he sayd
I spake agayneste the kynges injvntyones, & as trevly
as the lorde lyueth, I reioysyd that I was betten for

chrystes sake, & wepte not one taare out of myne eyes
& I thynke I felte not the strypes my reioysynge was so
mvche, & then my father sawe that wen he had beten
me Inofe[3] he let me goo & I wente to bede agayne, &
shede not one tare out of myne eyes, suerly sayd my
father, he is paste grace for he wepeth not for then was
he in twyse so moche rage, & sayd, fette me an havlter
I will suerly hange hym vp, for as good I hange hym vp
as another shovlde, & when he sawe that nobody wolde
goo he went downe, into his shoppe & brovght vp an
havlter, & the whyles he went a thou thefe, sayd my
mother, howe haste thow angeryd thy father, I neuer
sawe hym so angary, mother sayed I, I am the more
sorryer that he sholde be so angary for this matter,
& then began I to wepe for the grefe of the lake of knowledge in them, then sayed my mother, thomas Jeffary
aryse, & make the reddy for I cannot tell what he will
doo in his anger, & he sat vp in his bed pvttyng on of his
clothis & my father cometh vp with ye havlter & my
mother intretyd hym to lette me alone but in no wise he
wolde be intretyd but pvtte the havlter aboute my neke
I lyinge in my bedde & pvlled me with the havlter
behynde the sayd Thomas Jeffaryes bake almoste clene
ovt of my bede then my mother cryed out & pullyd hym
by the arme awaye, & my brother rycherd cryed out
that laye on the other syde of me, & then my father let
goo his hovlde & let me alone & wente to bede.

I thynke vj. dayes after my necke greved me with the
pvllyng of the havlter.[4]

[3] Enough.

[4] This is written in the margin, as is also the following sentence,
part of which has been rendered illegible in mounting the leaf :—
' wepyng tares . . . vrete this to thynke . . . lake of knowledge
. . . my father and mother they hade thought they had done god
good servis at that tyme, I troste he hath forgeuen them.'

XLV. THE GREAT BIBLE CONDEMNED

From Wilkins's *Concilia*, vol. iii, pp. 860 sq.

Convocatio praelatorum et cleri provinciae Cantuar. in domo capitulari ecclesiae S. Pauli London. 20. Januarii, congregata. Ex reg. convoc. et Excerpt. Heylinianis, et reg. Cranmer fol. 9.

In prima hujus convocationis sessione sacra, et quae sub auspiciis tractari solent, peragebantur. In secunda (Jan. 27) postquam Ric. Gwent, prolocutor, esset confirmatus, reverendissimus ex parte regis exposuit utrique domui, ' Quod regiae intentionis sit, quod ipsi patres, praelati, et clerus de rebus religionis lapsis et ruentibus consulant, ac de remediis congruis exhibendis inter se deliberent, et quae reformanda et corrigenda duxerint, inter se corrigant et reforment ; denuncians iis, quod in Testamento tam Veteri quam Novo in lingua Anglicana habentur multa, quae reformatione indigent ; proinde velle, ut prolocutor cum clero ad inferiorem domum se conferant, et inter se conveniant de dictis libris examinandis, quodque nonnulli periti etiam designentur ad canones et alias leges de simonia vitanda et coercenda condendos.'

In tertia sessione (Febr. 3.) post discursum de versione Bibliorum habitum, ' reverendissimus rogavit singulos, utrum sine scandalo et errore ac offensione manifesta Christi fidelium magnam Bibliam in Anglico sermone tralatam vellent retinere. Visum est majori parti eorundem dictam Bibliam non posse retineri, nisi prius debite castigetur et examinetur juxta eam Bibliam, quae communiter in ecclesia Anglicana legitur. Postea prolocutor et clerus comparens, exhibuerunt reverendissimo

quandam constitutionem provincialem per eos et in
vulgari et Latino sermone conceptam de simoniacis ;
cujus considerationem ipse in aliud tempus distulit,
clerique tempus ad exhibenda notata et errata in Veteri
Testamento protraxit.'

In quarta sessione (Feb. 10) nihil actum est.   In
quinta (Febr. 13) ' post colloquium inter episcopos
habitum de modo et forma procedendi in et circa examen
sacri voluminis, prolocutor intrans praesentavit librum,
continentem notata per eos ex Veteri Testamento in
diversis paginis, quae commisit rever. et patrum acri
judicio examinanda.   In coetu selecto pro examinandis
Bibliis, Novum Testamentum tradebatur episcopis
Dunelm. Winton. Hereford, Roffen. et Westmon. cum
doctoribus Wotton, Day, Coren, Wilson, Leighton, May
et aliis e domo inferiori convocationis : Vetus Testamentum archiepisc. Ebor. episcopo Elien. cum Redman,
Taylor, Haynes, Robertson, Cocks, etc. viris in Hebraica,
Graeca, Latina et Anglicana peritis. . . .

(Febr. 17) Prolocutore autem intrante, antequam
discessissent membra ejus, episcopus Winton. publice
legebat verba Latina in sacro volumine contenta, quae
voluit pro eorum germano et nativo intellectu et rei
majestate, quoad poterit vel in sua natura retineri,
vel quam accommodatissime fieri possit in Anglicum
sermonem verti.'   Quaenam illa fuerint ex Fullero
(Church Hist. p. 236) docemur.

Abridged Translation

The Archbishop's speech asks the clergy in the king's
name to come to the aid of the Church in its stress, and
denounces the English Old and New Testament as need-

ing many reforms; there was therefore to be a meeting of the two houses to make arrangements for examining the said books. In the third session after a discussion the Archbishop asked members individually whether without scandal error and manifest offence of Christ's faithful they voted to retain the Great Bible in the English speech. The majority resolved that the said Bible could not be retained until first duly purged and examined side by side with the (Latin) Bible commonly read in the English Church. . . . The day for bringing up passages marked as erroneous in the Old Testament was deferred. In the fifth session after a conversation among the Bishops as to the manner and form of proceeding with the examination of the sacred volume, the prolocutor entered and presented a book containing passages out of the Old Testament marked by the clergy in various pages, which he committed to be rigorously examined by the most reverend and the fathers (i. e. the Archbishop and Bishops). In committee for examining the Bible the New Testament was entrusted to the Bishops of Durham, Winchester, Hereford, Rochester and Westminstei, with Doctors Wotton, Day, Coren, Wilson, May, and others of the Lower House of Convocation. The Old Testament to the Archbishop of York and the Bishop of Ely, with Redman, Taylor, Haynes, Robertson, Cocks, &c., men skilled in Hebrew, Greek, Latin, and English. . . . On the prolocutor entering before they dissolved, the Bishop of Winchester publicly read the Latin words in the Sacred Volume which he desired for their germane and native meaning and for the majesty of their matter might be retained as far as possible in their own nature or be turned into English speech as closely as possible.[2]

[2] The words as given by Fuller are : Ecclesia, Poenitentia,

XLVI. PREFACE TO THE GENEVA NEW
TESTAMENT

To the Reader Mercie and peace through Christ
our Saviour

As the life of a true Christian is moste subiect to the
reprehension of the worlde : so all his actions, and entre-
prises, be they neuer so commendable, moue the wicked
rather to grudge and murmure, then to glorifie God who
is autor of the same. Which euil God hath left to his
Churche, as a necessarie exercise, aswel that man sholde
not be puffed vp with opinion of the gifts that he receaueth
of his heauenly Father : as also that seing how he euer
mainteyneth the same in despite of all outrageous
tyrannie, he might be more assured of Gods diuine
prouidence, and louing kyndenes towards his elect. For

Pontifex, Ancilla, Contritus, Olocausta, Justitia, Justificare
Idiota, Elementa, Baptizare, Martyr, Adorare, Dignus, San-
dalium, Simplex, Sapientia, Pietas, Presbyter, Lites, Servus,
Opera, Sacrificium, Tetrarcha, Sacramentum, Simulachrum,
Gloria, Conflictationes, Ceremonia, Mysterium, Religio, Spiritus
Sanctus, Spiritus, Merces, Confiteor tibi Pater, Panis proposi-
tionis, Communio, Perseverare, Dilectus, Didragma, Hospitalitas,
Episcopus, Gratia, Charitas, Tyrannus, Concupiscentia, Bene-
dictio, Humilis, Humilitas, Scientia, Gentilis, Synagoga, Ejicere,
Misericordia, Complacui, Increpare, Distribueretur, Orbis, Incul-
patus, Senior, Apocalypsis, Satisfactio, Contentio, Conscientia,
Peccatum, Peccator, Idolum, Prudentia, Prudenter, Cisera,
Apostolus, Apostolatus, Egenus, Stater, Societas, Zizania, Chri-
stus, Conversari, Profiteor, Impositio manuum, Idololatria,
Dominus, Sanctus, Confessio, Imitator, Pascha, Innumerabilis,
Inenarrabilis, Infidelis, Paganus, Commilito, Virtutes, Parabola,
Magnifico, Oriens, Subditus, Dominationes, Throni, Potestates
Hostia.

this cause we se that in the Churche of Christ ther are
thre kyndes of men : some are malicious despicers of the
worde, and graces of God, who turne all things into poison,
and a farther hardening of their hearts : others do not
openly resiste and contemne the Gospel, because they are
stroken as it were in a trance with the maiestie therof,
yet ether they quarell and cauell, or els deride and mocke
at whatsoeuer thing is done for the aduancement of
the same. The thirde sort are the simple lambes, which
partely are already in the folde of Christ, and so heare
willingly their Shepeherds voyce, and partly wandering
astray by ignorance, tary the tyme tyll the Shepherde
fynde them and bring them vnto his flocke. To this
kynde of people, in this translation I chiefly had respect,
as moued with zeale, conselled by the godly, and drawen
by [1] occasion, both of the place where God hath appointed
vs to dwel, and also of the store of heauenly learning &
iudgement, which so abundeth in this Citie of Geneva,
that iustely it may be called the patron and mirrour of
true religion and godlynes. To these therfore which are
of the flocke of Christ which knowe their Fathers wil, and
are affectioned to the trueth, I rendre a reason of my
doing in fewe lines. First as touching the perusing of
the text, it was diligently reuised by the moste approued
Greke examples, and conference of translations in other
tonges as the learned may easely iudge, both by the
faithful rendering of the sentence, and also by the proprietie of the wordes, and perspicuitie of the phrase.
Forthermore that the Reader might be by all meanes
proffited, I haue deuided the text into verses and sections,
according to the best editions in other langages, and
also, as to this day the ancient Greke copies mencion, it
was wont to be vsed. And because the Hebrewe and

[1] Misprinted ' dy '.

Greke phrases, which are strange to rendre in other
tongues, and also short, shulde not be so harde, I haue
sometyme interpreted them without any whit diminishing the grace of the sense, as our langage doth vse them,
and sometyme haue put to that worde, which lacking
made the sentence obscure, but haue set it in such letters
as may easely be discerned from the commun text. As
concerning the Annotations, wherunto these letters,
a, b, c, &c., leade vs, I haue endeuored so to proffit all
therby, that both the learned and others might be holpen :
for to my knollage I haue omitted nothing vnexpounded,
wherby he that is anything exercised in the Scriptures
of God, might iustely complayn of hardenes : and also
in respect of them that haue more proffited in the same
I haue explicat all suche places by the best learned interpreters ; as ether were falsely expounded by some or
els absurdely applyed by others : so that by this meanes
both they which haue not abilitie to by the Commentaries
upon the Newe testament, and they also which haue not
opportunitie and leasure to reade them because of their
prolixitie may vse this booke in stede therof, and some
tyme wher the place is not greatly harde, I haue noted
with this marke ″, that which may serue to the edification
of the Reader : adding also suche commone places, as
may cause him better to take hede to the doctrine.
Moreouer, the diuerse readings according to diuerse Greke
copies, which stande but in one worde, may be knowen
by this note ″, and if the bookes do alter in the sentence
then is it noted with this starre *, as the cotations are.
Last of all remayne the arguments, aswel they which
conteyne the summe of euery chapter, as the other
which are placed before the bookes and epistles : wherof
the commoditie is so great, that they may serue in stede
of a Commentarie to the Reader : for many reade the

Scriptures with myndes to proffit, but because they do
not consider the scope and purpose wherfore the holy
Gost so writeth and to what ende (which thing the Arguments do faithfully expresse) they either bestowe their
tyme without fruit, or els defraude them selues of a great
deale which they might atteyne vnto otherwise.   To the
intent therfore that, not onely they which are already
aduanced in the knollage of the Scriptures, but also the
simple and vnlearned might be forthered hereby, I haue
so moderat them with playnenes and breuitie, that the
verie ignorant may easely vnderstande them and beare
them in memorie.   And for this cause I haue applied
but one argument to the foure Euangelists, chiefely for
because that all writing of one matter, thogh by euery
one diuersly handeled, they required no diuersitie of
arguments.   Thus in fewe wordes I haue declared as
touching the chiefe pointes, beseching God so to inflame
our hearts with the desire to knowe his diuine wil, that
we may meditate in his holy worde both day and night,
wherin he hath reueiled it, and hauing atteyned thervnto
may so practise it in all our actions, that as we growe
in the ripenes of our Christian age, so we may glorifie
him more and more rendring to him eternal thankes
and praises for his heauenly and inestimable giftes
bestowed vpon his Churche, that all thogh Satan, Antichrist, and all his ennemies rage and burste, yet are they
not able to suppresse them, nether wil he diminishe
them : for seing he doth not onely brydel his ennemies
furie, but causeth them to defende and preserue his
gifts for the vse of his Churche (as we se the Jewes,
Christs professed ennemies preserue the olde testament
in moste integritie) what shulde we doute of his bontiful
liberalitie towards vs ? or why do we not rather with all
humilitie and submission of mynde obey him, loue and

feare him which is God blessed for euer ? To whome with
the Sonne and holy Gost be praise, honour & glorie.
Amen.

XLVII. PREFACE TO THE GENEVA BIBLE

To our Beloved in the Lord the Brethren of
England, Scotland, Ireland, &c., Grace, mercie, and
peace, through Christ Iesus.

Besides the manifolde and continual benefites which
almightie God bestoweth vpon vs, bothe corporal and
spiritual, we are especially bounde (deare brethren) to
giue him thankes without ceasing for his great grace and
vnspeakable mercies, in that it hath pleased him to call
vs vnto this meruelous light of his Gospel, and mercifully
to regarde vs after so horrible backesliding and falling
away from Christ to Antichrist, from light to darcknes,
from the liuing God to dumme and dead idoles, and that
after so cruel murther of Gods Saintes, as alas, hathe bene
among vs, we are not altogether cast of, as were the
Israelites, and many others for the like, or not so manifest
wickednes, but receyued agayne to grace with moste
euident signes and tokens of Gods especial loue and
fauour. To the intent therefore that we may not be
vnmyndeful of these great mercies, but seke by all meanes
(according to our duetie) to be thankeful for the same,
it behoueth vs so to walke in his feare and loue, that all
the daies of our life we may procure the glorie of his holy
name. Now forasmuche as this thing chefely is atteyned
by the knollage and practising of the worde of God
(which is the light to our paths, the keye of the kingdome
of heauen, our comfort in affliction, our shielde and
sworde against Satan, the schoole of all wisdome, the
glasse wherein we beholde Gods face, the testimonie of

his fauour, and the only foode and nourishment of our soules) we thoght that we colde bestowe our labours & studie in nothing which colde be more acceptable to God and comfortable to his Churche then in the translating of the holy Scriptures into our natiue tongue : the which thing albeit that diuers heretofore haue indeuored to atchieue yet considering the infancie of those tymes and imperfect knollage of the tongues, in respect of this ripe age and cleare light which God hath now reueiled, the translations required greatly to be perused and reformed. Not that we vendicat any thing to our selues aboue the least of our brethren (for God knoweth with what feare and trembling we haue bene now, for the space of two yeres and more day and night occupied herein) but being earnestly desired, and by diuers, whose learning and godynes we reuerence, exhorted, and also incouraged by the ready willes of suche, whose heartes God likewise touched, not to spare any charges for the fortherance of suche a benefite and fauour of God toward his Churche (thogh the tyme then was moste dangerous and the persecution sharpe and furious) we submitted our selues at length to their godly iudgementes, and seing the great oportunitie and occasions, which God presented vnto vs in this Churche,[1] by reason of so many godly and learned men ; and suche diuersities of translations in diuers tongues, we undertoke this great and wonderful worke (with all reuerence, as in the presence of God, as intreating the worde of God, whereunto we thinke our selues vnsufficient) which now God according to his diuine prouidence and mercie hath directed to a moste prosperous end. And this we may with good conscience protest, that we haue in euery point and worde, according to the measure of that knollage which it pleased al mightie God to giue

[1] i.e. at Geneva.

vs, faithfully rendred the text, and in all hard places
moste syncerely expounded the same. For God is our
witnes that we haue by all meanes indeuored to set
forthe the puritie of the worde and right sense of the
holy Gost for the edifying of the brethren in faith and
charitie.

Now as we haue chiefely obserued the sense, and
laboured alwaies to restore it to all integritie, so haue
we moste reuerently kept the proprietie of the wordes,
considering that the Apostles who spake and wrote to
the Gentiles in the Greke tongue, rather constrayned
them to the liuely phrase of the Ebrewe, then entreprised
farre by mollifying their langage to speake as the Gentils
did. And for this and other causes we haue in many
places reserued the Ebrewe phrases, notwithstanding
that thei may seeme somewhat hard in their eares that
are not wel practised and also delite in the swete sounding
phrases of the holy Scriptures. Yet lest ether the simple
shulde be discouraged, or the malicious haue any occasion
of iust cauillation, seing some translations read after one
sort, and some after another, whereas all may serue to
good purpose and edification, we haue in the margent
noted that diuersitie of speache or reading which may
also seme agreable to the mynde of the holy Gost and
propre for our langage with this marke x.

Agayne where as the Ebrewe speache semed hardly
to agre with ours, we haue noted it, in the margent after
this sort ", vsing that which was more intelligible. And
albeit that many of the Ebrewe names be altered from
the olde text, and restored to the true writing and first
original, whereof thei haue their signification, yet in
the vsual names litle is changed for feare of troubling
the simple readers. Moreouer whereas the necessitie of
the sentence required any thing to be added (for suche

is the grace and proprietie of the Ebrewe and Greke tongues, that it can not but ether by circumlocution, or by adding the verbe or some worde be vnderstand of them that are not wel practised therein) we haue put it in the text with another kynde of lettre, that it may easely be discerned from the common lettre. As touching the diuision of the verses, we haue followed the Ebrewe examples, which have so euen from the begynning distinct them. Which thing as it is moste profitable for memorie : so doeth it agre with the best translations, and is moste easie to finde out both by the best Concordances, and also by the cotations which we haue dilygently herein perused and set forthe by this starre *. Besides this, the principal matters are noted and distincted by this marke ¶. Yea and the argumentes bothe for the booke and for the chapters with the numbre of the verse are added, that by all meanes the reader might be holpen. For the which cause also we haue set ouer the head of euery page some notable worde or sentence which may greatly further aswel for memorie, as for the chief point of the page. And considering how hard a thing it is to vnderstand the holy Scriptures, and what errors, sectes and heresies growe dailie for lacke of the true knollage thereof, and how many are discouraged (as thei pretend) because thei can not atteine to the true and simple meaning of the same, we haue also indeuored bothe by the diligent reading of the best commentaries, and also by the conference with the godly and learned brethren, to gather brief annotations vpon all the hard places, aswel for the vnderstanding of suche wordes as are obscure, and for the declaration of the text, as for the application of the same as may most apperteine to Gods glorie and the edification of his Churche. Forthermore whereas certeyne places in the bookes of Moses, of

the Kings and Ezekiel semed so darke that by no description thei colde be made easie to the simple reader, we
haue so set them forthe with figures and notes for the
ful declaration thereof, that thei which can not by
iudgement, being holpen by the annotations noted by
the letters a b c. &c. atteyn therevnto, yet by the per-
spectiue, and as it were by the eye may sufficiently knowe
the true meaning of all suche places.   Wherevnto also
we haue added certeyne mappes of Cosmographie which
necessarely serue for the perfect vnderstanding and
memorie of diuers places and countreys, partely described,
and partely by occasion touched, bothe in the olde and
newe Testament.   Finally that nothing might lacke
which might be boght by labors, for the increase of
knowlage and fortherance of Gods glorie, we haue
adjoyned two moste profitable tables, the one seruing
for the interpretation of the Ebrewe names : and the
other conteyning all the chefe and principal matters of
the whole Bible : so that nothing (as we trust) that any
colde iustely desire, is omitted.   Therefore, as brethren
that are partakers of the same hope and saluation with
vs, we beseche you, that this riche perle and inestimable
treasure may not be offred in vayne, but as sent from
God to the people of God, for the increase of his kingdome,
the comfort of his Churche, and discharge of our conscience, whome it hath pleased him to raise vp for this
purpose, so you wolde willingly receyue the worde of
God, earnestly studie it, and in all your life practise it,
that you may now appeare in dede to be the people of
God, not walking any more according to this worlde,
but in the frutes of the Spirit, that God in vs may be
fully glorified through Christ Iesus our Lord, who
lyueth and reigneth for euer.   Amen.   From Geneua,
10 April. 1560.

XLVIII.   PRIVILEGE AND LICENCE TO JOHN BODLEY FOR PRINTING THE GENEVA BIBLE FOR SEVEN YEARS

Printed from the original, Patent Roll, 3 Elizabeth, part 13 (34), 1.

Elizabeth by the grace of god, &c., To all maner of printers booke-sellers and other our officers ministers and subiectes greating. We do youe to understande that of our grace especiall. We haue graunted and geven priuiledge and licence and by thes presentes for us our heires and successors do graunte and geue priuilege and lycence vnto our welbeloued subiecte John Bodeleigh and his assignes for terme of seven yeares next ensuyng the date of thes our lettres patent to imprint or cause to be emprinted the Inglysshe bible with annotacions faithfully translated and fynished in thes present yeare of our lord god a thousand fyve hundreth and threscore, and dedicated to vs. straightly forbidding and com- manding by thes presentes all and singuler our subiectes aswell printers as bokesellers as all other person within our Realmes and dominions whatsoever they be, in anie maner to imprint or cause to be emprinted anie of the forseid englisshe bibles that the said John Bodeleigh shal by auctoritie of this our licence imprint or cause to be emprinted or any parte of them, but onely the said John Bodeleigh and his assignes vpon payne of our high Indignacion and displeasure, And that euery offender theren shall forfeit to our vse fortie shillinges of lawfull money of Englond for euery suche bible or bibles at anie tyme so imprinted contrary to the true meanyng of this our presente licence and priuilege, ouer and besides

all suche booke or bookes so imprinted to be forfeited
to whom soeuer shall susteyne the charges and sue the
said forfeiture on our behalf.   Prouided that the bible
to be emprinted may be so ordered in the edicion thereof
as may be seme expedient by the aduise of our trusty and
welbeloued the bisshopps of Canterbory and London.[1]
In witnes whereof &c. Witnes the quene at Westminster
the viij day of Januarye.[2]   per breue de priuato sigillo.

XLIX.   PARKER AND GRINDAL ON THE RENEWAL OF BODLEY'S PRIVILEGE

From British Museum, Lansdowne MS. viii. Art. 82 [p. 205].

Being enformed by this berer John Bodleygh that
vppon his late sute to you for the renewing of his privilege
with longer tearme,[1] for the reimprintinge of the late
Geneva Bible by him and his associates sett foorthe,
you suspended to give your furderaunce vntill you had
hearde owre advise.   So it is that we thinke so well óf
the first impression, and reviewe of those whiche have
sithens travailed therin, that we wishe it wold please
you to be a meane that twelve yeres longer tearme maye

---

[1] In the absence of any other explanation of the failure of
John Bodley to make any use of this licence it seems reasonable
to attribute it to this clause, which enabled the Archbishop of
Canterbury and Bishop of London to make any conditions, such
as the omission of notes which they considered objectionable,
that they might please.

[2] The year being reckoned from Lady Day, the date January 8
[1561] would be the same year as that in which the Geneva Bible
was printed (1560).

[1] Over four of the seven years for which Bodley had obtained
a privilege had now elapsed, and he clearly wanted to keep his
rights alive in the hope of being able to come to terms with the
Archbishop.

be by speciall privilege graunted him, in consideracion of the charges by him and his associates in the first impression, and the reviewe sithens susteyned.[2] For thoughe one other speciall bible for the churches be meant by vs to be set forthe as convenient tyme and leysor hereafter will permytte : yet shall it nothing hindre but rather do moche good to have diversitie of translacions and readinges. And if his licence, herafter to be made, goe simplye foorthe without proviso of our oversight as we thinke it maye so passe well ynoughe,[3] yet shall we take suche ordre in writing withe the partie, that no impression shall passe but by owr direcion, consent, and advise. Thus ending we commende you to Allmightie god. From Lambethe this ixth of Marche 1565.

Yor in Christe,

Matthue Cantuar

Edm. London.[4]

[2] This suggests that the Geneva Bible had been revised, at Bodley's expense, in the hope of meeting the Archbishop's wishes.

[3] i. e. the clause in the original privilege ' Prouided that the bible to be emprinted may be so ordered in the edicion thereof as may seme expedient by the aduise of our trusty and wel-beloued the bisshopps of Canterbory and London ' might be omitted—a concession, perhaps to Puritan feelings, which Parker owing to the strength of his position could afford to make.

[4] Addressed : ' To the honorable Sir William Cecill knight principall Secretarie to the Quenes Maiestie ' ; endorsed : ' 9 Martii 1565. Archb. of Cantuar & B. of Lond. for John Bodlegh for printing of the Geneva bible.'

L. THE PREPARATION OF THE BISHOPS' BIBLE

A. LETTER OF RICHARD COX, BISHOP OF ELY, TO CECIL

From the original in the Record Office (*Domestic State Papers*, Elizabeth, vol. xxi, Article 18).

A nother thing ther is worthy to be consydered, the translation of the bible to be committed to mete men and to be vewed ouer and amended. I called apon it in bothe my masters tymes sed frustra. Yet god be praised, ye haue men hable to do it thoroughly. Thus muche I signifie to you because god hath apoynted you a speciall instrumente to the furtheraunce of his heavenly truthe, vnder so gratiouse a soverayn, who I trust doth not mislyke the apologie

.　　.　　.　　.　　.　　.　　.　　.

From Downham the xix of January 1561.

Your hartyly assured

Richarde Ely.[1]

B. PARKER INVITES CECIL TO TAKE PART IN THE REVISION

From the original in the Record Office (*Domestic State Papers*, Elizabeth, vol. xli, Article 33).

Sir I haue destributed the bible in partes to dyuerse men, I am desierus yf ye coud spare so moche leysur eyther in mornyng or evenyng : we had one epistle of

[1] Addressed : 'To the most honorable Sir William Cecill knight Secretary to the Quenes maiestie'; endorsed in two hands. 19 Januar. B. of Ely & my master. In commendacion of Apologia [pro] Ecclesia Anglicana. 1561.'

S. Paul or peter, or Jamys of your pervsinge to thentent
that ye maye be one of the buylders of this good worke
in christes churche, although otherwise we account youe
a comon paterne to christes blessed word & religion, thus
God kepe your honor in helthe, from my house this xxvj
of novembre

Your honors

Matth. Cant.[1]

C. STRYPE'S SUMMARY OF OTHER CORRESPONDENCE

From the *Life and Acts of Matthew Parker*.   By John Strype,
Oxford, 1821, vol. i, pp. 415–17.

Edwin, Bishop of Worcester, who, as he was an
excellent preacher, so a man well skilled in the original
languages, was one of the Bishops appointed to this
work.   His part being finished, he sent it back to the
Archbishop, with his letter dated from Worcester,
Feb. 6.   Which, because it may give us some light into
this good design, I will here set down.

'My duty remembered ; According to your Grace's
letter of instruction, I have perused the book you sent
me, and with good diligence : having also, in conference
with some other, considered of the same, in such sort,
I trust, as your Grace will not mislike of.   I have sent
up with it my Clerk, whose hand I used in writing forth
the corrections and marginal notes.   When it shall
please your Grace to set over the Book to be viewed by
some one of your Chaplains, my said Clerk shall attend
a day or two, to make it plain unto him, how my notes
are to be placed.

[1] Addressed : ' To ye right honorable Sir W. Cecill principal
Secretary to the Queens Maiestie ' ; endorsed : ' 26 Novembre
1566. Archb. of Cantuar to my master.   Translacion of ye Bible.'

' In mine opinion, your Grace shall do well to make the whole Bible to be diligently surveyed by some well learned, before it be put to print ; and also to have skilful and diligent correctors at the printing of it, that it may be done in such perfection, that the adversaries can have no occasion to quarrel with it. Which thing will require a time. *Sed sat cito, si sat bene.* The setters forth of this our common translation followed Munster [1] too much, who doubtless was a very negligent man in his doings, and often swerved very much from the Hebrew.

' Thus, trusting that your Grace will take in good part my trifles, wherein wanted no good will, I commend the same to the grace of Almighty God. From my house at Worcester.

' Your Grace's in Christ at commandment,

' Ed. Wigorn.'

And in another letter, the same pious Bishop put the Archbishop in mind of this great work, to proceed earnestly forward in it. ' Your Grace,' said he, ' should much benefit the Church, in hastening forward the Bible which you have in hand : those that we have be not only false printed, but also give great offence to many, by reason of the depravity in reading.'

To Guest, Bishop of Rochester, the Archbishop sent the Book of Psalms to revise : and he sent it back again with his notes and advertisements, as the Bishop of Worcester had done. In his letter to the Archbishop he said, ' he had not altered the translation but where it gave occasion of an error. As at the first Psalm, at the

---

[1] i. e. Sebastian Münster, the author of a new Latin version of the Old Testament, first printed at Basel, 1534-5.

beginning, I turn the preterperfect tense into the present tense : because the sense is too harsh in the preterperfect tense. Where in the New Testament one piece of a Psalm is reported, I translate it in the Psalms according to the translation thereof in the New Testament, for the avoiding of the offence that may rise to the people upon divers translations.[2] Where two great letters be joined together, or where one great letter is twice put, it signifieth that both the sentences or the words be expounded together.'

To Parkhurst, Bishop of Norwich, the Archbishop sent another part of the Bible, to make his notes and advertisements upon. Who wrote back to the Archbishop, that he would travail therein with such diligence and expedition as he might.

Davies, Bishop of St. David's, had another portion. And he wrote to the Archbishop that he was in hand with that part of the Bible he sent him. And again, not long after, in the year 1566, he wrote the Archbishop, that he would finish it with as much speed as he could ; and that he bestowed, for his performance of the same, all such time as he could spare.

This Bishop was now very busy in translating the Bible into Welsh, together with William Salisbury, Bishop of Man, a man very learned in the British antiquities.

This business in correcting the former translation of the Bible, went forward along the next year 1566. Cox, Bishop of Ely, who seems to have had another part of the holy Scripture committed to him, in a letter dated May 3, 1566, had these words concerning this noble

[2] Probably because these views did not commend themselves to Parker, Bishop Guest's work seems not to have been used. See Introduction, p. 31.

work : ' I trust your Grace is well forward with the Bible by this time. I perceive the greatest burden will lie upon your neck, touching care and travail. I would wish that such usual words as we English people be acquainted with might still remain in their form and sound, so far forth as the Hebrew will well bear ; ink-horn terms to be avoided. The translation of the verbs in the Psalms to be used uniformly in one tense, &c. And if ye translate *bonitas* or *misericordia*, to use it likewise in all places of the Psalms, &c. God send this good travail a blessed success.'

LI. PARKER ANNOUNCES TO CECIL THE COMPLETION OF THE BISHOPS' BIBLE

From the original in the Record Office (*Domestic State Papers*, Elizabeth, vol. xlvii, No. 78).[1]

Salutem in Christo. Sir I have receyved your lettres, and shall performe that yowe desier, concerning Mr. Welles when he cometh to me or any of his factors, I here his knowledge and honestye to be well reported. Sir, after much toyle of the Printer and sum Labors taken of sum parties for the setting owte and Recognising of the Englishe bible, we be nowe come to a conclusion for the substance of the booke. Sum ornamentes of the same [2] be yet lacking, prayeng your Honor to beare in pacience till yt be fully reedy. I do meane by gods

[1] Addressed : ' To the right honorable Sir William Cicell knight Principall Secretarye to the Quenes maiestie. At the Cowrte ; endorsed : ' 22 Septembre 1568. Tharchbishop of Canterbury to my Master. Bible.'

[2] Almost certainly the engraved title-page and portraits of Leicester and Cecil (now Lord Burghley), which would be printed by a separate impression.

grace, yf my health will serve me better than yt is at this tyme, to present the Quenes highnes with the first, as sone as I can here her Maiestie to be come to Hampton Courte which we here will be within eight or nyne dayes. Which god prosper, and sent to your honor grace and health as I wishe to my selfe. From my howse at Lambith, this xxij of September

Your Honors loving Frende

Matth. Cant.

LII. PRESENTATION OF THE BISHOPS' BIBLE TO THE QUEEN, AND STORY OF THE REVISION

A. ARCHBISHOP PARKER TO CECIL

From the original in the Record Office (*Domestic State Papers*, Elizabeth, vol. xlviii, 6).[1]

Sir after my right hartie Comendacions, I was in purpose to have offred to the Quenes highnes the first fruites of our Labors in the recognising the Bible, But I feale my health to be such, that as yet I dare not adventure. Whervppon for that I wold not have the Queens highnes and your honor to be long delayed, nor the poore printer after his great charges to be longer deferred, I have caused one booke to be bound as you see which I hartelye pray yow to present favorablie to the Queens Maiestie, with your frendlie excuse of my

[1] Addressed : 'To the right honorable Sir William Cecyll knight principall Secretary to the Queen's maiestie and one of hir prevy counseyle be it deliuered ' ; endorsed : ' 5 October 1568, Archb. of Canterbury to my master with the bible newly sett forth.'

disabylitie, in not coming my self. I haue also wrytten
to the Queens Maiestie, the Copie wherof I have sent yow
the rather to vse your oportunitie of deliuerie, yf your
Prudence shall not think them tolerable. And bicause
I wold yow knewe all, I here send yow a note to signifie :
who first traueiled in the diuerse bookes, though after
them sum other perusing was had, the lettres of their
names be partlie affixed in the ende of their bookes,
Which I thought a polecie to showe them, to make them
more diligent, as Awnswerable for their doinges. I have
remembred yow of such observacions as my first lettres
sent to them (by your advise) did signifie. Yt may be
that in so long a worke thinges have scaped which may
be Lawfull to euerie man cum bona venia to amend whan
they find them non omnia possumus omnes. The
Printer hath honestlie done his diligence, yf your honor
wold obteine of the Queens highnes, that the edicion
might be Licensed and only comended in publike reading
in Churches, to drawe to one vniformitie, yt weare no
greate cost to the most parishes and a Relief to him for
his great charges susteined. The Psalters might remayn
in Queres as they be much multiplied but wher of ther
owne accord they wold vse this Translacion.[2] Sir,
I pray your honor be a meane that Jug only may have
the preferment of this edicion,[3] for yf any other shuld
Lurche him to steale from him thes copies,[4] he weare

[2] i. e. Churches which had bought Psalters of the Great Bible
version for use in choir were not to be put to the expense of
buying new ones of the Bishops' version. In the second edition
(1572) the hold which the Psalter of the Great Bible had established was further recognized by that version being printed as
well as the newer one, and it has continued the liturgical psalter
unto this day.

[3] ' edition ' seems here used in the sense of ' version '.

[1] i. e. copyrights.

a great Loser in this first doing,[5] And Sir without doubt he hath well deserved to be preferred. A man wold not thinke that he had devoured so much payne as he hath susteined. Thus I wish your honor all grace vertue and helthe as to my self. From my house at Lambith this fifth of October.

Your Honors loving Frend

Matthue Cantuar.

B. Archbishop Parker to Queen Elizabeth

Printed from the original in the Record Office (*Domestic State Papers*, Elizabeth, vol. xlviii, 6, I).

After my most Lowlie submission to your Maiestie, with my hartie reioyce of your prosperous progresse and retorne, pleaseth yt your highnes to accept in good parte, the endevor and diligence, of sum of vs your chapleins, my brethren the Bisshoppes, with other certaine Learned men, in this newe edicion of the bible, I trust by comparisone of divers translacions put forth in your realme will apeare as well the workemanshippe of the printer, as the Circumspeccion of all such as have traveiled in the recognicion. Amonge divers observacions which have bin regarded in this recognition one was, not to make yt varye much from that translacion which was comonlye vsed by Publike order, except wher eyther the verytie of the hebrue & greke moved alteracion, or wher the text was by sum negligence mutilated from the originall. So that I trust your Loving subiectes shall se good cause in your Maiesties dayes to thanke god, and to reioyce, to see this his treasor of his holy worde, so set oute, as may be proved (So farforth as mortall mans knowledge can attaine to, or as farforth as god hath

---

[5] The word 'translacion' has been struck out before 'doing'.

hitherto revealed) to be faithfully handeled in the
vulgar tonge, besechinge your highnes, that yt may have
your gracious favor, License and proteccion to be
com[un]icated abrode, aswell for that in many Churches
they want their bookes, and have longe tyme loked for
this : as for that in certaine places be publikely vsed
sum translations which have not byn Labored in your
Realme having inspersed diverse preiudicall notis which
might have ben also well spared.[1] I have byn bolde in
the forniture with fewe wordes to expresse the incom-
perable valewe of this Treasor amonge many thinges
good profitable and bewtifull, ye have in possession, yet
this only necessarie, whereof so to thinke, and so to
beleve, maketh your Maiestie blessed, not only here in
this your gouernance, but yt shall advance your maiestie
to attaine at the last the blisse everlastinge, which after
a longe prosperous raigne over vs, Almightie god send
yow, as certainelie he will, for cherishinge that Juell
which he loveth best, of which is pronounced that
Quomodocumque Celum et terra transibunt verbum
tamen domini manebit in eternum. God preserve your
highnes in all grace and felicitie.

C. Parker's Note as to the Translators[1]

Printed from the original in the Record Office (*Domestic State
Papers*, Elizabeth, vol. xlviii, 6, II).

The sum of the scripture
The Tables of Christes line
The argument of the scriptures
The first Preface into the whole Bible } M. Cant.
The Preface into the psalter
The preface into the new Testament

[1] The allusion is of course to the Geneva Bible.
[1] See Introduction, p. 30.

Genesis ⎫ M. Cant.
Exodus ⎭

Leviticus ⎫ Cantuarie.
Numerus ⎭

Deuteronomius. W. Exon.

Josue ⎫
Judicum ⎪
Ruth ⎬ R. Meneuen.
Regum 1, 2 ⎭

Regum 3, 4 ⎫ Ed. Wigorn.
Paralipomena 1, 2 ⎭

Job ⎫ Cantuarie.
Proverbia ⎭

Ecclesiastes ⎫ Cantabrigie.
Cantica ⎭

Ecclesiasticus ⎫
Susanna ⎪
Baruc ⎬ J. Norwic.
Maccabeorum ⎭

Esdras ⎫
Judith ⎪
Tobias ⎬ W. Cicestren.
Sapiencia ⎭

Esaias ⎫
Hierimias ⎬ R. Winton.
Lamentaciones ⎭

Ezechiel ⎫ J. Lich. & Covent.
Daniel ⎭

Prophete ⎫ Ed. London.
Minores ⎭

Mattheus ⎫ M. Cant.
Marcus ⎭

Lucas ⎫ Ed. Peterb.
Johannes ⎭

Acta Apostolorum }
Ad. Romanos } R. Eliensis.

1 epistola Corin. D. Westmon.

2 epistola Corin. }
Ad Gallathas }
Ad Ephesios }
Ad Philepenses }
Ad Collossenses }
Ad Thessalonicenses } M. Cant.
Ad Timothium }
Ad Titum }
Ad Philemonem }
Ad Hebreos }

Epistolae Canonicae }
Apocalipsis } N. Lincoln.

Observacions respected of the Translators

Firste to followe the Commune Englishe Translacion. vsed in the Churches and not to receed from yt but wher yt varieth manifestlye from the Hebrue or Greke originall.

Item to vse such sections and devisions in the Textes as Pagnine in his Translacion vseth, & for the veritie of the Hebrue to followe the said Pagnine and Munster specially, And generally others learned in the tonges.

Item to make no bitter notis vppon any text, or yet to set downe any determinacion in places of controversie.

Item to note such Chapters and places as conteineth matter of Genealogies or other such places not edefieng, with some strike or note that the Reader may eschue them in his publike readinge.

Item that all such wordes as soundeth in the Olde Translacion to any offence of Lightnes or obscenitie be expressed with more convenient termes and phrases.

The printer hath bestowed his thickest Paper in the newe Testament bicause yt shalbe most occupied.

LIII. THE INCEPTION OF THE RHEIMS NEW TESTAMENT

Part of a Letter from Cardinal Allen to Dr. Vendeville

From *Letters and Memorials of William Cardinal Allen*, by T. F. Knox. 1882, p. 52 sqq.

Singulis diebus Dominicis et festis habentur conciones anglicae a provectioribus ad evangelium, epistolam vel historiam diei propriam, ubi inflammantur omnium animi ad pietatem in Deum et ad zelum in Angliam a schismate in viam salutis revocandum. Id autem anglice facimus ut vernaculae linguae facultatem majorem et gratiam, qua haeretici mire sibi placent et insigniter aliis simplicioribus nocent, assequamur. In quo genere vel imperiti alioquin haeretici multis doctioribus catholicis saepe praestant, quod hi in academiis et scholis educati non habent fere Scripturae textum nec allegant nisi latinum, quem cum pro concione indocta coguntur mox in vulgarem linguam vertere, quia statim alicujus versionis vulgaris verba non sunt, saepe parum accommodate et non sine ingrata haesitatione transferunt ; ubi adversarii ad unguem tenent ex haeretica aliqua versione omnia Scripturae loca quae pro ipsis facere videantur, et quadam composita fraude ac mutatione sacrorum verborum efficiunt tandem ut nihil

loqui videantur nisi ex Bibliis. Cui malo utrinque
mederi possit, si et nos haberemus aliquam catholicam
versionem Bibliorum ; omnes enim anglicae versiones
sunt corruptissimae. Quales in Belgio vestro habeatis
nescio ; certe nos si sua Sanctitas faciendum judicabit,
id etiam agemus ut fideliter, pure et genuine secundum
approbatam ecclesiae editionem Biblia vertantur ; cum
ad hanc rem viros jam habeamus aptissimos. Licet
enim optandum esset fortasse ut nunquam in barbaras
linguas Scripturae verterentur, tamen cum tanta sit
hodie vel ex haeresi vel aliunde curiositas hominum etiam
non malorum, et saepe etiam propter confutationem
adversariorum legendi necessitas, satius est ut fidelem
et catholicam habeant translationem, quam ut cum peri-
culo aut ad perditionem utantur corrupta ; praesertim
cum periculis ex difficiliorum quorundam locorum lectione
commodis quibusdam annotationibus occurri possit.

TRANSLATION

From *First and Second Diaries of the English College at Douay*.
By T. F. Knox. 1878, p. xl.

On every Sunday and festival English sermons are
preached by the more advanced students on the gospel,
epistle, or subject proper to the day. These discourses
are calculated to inflame the hearts of all with piety
towards God and zeal for the bringing back of England
from schism to the path of salvation. We preach in
English, in order to acquire greater power and grace in
the use of the vulgar tongue, a thing on which the heretics
plume themselves exceedingly, and by which they do great
injury to the simple folk. In this respect the heretics,
however ignorant they may be in other points, have the
advantage over many of the more learned catholics, who

having been educated in the universities and the schools do not commonly have at command the text of Scripture or quote it except in Latin. Hence when they are preaching to the unlearned, and are obliged on the spur of the moment to translate some passage which they have quoted into the vulgar tongue, they often do it inaccurately and with unpleasant hesitation, because either there is no English version of the words or it does not then and there occur to them. Our adversaries on the other hand have at their fingers' ends all those passages of Scripture which seem to make for them, and by a certain deceptive adaptation and alteration of the sacred words produce the effect of appearing to say nothing but what comes from the bible. This evil might be remedied if we too had some catholic version of the bible, for all the English versions are most corrupt. I do not know what kind you have in Belgium. But certainly we on our part, if his Holiness shall think proper, will undertake to produce a faithful, pure and genuine version of the bible, in accordance with the edition approved by the Church, for we already have men most fitted for the work. Perhaps indeed it would have been more desirable that the Scriptures had never been translated into barbarous tongues ; nevertheless at the present day, when either from heresy or other causes, the curiosity of men, even of those who are not bad, is so great, and there is often such need of reading the Scriptures in order to confute our opponents, it is better that there should be a faithful and catholic translation than that men should use a corrupt version to their peril or destruction ; the more so since the dangers which arise from reading certain more difficult passages may be obviated by suitable notes.

LIV. PREFACE TO THE RHEIMS NEW TESTAMENT

From the copy in the British Museum.

The Preface to the Reader treating of these three points : of the translation of Holy Scriptures into the vulgar tongues, and namely into English ; of the causes why this new Testament is translated according to the auncient vulgar Latin text : & of the maner of translating the same.

The holy Bible long since [1] translated by vs into English, and the old Testament lying by vs for lacke of good meanes to publish the whole [2] in such sort as a worke of so great charge and importance requireth : we have yet through Gods goodnes at length fully finished for thee (most Christian reader) all the NEW TESTAMENT, which is the principal, most profitable & comfortable peece of holy writte : and, as wel for all other institution of life and doctrine, as specially for deciding the doubtes of these daies, more propre and pregnant then the other part not yet printed.

Which translation we doe not for all that publish, vpon erroneous opinion of necessitie, that the holy Scriptures should alwaies be in our mother tonge, or that they ought, or were ordained by God, to be read indifferently of all, or could be easily vnderstood of euery one that readeth or heareth them in a knowen language : or that they were not often through mans malice or

Translation of the Scriptures into the vulgar tongues, not absolutely necessarie or profitable, but according to the time.

---

[1] According to the College Diaries it was begun on or about March 16, 1578, and finished in March 1582.

[2] The Old Testament was not printed until 1609.

infirmitie, pernicious and much hurtful to many : or that we generally and absolutely deemed it more conuenient in it self, & more agreable to Gods word and honour or edification of the faithful, to haue them turned into vulgar tonges, then to be kept & studied only in the Ecclesiastical learned languages : Not for these nor any such like causes doe we translate this sacred booke, but vpon special consideration of the present time, state, and condition of our countrie, vnto which, diuers thinges are either necessarie, or profitable and medicinable now, that otherwise in the peace of the Church were neither much requisite, nor perchance wholy tolerable. . . .

[b. iij recto]

Now TO GIVE thee also intelligence in particular, most gentle Reader, of such thinges as it behoueth thee specially to know concerning our Translation : We translate the old vulgar Latin text, not the common Greeke text, for these causes.

Many causes why this new Testament is translated according to the auncient vulgar Latin text.

1. It is so auncient, that it was vsed in the Church of God aboue 1300 yeres agoe, as appeareth by the fathers of those times.

It is most auncient.

2. It is that (by the common receiued opinion and by all probabilitie) which S. Hierom. afterward corrected according to the Greeke, by the appointment of Damasus then Pope, as he maketh mention in his preface before the foure Euangelistes, vnto the said Damasus : and *in Catalogo in fine*, and *ep*. 102.

Corrected by S. Hierom.

3. Consequently it is the same which S. Augustine so commendeth and alloweth in an Epistle to S. Hierom.[3]

Commended by S. Augustine.

[3] Note : Ep. 10.

4. It is that, which for the most part euer since hath been vsed in the Churches seruice, expounded in sermons, alleaged and interpreted in the Commentaries and writings of the auncient fathers of the Latin Church.

Vsed and expounded by the fathers.

5. The holy Councel of Trent, for these and many other important considerations, hath declared [4] and defined this onely of al other latin translations, to be authentical, and so onely to be vsed and taken in publike lessons, disputations, preachings, and expositions, and that no man presume upon any pretence to reiect or refuse the same.

Only authenticated by the holy Councel of Trent.

6. It is the grauest, sincerest, of greatest maiestie, least partialitie, as being without al respect of controuersies and contentions, specially these of our time ; as appeareth by those places which Erasmus and others at this day translate much more to the aduantage of the Catholike cause.

Most graue, least partial.

7. It is so exact and precise according to the Greeke, both the phrase and the word, that delicate Heretikes therfore reprehend it of rudenes. And that it followeth the Greeke far more exactly then the Protestants translations, beside infinite other places, we appeale to these. Tit. 3. 14. *Curent bonis operibus praeesse*, προίστασθαι Eng. bib. 1577 *to mainteine good workes*, and Hebr. 10. 20. *Viam nobis initiavit*, ἐνεκαίνεσεν. English bib. *be prepared*. So in these wordes, *Iustificationes, Traditiones, Idola* &c. In al which they come not neere the Greeke, but auoid it of purpose.

Precise in following the Greek.

8. The Aduersaries them selues, namely Beza, preferre it before al the rest. *In praefat. no. Test. an* 1556. And againe he saith,

Preferred by Beza himself.

[4] Note : Sess. 4.

that the old Interpreter translated very religiously. *Annot. in* 1. *Luc. v.* 1.

9. In the rest, there is such diuersitie and dissension, and no end of reprehending one an other, and translating euery man according to his fantasie, that Luther [5] said, If the world should stand any long time, we must receiue

Al the rest mis-liked of the Sec-taries themselues, eche reprehending another.

againe (which he thought absurd) the Decrees of Councels, for preseruing the vnitie of faith, because of so diuers in-terpretations of the Scripture. And Beza (in the place aboue mentioned) noteth the itching ambition of his fellow-translators, that had much rather disagree and dissent from the best, then seeme them selues to haue said or written nothing. And Bezas translation it self, being so esteemed in our countrie, that the Geneua [6] English Testament be translated according to the same, yet sometime goeth so wide from the Greeke, and from the meaning of the holy Ghost, that them selues which protest to translate it, dare not folow it. For example, *Luc.* 3. 36. They haue put these wordes, *The sonne of Cainan,* which he wittingly and wilfully left out ; and *Act.* 1. 14, they say, *With the women,* agreably to the vulgar Latin : where he saith. *Cum vxoribus, with their wiues.*

It is truer than the vulgar Greek text it selfe.

10. It is not onely better then al other Latin translations, but then the Greeke text it self, in those places where they disagree.

[c iii recto :]

IN THIS OUR TRANSLATION. because we wish it to be most sincere, as becometh a Catholike translation,

[5] Note : Cochla. c. 11. de cano, Script. authoritate.

[6] Note : The new Test. printed the yere 1580 in the title.

and have endeuoured so to make it ; we are very precise
& religious in folowing our copie, the old vulgar approued Latin : not onely in sense, which we hope we
alwaies doe, but sometime in the very wordes also and
phrases, which may seeme to the vulgar Reader & to
common English eares not yet acquainted therewith,
rudenesse or ignorance : but to the discrete Reader that
deepely weigheth and considereth the importance of
sacred wordes and speaches, and how easily the volun-
tarie Translatour may misse the true sense of the Holy
Ghost, we doubt not but our consideration and doing
therein, shal seeme reasonable and necessarie : yea and
that al sortes of Catholike Readers wil in shorte time
thinke that familiar, which at the first may seeme
strange & wil esteeme it more, when they shal [7] otherwise be taught to vnderstand it, then if it were the common knowen English.

For example, we translate often
thus, *Amen, Amen I say vnto you.*
Which as yet seemeth strange, but
after a while it wil be as familiar, as

Certaine wordes
not English nor as
yet familiar in the
English tongue.

Amen in the end of al praiers and Psalmes, and euen as
when we end with, *Amen*, it soundeth far better then
So be it : so in the beginning, *Amen
Amen*, must needes by vse and custom

Amen.

sound far better, then, *Verily verily.* Which in deede
doth not expresse the asseueration and assurance signified
in this Hebrue word, besides that it is the solemne and
vsual word of our Sauiour [8] to expresse a vehement
asseueration, and therfore is not changed, neither in the
Syriake nor Greeke, nor vulgar Latin Testament, but is
preserued and vsed of the Euangelistes and Apostles

[7] Note : *See the last Table at the end of the booke.*
[8] Note : See *annot. Io. c.* 8. *v.* 34 *& Apoc.* c. 19. v. 4.

them selues, euen as Christ spake it, *propter sanctiorem authoritatem*, as S. Augustine saith of this and of *Allelu-ia, for the more holy and sacred authoritie thereof, li 2. Doct. Christ. c.* 11.   And therfore do we keepe the word

Alleluia.

Allelu-ia. Apoc. 19. as it is both in Greeke and Latin yea and in al the English translations, though in their bookes of common praier they translate it, *Praise ye the Lord.* Againe, if *Hosanna, Raca, Belial*, and such like be yet vntranslated in the English Bibles,[9] why may not we say *Corbana*,

Parasceue.

and *Parasceve* : specially when they Englishing this later thus, *the preparation of the Sabboth* put three wordes more into the text, then the Greeke word doth signifie. *Mat.* 27. 62. And others saying thus, After the day *of preparing*, make a cold translation and short of the sense : as if they should translate, Sabboth, *the resting*, for, *Parasceve*[10] is as solemne a word for the Sabboth eue, as *Sabboth* is for the Iewes seuenth day, and now among Christians much more solemner, taken for Good-friday onely.   These wordes then we thought it far better to keepe in the text, and to tel their signification in the margent or in a table for that purpose, then to disgrace bothe the text & them with translating them.   Such are also these wordes,

Pasche, Azymes.

The Pasche, The feast of Azymes, The bread of Proposition.   Which they translate [11] *The Passeouer, The feast of sweete bread, The shew bread.*   But if *Pentecost* Act. 2. be yet vntranslated in their bibles, and seemeth not strange : why should not *Pasche* and *Azymes* so remaine also, being solemne feastes, as Pentecost was ? or why should they English

9 Note : *No. Test. an.* 1580, *Bib. an* 1577.
10 Note : *Mar.* 14. v. 42.
11 Note : *Bib.* 1577. Mat. 26. 17.

one rather then the other ? specially whereas *Passeouer*
at the first was as strange, as *Pasche* may seeme now,
and perhaps as many now vnderstand *Pasche*, as *Passeouer*, and as for *Azymes*, when they English it, *the feast
of sweete bread*, it is a false interpretation of the word,
& nothing expresseth that which belongeth to the feast,
concerning vnleauened bread. And as for their terme
of *shew bread*, it is very strange and ridiculous. Againe,
if *Proselyte* be a receiued word in the English bibles
Mat. 23. *Act.* 2 : why may not we be bold to say, *Neo-
phyte.* 1. Tim. 3. ? specially when they translating it
into English do falsely expresse the signification of the
word thus, *a yong scholer*. Whereas it is a peculiar word
to signifie them that were lately baptized, as *Cate-
chumenus*, signifieth the newely instructed in faith not
yet baptized, who is also a yong scholar rather then the
other, and many that haue been old scholars, may be
Neophytes by differring baptisme. And if *Phylacteries* be
allowed for English *Mat.* 23. we hope that *Didragmes*
also, *Prepuce, Paraclete*, and such like, wil easily grow
to be currant and familiar. And in good sooth there is
in al these such necessitie, that they can not conueniently
be translated, as when S. Paul [12] saith, *concisio, non
circumcisio* : how can we but folow his very wordes
and allusion ? And how is it possible to expresse
Euangelizo, but as we do, *Euan-
gelize* ? for *Euangelium* being the
Gospel, what is, *Euangelizo* or *to
Euangelize*, but to shew the glad tydings of the Gospel, of the time of
grace, of al Christes benefites ? Al

Why we say *our
Lord*, not *the Lord*
(but in certaine
cases) see the An-
notations 1. *Tim.* 6
pag. 585.

which signification is lost, by translating as the English
bibles do, *I bring you good tydings*. Luc. 2. 10. Therfore

[12] Note : *Phil.* 3.

we say *Depositum* 1 Tim. 6. and, He *exinanited* him self,
Philip. 2. and, You haue *reflorished*, Philip. 4. and, *to
exhaust*, Hebr. 9. 28. because we can not possibly attaine
to expresse these wordes fully in English, and we thinke
much better, that the reader staying at the difficultie of
them, should take an occasion to looke in the table folowing, or otherwise to aske the ful meaning of them, then
by putting some vsual English wordes that expresse
them not, so to deceiue the reader. Sometime also we
doe it for an other cause, as when we say, *The aduent of
our Lord*, and *Imposing of handes.* because one is a
solemne time, the other a solemne action in the Catholike
Church : to signifie to the people,
that these and such like names come
out of the very Latin text of the
Scripture. So did *Penance, doing
penance, Chalice, Priest, Deacon, Traditions, aultar, host*,
and the like (which we exactly keepe as Catholic termes)
procede euen from the very wordes of Scripture.

Catholike termes
proceding from the
very text of Scrip-
ture.

Moreouer, we presume not in hard places to mollifie
the speaches or phrases, but religiously keepe them
word for word, and point for point, for feare of missing,
or restraining the sense of the holy
Ghost to our phantasie, as Eph. 6.
*Against the spirituals of wickednes in
the celestials.* and *What to me and thee woman* ? [13] whereof
see the Annotation vpon this place. and 1 Pet. 2. *As
infants euen now borne, reasonable, milke without guile
desire ye*, We do so place *reasonable*, of purpose, that it
may be indifferent both to infants going before, as in
our Latin text : or to milke that foloweth after, as in
other Latin copies and in the Greeke, Io. 3. we translate,
The spirit breatheth where he wil &c. leauing it indifferent

Certain hard
speaches and
phrases.

to signifie either the holy Ghost, or winde : which the Protestants translating, *winde*, take away the other sense more common and vsual in the auncient fathers. We translate *Luc* 8. 23, *They were* *filled*, not adding of our owne, *with water* to mollifie the sentence, as the Protestants doe, and c. 21. *This is the chalice, the new Testament &c* not, *This chalice is the new Testament.* likewise Mar. 13, *Those daies shal be such tribulation &c* not as the Aduersaries, *In those daies*, both our text and theirs being otherwise. likewise Iac. 4. 6. *And giueth greater grace*, leauing it indifferent to the *Scripture*, or to the *holy Ghost*, both going before. Whereas the Aduersaries to to boldly & presumptuously adde, saying, *The Scripture giueth*, taking away the other sense, which is far more probable, likewise *Heb.* 12. 21. we translate, *So terrible was it which was seen, Moyses said &c.* neither doth Greeke or Latin permit vs to adde, *that* Moyses said, as the Protestants presume to doe, So we say, *Men brethren, A widow woman, A woman a sister, Iames of Alphaeus*, and the like. Sometime also [14] we folow of purpose the Scripture phrase, as, *The hel of fire*,[15] according to Greeke and Latin, which we might say perhaps, *the firyhel*, by the Hebrue phrase in such speaches, but not, *hel fire*, as commonly it is translated Likewise *Luc* 4. 36. What *word* is this, that in power and authoritie he commaundeth the vncleane spirits ? as also *Luc* 2. Let vs passe ouer, and see the *word* that is done. Where we might say, *thing*, by the Hebrue phrase, but there is a certaine maiestie and more signification in these speaches, and therfore both Greeke & Latin keepe them, although it is no more the Greeke or Latin phrase, then it is the Eng-

The Protestants presumptuous boldnes and libertie in translating.

---

[14] Note : Mat. 5.   [15] Note : *Gehenna ignis.*

lish. And why should we be squamish at new wordes or phrases in the Scripture, which are necessarie : when we do easily admit and folow new wordes coyned in court and in courtly or other secular writings ?

We adde the Greeke in the margent The Greeke added often in the margent for many causes. for diuers causes. Sometime when the sense is hard, that the learned reader may consider of it and see if he can helpe him selfe better then by our translation as Luc. 11. *Nolite extolli*, μὴ μετεωρίζεσθαι and againe, *Quod superest date eleemosynam*, τὰ ἐνόντα. Sometime to take away the ambiguitie of the Latin or English, as Luc. 11. *Et domus supra domum cadet* which we must needes English, *and house upon house, shal fall* by the Greeke, the sense is not, one house shal fal vpon an other, but, if one house rise vpon it self, that is, against it self, it shal perish, according as he speaketh of a kingdom deuided against it self, in the wordes before, And Act. 14. *Sacerdos Iouis qui erat*, in the Greeke, *qui*, is referred to Jupiter. Sometime to satisfie the reader that might otherwise conceiue the translation to be false, as *Philip* 4 *v* 6. *But in euerything by praier, &c.* ἐν παντὶ προσευχῇ not, *in al praier*, as in the Latin it may seeme. Sometime when the Latin neither doth, nor can, reache to the signification of the Greeke word, we adde the Greeke also as more significant. *Illi soli seruies*,[16] *him only shalt thou serue*, λατρεύσεις And *Act.* 6. Nicolas *a stranger* of Antioche, προσέλυτος and, *Ro.* 9. *The seruice*, ἡ λατρεία and *Eph* 1. to *perfite instaurare omnia in Christo*, ἀνακεφαλαιώσασθαι And *Wherein he hath gratified us*, ἐχαρίτωσεν & Eph. 6. *Put on the armour*, πανοπλίαν and a number the like. Sometime, when the Greeke hath two senses, and

[16] Note : *Mat.* 4.

the Latin but one, we adde the Greeke. 2. Cor. 1.
By the exhortation wherewith we also are exhorted, the
Greeke signifieth also *consolation &c.* and 2. Cor. 10.
But hauing hope of your faith increasing, to be &c. where
the Greeke may also signifie, *as* or *when your faith in-*
creaseth. Sometime [17] for aduantage of the Catholike
cause, when the Greeke maketh vs more then the Latin,
as, Seniores, πρεσβυτέρους. *Vt digni habeamini*, ἵνα
ἀξιωθῆτε *Qui effundetur*, τὸ ἐκχευόμενον, *Praecepta*, παρα-
δόσεις. & Io. 21. ποίμαινε, *Pasce & rege.* And sometime
to shew the false translation of the Heretike, as when
Beza saith *Hoc poculum in meo sanguine qui*, τὸ
ποτήριον ἐν τῷ αἵματι τὸ ἐκχρευόμενον Luc. 22. & *Quem*
oportet coelo contineri, ὃν δεῖ οὐρανὸν δεχεσθαι, *Act.* 3.   Thus
we vse the Greeke diuers waies, & esteeme of it as it
is worthie, & take al commodities thereof for the better
vnderstanding of the Latin, which being a translation,
can not alwaies attaine to the ful sense of the principal
tonge, as we see in al translations.

Item we adde the Latin word some-   The Latin text
time in the margent, when either we   sometimes noted in
can not fully expresse it (as *Act.* 8   the margent.
They tooke order for Steuens funeral, *Curauerunt*
Stephanum, and, Al take not this word, *Non omnes*
capiunt) or when the reader might thinke, it can not be
as we translate, as, *Luc.* 8. A storme of winde descended
into the lake, and *they were filled*, *& complebantur*, and
Io. 5. when Iesus knew that he had now a long time, *quia*
iam multum tempus haberet, meaning, in his infirmitie.

This precise folowing of our Latin text, in neither
adding nor diminishing, is the cause why we say not
in the title of bookes, in the first page, S. Mathew,
S. Paul : because it is so neither in Greeke nor Latin,

[7] Note : *Act.* 15. 2 *Thes.* 2. 1 *Cor .*11.

though in the toppes of the leaues folowing, where we
may be bolder, we adde S. Matthew
&c to satisfie the reader. Much vnlike
to the Protestants our Aduersaries,
which make no scruple [18] to leaue out
the name of Paul in the title of the
Epistle to the Hebrues, though it be in euery Greeke
booke which they translate. And their most authorised
English Bibles leaue out (Catholike) in the title of
S. Iames Epistle and the rest, which were famously
knowen in the primitiue Church by the name of *Catholicae
Epistolae*, Euseb. hist. Eccl. li 2. c 22.

In the beginning
of bookes Matthew,
Paul, &c. not S.
Matthew, S. Paul
&c.

Another reading
in the margent.
Item we giue the Reader in places
of some importance, an other reading
in the margent, specially when the Greeke is agreable to
the same, as Io. 4, *transiet de morte ad vitam*. Other Latin
copies haue, *transiit*, and so it is in the Greeke.

We binde not our selues to the pointes of any one
copie, print, or edition of the vulgar Latin, in places of
no controuersie, but folow the pointing most agreable to
the Greeke and to the fathers commentaries. As Col. 1. 10.
*Ambulantes dignè Deo, per omnia placentes. Walking
worthy of God, in al things pleasing,*

The pointing
sometimes altered.
ἀξίως τοῦ κυρίου εἰς πᾶσαν ἀρέσκειαν.
Eph. 1. 17. We point this, *Deus Domini nostri Iesu
Christi, pater gloriae.* as in the Greeke, and S. Chrysostom,
& S. Hierom both in text and commentaries. Which the
Catholike reader specially must marke, lest he finde
fault, when he seeth our translation disagree in such
places from the pointing of his Latin Testament.

We translate sometime the word that is in the
Latin margent, and not that in the text, when by the
Greeke or the fathers we see it is a manifest fault of

[18] Note : Bib. an 1579, 1580 an 1577, 1562.

the writers heretofore, that mistooke one word for an other. As, *In fine*, not *in fide*, 1 Pet. 3. v. 8. *praesentium*, not, *praescientium*, 2 Pet. 1. v. 16. Heb. 13. *latuerunt*, not, *placuerunt*.

The margent reading sometime preferred before the text

Thus we haue endeuoured by al meanes to satisfie the indifferent reader, and to helpe his vnderstanding euery way, both in the text, and by Annotations ; and withal to deale most sincerely before God and man, in translating and expounding the most sacred Text of the holy Testament. Fare wel good Reader, and if we profit the any whit by our poore paines let vs for Gods sake be partakers of thy deuout praiers, and together with humble and contrite hart call vpon our Sauiour Christ to cease these troubles & stormes of his derest spouse : in the meane time comforting our selues with this saying of S. Augustine : *That Heretikes, when they receiue power corporally to afflict the Church, doe exercise her patience : but when they oppugne her onely by their euil doctrine or opinion, then they exercise her wisedomes.* De ciuit. Dei li 18. ca. 51.

LVI. JUGGE AND BARKER AND THEIR PATRONS

A. The copie of the Quenes maiesties High Commissioners order taken between Mr Richard Jugge and others of the Companie of Stationers as hereafter foloweth [1]

Sexto die mensis junii Anno Domini 1575. Coram reverendo patre Domino Edwino London. Episcopo

[1] This and the next two documents and also No. LXI I owe to the kindness of Mr. Charles Rivington, Clerk to the Stationers' Company. The date of the first, just three weeks after Archbishop Parker's death, is very significant.

ac venerabilibus viris, Roberto Monnson armiger. uno justiciar. domine Regine de communi banco petro Osborne Armiger. et John Hannon legum doctor. Commissioner regiis in causis ecclesiasticis et legitime assignat. in presencia mei Willim Bedell Registrar &c.

At which daye and place after longe hearinge and debatinge of the grieves and differences between the Stationers of London as namely then present Humfrey Toye Luke Harrison ffrauncis Coldock and George Bisshopp declaring their grieves therein on their partie, and Richard Jugge also Stationer hir maiesties prynter on the other partie, Touchinge the printinge of the Bible and Testament. Yt was ordered by the sayd Commissioners by assent of the parties present That from henceforthe the sayd Richard Jugge only shall have without interrupcion the printinge of the Byble in Quarto and the Testament in decimo Sexto ; And all other Bibles in folio and Testaments (excepted as before) to be at the liberty of the printinge of the rest of the Stationers and he the said Richard Jugge also without contradiction of any person to have the printinge of the rest as aforesaid

B. The Beginning of the Bible Stock

Ninth June 1575

Whereas on the Sixth daie of this instant month of June yt was ordered by the Quenes maiesties Comissioner in Causes ecclesiasticall by assent of Richard Jugge Stationer hir maiesties Printer and certen other Stationers then present, That the said Richard Jugge onelie shall have without interrupcion the printinge of the byble in Quarto and the testament in decimo Sexto. And all other bibles in folio and testaments (excepted as before) to be at the libertie of the printinge of the rest of the

Stationers. And he the saide Richard Jugge also without contradiction of any person, to have the printinge of the reste as aforesaid. As by the same order (a trewe copie whereof is before entred into this present booke) more plainelie maie appeare

For good order and quietness to be had and used touchinge the saide Bibles and Testaments so licenced to be printed in comon, yt was thoughte meete and convenient, and also ordeined established and decreed on the nyneth daie of June aforesaide, by the Master Wardens and Assistants of the saide Arte or misterie of Stationers, and with the assent of all the persons here undernamed, That noe person or persons, at anye tyme hereafter shall printe or cause to be printed, any of the saide Bibles or Testaments ordered to be printed in comon as aforesaide unles he or they (which so will printe or cause to be printed any of the same Bibles or testaments) shall before the printinge thereof : as well present [1] every suche Bible and testament so to be printed, to suche of the master wardens and assistants of the saide arte or misterie as shal be noe parties nor partners to or in the imprintinge thereof : As also have and obteyne their licence for the imprintinge of the same, to the intent that the same master wardens and assistants in the grauntinge of every suche licence, maie jnioyne and take order with the partie and parties to whome any suche licence shal be graunted, for the good and sufficient imprintinge of everye suche Bible & testament so to be presented as well with good paper and good woorkemanshippe, as with good correction

And that also upon the finishinge of every impression of any of the saide bibles or Testaments so to be presented and licenced : the parties and partners of the same, shall

[1] 'Exhibit,' not 'give.'

before any of the same be putt to sale : bringe give and deliver one whole and perfecte booke thereof to the master wardens and assistants of the saide arte or misterie beinge noe partners therein, to the ende that they maie see and viewe the same if it be done woorkmanlie and orderlie in all poynts accordinge to the true meaninge of this present order and decree everie of which booke so to be viewed shall remaine in the saide hall to the use of the saide whole Companie forever

Whereupon John Walley John Judson William Norton Humfrey Toye John Harrison Lucas Harrison George Bisshoppe Garret Dewce Richard Watkins and Frauncis Coldock on the saide nyneth daie of June, did present unto the master and wardens and others of the assistants of the saide arte or misterie accordinge to the saide order, one Englishe bible in folio of the Pica letter, a newe Testament in Englishe in Octavo of the longe primer letter, and one other Jnglishe new testament in Quarto of the Englishe or pica letter, And were licenced accordinge to the same order, to ymprinte one impression of the same sevrall bookes, in folio and octavo

And the saide Richard Jugge hath assented notwithstandinge that the newe Testament in Quarto (as he sayeth) his parcell of the bible in quarto by the saide order of the Comissioners is lefte to remayne to him alone, that the imprintinge of the saide Testament in Quarto shalbe likewise permitted, and by the order of the saide companie it is also the saide nyneth daie, so licenced to the parties abovesaide. And further it is likewise ordered and agreed by the saide master wardens and assistants on the saide nynth daie of June, and the saide John Walley William Norton Humfrey Toye John Harrison Lucas Harrison George Bisshopp Garret Dewce Richard Watkins and Frauncis Coldock, and also John Wighte,

for them and their assigns have hereunto submitted
themselves, and consented and faithfullie promised to
be contented with and to obey and observe the orders
followinge, yiz. That if any complainte or controversie
shall at any time arise or be made or occasioned by or
amongst any of the saide persons now licenced or hereafter to be licenced to printe the saide bookes laste
mencioned, or any of the saide bookes ordered to be
printed in comon as aforesaid : or any printer, or other
person that shall have to doe in the woorkemanshippe or
utterance thereof, or any other person whiche the said
persons licenced shall ioyne with them in any parte of
the charge or proffit : for or touchinge their or any of
their dealings or doings in the printinge utteringe or
Sellinge of the same bookes or any of them, that then
every person and persons, whoe shalbe occasions thereof,
or whome it shal in any wise concerne, shall stande to
abide obey observe and performe, suche ende order and
determinacion, as in and for evry or any suche complainte
or controversie, shalbe made by the master wardens
and assistants of the saide arte or misterie beinge noe
parties nor partners thereto as aforesaide

And that any person or persons whiche hereafter shall
or will accordinge to theis ordenances and decrees ymprint
or cause to be imprinted any of the saide Bibles or
Testaments ordered to be printed in comon as aforesaide,
shal not at anie tyme put to sale or cause to be put to
sale any of the same bookes, to any person or persons
beinge not a freeman, or brother of the saide companie,
at suche rates as maie be preiudice hurte hinderance or
losse to the usuall and reasonable maner of Sale by other
Stationers that shall sell the same againe by retaile

And that no suche person or persons as shall so printe
or cause to be printed any suche Bible or Testament,

shall at anye tyme after he or they shall have putt any of the same to Sale : by any meanes, by reason of scarcitie thereof when the moste of them be uttered and Sold, or for any other occasion, encrease and enhaunce or cause to be encreased or enhaunced to any freeman or brother of the saide companie, the firste price whiche he or they shall have made of the same bookes at the firste puttinge to sale thereof, whiche firste price to the Companie they shall cause to be entered in the hall of the Companie before the puttinge of any of the same bookes to Sale

And moreover that evry offendor and offendors of or in theis present orders and decrees and other the premisses or any of them, from and after due proofe made of his or their offence, shalbe for ever barred excluded and amoved from printinge and beinge partner in the printinge of any of the said Bibles or Testaments ordered to be printed in comon as aforesaide ; and from havinge any further interest or benefit therein : And shall also forfeite and lose all his and their interest parte and parts therein, to be employed and disposed at the discrecion of the master wardens and assistants of the saide companie then beinge and havinge no parte in the printinge of the same bookes : or to be (upon reasonable consideracions) to him restored, as the saide master wardens and assistants with the assent of the rest of the partners shall think meete

C. Barker's satisfaction to Jugge.

IX° die Junij 1575.

Whereas Christofer Barker citizen and Draper of London hathe obteyned a graunt and licence in writinge under the handes of seven of the Quenes maiesties

honrable privie counsell [1] accordinge to hir highnes
jniuntions, for the printinge of theise Twoo Bookes
hereafter mencioned That is to saye. A Byble in
Englishe with notes in the same which was dedicated
unto hir maiestie in the ffirst yere of hir highnes reign
and commenly called or knowen by the name of the
Geneva Byble and a Testament to be translated out of
the latin tonge into the Englishe (the Latin copie thereof
by hir highnes privledge) belonginge to one Thomas
Vautrolier a frenchman. And whereas hir maiesties highe
comissioners in causes ecclesiasticall in consideracion
of the greate charges costs and expenses which Richard
Jugge hir Maiesties servant and printer nowe master of
the Companie of Stationers of the Citie of London (by
and upon comaundement) hathe susteined in the printinge
of the Bibles and Testaments in Englishe, have licenced
and ordered to the same Richard Jugge the only impryn-
tinge of evrye Englishe Byble in Quarto, and of evry
Jnglishe Testament in decimo sexto. As by a true copie
of the same order beinge before entred into this booke
moore at large appearethe. For and in consideracion
of which order and licence so made and gyven by the
saide highe comissioners and for diverse other goode and
reasonable causes and consideracions him the said Christofer Barker especially movinge he the same Christofer
in the nynth day of June in the yere of our Lord 1575 and
in the Sevententhe yere of the reigne of our sovreign
Ladie Quene Elizabeth about thhoure of eleven of ye
clocke in the forenone of the same day at and within the

---

[1] This would not be a patent, only an ordinary copyright
obtained in an unusually formal and dignified way. That seven
privy councillors thus supported Barker is very significant of the
determination that now Parker was dead the Geneva version
should have its turn.

said Stationers Hall in the presence of theise persons whose names are hereunto subscribed of his owne franke and free accord and good will, did gyve his hand and faythfull promise to the said Richard Jugge. And did covenaunte promise graunte and agree to and with the said Richard Jugge in manner and forme folowinge. That is to say. That he the said Christofer or any other person or persons by his assent meanes or procurement shall not at any tyme ymprint or cause to be ymprinted any maner of Englishe Testament in XVI° or any Englishe Byble in Quarto, or in any other volume or volumes whatsoever which shall or may be hurtfull or preiudiciall unto ye said Richard Jugge for or concerninge ye printinge utteringe or sellinge of any Byble in Quarto or any Testament in Decimo Sexto. And that he the said Richard Jugge shall and may have and enioye to his owne use the onely ymprintinge utteringe and sellinge of all Jnglishe Bybles in Quarto and of all Englishe Testaments in Decimo Sexto at all tymes without resistance hurt preiudice or interrupcion therein or thereto to be made done caused or procured in any wise by the said Christofer or any other by his assent meanes or procurement. And further that yf the said Christofer or his assignes shall at any tyme be comaunded by or from the Quenes maiestie or hir counsell or by any comissioner or comissioners in causes Ecclesiasticall or by any other person or persons authorised by hir highnes : to ymprint any Englishe Testament in XVI^to or any Englishe Byble in the volume called quarto, or in any other volume or size which may be hurtfull or preiudiciall to the said Richard Jugge as aforesaide. That then he the said Christofer Barker and his assignes imediately upon any suche comaundement to him or them gyven shall thereof gyve notice to the said Richard Jugge And shall quietly permit and suffer the same Richard Jugge at his owne charge and to and for his owne propre and onely use to ymprinte utter and sell evry suche Byble and Testament whiche the said Christofer or his assignes shalbe so comaunded to printe. The said Richard Jugge therefore alowinge unto the said Christofer for every suche booke Licenced to the said Christofer as abovesaid and so to be comaunded as aforesaid to be printed : at and upon evry ympression thereof to be made by the said Richard Jugge accordinge to the tenor of theis presents : only 1 quier of printed paper of evry shete of evry booke so to be printed amountinge in the whole to ffyve and twentie perfect bookes of evry suche whole impression thereof. Jn witnes whereof the persons hereunder named for a remembrance and testimonie of the truethe in the premisses hereunto have subscribed their names as witnesses thereof. Gyven the nynthe day of June in the year within written

Rychard Tottyll Wardens of
Wyllyam Cooke the said
Companie of Stationers.

Also about Tenne of the clocke in the forenoone of the eight daye of June in the said yere within wrytten. The saide Christofer Barker came to the house of the said Richard Jugge beside Newegate Market in London signifyenge unto the same Richard the seid graunte and licence abovemencioned to be made to the same Christofer. And then and there in the presence of the wife of the said Ric. Jugge and of Richard Watkins citizen and Stationer of London the same Christofer Barker did gyve his hand and faythfull promise unto the sayde Richard Jugge for all the same causes effects intents and purposes above and within wrytten concerninge the ymprintinge

Y

of the Byble in Quarto and the testament in Decimo Sexto.

by me Richard Watkyns

The said Richard Tottell Willm Cooke and Richard Watkins dyd sevrally subscribe as is above written in the presence of us whose names ensue viz.

Willm Seres

Jhon Daye

Thomas Marshe

John Waley

Jhon Judson

LVII. BARKER ESTABLISHES HIS MONOPOLY [1]

From the original Patent Roll, 19 Elizabeth, Part 8.

Regina omnibus ad quos etc. salutem. Sciatis quod nos de gratia nostra speciali ac ex certa scientia et mero motu nostris, necnon propter credibilem informacionem

[1] The purport of this very full patent is that the queen, in consideration of the skill shown by Christopher Barker in the art of printing, grants to him, for herself, her heirs and successors, the office of royal printer of all statutes, books, bills, acts of parliament, proclamations, injunctions, bibles, and new testaments, in the English tongue of any translation, with or without notes, whether previously in print or to be subsequently printed by her command. Also of all service-books ordered to be used in churches, and all other volumes, however called, ordered to be printed by [the Queen] or Parliament, whether in English or in English and some other language (save only Latin grammars) and makes Christopher Barker her printer, to exercise the office personally or by a sufficient deputy or deputies for his natural life. Wherefore she forbids all and sundry her subjects in or out of her dominions to print any book, &c., of which the printing is hereby given to the said Christopher Barker, or to cause any book of the said Christopher Barker's printing

nobis factam promptitudinis et dextre noticie que
dilectus subditus noster Christoferus Barker de civitate
London impressor habet et demonstravit in arte &
misterio impressionis dedimus et concessimus ac per presentes pro nobis heredibus et successoribus nostris damus
ac concedimus eidem Christofero Barker officium Impressoris nostri omnium et singulorum statutorum librorum
libellorum actuum parliamenti proclamacionum iniunctio-
num ac bibliorum et novorum testamentorum quorumcunque in lingua anglicana alicujus translacionis cum
notis aut sine notis antehac impressorum aut imposterum
per mandatum nostrum imprimendorum.   Necnon omnium aliorum librorum quorumcunque quos nos pro dei
servicio in Templis hujus Regni nostri Anglie uti manda-
vimus aut imposterum uti mandaverimus ac aliorum
voluminum ac rerum quorumcumque quocumque nomine
termino titulo aut sensu seu quibuscumque nominibus ter-
minis titulis aut sensibus nominentur vocentur vel cen-
seantur aut eorum aliquod nominetur, vocetur censeatur
aut imposterum nominabuntur, vocabuntur vel censebun-
tur seu per parliamentum regni nostri predicti in Angli-

to be printed abroad or at home, and imported or sold in England
under penalty of a fine of 40s. for every book so printed or sold
and seizure of the stock.   And she gives to Christopher Barker
and his assigns the right of seizing and arresting without let or
stay.   Moreover she gives the right of impressing skilled workmen
when needed for his service.   The said Christopher Barker to be
paid £6 13s. 4d. yearly, one half at Michaelmas, the other at
Easter.—A complete monopoly of printing English Bibles of every
kind was thus conferred, including adequate powers for enforcing
it.   As to Barker's personal position, however, the patent must
be read in connexion with his statement in 1582 (printed on
page 42), in which he writes of many of his friends disbursing
round sums of money for him, and the Memorandum printed
as No. LXI, where we find used the remarkable phrase 'parteners
in the previleges '.

cana lingua vel in Anglicana et alia lingua quacumque mixtis iam edit impressit vel excussit aut imposterum edendum excudendum & ad impressionem ponendum (exceptis solummodo rudimentis grammatice institucionis latine lingue) ac ipsum Christoferum Barker Impressorem nostrum omnium singulorum permissorum facimus ordinamus et constituimus per presentes habendo gaudendo occupando et exercendo officium predictum prefato Christofero Barker per se vel per sufficientem deputatum suum sive deputatos suos sufficientes durante vita sua naturali unacum omnibus proficuis commoditatibus advantagiis preeminentiis privilegiis eidem officio quoquomodo spectantibus sive pertinentibus. Quare prohibemus et vetamus ac inhibemus omnibus et singulari[bu]s subditis nostris quibuscunque ubivis gentium et locorum agentibus et ceteris aliis quibuscunque ne illi vel eorum aliquis per se vel per alium vel alios imprimat seu imprimi faciat vel faciant infra seu extra dominia nostra quecumque aliquod volumen librum aut opus seu aliqua volumina libros aut opera quecunque de quibus impressio per presentes per nos conceditur prefato Christofero Barker. Ac quod nullus aliquos libros volumina aut opus quodcumque in vernacula aut anglicana lingua aut anglicana cum aliis ut prefertur infra regna seu dominia nostra per prefatum Christoferum Barker impressa aut que in futuris erunt per ipsum impressa in partibus transmarinis aut in partibus forinsecis imprimi facient vel faciet nec ea seu eorum aliquod importet vel importent seu importari faciet vel facient aut ea vel eorum aliquod vendat vel vendant sub pena forisfacturis XL^s. legalis monete Anglie pro quolibet tali libro volumine vel opere sic imprimendo vel vendendo ac confiscationis et amissionis talium librorum voluminum operum materiarum et rerum quorumcunque et eorum cuius libet. Que quidem libri volumina materia et res quecumque sic impressoris vel imposterum contra tenorem presentium imprimenda aut infra hoc regnum nostrum sive dominia quecumque importanda & sicut praemittitur forisfaciendum et confiscandum nos concessimus ac aucthoritatem et potestatem per presentes pro nobis heredibus et successoribus nostris concedimus prefato Christofero Barker impressori nostro et assignatis suis apprehendendi capiendi seizendi et ad opus nostrum arestandi et confiscandi sine impedimento interrupcione dilatione contradiccione seu perturbacione quacumque vetantes insuper et firmiter prohibentes virtute et vigore presentium ne quis alius quocumque modo colore vel pretextu librum vel libros aut opera quecumque per dictum Christoferum Barker imprimenda de novo imprimere vel alibi impressa vendere aut emere presumat vel audeat quovismodo. Et insuper de ampliori gracia nostra concessimus et licenciam dedimus ac per presentes pro nobis heredibus et successoribus nostris concedimus et licenciam damus eidem Christofero Barker quod ipse vel assignati sui de tempore in tempus durante vita naturalis prefati Christopher Barker operarios de arte et misteriis impressionis capere apprehendere ac conducere possit vel possint ad operandum in arte predicta ad appunctament[um] sive assignationem dicti Christoferi Barker tali tempore et talibus temporibus durantibus quo vel quibus idem Christoferus Barker vel assignati sui hujusmodi operariis egebit vel egebunt. Concessimus etiam ac per presentes pro nobis heredibus ac successoribus nostris concedimus dicto Christofero Barker pro exercitio officii predicti feodum sive annuitatem sex librorum tredecim solidos et quatuor denariis : habendo et annuatim percipiendo predictum feodum sive annuitatem sex librorum tresdecim solidos et quatuor denariis prefato

Christofero Barker ad festum Sancti Michaelis archangeli et pasche equis portionibus solvendum durante vita sua naturali de Thesauro nostro ab receptis scaccariis nostri Westmonasteriensis per manus Thesaurari et camerari nostrorum pro tempore existentis mandantes etiam et per presentes firmiter injungendum precipientes omnibus et singulis maioris vice ballivis constabularum et aliis officiorum ministris et subditis nostris quibuscunque quod prefato Christofero et assignatis suis in execucione officii predicti ac factione omnium et singulorum in his lettris nostris patenti[bu]s specificat agendum de tempore in tempus quando necesse fuit sint intendentes attendent pariter & auxiliantes in omnibus presentibus decet eo quod expresse mencione etc. In cuius rei etc. Teste R. apud castrum de Windesore xxvii° die septembris

per breve de privato sigillo.

LVIII. BARKER'S CIRCULAR TO THE CITY COMPANIES

Broadside in the Library of the Society of Antiquaries

May it please you, whereas at my extreeme charges I haue lately imprinted a large Bible most faithfully translated, with large notes and expositions, especiallie vpon Job, the Psalmes, the Prophets and the newe Testament, and that the right honourable my L. Maior with the consent of his worshipfull brethren, hauing consideration of the same, hath made request as you know for the vtterance of some of them among the worshipfull and well disposed Citizens. And nowe I vnderstand that my Booke is mistaken for another Bible[1] which was begon before I had authoritie, as it

[1] But for this circular we should have been bound to believe that Barker began his career as Queen's Printer by printing not

is affirmed, which could not be finished but by my consent, and therefore hath the name to be printed by the assignement of Christopher Barker, and as I will not dispraise the said booke, so may I iustly affirme that there is in quantitie, paper, and workmanship, besides many other things therein conteined for the profite of the Reader, ten shillings difference to him that hath any iudgement at all, and yet if any be disposed to haue their bookes bossed, I wil bosse them at the same price mentioned in my articles Further if there be anie that is not willing to disburce present money, may haue time till Candlemas next, so that the Master and wardens be then answerable for so many bookes as shall be so deliuered, and where the beadle was appointed ijd. I thinke it to litle, and will alowe him for each booke iiijd and although here can rise no great gaine to me in this bargaine, yet must I needs thinke my selfe most bounden to this most honourable citie, to the vttermost of my possible power, besides the ordinarie duetie I owe thereunto.

Articles concerning the deliuery of the Bibles mentioned in the peticion of Christopher Barker Printer to the Queenes most excellent Maiestie.

First that your said suppliant shall deliuer to euery hall or company one large Bible with the argumentes to euery booke in the olde and newe Testaments, the summaries or contents of euery Chapter, the notes or expositions vpon all the hard places of the text, and also a Table of the principall matters therein conteined. Which Booke is dedicated to the Queenes most excellent

only several Geneva Bibles, but also a Bishops'. We learn here that he only printed the Geneva Bibles and that the Bishops' must have been printed in pursuance of the arrangement set forth in No. LVI A and B, which Barker was now able to override.

Maiestie, authorized by the Lordes and others of her Highnesse priuie counsell, confirmed and allowed by the L. Archbishops grace of Canterburie, the Bishop of Sarum her Maiesties high almner &c. Whereunto is added a Kalender historicall, the Booke of Common prayer with the administration of the Sacraments and other things most necessary.

Item that the clarkes of eche of the sayde Companies may take and set downe in writing the names of all such persons of the same companies as will graunt to buy of the said Bibles, and what nomber thereof they are minded to haue, and whether they will haue them bound or unbound.

And that euery of the said clarkes hauing so done, may certifie your said suppliant thereof, And he will thereupon bring the same bookes to the halles of eche of the sayd companies where the buyers may haue the same with asmuch conuenient speed as may be, paying for the same as foloweth.

Your said suppliant hauing bene at great charge aswell in preparing furniture as in retayning Iourneymen and three learned men for a long time for the printing of the said bibles, and correcting such small faultes as had escaped in the former prints thereof, so as if it were prised at xxxs. it were scarce sufficient, (his labour and cost being well considered) yet he is content for present money by this meane to take for euery of the same bibles bound xxiiijs. and for euery of the same vnbound xxs.

And for the paines of the clarkes of the same companies in taking and writing the names of the buyers of the same bookes and receyuing the money for the same, your said suppliant will giue to euery of them iiijd. for euery booke that is solde in their seuerall companies.

And in euery of the said companies where your said suppliant shal receyue xl. pound or aboue, he is content to giue to the hall thereof one bible for the vse of the whole companie at their assemblies in the same hall.

LIX. DRAFT FOR AN ACT OF PARLIAMENT FOR A NEW VERSION OF THE BIBLE [1]

From British Museum Add. MS. 34729, fol. 77

An act for the reducinge of diversities of Bibles now extant in the Englishe tongue to one setled vulgar translated from the originall.

For avoydinge of the multiplicitie of errors, that are rashly conceaved by the inferior and vulgar sorte by the varietie of the translacions of Bible to the most daungerous increase of papistrie and atheisme. And whereas many from the high to the lowe of all sortes have bene desierous greatly and a longe time to have the holy booke of god which for the olde testament is in Hebrewe for the new all originally in Greeke to be translated in such sorte, that such as studie it, shoulde in noe place be snared, which worke noe doubt the lordes spirituall of this Parliament with the painfull travailles of such of both Vniversities as they shall or may call vnto them, may with the grace of Allmightie god perfect, which will tende to her Majesties immortall fame beinge amongest the Christian princes universally knowen to be not inferior to any in the furtheringe and defendinge of the faith of [Christ, And whereas] the chiefest obstacle to the buildinge of this godly worke heretofore hath bene discerned to be for that noe compulsarie meanes hath bene

[1] This draft clearly belongs to the reign of Elizabeth, probably to the primacy of Whitgift, but with whom it originated appears not to be known.

had ne made whereby the students of both universities
may be compelled to assiste the saide lordes spirituall
in the painefull examinacion and execucion of the
saide worke, nor howe the charges of such students and
laborers in the same vyneyarde may from time to time be
competently defrayed Bee it therefore enacted by the
Queenes most excellent Majestie by the assent of the
Lords spirituall and temporall and the Commons in this
Parliament assembled and by the Aucthoritie of the
same that the lords spirituall of this Realme that now
are and in succession hereafter shalbe, or any Sixe or
more of them, whereof the Lorde Archbisshoppe of
Canterbury for the time beinge to be one may at their
pleasures from time to time assemble treate and deale
towchinge the accomplishment of the saide worke and
may by their letters call and appoint such students of
both universities to assist them in the same from time
to time as by them shalbe thought requisite, and to
allowe such sommes of money towards the charges and
paines of such students that shalbe imployed in or about
such worke to be levied by censure ecclesiasticall as to
the saide Lordes spirituall or any sixe or more of them
whereof the Archbishop of Canterburye for the time
beinge to be one shalbe thought meet, the saide charges
of such students and workers to be assessed levied and
gathered of such Cathedrall Churches and Colledges and
the revenues thereof as by the saide lordes spirituall, or
any sixe or more of them whereof the saide Archbisshoppe
of Canterbury to be one shalbe thought requisite and
vnder their handes and seales ordeyned or appointed,
and that it shall and may be lawfull to or for any temporall person by deede gift or will to bestowe any gifte
or legacy of mony or goodes towards the supportinge
of the saide charges, and such gifte or will to be put in

execucion by decree or censure of the Lorde Keeper of the greate seale of England or lorde Chauncellor for the time beinge, vppon any complaint or Informacion to him given in her Majesties Courte of Chauncery in that behalfe.

[Endorsed :] *The form of an Act* Concerninge translacion of the holie Bible from the originall hebrew and greeke. *To compel any of either University to come & assist in translating.* A[rch]B[ishop] Whitgift. Tempore Regin. Elizab.[2]

LX. THE ATTEMPT TO PROVIDE FOR THE TRANSLATORS OF 1611[1]

A. BISHOP BANCROFT CIRCULATES A LETTER FROM THE KING

Printed from Strype. (Reg. III. Whitgift, fol. 155)

After my hearty commendations unto your lordship I have received letters from his most excellent majesty, the tenor whereof followeth :—

Right trusty and well beloved, we greet you well. Whereas we have appointed certain learned men, to the number of four and fifty, for the translating of the Bible, and that in this number, divers of them have either no ecclesiastical preferment at all, or else so very small, as the same is far unmeet for men of their deserts, and yet we of ourself in any convenient time cannot well remedy it, therefore we do hereby require you, that presently you write in our name as well to the archbishop of York, as to the rest of the bishops of the province of Cant. signifying unto them, that we do will, and

[2] The words in italics are in a different handwriting to the remainder.

[1] Other documents concerning the version of 1611 are quoted textually in the Introduction.

straitly charge every one of them, as also the other
bishops of the province of York, as they tender our
good favour towards them, that (all excuses set apart)
when any prebend or parsonage, being rated in our book
of taxations, the prebend to twenty pound at the least
and the parsonage to the like sum and upwards, shall
next upon any occasion happen to be void, and to be
either of their patronage and gift, or the like parsonage
so void to be of the patronage or gift of any person
whatsoever, they do make stay thereof, and admit none
unto it, until certifying vs of the avoidance of it, and of
the name of the patron (if it be not of their own gift)
we may commend for the same some such of the learned
men, as we shall think fit to be preferred unto it : not
doubting of the bishops' readiness to satisfy us herein,
or that any of the laity, when we shall in time move
them to so good and religious an act, will be unwilling
to give us the like due contentment and satisfaction ;
we ourselves having taken the same order for such
prebends and benefices as shall be void in our gift.
What we write to you of others, you must apply it to
yourself, as also not forget to move the said archbishop
and all the bishops, with their deans and chapters of
both provinces, as touching the other point to be imparted otherwise by you unto them. Furthermore we
require you, to move all our bishops to inform themselves
of all such learned men within their several dioceses,
as having especiall skill in the Hebrew and Greek tongues,
have taken pains, in their private studies of the scriptures,
for the clearing of any obscurities either in the Hebrew
or in the Greek, or touching any difficulties or mistakings
in the former English translation, which we have now
commanded to be thoroughly viewed and amended, and
thereupon to write unto them, earnestly charging them,

and signifying our pleasure therein, that they send such their observations either to Mr. Lively, our Hebrew reader in Cambridge, or to Dr. Harding, our Hebrew reader in Oxford, or to Dr. Andrews, dean of Westminster, to be imparted to the rest of their several companies ; so that our said intended translation may have the help and furtherance of all our principal learned men within this our kingdom. Given under our signet at our palace of Westm. the two and twentieth of July, in the second year of our reign of England, France and Ireland, and of Scotland xxxvii.

Your lordship may see, how careful his majesty is for the providing of livings for these learned men : I doubt not therefore, but your lordship will have a due regard of his majesty's request herein, as it is fit and meet, and that you will take such order both with your chancellor, register, and such your lordship's officers, who shall have intelligence of the premises, as also with the dean and chapter of your cathedral church, whom his majesty likewise requireth to be put in mind of his pleasure herein, not forgetting the latter part of his majesty's letter, touching the informing of yourself of the fittest linguists within your diocese for to perform, and speedily to return that, which his majesty is so careful to have faithfully performed. I could wish your lordship would, for my discharge return me in some few lines, the time of the receipt of these letters, that I may discharge that duty, which his majesty, by these his letters, hath laid upon me ; and so I bid your lordship right heartily farewell.

From Fulham the 31st of July, MDCIV.

Your lordship's loving friend and brother,

R. London.

B. Bancroft's Exhortation to the Bishops to Subscribe

From the same. (Reg. III. Whitgift, fol. 156)

' Salutem in Christo.' My very good lord, as touching that clause in his majesty's letter, which is referred to my relation, this it is : there are many, as your lordship perceiveth, who are to be employed in this translating of the Bible, and sundry of them must of necessity have their charges borne, which his majesty was very ready of his most princely disposition to have borne : but some of my lords, as things now go, did hold it inconvenient, whereupon it was left to me, to move all my brethren, the bishops, and likewise every several dean and chapter, to contribute toward this work. Accordingly therefore to my duty, I heartily pray your lordship, not only to think yourself what is meet for you to give for this purpose, but likewise to acquaint your dean and chapter not only with the said clause of his majesty's letter, but likewise with the meaning of it, that they may agree upon such a sum, as they mean to contribute. I do not think that a thousand marks will finish the work, to be employed as is aforesaid, whereof your lordship, with your dean and chapter, having due consideration, I must require you in his majesty's name, according to his good pleasure in that behalf, that as soon as possibly you can, you send me word, what shall be expected from you and your said dean and chapter ; for I am to acquaint his majesty with every man's liberality towards this most godly work.

And thus not doubting of your especiall care for the accomplishing of the premises, and desiring your lordship to note the date to me of your receipt of this letter, I commit your lordship unto the tuition of the Almighty God. From Fulham this 31st of July MDCIV.

Your lordship's very loving friend and brother,

R. London.

LXI. THE BIBLE STOCK IN 1606[1]

Mr. Barker Master.

Mr. White) Wardens.
Mr. Leake)

1606   4 July

Memorandum that Mr. Barker in consideration that Mr. Dawson hath remitted and yeilded up unto hym all the full right & interest & Clayme to the printinge of the booke of holy Scripture called the Newe Testament in the volume called Octavo of Mr. Cheak's translacion hathe undertaken and agreed to pay unto the parteners in the previleges to their own proper use Foure hundred pounds either out of his Divids of his parte in the said privilege as they shall growe due untyll they amount to so muche Or else in some spedye sorte as he shall think convenient Be yt remembered that on this present day Mr. Barker hathe payd unto the said partners as well Twenty pounds whiche he receaved for the dividt of his parte upon the dividt made this day As also four score pounds moore in present money whiche maketh up one hundred pounds and is the first hundred pounds parcell of the said Foure hundred pounds

Mr. Barker.
Mr. Dawson.

Mr. Dawson yeildeth up the testament in 8 to Mr. Barker.

Mr. Barker undertaketh the payment of 400li to the ptners in the privilege to theire own use.

He now payeth the first 100li thereof.

[1] This very important document, most kindly supplied by Mr. Charles Rivington, invites more commentary than the date of its receipt allows. The surrender of the copyright of Sir John Cheke's version of the New Testament, though mentioned as the only consideration, was probably quite a minor one, as its pecuniary value would have been nearer four hundred pence than as many pounds. It reads as if Barker had been taking too large a share of the profits and that this was a settlement not improbably in anticipation of the outlay to be incurred on the new version.

LXII. REPORT ON THE MAKING OF THE VERSION OF 1611 PRESENTED TO THE SYNOD OF DORT

Sessione Septima.

xx Novembris, Die Martis ante meridiem.

Theologi Magnae Britanniae scripto explicarunt, quo consilio, quáque ratione negotium accuratissimę versionis Anglicanę à Serenissimo Rege Iacobo institutum fuerit, quę ratio in distribuendo opere fuerit observata : tum quę leges interpretibus fuerint prescripte ; ut inde ea, que nobis usui fore judicarentur, desumi possent. Exemplum ejus scripti hic subjicitur :

Modus quem Theologi Angli in versione Bibliorum sunt secuti.

Theologi Magnae Britanniae, quibus non est visum tantae quaestioni subitam et inopinatam responsionem adhibere, officii sui esse judicarunt, praematura deliberatione habita, quando quidem facta esset honorifica accuratissimae translationis Anglicanae mentio, à Serenissimo Rege Iacobo, magna cum cura, magnisque sumptibus nuper editae, notum facere huic celeberrimae Synodo, quo consilio, quaque ratione sacrum hoc negotium à Serenissima ejus Majestate praestitum fuerit.

Primo, in opere distribuendo hanc rationem observari voluit : totum corpus Bibliorum in sex partes fuit distributum : cuilibet parti transferendae destinati sunt septem vel octo viri primarij, Linguarum peritissimi.

Duae partes assignatae fuerunt Theologis quibusdam Londinensibus : quatuor vero partes reliquae divisae fuerunt aequaliter inter utriusque Academiae Theologos.

Post peractum à singulis pensum, ex hisce omnibus

duodecim selecti viri in unum locum convocati, integrum opus recognoverunt, ac recensuerunt.

Postremo, Reverendissimus Episcopus Wintoniensis, Bilsonus, una cum Doctore Smitho, nunc Episcopo Glocestriensi, viro eximio, et ab initio in toto hoc opere versatissimo, omnibus mature pensitatis & examinatis extremam manum huic versioni imposuerunt.

Leges Interpretibus praescriptae fuerunt hujusmodi :

Primo, cautum est, ut simpliciter nova versio non adornaretur, sed vetus, et ab Ecclesià diu recepta ab omnibus naevis et vitiis purgaretur ; idque hunc in finem, ne recederetur ab antiqua translatione, nisi originalis textus veritas, vel emphasis postularet.

Secundo, ut nullae annotationes margini apponerentur : sed, tantum loca parallela notarentur.

Tertio, ut ubi vox Hebraea vel Graeca geminum idoneum sensum admittit : alter in ipso contextu, alter in margine exprimeretur. Quod itidem factum, ubi varia lectio in exemplaribus probatis reperta est.

Quarto, Hebraismi et Graecismi difficiliores in margine repositi sint.

Quinto, in translatione Tobit et Iudithae, quando quidem magna discrepantia inter Graecum contextum et veterem vulgatam Latinam editionem reperiatur, Graecum potius contextum secuti sunt.

Sexto, ut quae ad sensum supplemendum ubivis necessario fuerunt contextui interserenda, alio, scilicet minusculo, charactere, distinguerentur.

Septimo, ut nova argumenta singulis libris, & novae periochae singulis capitibus praefigerentur.

Denique, absolutissima Geneologia et descriptio Terrae sanctae, huic opere conjungerentur.

Translation

The theologians of Great Britain offered a written explanation of the design and plan in accordance with which the business of the very accurate English version was instituted by the most Serene King James, of what plan was observed in distributing the work, and what rules were laid down for the translators ; with the intent that any points which might be judged useful to us might be taken from it. A copy of this document is subjoined.

Method which the English Theologians followed in the version of the Bible. The theologians of Great Britain, unwilling to give a sudden and unconsidered answer to so important a question, considered it their duty to hold an early consultation, and since honourable mention has been made of the very accurate English translation lately set forth, with great care and at great expense, by the most Serene King James, to notify to this numerously attended Synod the design and plan with which this sacred business was furnished by his most Serene Majesty.

Firstly, in the distribution of the work he willed this plan to be observed : the whole text of the Bible was distributed into six sections, and to the translation of each section there were nominated seven or eight men of distinction, skilled in languages.

Two sections were assigned to certain London theologians ; the four remaining sections were equally divided among the theologians of the two Universities.

After each section had finished its task twelve delegates, chosen from them all, met together and reviewed and revised the whole work.

Lastly, the very Reverend the Bishop of Winchester,

Bilson, together with Dr. Smith, now Bishop of Gloucester, a distinguished man, who had been deeply occupied in the whole work from the beginning, after all things had been maturely weighed and examined, put the finishing touch to this version.

The rules laid down for the translators were of this kind :

In the first place caution was given that an entirely new version was not to be furnished, but an old version, long received by the Church, to be purged from all blemishes and faults ; to this end there was to be no departure from the ancient translation, unless the truth of the original text or emphasis demanded.

Secondly, no notes were to be placed in the margin, but only parallel passages to be noted.

Thirdly, where a Hebrew or Greek word admits two meanings of a suitable kind, the one was to be expressed in the text, the other in the margin. The same to be done where a different reading was found in good copies.

Fourthly, the more difficult Hebraisms and Graecisms were consigned to the margin.

Fifthly, in the translation of Tobit and Judith, when any great discrepancy is found between the Greek text and the old vulgate Latin they followed the Greek text by preference.

Sixthly, that words which it was anywhere necessary to insert into the text to complete the meaning were to be distinguished by another type, small roman.

Seventhly, that new arguments should be prefixed to every book, and new headings to every chapter.

Lastly, that a very perfect Genealogy and map of the Holy Land should be joined to the work.

LXII. PREFACE TO THE VERSION OF 1611

THE TRANSLATORS TO THE READER

Zeale to promote the common good, whether it be by deuising any thing our selues, or reuising that which hath bene laboured by others, deserueth certainly much respect and esteeme, but yet findeth but cold intertainment in the world.   It is welcommed with suspicion in stead of loue, and with emulation in stead of thankes : and if there be any hole left for cauill to enter, (and cauill, if it doe not finde a hole, will make one) it is sure to bee misconstrued, and in danger to be condemned. This will easily be granted by as many as know story, or haue any experience. For, was there euer any thing proiected, that sauoured any way of newnesse or renewing, but the same endured many a storme of gaine-saying, or opposition ? A man would thinke that Ciuilitie, holesome Lawes, learning and eloquence, Synods, and Church-maintenance, (that we speake of no more things of this kinde) should be as safe as a Sanctuary, and ‖ out of shot,[1] as they say, that no man would lift vp the heele, no, nor dogge mooue his tongue against the motioners of them.   For by the first, we are distinguished from bruit-beasts led with sensualitie : By the second, we are bridled and restrained from outragious behauiour, and from doing of iniuries, whether by fraud or by violence : By the third, we are enabled to informe and reforme others, by the light and feeling that we haue attained vnto our selues : Briefly, by the fourth being brought together to a parle face to face, we sooner compose our differences then by writings,

The best things haue been calumniated.

---

[1] ἔξω βέλους.

which are endlesse : And lastly, that the Church be
sufficiently prouided for, is so agreeable to good reason
and conscience, that those mothers are holden to be lesse
cruell, that kill their children assoone as they are borne,
then those noursing fathers and mothers (wheresoeuer
they be) that withdraw from them who hang vpon their
breasts (and vpon whose breasts againe themselues doe
hang to receiue the Spirituall and sincere milke of the
word) liuelyhood and support fit for their estates. Thus
it is apparent, that these things which we speake of, are
of most necessary vse, and therefore, that none, either
without absurditie can speake against them, or without
note of wickednesse can spurne against them.

Yet for all that, the learned know that certaine worthy
men [2] haue bene brought to vntimely death for none
other fault, but for seeking to reduce their Countrey-men
to good order and discipline : and that in some Common-
weales [3] it was made a capitall crime, once to motion the
making of a new Law for the abrogating of an old, though
the same were most pernicious : And that certaine,[4]
which would be counted pillars of the State, and paternes
of Vertue and Prudence, could not be brought for a long
time to giue way to good Letters and refined speech, but
bare themselues as auerse from them, as from rocks or
boxes of poison : And fourthly, that hee [5] was no babe,
but a great clearke, that gaue foorth (and in writing to
remaine to posteritie) in passion peraduenture, but yet
he gaue foorth, that hee had not seene any profit to come
by any Synode, or meeting of the Clergie, but rather the
contrary : And lastly, against Church-maintenance and
allowance, in scuh sort, as the Embassadors and messen-
gers of the great King of Kings should be furnished, it is

---

[2] *Anacharsis with others.*   [3] *Locri.*   [4] *Cato the elder.*
[5] *Gregory the Diuine.*

not vnknowen what a fiction or fable (so it is esteemed,
and for no better by the reporter himselfe,[6] though
superstitious) was deuised ; Namely, that at such time
?s the professours and teachers of Christianitie in the
Church of Rome, then a true Church, were liberally
endowed, a voyce forsooth was heard from heauen,
saying ; Now is poison powred down into the Church, &c.
Thus not only as oft as we speake, as one saith, but also
as oft as we do any thing of note or consequence, we
subiect our selues to euery ones censure, and happy is
he that is least tossed vpon tongues ; for vtterly to
escape the snatch of them it is impossible. If any man
conceit, that this is the lot and portion of the meaner sort
onely, and that Princes are priuiledged by their high
estate, he is deceiued. As *the sword deuoureth aswell one
as the other*, as it is in *Samuel* ;[7] nay as the great Com-
mander charged his souldiers in a certaine battell, to
strike at no part of the enemie, but at the face ; And as
the King of *Syria* commanded his chiefe Captaines *to
fight neither with small nor great, saue onely against the
King of Israel* :[8] so it is too true, that Enuie striketh
most spitefully at the fairest, and at the chiefest. *Dauid*
was a worthy Prince, and no man to be compared to him
for his first deedes, and yet for as worthy an acte as euer
he did (euen for bringing backe the Arke of God in
solemnitie) he was scorned and scoffed at by his owne
wife.[9] *Solomon* was greater than *Dauid*, though not in
vertue, yet in power : and by his power and wisdome he
built a Temple to the LORD, such a one as was the glory
of the land of Israel, and the wonder of the whole world.
But was that his magnificence liked of by all ? We
doubt of it. Otherwise, why doe they lay it in his sonnes

[6] *Nauclerus.*   [7] 2. Sam. 11. 25.   [8] 1. King. 22. 31.
[9] 2. Sam. 6. 16.

dish, and call vnto him for ‖ easing of the burden,[10] *Make,*
say they, *the grieuous seruitude of thy father, and his sore
yoke, lighter.*[11] Belike he had charged them with some
leuies, and troubled them with some cariages ; Hereupon
they raise vp a tragedie, and wish in their heart the
Temple had neuer bene built. So hard a thing it is to
please all, euen when we please God best, and doe seeke
to approue our selues to euery ones conscience.

If wee will descend to later times, wee shall finde many
the like examples of such kind, or   The highest per-
rather vnkind acceptance. The first   sonages haue been
Romane Emperour [12] did neuer doe a   calumniated.
more pleasing deed to the learned, nor more profitable to
posteritie, for conseruing the record of times in true sup-
putation ; then when he corrected the Calender, and
ordered the yeere according to the course of the Sunne :
and yet this was imputed to him for noueltie, and arro-
gancie, and procured to him great obloquie.   So the
first Christened Emperour [13] (at the leastwise that openly
professed the faith himselfe, and allowed others to doe the
like) for strengthening the Empire at his great charges,
and prouiding for the Church, as he did, got for his labour
the name *Pupillus,*[14] as who would say, a wastefull
Prince, that had neede of a Guardian, or ouerseer.   So
the best Christened Emperour,[15] for the loue that he bare
vnto peace, thereby to enrich both himselfe and his
subiects, and because he did not seeke warre but find it,
was iudged to be no man at armes,[16] (though in deed he
excelled in feates of chiualrie, and shewed so much when
he was prouoked) and condemned for giuing himselfe to
his ease, and to his pleasure. To be short, the most

[10] σεισάχθειαν.   [11] 1. King. 12. 4.   [12] *C. Cæsar. Plutarch.*
[13] *Constantine.*   [14] *Aurel. Victor.*   [15] *Theodosius.*
[16] *Zosimus.*

learned Emperour of former times,[17] (at the least, the
greatest politician) what thanks had he for cutting off
the superfluities of the lawes, and digesting them into
some order and method ? This, that he hath been blotted
by some to bee an Epitomist, that is, one that extin-
guished worthy whole volumes, to bring his abridgements
into request.   This is the measure that hath been rendred
to excellent Princes in former times, euen, *Cum benè
facerent, malè audire*, For their good deedes to be euill
spoken of.   Neither is there any likelihood, that enuie
and malignitie died, and were buried with the ancient.
No, no, the reproofe of *Moses* taketh hold of most ages ;
*You are risen vp in your fathers stead, an increase of
sinfull men.*[18] *What is that that hath been done ? that
which shall be done : and there is no new thing vnder the*

His Maiesties
constancie, not-
withstanding
calumniation, for
the suruey of the
English transla-
tions.

Sunne,[19] saith the wiseman : and
S. *Steuen, As your fathers did, so doe
you.*[20]   This, and more to this purpose,
His Maiestie that now reigneth (and
long, and long may he reigne, and
his offspring for euer, *Himselfe and
children, and childrens children alwayes* [21]) knew full
well, according to the singular wisedome giuen vnto him
by God, and the rare learning and experience that he
hath attained vnto ; namely that whosoeuer attempteth
any thing for the publike (specially if it pertaine to
Religion, and to the opening and clearing of the word
of God) the same setteth himselfe vpon a stage to be
glouted vpon by euery euil eye, yea, he casteth himselfe headlong vpon pikes, to be gored by euery sharpe
tongue.   For he that medleth with mens Religion in
any part, medleth with their custome, nay, with their

[17] *Iustinian.*   [18] Numb 32. 14.   [19] Eccles. 1. 9.
[20] Acts 7. 51.   [21] Αὐτὸς, καὶ παῖδες, καὶ παίδων πάντοτε παῖδες.

freehold ; and though they finde no content in that
which they haue, yet they cannot abide to heare of
altering. Notwithstanding his Royall heart was not
daunted or discouraged for this or that colour, but stood
resolute, *as a statue immoueable, and an anuile not easie
to be beaten into plates*,[22] as one sayth ; he knew who had
chosen him to be a Souldier, or rather a Captaine, and
being assured that the course which he intended made
much for the glory of God, & the building vp of his
Church, he would not suffer it to be broken off for whatsoeuer speaches or practises. It doth certainely belong
vnto Kings, yea, it doth specially belong vnto them, to
haue care of Religion, yea, to know it aright, yea, to
professe it zealously, yea to promote it to the vttermost
of their power. This is their glory before all nations
which meane well, and this will bring vnto them a farre
most excellent weight of glory in the day of the Lord
Iesus. For the Scripture saith not in vaine, *Them that
honor me, I will honor*,[23] neither was it a vaine word that
Eusebius deliuered long agoe, that pietie towards God [24]
was the weapon, and the onely weapon that both preserued *Constantines* person, and auenged him of his
enemies.[25]

But now what pietie without trueth ? what trueth
(what sauing trueth) without the word   The praise of the
of God ? what word of God (whereof   holy Scriptures.
we may be sure) without the Scripture ? The Scriptures
we are commanded to search. Ioh. 5. 39. Esa. 8. 20.
They are commended that searched & studied them.
Act. 17. 11. and 8. 28, 29. They ar ereproued that were
vnskilful in them, or slow to beleeue them. *Mat.* 22. 29.
Luk. 24. 25. They can make vs wise vnto saluation.

---

[22] *Suidas.* ὥσπερ τὶς ἀνδριὰς ἀπερίτρεπτος καὶ ἄκμων ἀνήλατος.
[23] 1. Sam. 2. 30.   [24] θεοσέβεια.   [25] *Eusebius lib.* 10 *cap.* 8.

2. *Tim.* 3. 15. If we be ignorant, they will instruct vs ; if out of the way, they will bring vs home ; if out of order, they will reforme vs, if in heauines, comfort vs ; if dull, quicken vs ; if colde, inflame vs. *Tolle, lege ; Tolle, lege,*[26] Take vp and read, take vp and read the Scriptures, (for vnto them was the direction) it was said vnto S. *Augustine* by a supernaturall voyce. *Whatsoeuar is in the Scriptures, beleeue me,* saith the same S. *Augustine,*[27] *is high and diuine ; there is verily trueth, and a doctrine most fit for the refreshing and renewing of mens mindes, and truely so tempered, that euery one may draw from thence that which is sufficient for him, if hee come to draw with a deuout and pious minde, as true Religion requireth.* Thus S. *Augustine.* And S. *Hierome* [28] : *Ana scripturas, & amabit te sapientia &c.* Loue the Scriptures, and wisedome will loue thee. And S. *Cyrill* against *Iulian ;* [29] *Euen boyes that are bred vp in the Scriptures, become most religious, &c.* But what mention wee three or foure vses of the Scripture, whereas whatsoeuer is to be beleeued or practised, or hoped for, is contained in them ? or three or foure sentences of the Fathers, since whosoeuer is worthy the name of a Father, from Christs time downeward, hath likewise written not onely of the riches, but also of the perfection of the Scripture ? *I adore the fulnesse of the Scripture,* saith *Tertullian* against *Hermogenes.*[30] And againe, to *Apelles* an Heretike of the like stampe, he saith ; *I doe not admit that which thou bringest in* (or concludest) *of thine owne* (head or store, *de tuo*) without Scripture. So Saint *Iustin*

[26] *S. August confess.* lib. 8. *cap.* 12.
[27] *S. August. de vtilit. credendi cap.* 6.
[28] *S. Hieronym. ad Demetriad.*
[29] *S. Cyril.* 7°. *contra Iulianum.*
[30] *Tertul. aduers. Hermo.   Tertul de carne Christi.*

Martyr [31] before him ; *Wee must know by all meanes*, saith
hee, *that it is not lawfull* (or possible) *to learne* (any thing)
*of God or of right pietie, saue onely out of the Prophets, who
teach vs by diuine inspiration.*   So Saint *Basill* [32] after
*Tertullian, It is a manifest falling away from the Faith,
and a fault of presumption, either to reiect any of those
things that are written, or to bring in* (vpon the head of
them, ἐπεισάγειν) *any of those things that* are not written.
Wee omit to cite to the same effect, S. *Cyrill* B. of
Hierusalem in his 4. *Cataches.* Saint *Hierome* against
Heluidius, Saint *Augustine* in his 3. booke against the
letters of *Petilian*, and in very many other places of his
workes.   Also we forbeare to descend to latter Fathers,
because wee will not wearie the reader.   The Scriptures
then being acknowledged to bee so full and so perfect,
how can wee excuse our selues of negligence, if we doe
not studie them, of curiositie, if we be not content with
them ?   Men talke much of εἰρεσιώνη,[33] how many
sweete and goodly things it had hanging on it ; of the
Philosophers stone, that it turneth copper into gold ; of
Cornu-copia, that it had all things necessary for foode in
it ; of *Panaces* the herbe, that it was good for all diseases ;
of *Catholicon* the drugge, that it is in stead of all purges ;
of *Vulcans* armour, that it was an armour of proofe
against all thrusts, and all blowes, &c.   Well, that which
they falsly or vainely attributed to these things for bodily
good, wee may iustly and with full measure ascribe vnto
the Scripture, for spirituall.   It is not onely an armour,
but also a whole armorie of weapons, both offensiue, and

[31] *Iustin προτρεπτ. πρὸς ἑλλην. οἷόν τε.*

[32] *S. Ba:il. περὶ πίστεως. ὑπερηφανίας κατηγορία.*

[33] Ειρεσιώνη σῦκα φέρει, καὶ πίονας ἄρτους, καὶ μέλι ἐν κοτύλῃ, καὶ
ελαιον, &c.   An oliue bow wrapped about with wooll, wherevpon
did hang figs, & bread, and honie in a pot, & oyle.

defensiue ; whereby we may saue our selues and put the
enemie to flight. It is not an herbe, but a tree, or rather
a whole paradise of trees of life, which bring foorth fruit
euery moneth, and the fruit thereof is for meate, and
the leaues for medicine. It is not a pot of *Manna*, or
a cruse of oyle, which were for memorie only, or for a
meales meate or two, but as it were a showre of heauenly
bread sufficient for a whole host, be it neuer so great ;
and as it were a whole cellar full of oyle vessels ; whereby
all our necessities may be prouided for, and our debts
discharged. In a word, it is a Panary of holesome foode,
against fenowed traditions ; a Physions-shop [34] (Saint
Basill calleth it) of preseruatiues against poisoned
heresies ; a Pandect of profitable lawes, against rebellious
spirits ; a treasurie of most costly iewels, against beggarly
rudiments ; Finally a fountaine of most pure water
springing vp vnto euerlasting life. And what maruaile ?
The originall thereof being from heauen, not from earth ;
the authour being God, not man ; the enditer, the holy
spirit, not the wit of the Apostles or Prophets ; the Pen-
men such as were sanctified from the wombe, and
endewed with a principall portion of Gods spirit ; the
matter, veritie, pietie, puritie, vprightnesse ; the forme,
Gods word, Gods testimonie, Gods oracles, the word of
trueth, the word of saluation, &c. the effects, light of
vnderstanding, stablenesse of perswasion, repentance
from dead workes, newnesse of life, holinesse, peace, ioy
in the holy Ghost ; lastly, the end and reward of the
studie thereof, fellowship with the Saints, participation
of the heauenly nature, fruition of an inheritance immortall, vndefiled, and that neuer shall fade away : Happie
is the man that delighteth in the Scripture, and thrise
happie that meditateth in it day and night.

[34] κοινὸν ἰατρεῖον.   *S. Basil. in Psal. primum.*

But how shall men meditate in that, which they cannot vnderstand ? How shall they vnderstand that which is kept close in an vnknowen tongue ? as it is written, *Except I know the power of the voyce, I shall be to him that speaketh, a Barbarian, and he that speaketh, shalbe a Barbarian to me.*[35] The Apostle excepteth no tongue ; not Hebrewe the ancientest, not Greeke the most copious, not Latine the finest. Nature taught a naturall man to confesse, that all of vs in those tongues which wee doe not vnderstand, are plainely deafe ; wee may turne the deafe eare vnto them. The *Scythian* counted the *Athenian*, whom he did not vnderstand, barbarous : [36] so the *Romane* did the *Syrian*, and the *Iew*, (euen S. *Hierome*[37] himselfe calleth the Hebrew tongue barbarous, belike because it was strange to so many) so the Emperour of *Constantinople*[38] calleth the *Latine* tongue, barbarous, though Pope *Nicolas* do storme at it : [39] so the *Iewes* long before *Christ*, called all other nations, *Lognazim*, which is little better then barbarous. Therefore as one complaineth, that alwayes in the Senate of *Rome,* there was one or other that called for an interpreter : [40] so lest the Church be driuen to the like exigent, it is necessary to haue translations in a readinesse. Translation it is that openeth the window, to let in the light ; that breaketh the shell, that we may eat the kernel ; that putteth aside the curtaine, that we may looke into the most Holy place ; that remooueth the couer of the well, that wee may come by the water, euen as *Iacob* rolled away the stone from the mouth of the well, by which meanes the

[35] 1. Cor. 14.
[36] *Clem. Alex.* 1°. *Strom.*
[37] *S. Hieronym. Damaso.*
[38] *Michael, Theophili fil.*
[39] *2. Tom. Concil. ex edit. Petri Crab.*
[40] *Cicero* 5°. *de finibus.*

flockes of *Laban* were watered.[41] Indeede without translation into the vulgar tongue, the vnlearned are but like children at *Iacobs* well (which was deepe) without a bucket or some thing to draw with : [42] or as that person mentioned by *Esay*, to whom when a sealed booke was deliuered, with this motion, *Reade this, I pray thee*, hee was faine to make this answere, *I cannot, for it is sealed*.[43]

The translation of the olde Testament out of the Hebrew into Greeke.

While God would be knowen onely in *Iacob*, and haue his Name great in *Israel*, and in none other place, while the dew lay on *Gideons* fleece onely, and all the earth besides was drie ; [44] then for one and the same people, which spake all of them the language of *Canaan*, that is, *Hebrewe*, one and the same originall in *Hebrew* was sufficient. But when the fulnesse of time drew neere, that the Sunne of righteousnesse, the Sonne of God should come into the world, whom God ordeined to be a reconciliation through faith in his blood, not of the *Iew* onely, but also of the *Greeke*, yea, of all them that were scattered abroad ; then loe, it pleased the Lord to stirre vp the spirit of a *Greeke* Prince (*Greeke* for descent and language) euen of *Ptolome Philadelph* King of *Egypt*, to procure the translating of the Booke of God out of *Hebrew* into *Greeke*. This is the translation of the *Seuentie* Interpreters, commonly so called, which prepared the way for our Sauiour among the Gentiles by written preaching, as Saint *Iohn* Baptist did among the *Iewes* by vocall. For the *Grecians* being desirous of learning, were not wont to suffer bookes of worth to lye moulding in Kings Libraries, but had many of their seruants, ready scribes, to copie them out, and so they

[41] Gen. 29, 10.   [42] Ioh. 4. 11.   [43] Esay 29. 11.
[44] *See S. August. lib.* 12. *contra Faust. c.* 32.

were dispersed and made common.   Againe, the *Greeke* tongue was wellknowen and made familiar to most inhabitants in *Asia*, by reason of the conquest that there the *Grecians* had made, as also by the Colonies, which thither they had sent.   For the same causes also it was well vnderstood in many places of *Europe*, yea, and of *Affrike* too.   Therefore the word of God being set foorth in *Greeke*, becommeth hereby like a candle set vpon a candlesticke, which giueth light to all that are in the house, or like a proclamation sounded foorth in the market place, which most men presently take knowledge of ; and therefore that language was fittest to containe the Scriptures, both for the first Preachers of the Gospel to appeale vnto for witnesse, and for the learners also of those times to make search and triall by.   It is certaine, that that Translation was not so sound and so perfect, but that it needed in many places correction ; and who had bene so sufficient for this worke as the Apostles or Apostolike men ?   Yet it seemed good to the holy Ghost and to them, to take that which they found, (the same being for the greatest part true and sufficient) rather then by making a new, in that new world and greene age of the Church, to expose themselues to many exceptions and cauillations, as though they made a Translation to serue their owne turne, and therefore bearing witnesse to themselues, their witnesse not to be regarded.   This may be supposed to bee some cause, why the Translation of the *Seuentie* was allowed to passe for currant.   Notwithstanding, though it was commended generally, yet it did not fully content the learned, no not of the *Iewes*.[45] For not long after *Christ*, *Aquila* fell in hand with a new Translation, and after him *Theodotion*, and after him *Symmachus* : yea, there was a fift and a sixt edition, the

[45] *Epiphan. de mensur. & ponderibus.*

Authours wherof were not knowen. These with the
Seuentie made vp the *Hexapla*, and were worthily and to
great purpose compiled together by *Origen*. Howbeit
the Edition of the *Seuentie* went away with the credit,
and therefore not onely was placed in the midst by
Origen (for the worth and excellencie thereof aboue the
rest, as *Epiphanius* gathereth) but also was vsed by the
Greeke fathers for the ground and foundation of their
Commentaries.[46] Yea, *Epiphanius* aboue named doeth
attribute so much vnto it, that he holdeth the Authours
thereof not onely for Interpreters, but also for Prophets
in some respect : and *Iustinian* the Emperour enioyning
the *Iewes* his subiects to vse specially the Translation of
the *Seuentie*, rendreth this reason thereof, because they
were as it were enlightened with propheticall grace.[47]
Yet for all that, as the *Egyptians* are said of the Prophet
to bee men and not God, and their horses flesh and not
spirit : [48] so it is euident, (and Saint *Hierome* affirmeth
as much) [49] that the *Seuentie* were Interpreters, they
were not Prophets ; they did many things well, as
learned men ; but yet as men they stumbled and fell,
one while through ouersight, another while through
ignorance, yea, sometimes they may be noted to adde
to the Originall, and sometimes to take from it ; which
made the Apostles to leaue them many times, when they
left the *Hebrew*, and to deliuer the sence thereof according to the trueth of the word, as the spirit gaue them
vtterance. This may suffice touching the Greeke Translations of the old Testament.

There were also within a few hundreth yeeres after

[46] *See S. August* 2°. *de doctrin. Christian. c.* 15°.

[47] *Nouell. diatax.* 146. προφητικῆs ὥσπερ χάριτοs περιλαμψάσηs αὐτούs.

[48] *Esa.* 31. 3.

[49] *S. Hieron. de optimo genere interpret.*

CHRIST, translations many into the Latine tongue : for this tongue also was very fit to conuey the Law and the Gospel by, because in those times very many Countreys Translation out of Hebrew and Greeke into Latine. of the West, yea of the South, East and North, spake or vnderstood Latine, being made Prouinces to the *Romanes*. But now the Latine Translations were too many to be all good, for they were infinite (*Latini Interpretes nullo modo numerari possunt*, saith *S. Augustine*.[50]) Againe they were not out of the *Hebrew* fountaine (wee speake of the *Latine* Translations of the Old Testament) but out of the *Greeke* streame, therefore the *Greeke* being not altogether cleare, the *Latine* deriued from it must needs be muddie. This moued *S. Hierome* a most learned father, and the best linguist without controuersie, of his age, or of any that went before him, to vndertake the translating of the Old Testament, out of the very fountaines themselues ; which hee performed with that euidence of great learning, iudgement, industrie and faithfulnes, that he hath for euer bound the Church vnto him, in a debt of speciall remembrance and thankefulnesse.

Now though the Church were thus furnished with *Greeke* and *Latine* Translations, euen before the faith of CHRIST was generally embraced in the Empire : (for the learned know that euen in *S. Hieroms* The translating of the Scripture into the vulgar tongues. time, the Consul of *Rome* and his wife were both Ethnicks, and about the same time the greatest part of the Senate also [51]) yet for all that the godly-learned were not content to haue the Scriptures in the Language which themselues vnderstood, *Greeke* and *Latine*, (as the good Lepers were

<hr />

[50] *S. Augustin. de doctr. Christ. lib. 2. cap. 11.*

[51] *S. Hieronym. Marcell. Zosim.*

A a

not content to fare well themselues, but acquainted their neighbours with the store that God had sent, that they also might prouide for themselues [52]) but also for the behoofe and edifying of the vnlearned which hungred and thirsted after Righteousnesse, and had soules to be saued aswell as they, they prouided Translations into the vulgar for their Countreymen, insomuch that most nations vnder heauen did shortly after their conuersion, heare CHRIST speaking vnto them in their mother tongue, not by the voyce of their Minister onely, but also by the written word translated. If any doubt hereof, he may be satisfied by examples enough, if enough wil serue the turne. First *S. Hierome* saith, *Multarum gentiū linguis Scriptura antè translata, docet falsa esse quæ addita sunt, &c.*[53] *i. The Scripture being translated before in the languages of many Nations, doth shew that those things that were added* (by *Lucian* or *Hesychius*) *are false.* So *S. Hierome* in that place. The same *Hierome* elsewhere affirmeth that he, the time was, had set forth the translation of the *Seuenty, suæ linguæ hominibus.*[54] *i.* for his countreymen of *Dalmatia.* Which words not only *Erasmus* doth vnderstand to purport, that *S. Hierome* translated the Scripture into the *Dalmatian* tongue, but also *Sixtus Senensis,*[55] and *Alphonsus à Castro*[56] (that we speake of no more) men not to be excepted against by them of *Rome,* doe ingenuously confesse as much. So, *S. Chrysostome*[57] that liued in *S. Hieromes* time, giueth euidence with him : *The doctrine of* S. *Iohn* (saith he) *did not in such sort* (as the Philosophers did) *vanish away : but the Syrians, Egyptians,*

[52] 2. King. 7. 9. [53] *S. Hieron. præf. in* 4. *Euangel.*
[54] *S. Hieron. Sophronio.* [55] *Six. Sen. lib.* 4.
[56] *Alphon. à Castro lib.* 1. *ca.* 23.
[57] *S. Chrysost. in Iohan. cap.* 1. *hom.* 1.

*Indians, Persians, Ethiopians, and infinite other nations
being barbarous people, translated it into their (mother)
tongue, and haue learned to be (true) Philosophers,* he
meaneth Christians. To this may be added *Theodorit*,[58]
as next vnto him, both for antiquitie, and for learning.
His words be these, *Euery Countrey that is vnder the
Sunne, is full of these wordes* (of the Apostles and Prophets)
and the Hebrew tongue (he meaneth the Scriptures in the
Hebrew tongue) *is turned not onely into the Language of
the Grecians, but also of the Romanes, and Egyptians, and
Persians, and Indians, and Armenians, and Scythians,
and Sauromatians, and briefly into all the Languages that
any Nation vseth.* So he. In like maner, *Vlpilas* is
reported by *Paulus Diaconus* [59] and *Isidor* [60] (and before
them by *Sozomen* [61]) to haue translated the Scriptures
into the *Gothicke* tongue : *Iohn* Bishop of *Siuil* by
Vasseus,[62] to haue turned them into *Arabicke*, about the
yeere of our Lord 717 : *Beda* by *Cistertiensis*, to haue
turned a great part of them into *Saxon* : *Efnard* by
Trithemius, to haue abridged the French Psalter, as *Beda*
had done the *Hebrew*, about the yeere 800 : King *Alured*
by the said *Cistertiensis*,[63] to haue turned the Psalter into
Saxon : *Methodius* by *Auentinus* [64] (printed at *Ingolstad*)
to haue turned the Scriptures into ‖ *Sclauonian* : *Valdo*,
Bishop of *Frising* by *Beatus Rhenanus*, to haue caused
about that time, the Gospels to be translated into *Dutch*-
rithme, yet extant in the Library of *Corbinian* : *Valdus*,
by diuers to haue turned them himself, or to haue

[58] *Theodor.* 5. *Therapeut.*　　　　　[59] *P. Diacon. li.* 12.
[60] *Isidor. in Chron.*　　　　　[61] *Goth. Sozom. li.* 6. *cap.* 37.
[62] *Vaseus in Chron Hispan.*
[63] *Polydor. Virg.* 5. *histor. Anglorum testatur idem de Aluredo
nostro.*
[64] *Auentin. lib.* 4. *Circa annum 900. *B. Rhenan. rerum
German. lib.* 2.

gotten them turned into *French,* about the yeere 1160* :
Charles the 5. of that name, surnamed *The wise,* to
haue caused them to be turned into *French,* about
200. yeeres after *Valdus* his time, of which translation there be many copies yet extant, as witnesseth
Beroaldus.[65] Much about that time, euen in our King
Richard the seconds dayes, *Iohn Treuisa* translated them
into *English,* and many *English* Bibles in written hand
are yet to be seene with diuers, translated as it is very
probable, in that age. So the *Syrian* translation of the
New Testament is in most learned mens Libraries, of
Widminstadius his setting forth, and the Psalter in
Arabicke is with many, of *Augustinus Nebiensis* setting
foorth. So *Postel* affirmeth, that in his trauaile he saw
the Gospels in the *Ethiopian* tongue ; And *Ambrose
Thesius* alleageth the Psalter of the *Indians,* which he
testifieth to haue bene set forth by *Potken* in *Syrian*
characters. So that, to haue the Scriptures in the mother-
tongue is not a quaint conceit lately taken vp, either by
the Lord *Cromwell* in *England,*[66] or by the Lord *Radeuil*
in *Polonie,* or by the Lord *Vngnadius* in the Emperours
dominion, but hath bene thought vpon, and put in practise of old, euen from the first times of the conuersion of
any Nation ; no doubt, because it was esteemed most
profitable, to cause faith to grow in mens hearts the
sooner, and to make them to be able to say with the
words of the Psalme, *As we haue heard, so we haue seene.*[67]

Now the Church of Rome would seeme at the length
to beare a motherly affection towards her children, and
to allow them the Scriptures in their mother tongue :
but indeed it is a gift, not deseruing to be called a gift,
an vnprofitable gift : [68] they must first get a Licence in

[65] *Beroald.*   [66] *Thuan.*   [67] Psal. 48. 8.
[68] δῶρον ἄδωρον κοὐκ ὀνήσιμον. *Sophocles.*

writing before they may vse them, and to get that, they must approue themselues to their Confessor, that is, to be such as are, if not frozen in the dregs, yet sowred with the leauen of their superstition. Howbeit, it seemed too much to *Clement the* 8. that there should be

The vnwillingnes of our chiefe Aduersaries, that the Scriptures should be diuulged in the mother tongue, &c.

any Licence granted to haue them in the vulgar tongue, and therefore he ouerruleth and frustrateth the grant of *Pius* the fourth.[69] So much are they afraid of the light of the Scripture, (*Lucifugæ Scripturarum*, as *Tertullian* speaketh [70]) that they will not trust the people with it, no not as it is set foorth by their owne sworne men, no not with the Licence of their owne Bishops and Inquisitors. Yea, so vnwilling they are to communicate the Scriptures to the peoples vnderstanding in any sort, that they are not ashamed to confesse, that wee forced them to translate it into English against their wills. This seemeth to argue a bad cause, or a bad conscience, or both. Sure we are, that it is not he that hath good gold, that is afraid to bring it to the touch-stone, but he that hath the counterfeit : neither is it the true man that shunneth the light, but the malefactour, lest his deedes should be reproued : neither is it the plaine dealing Merchant that is vnwilling to haue the waights, or the meteyard brought in place, but he that vseth deceit. But we will let them alone for this fault, and returne to translation.

Many mens mouths haue bene open a good while and yet are not stopped) with speeches about the

---

[69] See the obseruation (set forth by Clemen. his authority) vpon the 4. rule of Pius the 4. his making in the Index, *lib. prohib. pag.* 15. *ver.* 5.

[70] *Tertul. de resur. carnis.*   Ioan 3. 20.

Translation so long in hand, or rather perusals of

The speaches and reasons, both of our brethren, and of our Aduersaries against this worke.

Translations made before : and aske what may be the reason, what the necessitie of the employment : Hath the Church bene deceiued, say they, all this while ?   Hath her sweet bread bene mingled with leauen, her siluer with drosse, her wine with water, her milke with lime ? (*Lacte gypsum malè miscetur*, saith *S. Ireney*,[71]) We hoped that we had bene in the right way, that we had had the Oracles of God deliuered vnto vs, and that though all the world had cause to be offended and to complaine, yet that we had none.   Hath the nurse holden out the breast, and nothing but winde in it ?   Hath the bread bene deliuered by the fathers of the Church, and the same proued to be *lapidosus*, as *Seneca* speaketh ?   What is it to handle the word of God deceitfully, if this be not ? Thus certaine brethren.   Also the aduersaries of *Iudah* and *Hierusalem*, like *Sanballat* in *Nehemiah*, mocke as we heare, both at the worke and workemen, saying ; *What doe these weake Iewes, &c. will they make the stones whole againe out of the heapes of dust which are burnt ? although they build, yet if a foxe goe vp, he shall euen breake downe their stony wall.*[72]   Was their Translation good before ?   Why doe they now mend it ?   Was it not good ? Why then was it obtruded to the people ?   Yea, why did the Catholicks (meaning Popish *Romanists*) alwayes goe in ieopardie, for refusing to goe to heare it ?   Nay, if it must be translated into English, Catholicks are fittest to doe it.   They haue learning, and they know when a thing is well, they can *manum de tabulâ*.   Wee will answere them both briefly :   and the former, being brethren, thus, with *S. Hierome, Damnamus veteres ?*

[71] *S. Iren. 3. lib. cap.* 19.   [72] Neh. 4. 3.

Minimè, sed post priorum studia in domo Domini quod possumus laboramus.[73] That is, *Doe we condemne the ancient ? In no case : but after the endeuours of them that were before vs, wee take the best paines we can in the house of God.* As if hee said, Being prouoked by the example of the learned that liued before my time, I haue thought it my duetie, to assay whether my talent in the knowledge of the tongues, may be profitable in any measure to Gods Church, lest I should seeme to haue laboured in them in vaine, and lest I should be thought to glory in men, (although ancient,) aboue that which was in them. Thus *S. Hierome* may be thought to speake.

And to the same effect say wee, that we are so farre off from condemning any of their labours that traueiled before vs in this A satisfaction to our brethren. kinde, either in this land or beyond sea, either in King *Henries* time, or King *Edwards* (if there were any translation, or correction of a translation in his time) or Queene *Elizabeths* of euer-renoumed memorie, that we acknowledge them to haue beene raised vp of God, for the building and furnishing of his Church, and that they deserue to be had of vs and of posteritie in euerlasting remembrance. The Iudgement of *Aristotle* is worthy and well knowen : [74] *If Timotheus had not bene, we had not had much sweet musicke ; but if Phrynis (Timotheus his master) had not beene, wee had not had Timotheus.* Therefore blessed be they, and most honoured be their name, that breake the yce, and giueth onset vpon that which helpeth forward to the sauing of soules. Now what can bee more auaileable thereto, then to deliuer Gods booke vnto Gods people in a tongue which they vnderstand ? Since of an hidden treasure, and of a fountaine that is

[73] *S. Hieron. Apolog. aduers. Ruffin.*
[74] *Arist. 2. metaphys. cap. 1.*

sealed, there is no profit, as *Ptolomee Philadelph* wrote
to the Rabbins or masters of the Iewes, as witnesseth
Epiphanius : [75] and as S. *Augustine* saith ; *A man had
rather be with his dog then with a stranger* [76] (whose tongue
is strange vnto him.) Yet for all that, as nothing is
begun and perfited at the same time, and the later
thoughts are thought to be the wiser : so, if we building
vpon their foundation that went before vs, and being
holpen by their labours, doe endeuour to make that better
which they left so good ; no man, we are sure, hath cause
to mislike vs ; they, we perswade our selues, if they were
aliue, would thanke vs. The vintage of *Abiezer*, that
strake the stroake : yet the gleaning of grapes of
Ephraim was not to be despised. See *Iudges* 8. *verse* 2.[77]
Ioash the king of *Israel* did not satisfie himselfe, till he
had smitten the ground three times ; [78] and yet hee
offended the Prophet, for giuing ouer then. *Aquila*, of
whom wee spake before, translated the Bible as carefully, and as skilfully as he could ; and yet he thought
good to goe ouer it againe, and then it got the credit
with the Iewes, to be called κατὰ ἀκρίβειαν, that is, accu-
ratly done, as Saint *Hierome* witnesseth.[79] How many
bookes of profane learning haue bene gone ouer againe
and againe, by the same translators, by others ? Of one
and the same booke of *Aristotles* Ethikes, there are
extant not so few as sixe or seuen seuerall translations.
Now if this cost may bee bestowed vpon the goord,
which affordeth vs a little shade, and which to day
flourisheth, but to morrow is cut downe ; what may we
bestow, nay what ought we not to bestow vpon the Vine,

[75] *S. Epiphan. loco antè citato.*
[76] *S. Augustin. lib.* 19. *de ciuit. Dei c.* 7.
[77] Iudges 8. 2.   [78] 2 Kings 13. 18. 19.
[79] *S. Hieron. in Ezech. cap.* 3.

the fruite whereof maketh glad the conscience of man,
and the stemme whereof abideth for euer ? And this is
the word of God, which we translate. *What is the chaffe
to the wheat, saith the Lord ?*[80] *Tanti vitreum, quanti
verum margaritum* [81] (saith *Tertullian*,) if a toy of glasse
be of that rekoning with vs, how ought wee to value the
true pearle ? Therefore let no mans eye be euill, because
his Maiesties is good ; neither let any be grieued, that
wee haue a Prince that seeketh the increase of the
spirituall wealth of Israel (let *Sanballats* and *Tobiahs* doe
so, which therefore doe beare their iust reproofe (but let
vs rather blesse God from the ground of our heart, for
working this religious care in him, to haue the translations
of the Bible maturely considered of and examined.
For by this meanes it commeth to passe, that whatsoeuer
is sound alreadie (and all is sound for substance, in one
or other of our editions, and the worst of ours farre
better then their autentike vulgar) the same will shine
as gold more brightly, being rubbed and polished ; also,
if any thing be halting, or superfluous, or not so agreeable
to the originall, the same may bee corrected, and the
trueth set in place. And what can the King command to
bee done, that will bring him more true honour then this ?
and wherein could they that haue beene set a worke,
approue their duetie to the King, yea their obedience to
God, and loue to his Saints more, then by yeelding their
seruice, and all that is within them, for the furnishing
of the worke ? But besides all this, they were the principall motiues of it, and therefore ought least to quarrell it :
for the very Historicall trueth is, that vpon the importunate petitions of the Puritanes, at his Maiesties

[80] Ierem. 23. 28.
[81] *Tertul. ad Martyr.   Si tanti vilissimum vitrum, quanti
pretiosissimum Margaritum : Hieron. ad Saluin.*

comming to this Crowne, the Conference at Hampton
Court hauing bene appointed for hearing their complaints : when by force of reason they were put from all
other grounds, they had recourse at the last, to this
shift, that they could not with good conscience subscribe
to the Communion booke, since it maintained the Bible
as it was there translated, which was as they said,
a most corrupted translation.   And although this was
iudged to be but a very poore and emptie shift ; yet euen
hereupon did his Maiestie beginne to bethinke himselfe
of the good that might ensue by a new translation, and
presently after gaue order for this Translation which is
now presented vnto thee.   Thus much to satisfie our
scrupulous Brethren.

Now to the later we answere ; that wee doe not deny,

An answere to the   nay wee affirme and auow, that the
imputations of our   very meanest translation of the Bible in
aduersaries.   English, set foorth by men of our profession (for wee haue seene none of theirs of the whole Bible
as yet) containeth the word of God, nay, is the word of
God. As the Kings Speech which hee vttered in Parliament,
being translated into *French, Dutch, Italian* and *Latine,* is
still the Kings Speech, though it be not interpreted by
euery Translator with the like grace, nor peraduenture so
fitly for phrase, nor so expresly for sence, euery where. For
it is confessed, that things are to take their denomination
of the greater part ; and a naturall man could say, *Verùm
vbi multa nitent in carmine, non ego paucis offendor maculis,
&c.*[82]   A man may be counted a vertuous man, though
hee haue made many slips in his life, (els, there were none
vertuous, for *in many things we offend all*[83]) also a comely
man and louely, though hee haue some warts vpon his
hand, yea, not onely freakles vpon his face, but also

[82] *Horace.*   [83] Iames 3. 2.

skarres. No cause therefore why the word translated should bee denied to be the word, or forbidden to be currant, notwithstanding that some imperfections and blemishes may be noted in the setting foorth of it. For what euer was perfect vnder the Sunne, where Apostles or Apostolike men, that is, men indued with an extraordinary measure of Gods spirit, and priuiledged with the priuiledge of infallibilitie, had not their hand ? The Romanistes therefore in refusing to heare, and daring to burne the Word translated, did no lesse then despite the spirit of grace, from whom originally it proceeded, and whose sense and meaning, as well as mans weakenesse would enable, it did expresse. Iudge by an example or two. *Plutarch* writeth,[84] that after that *Rome* had beene burnt by the *Galles*, they fell soone to builde it againe : but doing it in haste, they did not cast the streets, nor proportion the houses in such comely fashion, as had bene most sightly and conuenient ; was *Catiline* therefore an honest man, or a good Patriot, that sought to bring it to a combustion ? or *Nero* a good Prince, that did indeed set it on fire ? So, by the story of *Ezrah*, and the prophesie of *Haggai* it may be gathered, that the Temple built by *Zerubbabel* after the returne from *Babylon*, was by no meanes to bee compared to the former built by *Solomon* (for they that remembred the former, wept when they considered the later) [85] notwithstanding, might this later either haue bene abhorred and forsaken by the *Iewes*, or prophaned by the *Greekes* ? The like wee are to thinke of Translations. The translation of the *Seuentie* dissenteth from the Originall in many places, neither doeth it come neere it, for perspicuitie, grauitie, maiestie ; yet which of the Apostles did condemne it ? Condemne it ? Nay, they vsed it, (as it is apparent, and as Saint *Hierome* and

<hr />

[84] *Plutarch. in Camillo.*   [85] Ezrah 3. 12.

most learned men doe confesse) which they would not
haue done, nor by their example of vsing it, so grace and
commend it to the Church, if it had bene vnworthy the
appellation and name of the word of God. And whereas
they vrge for their second defence of their vilifying and
abusing of the *English* Bibles, or some pieces thereof,
which they meete with, for that heretikes (forsooth) were
the Authours of the translations, (heretikes they call vs
by the same right that they call themselues Catholikes,
both being wrong) wee marueile what diuinitie taught
them so. Wee are sure *Tertullian* was of another minde :
Ex personis probamus fidem, an ex fide personas ? [86] Doe
we trie mens faith by their persons ? we should trie
their persons by their faith. Also S. *Augustine* was of
an other minde : for he lighting vpon certaine rules made
by *Tychonius* a *Donatist*, for the better vnderstanding of
the word, was not ashamed to make vse of them, yea, to
insert them into his owne booke, with giuing commendation to them so farre foorth as they were worthy to be
commended, as is to be seene in S. *Augustines* third
booke *De doctrinâ Christianâ.*[87] To be short, *Origen*, and
the whole Church of God for certain hundred yeeres, were
of an other minde : for they were so farre from treading
vnder foote, (much more from burning) the Translation
of *Aquila* a Proselite, that is, one that had turned *Iew* ;
of *Symmachus*, and *Theodotion*, both *Ebionites*, that is,
most vile heretikes, that they ioyned them together with
the *Hebrew* Originall, and the Translation of the *Seuentie*
(as hath bene before signified out of *Epiphanius*) and
set them forth openly to be considered of and perused
by all. But we weary the vnlearned, who need not

[86] *Tertul. de præscript. contra hæreses.*
[87] *S. August. 3. de doct. Christ. cap. 30.*

know so much, and trouble the learned, who know it already.

Yet before we end, we must answere a third cauill and obiection of theirs against vs, for altering and amending our Translations so oft ; wherein truely they deale hardly, and strangely with vs.   For to whom euer was it imputed for a fault (by such as were wise) to goe ouer that which hee had done, and to amend it where he saw cause ? Saint *Augustine* [88] was not afraide to exhort S. *Hierome* to a *Palinodia* or recantation ; the same S. *Augustine* [89] was not ashamed to retractate, we might say reuoke, many things that had passed him, and doth euen glory that he seeth his infirmities.[90]   If we will be sonnes of the Trueth, we must consider what it speaketh, and trample vpon our owne credit, yea, and vpon other mens too, if either be any way an hinderance to it.   This to the cause : then to the persons we say, that of all men they ought to bee most silent in this case.   For what varieties haue they, and what alterations haue they made, not onely of their Seruice bookes, Portesses and Breuiaries, but also of their *Latine* Translation ?   The Seruice booke supposed to be made by S. *Ambrose* (*Officium Ambrosianum*) was a great while in speciall vse and request : but Pope *Hadrian* calling a Councill [91] with the ayde of *Charles* the Emperour, abolished it, yea, burnt it, and commanded the Seruice-booke of Saint *Gregorie* vniuersally to be vsed.   Well, *Officium Gregorianum* gets by this meanes to be in credit, but doeth it continue without change or altering ? No, the very *Romane* Seruice was of two fashions, the New fashion, and the Old, (the one vsed in one Church, the other in another) as is to bee seene in

[88] *S. Aug. Epist. 9.*   [89] *S. Aug. lib. Retractat.*
[90] *Video interdum vitia mea, S Aug. Epist. 8.*
[91] *Durand. lib. 5. cap. 2.*

Pamelius a Romanist, his Preface, before *Micrologus*.
The same *Pamelius* reporteth out of *Radulphus de Riuo*,
that about the yeere of our Lord, 1277. Pope *Nicolas* the
third remoued out of the Churches of *Rome*, the more
ancient bookes (of Seruice) and brought into vse the
Missals of the Friers Minorites, and commaunded them
to bee obserued there ; insomuch that about an hundred
yeeres after, when the aboue named *Radulphus* happened
to be at *Rome*, he found all the bookes to be new, (of the
new stampe.) Neither was there this chopping and
changing in the more ancient times onely, but also of late :
Pius Quintus himselfe confesseth, that euery Bishopricke
almost had a peculiar kind of seruice, most vnlike to that
which others had : which moued him to abolish all other
Breuiaries, though neuer so ancient, and priuiledged and
published by Bishops in their Dioceses, and to establish
and ratifie that onely which was of his owne setting foorth,
in the yeere 1568.   Now, when the father of their Church,
who gladly would heale the soare of the daughter of his
people softly and sleightly, and make the best of it,
findeth so great fault with them for their oddes and
iarring ; we hope the children haue no great cause to
vaunt of their vniformitie.   But the difference that
appeareth betweene our Translations, and our often
correcting of them, is the thing that wee are specially
charged with ; let vs see therefore whether they themselues bee without fault this way, (if it be to be counted
a fault, to correct) and whether they bee fit men to
throw stones at vs :   *O tandem maior parcas insane
minori*:[92] they that are lesse sound themselues, ought not
to obiect infirmities to others.   If we should tell them
that *Valla, Stapulensis, Erasmus,* and *Viues* found fault
with their vulgar Translation, and consequently wished

[92] *Horat.*

the same to be mended, or a new one to be made, they
would answere peraduenture, that we produced their
enemies for witnesses against them ; albeit, they were
in no other sort enemies, then as *S. Paul* was to the
Galatians,[93] for telling them the trueth : and it were to
be wished, that they had dared to tell it them plainlier
and oftner. But what will they say to this, that Pope
Leo the Tenth allowed *Erasmus* Translation of the New
Testament, so much different from the vulgar, by his
Apostolike Letter & Bull ; [94] that the same *Leo* exhorted
Pagnin to translate the whole Bible, and bare whatsoeuer
charges was necessary for the worke ? Surely, as the
Apostle reasoneth to the *Hebrewes*, that *if the former Law
and Testament had bene sufficient, there had beene no need
of the latter* : [95] so we may say, that if the olde vulgar had
bene at all points allowable, to small purpose had labour
and charges bene vndergone, about framing of a new.
If they say, it was one Popes priuate opinion, and that he
consulted onely himselfe ; then wee are able to goe further
with them, and to auerre, that more of their chiefe men
of all sorts, euen their owne *Trent*-champions *Paiua* &
Vega, and their owne Inquisitors, *Hieronymus ab Oleastro*,
and their own Bishop *Isidorus Clarius*, and their owne
Cardinall *Thomas à Vio Caietan*, doe either make new
Translations themselues,[96] or follow new ones of other
mens making, or note the vulgar Interpretor for halting ;
none of them feare to dissent from him, nor yet to except
against him. And call they this an vniforme tenour of
text and iudgement about the text, so many of their
Worthies disclaiming the now receiued conceit ? Nay,
we wil yet come neerer the quicke : doth not their *Paris*-
edition differ from the *Louaine*, and *Hentenius* his from

[93] *Galat.* 4. 16.   [94] *Sixtus Senens.*
[95] Heb. 7. 11. & 8. 7.   [96] *Sixtus* 5. *præfat. fixa Biblijs.*

them both, and yet all of them allowed by authoritie ? Nay, doth not *Sixtus Quintus* confesse, that certaine Catholikes (he meaneth certaine of his owne side) were in such an humor of translating the Scriptures into *Latine*, that Satan taking occasion by them, though they thought of no such matter, did striue what he could, out of so vncertaine and manifold a varietie of Translations, so to mingle all things, that nothing might seeme to be left certaine and firme in them, &c ? Nay further, did not the same *Sixtus* ordaine by an inuiolable decree, and that with the counsell and consent of his Cardinals, that the *Latine* edition of the olde and new Testament, which the Councill of *Trent* would haue to be authenticke, is the same without controuersie which he then set forth, being diligently corrected and printed in the Printing-house of *Vatican ?* Thus *Sixtus* in his Preface before his Bible. And yet *Clement* the eight his immediate successour, publisheth another edition of the Bible, containing in it infinite differences from that of *Sixtus*, (and many of them waightie and materiall) and yet this must be authentike by all meanes. What is to haue the faith of our glorious Lord IESVS CHRIST with Yea and Nay, if this be not ? Againe, what is sweet harmonie and consent, if this be ? Therfore, as *Demaratus* of *Corinth* aduised a great King, before he talked of the dissensions among the *Grecians*, to compose his domesticke broiles (for at that time his Queene and his sonne and heire were at deadly fuide with him) so all the while that our aduersaries doe make so many and so various editions themselues, and doe iarre so much about the worth and authoritie of them, they can with no show of equitie challenge vs for changing and correcting.

But it is high time to leaue them, and to shew in briefe what wee proposed to our selues, and what course we

held in this our perusall and suruay of the Bible.   Truly
(good Christian Reader) wee neuer
thought from the beginning, that we
should neede to make a new Translation, nor yet to make of a bad one a

good one, (for then the imputation of *Sixtus* had bene
true in some sort, that our people had bene fed with
gall of Dragons in stead of wine, with whey in stead
of milke :) but to make a good one better, or out of
many good ones, one principall good one, not iustly to
be excepted against ; that hath bene our indeauour,
that our marke.   To that purpose there were many
chosen, that were greater in other mens eyes then in
their owne, and that sought the truth rather then their
own praise.   Againe, they came or were thought to come
to the worke, not *exercendi causâ* (as one saith) but *exer-
citati*, that is, learned, not to learne :   For the chiefe
ouerseer and ἐργοδιώκτης vnder his Maiestie, to whom not
onely we, but also our whole Church was much bound,
knew by his wisedom, which thing also *Nazianzen*[97] taught
so long agoe, that it is a preposterous order to teach
first and to learne after, yea that τὸ ἐν πιθῳ κεραμίαν
μανθάνειν to learne and practise together, is neither
commendable for the workeman, nor safe for the worke.
Therefore such were thought vpon, as could say modestly
with Saint *Hierome, Et Hebræum Sermonem ex parte
didicimus, & in Latino penè ab ipsis incunabulis &c.
detriti sumus.   Both we haue learned the Hebrew tongue in
part, and in the Latine wee haue beene exercised almost
from our verie cradle.   S. Hierome* maketh no mention of
the *Greeke* tongue, wherein yet hee did excell, because
hee translated not the old Testament out of *Greeke,* but
out of *Hebrewe.*   And in what sort did these assemble ?

[97] *Nazianzen. εἰς ῥν. ἐπισκ. παρουσ. Idem in Apologet.*

In the trust of their owne knowledge, or of their sharpe-
nesse of wit, or deepenesse of iudgement, as it were in an
arme of flesh ? At no hand. They trusted in him that
hath the key of *Dauid,* opening and no man shutting ;
they prayed to the Lord the Father of our Lord, to the
effect that S. *Augustine* did ; *O let thy Scriptures be my*
pure delight, let me not be deceiued in them, neither let me
deceiue by them.[98] In this confidence, and with this
deuotion did they assemble together ; not too many,
lest one should trouble another ; and yet many, lest
many things haply might escape them. If you aske
what they had before them, truely it was the *Hebrew* text
of the Olde Testament, the *Greeke* of the New. These
are the two golden pipes, or rather conduits, where
through the oliue branches emptie themselues into the
golde.   Saint *Augustine* calleth them precedent, or
originall tongues ;[99] Saint *Hierome,* fountaines.[100] The
same Saint *Hierome* affirmeth,[101] and *Gratian* hath not
spared to put it into his Decree.   That, *as the credit of the*
olde Bookes (he meaneth of the Old Testament) *is to be*
tryed by the Hebrewe Volumes, so of the New by the
Greeke tongue, he meaneth by the originall *Greeke.*   If
trueth be to be tried by these tongues, then whence should
a Translation be made, but out of them ? These tongues
therefore, the Scriptures wee say in those tongues, wee
set before vs to translate, being the tongues wherein God
was pleased to speake to his Church by his Prophets and
Apostles. Neither did we run ouer the worke with that
posting haste that the *Septuagint* did, if that be true
which is reported of them, that they finished it in 72

----

[98] *S. Aug. lib.* 11. *Confess. cap.* 2.
[99] *S. August.* 3. *de doctr. c.* 3, *&c.*
[100] *S. Hieron. ad Suniam & Fretel.*
[101] *S. Hieron. ad Lucinium, Dist.* 9 *vt veterum.*

dayes ; [102] neither were we barred or hindered from going ouer it againe, hauing once done it, like S. *Hierome*,[103] if that be true which himselfe reporteth, that he could no sooner write any thing, but presently it was caught from him, and published, and he could not haue leaue to mend it : neither, to be short, were we the first that fell in hand with translating the Scripture into English, and consequently destitute of former helpes, as it is written of *Origen*, that hee was the first in a maner, that put his hand to write Commentaries vpon the Scriptures, and therefore no marueile, if he ouershot himselfe many times. None of these things : the worke hath not bene hudled vp in 72. dayes, but hath cost the workemen, as light as it seemeth, the paines of twise seuen times seuentie two dayes and more : matters of such weight and consequence are to bee speeded with maturitie : for in a businesse of moment a man feareth not the blame of conuenient slacknesse.[104] Neither did wee thinke much to consult the Translators or Commentators, *Chaldee, Hebrewe, Syrian, Greeke,* or *Latine,* no nor the *Spanish, French, Italian,* or *Dutch ;* neither did we disdaine to reuise that which we had done, and to bring backe to the anuill that which we had hammered : but hauing and vsing as great helpes as were needfull, and fearing no reproch for slownesse, nor coueting praise for expedition, wee haue at the length, through the good hand of the Lord vpon us, brought the worke to that passe that you see.

Some peraduenture would haue no varietie of sences to be set in the margine, lest the authoritie of the Scriptures for deciding of controuersies by that shew of vncertaintie, should somewhat be shaken. But we hold their

[102] *Ioseph. Antiq. lib.* 12.
[103] *S. Hieron. ad Pammac. pro libr. aduers. Iouinian* πρωτόπειροι.
[104] φιλεῖ γὰρ ὀκνεῖν πράγμ' ἀνὴρ πράσσων μέγα. *Sophoc. in Elect.*

iudgmēt not to be so sound in this point. For though,

Reasons mouing vs to set diuersitie of sences in the margin, where there is great probability for each. *whatsoeuer things are necessary are manifest,* as *S. Chrysostome* saith,[105] and as *S. Augustine,*[106] *In those things that are plainely set downe in the Scriptures, all such matters are found that concerne Faith, hope, and Charitie.* Yet for all that it cannot be dissembled, that partly to exercise and whet our wits, partly to weane the curious from loathing of them for their euery-where-plainenesse, partly also to stirre vp our deuotion to craue the assistance of Gods spirit by prayer, and lastly, that we might be forward to seeke ayd of our brethren by conference, and neuer scorne those that be not in all respects so complete as they should bee, being to seeke in many things our selues, it hath pleased God in his diuine prouidence, heere and there to scatter wordes and sentences of that difficultie and doubtfulnesse, not in doctrinall points that concerne saluation, (for in such it hath beene vouched that the Scriptures are plaine) but in matters of lesse moment, that fearefulnesse would better beseeme vs then confidence, and if we will resolue, to resolue vpon modestie with *S. Augustine,* (though not in this same case altogether, yet vpon the same ground) *Melius est dubitare de occultis, quam litigare de incertis,*[107] it is better to make doubt of those things which are secret, then to striue about those things that are vncertaine. There be many words in the Scriptures, which be neuer found there but once, (hauing neither brother nor neighbour, as the *Hebrewes* speake) so that we cannot be holpen by conference of places. Againe, there be many rare names of

---

[105] πάντα τὰ ἀναγκαῖα δῆλα. *S. Chrysost. in* 2. *Thess. cap.* 2.

[106] *S. Aug.* 2. *de doctr. Christ. cap.* 9.

[107] *S. August. li.* 8. *de Genes. ad liter. cap.* 5. ἅπαξ λεγόμενα.

certaine birds, beastes and precious stones, &c. concerning which the *Hebrewes* themselues are so diuided among themselues for iudgement, that they may seeme to haue defined this or that, rather because they would say somthing, thē because they were sure of that which they said, as *S. Hierome* somewhere saith of the *Septuagint.* Now in such a case, doth not a margine do well to admonish the Reader to seeke further, and not to conclude or dogmatize vpon this or that peremptorily ? For as it is a fault of incredulitie, to doubt of those things that are euident : so to determine of such things as the Spirit of God hath left (euen in the iudgment of the iudicious) questionable, can be no lesse then presumption. Therfore as S. *Augustine* saith,[108] that varietie of Translations is profitable for the finding out of the sense of the Scriptures : so diuersitie of signification and sense in the margine, where the text is not so cleare, must needes doe good, yea, is necessary, as we are perswaded. We know that *Sixtus Quintus* [109] expresly forbiddeth, that any varietie of readings of their vulgar edition, should be put in the margine, (which though it be not altogether the same thing to that we haue in hand, yet it looketh that way) but we thinke he hath not all of his owne side his fauourers, for this conceit. They that are wise, had rather haue their iudgements at libertie in differences of readings, then to be captiuated to one, when it may be the other. If they were sure that their hie Priest had all lawes shut vp in his brest, as *Paul* the second bragged,[110] and that he were as free from errour by speciall priuiledge, as the Dictators of *Rome* were made by law inuiolable, it were an other matter ; then his word were an Oracle, his opinion a decision. But the eyes of the world are now open.

[108] *S. Aug.* 2°. *de doctr. Christian. cap.* 14.
[109] *Sixtus* 5. *præf. Bibliæ.*   [110] *Plat.in Paulo secundo.*

God be thanked, and haue bene a great while, they find that he is subiect to the same affections and infirmities that others be, that his skin is penetrable,[111] and therefore so much as he prooueth, not as much as he claimeth, they grant and embrace.

An other thing we thinke good to admonish thee of (gentle Reader) that wee haue not tyed our selues to an vniformitie of phrasing, or to an identitie of words, as some peraduenture would wish that we had done, because they obserue, that some learned men some where, haue beene as exact as they could that way. Truly, that we might not varie from the sense of that which we had translated before, if the word signified the same thing in both places [112] (for there bee some wordes that bee not of the same sense euery where) we were especially carefull, and made a conscience, according to our duetie. But, that we should expresse the same notion in the same particular word ; as for example, if we translate the *Hebrew* or *Greeke* word once by *Purpose*, neuer to call it *Intent* ; if one where *Iourneying*, neuer *Traueiling* ; if one where *Thinke*, neuer *Suppose ;* if one where *Paine*, neuer *Ache* ; if one where *Ioy*, neuer *Gladnesse*, &c. Thus to minse the matter, wee thought to sauour more of curiositie then wisedome, and that rather it would breed scorne in the Atheist, then bring profite to the godly Reader. For is the kingdome of God become words or syllables ? why should wee be in bondage to them if we may be free, vse one precisely when wee may vse another no lesse fit, as commodiously ? A godly Father in the Primitiue time shewed himselfe greatly moued,[113] that one of newfanglenes called κράββατον σκίμπους, though

[111] ὁμοιοπαθὴς. τρωτός γ' οἱ χρὼς ἐστί.   [112] πολύσημα.
[113] Abed. *Niceph. Calist. lib.* 8. *cap.* 42.

the difference be little or none ; and another reporteth,[114] that he was much abused for turning *Cucurbita* (to which reading the people had beene vsed) into *Hedera*.   Now if this happen in better times, and vpon so small occasions, wee might iustly feare hard censure, if generally wee should make verball and vnnecessary changings.   We might also be charged (by scoffers) with some vnequall dealing towards a great number of good English wordes. For as it is written of a certaine great Philosopher, that he should say, that those logs were happie that were made images to be worshipped ; for their fellowes, as good as they, lay for blockes behinde the fire : so if wee should say, as it were, vnto certaine words, Stand vp higher, haue a place in the Bible alwayes, and to others of like qualitie, Get ye hence, be banished for euer, wee might be taxed peraduenture with S. *Iames* his words, namely, *To be partiall in our selues and iudges of euill thoughts*.   Adde hereunto, that nicenesse in wordes [115] was alwayes counted the next step to trifling,[116] and so was to bee curious about names too : [117] also that we cannot follow a better patterne for elocution then God himselfe ; therefore hee vsing diuers words, in his holy writ, and indifferently for one thing in nature : we, if wee will not be superstitious, may vse the same libertie in our English versions out of *Hebrew* & *Greeke*, for that copie or store that he hath giuen vs.   Lastly, wee haue on the one side auoided the scrupulositie of the Puritanes, who leaue the olde Ecclesiasticall words, and betake them to other, as when they put *washing* for *Baptisme*, and *Congregation* in stead of *Church* : as also on the other side we haue

---

[114] *S. Hieron. in. 4. Ionæ.*   See *S. Aug. epist* : 10.

[115] λεπτολογία.   [116] ἀδολεσχία.

[117] τὸ σπουδάζειν ἐπὶ ὀνόμασι.   See *Euseb.* προπαρασκευ. *li.* 12. *ex Platon.*

shunned the obscuritie of the Papists, in their *Azimes Tunike*, *Rational*, *Holocausts*, *Præpuce*, *Pasche*, and a number of such like, whereof their late Translation is full, and that of purpose to darken the sence, that since they must needs translate the Bible, yet by the language thereof, it may bee kept from being vnderstood. But we desire that the Scripture may speake like it selfe, as in the language of *Canaan*, that it may bee vnderstood euen of the very vulgar.

Many other things we might giue thee warning of (gentle Reader) if wee had not exceeded the measure of a Preface alreadie. It remaineth, that we commend thee to God, and to the Spirit of his grace, which is able to build further then we can aske or thinke. Hee remoueth the scales from our eyes, the vaile from our hearts, opening our wits that wee may vnderstand his word, enlarging our hearts, yea correcting our affections, that we may loue it aboue gold and siluer, yea that we may loue it to the end. Ye are brought vnto fountaines of liuing water which yee digged not ; doe not cast earth into them with the Philistines,[118] neither preferre broken pits before them with the wicked Iewes.[119] Others haue laboured, and you may enter into their labours ; O re- ceiue not so great things in vaine, O despise not so great saluation ! Be not like swine to treade vnder foote so precious things, neither yet like dogs to teare and abuse holy things. Say not to our Sauiour with the *Gergesites*, Depart out of our coasts ; [120] neither yet with *Esau* sell your birthright for a messe of potage.[121] If light be come into the world, loue not darkenesse more then light ; if foode, if clothing be offered, goe not naked, starue not

---

[118] Gen. 26. 15.   [119] Ierem. 2. 13.   [120] Matth. 8. 34.
[121] Hebr. 12 16.

your selues. Remember the aduise of *Nazianzene*,[122] *It is a grieuous thing* (or dangerous) *to neglect a great faire, and to seeke to make markets afterwards* : also the encouragement of S. *Chrysostome*,[123] *It is altogether impossible, that he that is sober* (*and watchfull*) *should at any time be neglected* : Lastly, the admonition and menacing of S. *Augustine*.[124] *They that despise Gods will inuiting them, shal feele Gods will taking vengeance of them.* It is a fearefull thing to fall into the hands of the liuing God ; but [125] a blessed thing it is, and will bring vs to euerlasting blessedness in the end, when God speaketh vnto vs, to hearken ; when he setteth his word before vs, to reade it ; when hee stretcheth out his hand and calleth, to answere, Here am I ; here we are to doe thy will, O God. The Lord worke a care and conscience in vs to know him and serue him, that we may be acknowledged of him at the appearing of our Lord Iesus Christ, to whom with the holy Ghost, be all prayse and thankesgiuing. Amen.

---

[122] *Nazianz.* περὶ ἁγ. βαπτ. δεινὸν πανήγυριν παρελθεῖν καὶ τηνικαῦτα πραγματείαν ἐπιζητεῖν.

[123] *S. Chrysost. in epist. ad Rom. Cap.* 14. *orat.* 26. *in* ἠθικ. ἀμήχανον σφόδρα ἀμήχανον.

[124] *S. August. ad artic. sibi falsè obiect. Artic.* 16.

[125] Heb. 10. 31.

INDEX

Abbot, George, Dean of Westminster, 52.

Ælfric, 3.

Aglionby, J., 53.

Alley, William, Bishop of Exeter, 30.

Andrewes, Lancelot, Bishop of Winchester, 49.

Andrewes, Roger, 50, 51.

Antwerp, printing at, 7-10, 14, 36, 92, 135-49, 169, 170, 175, 184, 185, 198, 200, 225.

Antwerp Polyglott, the, 61.

Allen, Cardinal, 33, 34, 36, 298.

Amsterdam, 74.

Anderson, Christopher, 104.

Authorized Version of 1611 : history of its production, 37-64 ; list of the translators, 49-53 ; rules observed in the translation, 53-5 ; contemporary account by one of the revisers, 55-6 ; payment of translators, 56-7 ; was this Version ever authorized ? 58-60 ; bibliographical description, 61-6 ; later history, 65-76 ; Bishop Bancroft circulates a letter from King James as to provision for the translators, 331-4 ; Bancroft's exhortation to the Bishops to subscribe, 334 ; account of the making of the version laid before the Synod of Dort, 336-9 ; the translators' Preface to the Reader, 340-77.

Awdeley, Lord Chancellor, 231.

Badius, Conrad, printer of Geneva, 25.

Ball, William, 57.

Bancroft, Richard, Bishop of London : his interest in the 1611 version, 47-8, 58, circulates a letter from King James to procure provision for the translators of the 1611 version, 331-3 ; his exhortation to the Bishops to subscribe, 334-5.

Baptist College, Bristol, 5.

Barker, Charles, printer, 57.

Barker, Christopher, printer : prints the Geneva version and the Bishops' Bible, 41-4 ; licensed to print Bibles and gives satisfaction to Richard Jugge, 318-22 ; establishes his monopoly of Bible printing, 42-3, 322-6 ; his circular to the City Companies, 326-9 ; his agreement with the Bible Stock, 335.

Barker, Matthew, printer, 57.

Barker, Robert (son of Christopher Barker), printer, 44 ; said to have paid for the translation of the 1611 version, 57 ; its first printer, 62, 68, 74.

Barker, Robert (2), printer, 57.

Barlow, Jerome, 120.

Barlow, William, Bishop of Chichester, 30, 47.

Barlow, William, Dean of Chester, 52, 53.

Baskett, J., printer, 75.

Becon, Thomas, 31.

Bedwell, William, 49, 50.

Bentham, Thomas, Bishop of Coventry and Lichfield, 31.

Bergen-op-Zoom, 175.

Berthelet, Thomas, printer, 23, 24, 163, 169, 242.

Beza, 28, 41, 303.

Bible, the English : prohibition of English translations from the time of Wyclif unless authorized by a Bishop or a Provincial Council, 3, 79–81 ; Sir Thomas More on prohibition, 81–3 ; More's plan for a limited circulation, 84–6 ; the printing of the first New Testaments, 99–108 ; the news sent to the King, 108–110 ; episcopal prohibition, 131–5 ; the search for English New Testaments at Antwerp, 135–49 ; the Bishop of London's attempt to buy up the translation, 150–3 ; Nix, Bishop of Norwich, refunds the Archbishop of Canterbury part of his outlay on New Testaments, 153–5 ; the confession of Robert Necton as to buying and selling New Testaments, 155–9 ; Bishop Nix implores the King's help in suppression, 159–61 ; the King consults his Council and the Bishops, 161–3 ; the King's Proclamation, forbidding the translation and possession of Holy Scripture in the English tongue, 163–9; the Bishops' petition for an English Bible, 9, 175–7 ; the projected Version, 196–8 ; Fox's account of the first Bibles, 223–32 ; King's Proclamation, forbidding importation without licence, 240–2 ; patent for Bible printing granted to Cromwell, 258–9 ; King's Proclamation for the English Bible to be set up in churches 261–5 ; Draft for a Proclamation as to the reading of the Bible in churches, 265–6 ; an admonition by the Bishop of London to all readers, 267–8 ; narrative of William Maldon, persecuted by his father for reading the Scripture, 268–71 ; the Great Bible condemned in Convocation, 272–5 ; Jugge and Barker as Bible printers, and the Company of Stationers, 313–14 ; the beginning of the Bible Stock, 41, 314–15 ; the Bible Stock in 1606, 335 ; Christopher Barker's licence and his satisfaction to Jugge, 318–22 ; Barker establishes his monopoly, 322–6 ; Barker's circular to the City Companies, 326–9 ; Draft for an Act of Parliament for a new version of the Bible, 329–31 ; attempt to provide for the translators of the 1611 version, 331–4.
    See also under Authorized Version ; Bishops' Bible ; Coverdale ; Douai Version ; Great Bible ; Geneva Bible ; Matthew ; Rheims New Testament ; Tyndale ; Wyclif.

Bible Society : rare editions of English Bibles in possession of, 73, 74.

Bickley, Thomas, 32.

Bilson, Bishop of Winchester, 58.

Birckmann, Arnold, 101, 106.

Birckmann, Francis, 136, 158.

Bishops' Bible : history of its production, 29–33, 41, 43, 44 ; list of the revisers, 30–1 ; the petition of Convocation for an English translation, 175–7 ; the projected version approved by Cromwell, 196–8 ; Committee appointed to examine former translations, 273–4 ; letter from the Bishop of Ely to Cecil, 287 ; Parker invites Cecil to take part in the revision, 287–8 ; Strype's summary of other correspondence as to preparation of the Bible, 288–91 ; Parker announces to Cecil the completion of the work, 291–2 ; presentation of the Bible to Queen Elizabeth and story of the revision, 37, 292–5 ; Parker's note as to the translators, 295–7 ; rules observed in translation, 297.

Blayney, Dr., of Oxford, revises the 1611 text, 76.

Bodley, John, receives an exclusive patent for printing the Geneva Bible for seven years, 27, 28, 284–5 ; asks for an extension of the privilege, 39 ; Parker and Grindal recommend extension, 285–6.

Boel, Cornelis, 62.

Bonner, Edmund, Bishop of London : promotes the printing of the Bible in English, 21, 223–31, 240 ; changes his views, 231 ; his admonition to all readers of the Bible in the English tongue, 267–8.

Boys, Dr. John, 50, 52, 55, 56, 60, 75.

Branthwait, Dr. William, 50, 51.

Brett, Richard, 50, 51.

Bristow, Richard, 34.

British Museum, rare editions of the Scriptures at, 8, 10, 186.

Bucer, Martin, 24.

Bugenhagen, Johann, 100, 104.

Burleigh, Lord, 33.

Bullingham, Nicholas, Bishop of Lincoln, 31.

Burley, Dr. Francis, 49, 50.

Byng, Andrew, 50, 51.

Calvin, 24.

Cambridge, 56, 75, 161, 164.

Campion, Edmund, 34.

Canterbury, Synod of, 176.

Carleton, Dr. James G., 37.

Castillon, French Ambassador in England, 249, 251.

Caxton, William, 2, 3.

Cecil, Sir William, 29, 37, 39, 286–8, 290.

Chaderton, Laurence, 50, 51.

Charles V, Emperor, 251.

Cheke, Sir John : his version of the New Testament, 335.

Christiern, King of Denmark, 99, 104.

Clark, Dr. Richard, 49, 50.

Cochlaeus : see Dobneck.

Cologne, printing at, 4, 5, 99, 102, 104, 106, 111, 122, 156.

Constantine, George, 152-3, 155–6.

Coverdale, Miles : his version of the Bible, 10–14 ; financial help given by Jacob van Meteren, 12, 198–200 ; edits the Great Bible, 17, 226, 229, 234, 247 ; Coverdale's account of his work, 17–19, 200–6, 234–6, 237–40, 245–6 ; his Latin-English New Testament, following the Vulgate text, 206–14, 224, 232, 243, 245.

Cox, Richard, Bishop of Ely : assists in translation of the Bishops' Bible, 29, 31, 287, 290.

Cranmer, Thomas, Archbishop of Canterbury : shows favour to Matthew's Bible, 16, 214–8, 221-2, 228 ; connexion with the Bishops' Bible, 177, 197–8 ; writes Prologue to second edition of the Great Bible, 22–3 ; discusses price and copyright of the Great Bible, 257–8.

Crispin, John, 39.

Cromwell, Richard, 244.

Cromwell, Thomas, Earl of Essex : encourages Bible translation, 15, 16, 170 ; favours the publication of Matthew's Bible, 16, 214–22, 228 ; provides funds for the Great Bible, 17 ; his interest in the work, 18–20, 206, 223, 227, 229, 232, 234–40, 243–58 ; his injunctions for setting up the Bible in the churches, 21, 261–2 ; secures the patent for printing, 22, 258–9 ; his arrangements for translation of the New Testament, 196 ; his fall from power, 229–31.

Curtis, Thomas, 76.

Dakins, William, 52, 53.
Davidson, Dr., Archbishop of Canterbury, 66.
Davies, Richard, Bishop of St. David's, 30, 290.
Day, John, printer, 174.
Demetrius, Emanuel, 198–9.
de Montmorency, Anne, Constable of France, 240, 249, 254, 255.
de Valera, Cipriano, 61.
Dillingham, Francis, 50, 51.
Diodati, 61.
Dobneck, Johann (Cochlaeus), 4, 5, 99, 102, 103, 105, 107.
Dort, 74 ; Synod of, 56, 58, 336–9.
Douai, English College at, 33, 36.
Douai Version of the Old Testament, 36–7.
Downes, Andrew, 50, 52, 55, 61.
Duff, Mr. Gordon, 135–6, 220.
Duport, Dr. John, 50, 51.

Edward VI, 24, 47, 121.
Edwin, Bishop of Worcester, 288–9.
Elizabeth, Queen, 25, 27, 28, 45 ; presentation of the Bishops' Bible to, 29, 292–5.
Elles, Richard, Dean of Worcester, 52.
Emmerson, Margaret van, 92.
Emperour, Martin (otherwise Martin Caesar or Keysere), printer of Antwerp, 8, 10.
Endhoven, Catharyn, 184, 185.

Endhoven, Christoffel van, printer of Antwerp, 7, 8, 135, 143, 146, 158, 191.
Endhoven, Hans van, 191.
Erasmus, 4, 5, 17, 35, 87, 96.

Fagius, Paul, 24.
Fairclough, Richard, 50, 51.
Fenton, Roger, 52, 53.
Fish, Simon, 155, 158, 165.
Fisher, Bishop, 103.
Fogny, John, printer of Rheims, 35.
Fox, John, 19, 38, 86, 110, 136, 155, 174, 223, 268.
Francis I, King of France : permits the Great Bible to be printed in Paris, 223, 226 ; his licence to Grafton and Whitchurch, 232–4.
Frankfort, 100, 105, 170.
Frith, John, 165, 173–4 ; his friendship with Tyndale, 89, 110, 111 ; defends Tyndale and his work against More, 172–4.
Froschouer, Christopher, printer of Zurich, 12, 13.
Fry, Francis, 70.
Fulke, Dr. William, 37.

Gardiner, Stephen, Bishop of Winchester, 20, 196, 227, 231, 235.
Garvais, Friar Henry, 246, 248.
Geneva Bible, 24–8 ; printed in London, 39 ; excluded by Parker, 40, 44, 74 ; its popularity, 43–5, 73–4 ; Preface to the Geneva New Testament, 275–9 ; Preface to the Geneva Bible, 279–84 ; privilege and licence to John Bodley for printing the Geneva Bible for seven years, 27, 28, 284–5 ; Bodley seeks renewal of privilege, 39, 285–6.
Gilby, Anthony, 27.
Gilford, Sir Henry, 87.
Ginsburg, Dr. Christian, 12, 13.

Goad, Dr., 75.

Gold, Henry, 122.

Goodman, Gabriel, Dean of Westminster, 31.

Grafton, Richard, grocer and printer, 195, 265 ; arranges for publication of Matthew's Bible, 15, 17, 218–22, 230 ; and of the Great Bible, 21, 23, 66, 223–40, 243–5 ; the French King's licence to print in Paris, 232–4.

Gray, William, 235, 237.

Greenwich, 260.

Great Bible, 17–24, 28, 32, 33 ; Fox's account of the printing of the edition of 1539, 19–20, 223–32 ; the French King's licence to Grafton and Whitchurch, 232–4 ; reports as to progress, 17–19, 22, 234–40, 243–6 ; Bishop Bonner's support, 19, 240 ; Bibles confiscated, and citation of François Regnault for printing the Bible in Paris, 246–8 ; letters from the French Ambassador in England to the Constable of France, 18, 249–51, 255–6 ; letter from the Imperial Ambassador in England to the Emperor Charles V, 251–3 ; letter from the Grand Constable of France to the French Ambassador in England, 254 ; price and copyright of the Bible, 22, 257 ; patent for selling the Bible granted to Anthony Marler, 260–1 ; Preface by Cranmer, 22–3 ; condemned in Convocation, 272–5.

Grindal, Edmund, Bishop of London, supports Bodley's privilege to print Geneva Bibles, 27, 39 ; one of the translators of the Bishop's Bible, 31 ; suspension of, 43.

Guest, Bishop of Rochester, 31, 289.

Haberdashers' Company, 21.

Hackett, John : searches at Antwerp for English New Testaments and heretical books, 92, 135–49.

Haghen, Godfrid van der, 9.

Halle's Chronicle, 15, 195.

Hamburg, 4, 10, 170, 228.

Hampton Court Conference, 45–7, 58.

Harding, Dr. John, 50, 51.

Harmer, John, 52, 53.

Harrison, Luke, 41.

Harrison, R., printer, 28.

Harrison, Thomas, 50, 51.

Hebblethwayte, William, 87, 97.

Henry VIII, 24, 47, 99, 102, 104 ; his Answer to Martin Luther, 117–8 ; consults his Council and the Bishops as to surreptitious translations, 161–3 ; endeavours to get Tyndale to retract, 169 ; the petition of Convocation to, 175–7 ; Coverdale's dedication of his Latin-English New Testament to, 206 ; Matthew's Bible dedicated to, 215, 228 ; favours the production of the Great Bible, 223 ; his Proclamation forbidding the circulation of books without licence, 240–2 ; his Proclamation for the English Bible to be set up in churches, 261–5 ; Draft Proclamation as to reading the Bible, 265–6.

Heze, Dietrich, 102, 106.

Hogenberg, Franciscus, 32.

Holbein, Hans, engraves title-page for the Great Bible, 22.

Holland, Dr. Thomas, 50, 51.

Hollybush, Johan, 136, 158, 206, 220.

Home, Robert, Bishop of Winchester, 30.

Hutchinson, Dr. Ralph, 52, 53.

Hutten, L., 53.

James I : calls together the Hampton Court Conference, 45–58 ; pushes forward the work of revision, 48 ; his order for translation, 49–54 ; endeavours to secure payment for the translators, 57.

Jerome, St., 35, 36.

John of Trevisa, 2.

Jones, Hugh, Bishop of Llandaff, 31.

Joye, George, 152, 162 ; edits an unauthorized version of Tyndale's New Testament, 6–8 ; seeks to obtain a licence from the King to translate Scripture, 174–5 ; Tyndale complains of Joye's unauthorized revision of his translation of the New Testament, 178–84 ; Joye's answer, 185–7 ; reconciliation and fresh quarrel, 188–95.

Juda, Leo, 12, 28.

Jugge, John, printer, 42.

Jugge, Richard, printer, 42, 59 ; commended for his printing of the Bishops' Bible, 32 ; monopoly secured to him, 40–1 ; dispute with the Stationers' Company, 313–4 ; beginning of the Bible Stock, 314–8 ; Barker's satisfaction to Jugge, 318–22.

Junius, Franciscus, 61.

Kilbye, Dr. Richard, 50, 51.

King, Geoffrey, 50.

Kingdon, Dr., 232.

Knox, T. F., 298, 299.

Latimer, Hugh, Bishop of Worcester, 262.

Laud, Archbishop, 66.

Lawney, Thomas, 196–8.

Layfield, Dr. John, 49, 50.

Lee, Edward, Archbishop of York, 108.

Leicester, Earl of, 32, 291.

Lively, Edward, 50.

Lobley, Michael, 225.

Luft, Hans, printer, 10, 92, 119.

Luther, Martin, 5, 10, 91, 99, 100, 104–6, 108–9, 117, 126–7, 129, 172, 202.

Lynne, Walter, printer, 121.

Mainz, 5, 102, 107.

Maldon, William, narrative of, 268–71.

Marburg, 92, 170.

Margaret of Savoy, 136.

Marillac, Charles, French Ambassador in England, 254, 255.

Marler, Anthony, gives financial support towards the production of the Great Bible, 21 ; concerned in its sale, 22, 260–1.

Martin, Gregory, 34, 36, 37.

Mary, Queen, 24.

Matthew, Thomas : his version of the Bible, 14–17, 18 ; Cranmer recommends the version to Cromwell, 214–7 ; Grafton's arrangements for publication, 218–22 ; Foxe's account of, 228–9.

Mede, Dr. Joseph, 75.

Meteren, Cornelius van, 200.

Meteren, Emanuel van, 198–9.

Meteren, Jacob van : story of financial help given by him to Coverdale in the production of the 1535 Bible, 12, 198–200.

Monmouth, H., 4, 88.

Montanus, Arias, 61.

More, Sir Thomas : his Dialogue on the prohibition of English translations of the Scriptures, 81–4 ; his plan for a limited circulation, 84–6 ; criticizes Tyndale's translation, 126–31 ; his controversy with Tyndale, 162, 172–3, 175.

Mummuth, H., *see* Monmouth.

Münster, Sebastian, 17, 28, 298.

Necton, Robert, 111 ; confession as to buying and selling New Testaments in English, 135, 155–9.

Necton, Thomas, 155.

New Testament : *see* Bible.

Nicholas of Hereford, 1.

Nicholson, James, printer, of Southwark, 13, 14, 136, 206, 220, 243.

Nix, Richard, Bishop of Norwich : refunds the Archbishop of Canterbury part of his outlay on New Testaments, 153 ; implores the King's help, 159–61.

Norton, William, printer, 41.

Nuremberg, 100, 105.

Olivetan, 28.

Ortelius, Abraham, 200.

Osiander, Andreas, 100, 105.

Overall, John, Bishop of Coventry, 49.

Oxford, 1–3, 56, 75–6, 79, 164.

Packington, Augustine, buys up Tyndale's translation of the New Testament, 150–2.

Pagninus, S., 28.

Paris, printing at, 198, 223–36, 246–50.

Paris, Dr. Thomas, of Cambridge, revises the 1611 text, 76.

Parker, Matthew, Archbishop of Canterbury : his attitude towards the Genevan version, 27, 28, 39, 40, 44 ; his interest in the Bishops' Bible, 30–1, 39, 59, 290 ; commends Jugge, 32, 37, 40 ; announces to Cecil completion of the Bishops' Bible, 291–4 ; presents the Bible to Queen Elizabeth, 294–5 ; his note as to the translators, 295–8.

Parkhurst, John, Bishop of Salisbury, 30, 290.

Perin, Dr. John, 52, 53.

Perne, Andrew, Dean of Ely, 30.

Petit, T., printer, 23, 24.

Pierson, Andrew, 30.

Plomer, Mr. H. R., vi, 22, 57, 68.

Pocock, Mr. N., 74.

Pole, Cardinal, 18.

Poyntz, Thomas, 9, 15, 232.

Puritans and the Hampton Court Conference, 45–7.

Purvey, John, 1, 2.

Quentell, Peter, printer of Cologne, 5, 101, 106, 111.

Rabbett, Michael, 52, 53.

Radcliffe, Dr. Jeremiah, 50, 52.

Raimond, John, printer, 135.

Ravens, Dr., 52, 53.

Ravis, Thomas, Dean of Christ Church, 52.

Rebul, Antoine, 27.

Redman, R., printer, 23.

Regnault, François, printer of Paris, 17, 239 ; cited for printing the Great Bible, 246–9.

Reynolds, Dr. John, 45–7, 50, 51.

Rheims New Testament, 33–7 ; its inception, 298–300 ; story of the translation, from the Preface, 301–13.

Richardson, Dr. John, 50, 51.

Ridley, Robert, criticizes Tyndale's version of the New Testament, 111, 122–6.

Rinck, Hermann, 103, 107, 108.

Rivington, Mr. Charles, 313, 335.

Rogers, John, 15, 228.

Roy, William, 4 ; his quarrel with Tyndale, 119–21.

Rupert, Abbot of Deutz, 100, 102, 105, 106.

Ruremond, Hans van, printer of Antwerp, 9, 135–6, 158, 220.

St. Paul's, London, 5, 79, 177, 225.

Salisbury, William, Bishop of Man, 290.

Sampson, Thomas, 27.

Sanderson, Thomas, 52, 53.

Sandys, Edwin, Bishop of Worcester, 30.

Saravia, Dr., 49, 50.

Savile, Sir Henry, 52.

Scambler, Edmund, Bishop of Peterborough, 31.

Schoeffer, Peter, printer, of Worms, 5.

Schott, Johann, printer, of Strassburg, 121.

Scrivener, Dr. F. H. A., 71-2, 75.

Selborne, Lord Chancellor, on the authorization of the 1611 version, 58-9.

Selden, John, 61.

Sion, Bridgetine house of, at Isleworth, 3.

Smith, Miles, Bishop of Gloucester, 50, 51, 58.

Smith, Rev. Walter E., 69.

Spalding, Robert, 50, 51.

Sparke, Michael, 65, 75.

Speed, John : his Genealogies of Scripture, 63, 339.

Spenser, Dr. John, 52, 53.

Stationers' Company, 41, 56, 225, 313-22.

Steele, Mr. Robert, 18, 121.

Stokesley, John, Bishop of London, 163, 196-7, 225.

Strassburg, 121, 174.

Strype's *Memorials*, 29, 31, 155, 288.

Sutor, Petrus, 124.

Taverner, Richard, his version of the Bible, 23, 24.

Tedder, Mr. H. R., 12.

Thompson, Giles, Dean of Windsor, 52.

Tighe, Dr. Robert, 49, 50.

Tomson, Laurence, 28, 42.

Tomson, Richard, 49, 50.

Tremellius, 61.

Tritheim, Johann, 100, 105.

Tuke, Sir Brian, 137, 140, 141, 148.

Tunstall, Cuthbert, Bishop of London : declines to encourage Tyndale, 4, 87 ; prohibits the circulation of Tyndale's translation, 131-5 ; endeavours to suppress the New Testament by purchase, 150-3 ; burns New Testaments in St. Paul's churchyard, 163.

Tyndale, William : his translations of the New Testament, 3-10, 24 ; translates portions of the Old Testament, 10-11 ; Fox's account of Tyndale's translations, 89-92 ; Tyndale's own story of his translation of the New Testament, 93-8 ; the printing of the first New Testaments, 99-108 ; the news sent to the King, 108-10 ; the supposed trial version of St. Matthew, 110-11 ; the beginning of the Prologue to the first New Testament, 111-4 ; Epilogue to the second New Testament, 114-7 ; Henry VIII's belief that Tyndale was instigated by Luther, 117-8 ; Tyndale and his fellow ' apostate ' William Roy, 119-21 ; an expert contemporary criticism of Tyndale's version, 122-6 ; the criticisms of Sir Thomas More, 126-31 ; episcopal prohibition, 131-5 ; the Bishop of London buys up the translation, 150-3 ; Stephen Vaughan's attempt to persuade Tyndale to submit to the King's command, 169-72 ; Frith's defence of Tyndale and his work, 172-5 ; Tyndale complains as to George Joye's unauthorized revision of his New Testament, 178–84 ; Joye's answer, 185–7 ; reconciliation and fresh disagreement, 188–90 ; Joye's narrative of the quarrel, 190–5 ; Halle's account of Tyndale's work as a translator, 195–6 ; his share in Matthew's Bible, 228–9.

Vaughan, Stephen : endeavours to persuade Tyndale to retract, 169–72.
Vautrollier, Thomas, printer, 41.
Vendeville, Dr., 33, 298.
Vilvorde, Tyndale's imprisonment and death at, 9.

Walker, Dr. Anthony, 55, 56.
Walsh, Sir John, 86–7.
Walsingham, Sir Francis, 41, 43.
Wanley, Humphrey, 175.
Ward, Dr. Samuel, 50, 52, 56, 75.
Waterton, Daniel, 1, 2.
Westcott, Bishop, 32.
Whitchurch, Edward, printer, 265 ; partner with Grafton in the printing and publication of the Great Bible, 15, 23, 66, 198, 223–40.
Whitgift, John, Archbishop of Canterbury, 43, 45, 59, 329.
Whittingham, William : translates the New Testament, 24 ; probable originator of the Geneva Bible, 25 ; his system of translation and annotation, 25–6 ; its effect on the 1611 version, 27.
Wilkes, Thomas, 42.
Wilson, Lea, 70.
Wittenberg, 99, 103, 104.
Wolsey, Cardinal, 10, 121, 135, 137, 141, 148.
Worcester, Chapter of, 65.
Worms, printing at, 4–6, 93, 108, 111, 122, 153, 157, 191.
Wright, Dr. Aldis, 32.
Wyclif, John, first English translations of the Bible ascribed to, 1–3 ; works prohibited, 79–81, 173.

Zurich, printing at, 12, 13.
Zwinglius, 12, 173.